A HISTORY
OF FINLAND

A HISTORY OF FINLAND

EINO JUTIKKALA
with KAUKO PIRINEN

Translated
by Paul Sjöblom

New and revised edition

DORSET PRESS
New York

This revised edition published by Dorset Press,
a division of Marboro Books Corporation,
by arrangement with
William Heinemann Ltd.
1988 Dorset Press

ISBN 0-88029-260-1
(formerly ISBN 434-37660-0)

Printed in the United States of America
M 9 8 7 6 5 4 3 2 1

Contents

Authors' note

The first three chapters were written by Professor Kauko Pirinen and the rest by myself. The translation from the original Finnish was done by Paul Sjöblom.

Minor revisions were made in the second edition. In the third edition, chapter 10 has been further revised and considerably enlarged.

Helsinki
March 1979

E.J.

A HISTORY OF FINLAND

1

The Settlement
of Finland Begins

The Origin of Finland

About twelve thousand years ago, Finland was almost totally buried under a
continental ice sheet, just as Greenland is today. Gradually, the ice sheet melted,
and its southern margin retreated farther and farther north. As the ice load
grew thinner and vanished, the earth's crust began to rise—a process that has
continued to this day, most markedly along the Gulf of Bothnia. During that
process, the Finnish peninsula slowly rose out of the sea, first forming solitary
islands, then chains of islands, and, finally, a clearly defined extension of the
continent.

The retreating glacier striated the bedrock, leaving behind it vivid evidence of
the ancient geologic process; and, during the melting stage, clay accumulated in
annual layers, and pollen grains were preserved in peat, thus bearing further
witness to the vicissitudes of Nature.

Through the study of such phenomena, geologists have been able to deduce
the origins of Finland. During extremely cold periods between 9.000 and 8.000
B.C., the continental ice sheet halted in its retreat three times and remained
stationary for centuries. This led to the formation of two chains of eskers out of
gravel and sand that were transported by streams of melting ice. These two
separate ridges, known as the Salpausselkä ranges, run east and west across the
entire breadth of Finland.

During the final stages of the Ice Age, the body of water that eventually
evolved into the Baltic Sea was a lake. From this vast stretch of water, a huge
labyrinthine lake separated inside the land mass that was to become the Finnish
peninsula and formed the tens of thousands of lakes of present-day Finland, as
the eart's crust rose. However, the ground did not rise at an even rate
everywhere, and, at times, the level of the sea rose, also forcing rivers into new
discharge channels and submerging extensive areas of land again. It was during
these upheavals of Nature that a number of the most ancient inhabited localities
in the country vanished.

While the continental ice sheet and great bodies of water still covered most of
Finland, a tundra, overgrown with dwarf birch, bordered the glacial margin,
both in the north and in the south. There, wild reindeer, Arctic fur-bearing

animals, and—in the coastal waters—fish, offered primitive hunters and fishermen a chance to eke out a livelihood. From those coastal regions of the Arctic Ocean, north of the present national boundary of Finland, have come the most ancient relics of human culture ever discovered by Finnish archaeologists. These date back to approximately 8.000 B.C. The oldest relics ever found in southern Finland are of slightly later origin, dating perhaps from 7.200 B.C. In those ancient times, there lived on the Finnish coast a simple people who made weapons of stone and bone, and who practiced hunting and fishing. Evidently, these earliest known inhabitants of Finland had arrived by land from eastern Europe.

About 5.000 B.C., the Finnish climate became damp and warm. As a result, extensive groves of hazel, elm, oak, and linden trees grew, all of which are encountered today only at scattered intervals in southern Finland. In the Finnish lakes even the edible water chestnut *Trapa natans* thrived, though now it is found only in central and southern Europe. Under such propitious circumstances, Stone Age man moved his abode northward and gradually spread over the whole peninsula. There is evidence which indicates that, even in those remote times, trade relations were maintained with alien peoples. For example, some of the stone weapons of the era are made of types of stone that do not occur in Finland.

Around the year 3.000 B.C., a new Stone Age culture, known as the Comb-Ceramic culture, spread throughout Finland. It took its name from an art that was introduced into Finland fully developed: the art of pottery-making. The name of that culture also derived from the fact bases which are decorated with a comblike stamp. The race which created that pottery was still totally dependent on hunting and fishing for a living. The only domestic animal was the dog. The dwelling places, which were changed frequently, were situated near waters that abounded in fish—generally on open, sandy beaches. Trade relations appear to have been maintained mostly with peoples in the east and the southeast; flint was brought over from Russia, amber from East Prussia. The Comb-Ceramic culture belongs to the great northeastern European group of hunting and fishing cultures that extended from the Vistula River to the Arctic Ocean and all the way to Siberia.

Archaeologists consider a culture new when its relics are found to have undergone a decisive change in character, but they cannot definitely determine whether the reason for the change was an entirely new population, an alien conquest, or simply a peaceful cultural interchange. The Comb-Ceramic people inherited their stone implements from an older, pre-Ceramic culture, which, at least, signifies that an unbroken contact with the earlier inhabitants of the country had existed. Some researchers assume that, during the middle phase of the Comb-Ceramic culture, new racial types from the plains of eastern Europe and from the Baltic regions merged with the indigenous population. On the basis of findings made east of Finland, anthropologists have ascertained that the Comb-Ceramic population was a short, longskulled race with an admixture of short-skulled "Mongoloid" types. The inhabitants of Finland probably had a different origin from those of Scandinavia. This assumption is based on the fact that, because of his poor navigational ability, Stone Age man traveled mostly overland.

The Comb-Ceramic period was followed in southwestern Finland by the so-called Battle Ax culture (approximately 1800—1600 B.C.), which, because of the ornamentation found on its pottery, is also known as the Cord-Ceramic culture. The Battle Ax culture, the chief center of which was situated in the middle of the continent, is generally associated with the migrations of the Indo-Europeans. Racially, the Battle Ax people were, according to data obtained from neighbouring areas, a long-skulled, European type. Moreover, the sharp contrast between the two cultures indicates that a new population had migrated to Finland in the interim, presumably from the Baltic region. The Battle Ax culture has received its name from the boat-shaped battle axes that were prevalent at the time. During the period of that culture's predominance, a considerable stoneimplement industry that used native raw materials, developed in Finland.

Also, those Battle Ax people evidently had already reached the agricultural stage, though the tending of cattle seems to have been more important to them than the raising of crops. Some form of religious life is indicated by the relics of these people. The dead were buried according to strict rites, usually in single graves, and interred with them were certain tools, pieces of pottery, and axes. Particular axes, decorated with the heads of animals, apparently were associated with hunting magic.

The Battle Ax people were excellent sailors, and they maintained active relations with the country of Sweden, which was occupied by people who practiced the same culture. Thus, by the end of the Stone Age, the culture of western Finland had lost its continental character and had become oriented toward the sea and the west. The western cultural orientation and the adoption of agriculture were revolutionary changes which make that brief and remote phase a significant one in Finnish history. The hybrid culture that evolved when the culturally dominant, but apparently numerically small, Battle Ax people merged with the primordial stock also followed the same western orientation. But this so-called Kiukainen culture of 1600—1200 B.C. (the name derives from the site of archaeological finds) also maintained contacts with tribes who dwelt in regions to the east. Thus, the sharp cultural boundary that had formed during the Battle Ax period between western and eastern Finland—the latter of which continued to be oriented toward the continental cultures of eastern Europe—was weakened.

About 1300 B.C., bronze, the earliest known metal, was introduced to Finland from the west. A few hundred years later, it also was brought to Finland from the east. At that time, bronze was wholly an imported commodity in Finland, for the copper resources of the country were not yet known. Bronze Age finds in Finland are very scanty. They total only slightly more than a hundred bronze objects. Molds for casting the metal and pieces of pottery also have been found. Findings of some importance in western Finland that date back to the Bronze Age have been made in a narrow zone along the coast.

The Bronze Age culture was commercial in character, having been oriented chiefly toward Scandinavia. Scholars have disagreed as to whether this culture was maintained in Finland by a foreign, Scandinavian population or whether the shift from the Stone Age to the Bronze Age represented a cultural loan. Evidently, however, the coastal region had been settled by a small ruling class,

11

consisting primarily of merchants, while the original native stock remained the same. Along the coast, the latter gradually adopted the use of bronze, whereas the inhabitants of the interior continued to hunt and fish in the old way with implements of bone and stone.

The last period from which Bronze Age relics have been found in western Finland was about 500 B.C. The corresponding period in eastern Finland came roughly a hundred years later. It was in those times that the climate in northern Europe deteriorated. The forests of deciduous trees disappeared, and the spruce usurped their place. The population evidently dwindled, also, though the country was not wholly abandoned.

Of course, the disappearance of bronze implements also could have been caused by the cessation of trade with other countries. This would have forced the inhabitants to fabricate their implements from wood, horn, or bone, as the Lapps did in later times.

Since the Stone Age inhabitants of Finland previously had known agriculture, there is no reason to suppose that they would have reverted to a nomadic existence. But it was not until the arrival of the Finns that a renaissance of culture and the permanent settlement of the country took place.

The Origin of the Finns

The language of the Finns differs radically from nearly all the other languages of the West. Although the Finns embraced Western culture at a very early date (a culture that evolved chiefly among peoples belonging to the Indo-European linguistic family), the Finnish language belongs to a completely different linguistic group, known as the Finno-Ugrian. Less than twenty million people speak the languages in this group. Among them are three highly civilized nations: the Estonians, the Finns, and the Hungarians. In spite of the small size of this group, the extreme tips of its wings are as far apart as those of the Indo-European language group. Finnish is no more closely related to Hungarian than, for instance, English is to Russian. On the other hand, Finnish and Estonian are so nearly alike that Finns and their kinsmen living across the Gulf of Finland can, to some extent, understand each others' speech. The Finno-Ugrian linguistic family is related to the tongues spoken by the scattered tribes of Samoyeds on both the European and Asiatic sides of the Soviet Union in the far North. Together, they are called the Uralic family of languages. Finnish has no other linguistic ties that can be traced with certainty.

Formerly, it was assumed that language and race were so closely allied that a relationship between languages proved a kinship between the peoples who speak them. Today, distinctions are drawn between language and race. The Finns and the Hungarians are not blood relatives—not to any appreciable degree, at least—whereas the Finns and the Estonians are quite closely related. Both of the latter belong to the so-called East Baltic race, which is relatively short-skulled and of medium height. However, among the Finns, especially among the inhabitants of western Finland, there are many representatives of the "Nordic" racial type, which is characterized by a long skull and tall stature.

Although the great mutual independence of language and race has been demonstrated, philologists still deal with such concepts as a primordial Finno-Ugrian (and, before that, Uralic) home, parent language, and parent race. Their assumption is that at some time in the remote past, somewhere, there must have lived a people who spoke the common Finno-Ugrian parent tongue, and that the present racial differences among the nations belonging to the Finno-Ugrian linguistic family came about through their intermixture with alien strains.

The primordial home of the parent race is generally situated somewhere in central Russia, around the middle course of the Volga, but the area might have been considerably broader in extent. It was in this region that, according to the philologists, the forebears of the Finns and the Hungarians parted several thousands of years ago. A few more partings of the ways took place later, before the westernmost branch of the Finnish race wandered to the shores of the Baltic. There, those Baltic Finns, comprising the proto-Finnic stock, came into contact, first with the Latgals (ancient Latvians) and the Lithuanians, then with Germans (presumably Goths living around the mouth of the Vistula), and finally also with Slavs. As a result, the proto-Finns, who, upon their arrival on the Baltic coast, were familiar with farming methods but mostly led the life of nomadic hunters and fishermen, turned into a firmly rooted agricultural people. They learned the use of metals and the art of navigation, and they organized themselves on the basis of permanently established communities. This evolutionary stage, during which the Finns developed into a seafaring nation on an estimable level of civilization along western lines, is evidenced by many ancient loan words preserved in the conservative Finnish language almost in their original form (for example: Finnish, *kuningas*, Gothic, *kuningaz*, both of which mean "king").

It has proved somewhat difficult to adjust the picture of the primordial home the Finnish race created by philology to findings of archaeological research. There has been controversy over whether the archaeological evidence uncovered in the Baltic countries points to a migratory trend from the east that might explain the advent of the Baltic Finns. Apparently, the ancestors of the Finns settled along the Baltic coast as early as the second pre-Christian chiliad, or about a thousand years earlier than previously supposed.

The Comb-Ceramic inhabitants of Finland are believed by many scholars to have been of Finno-Urgian stock (though not Baltic Finns proper), whereas the tendency has been to connect the long-skulled type that is encountered in western Finland with the Battle Ax people, granting the contribution also made by Swedish colonists of later times. There is no reason to identify the later Stone Age population of Finland—which was, perhaps, racially divided between the western and eastern parts of the country—wholly with the Lapps, despite the fact that Lapps still roamed about central Finland as late as historical times. For centuries, evidently, the Lapps, whose features bear a definite Mongolian stamp, led their nomadic existence to the north of the regions inhabited by the Finns. they eventually adopted a Finno-Ugrian tongue. Their arrival in northern Finland and northern Scandinavia can be dated archeologically, and it seems to have taken place during the closing stage of the Bronze Age, when the cultural sphere of Finland became clearly separated into northern and southern sectors.

The earliest reference to "Finns" in historical records apparently concerns the aboriginal inhabitants of Finland. In about 100 A.D., the Roman historian Tacitus portrayed, for the benefit of his debilitated compatriots, the wild and primitive people called *Fenni* who were content to exist without the comforts of civilization. Tacitus' description of the Fenni does not fit the proto-Finns, but it does fit the Lapps, as well as the Stone Age man of Finland. Considering that the Norwegians to this very day call the Lapps by a corresponding name (*Finner*), it is not unlikely that this appellation and that of the country were applied even before the arrival of the Baltic Finns. (Incidentally, the names by which the Finns call themselves and their land, *Suomalaiset* and *Suomi*, have not been satisfactorily explained.)

At the time Tacitus wrote his book, Finland was already receiving its new inhabitants. Isolated relics of the Iron Age indicate that expeditions to Finland were being made from the southern side of the Gulf of Finland as early as the last few centuries before the Christian era. Migrations, culminating in the establishment of permanent settlements, began at about the time of the birth of Christ. The great world power Rome extended its commercial influence as far as remote Finland in those days, with the Goths acting as intermediaries. Material evidence has been found in the from of Roman artifacts, such as iron swords and wine bowls. All that the ancient inhabitants of Finland could deliver in exchange probably was furs, although no trace of this commodity has been left among archaeological finds. Furs were thicker and of better quality in the north, and, for this reason, it was worth traveling even greater distances to procure them. Fur-traders and hunters from the southern side of the Gulf of Finland gradually settled permanently along the southwestern and western coasts of Finland, and later penetrated the interior of Tavastia (Häme), up the Kokemäki river system.

On the other hand, that part of the Finnish coast that was opposite the most prosperous population centers in Estonia remained unsettled, presumably because it was claimed by the Esths as a game preserve. The migrations from Estonia continued for centuries, but by the end of the Roman Iron Age (400 A.D.), an independent society consisting of those settlers began to develop in Finland. Iron, which, at first, had been imported from other lands, now was extracted from ores that were found in the bogs and lakes of the country.

Contrary to the burial custom brought over from Estonia, the remains of cremated bodies now were buried under heaps of stones mixed with earth, which resembled the burial cairns of the Bronze Age. On the strength of this evidence, some researchers have concluded that the Baltic Finns who migrated into Finland were outnumbered by the aboriginal inhabitants. But because of their higher cultural level, the Finns were able to absorb the aboriginal stock, although the latter's customs prevailed. Another theory is that, besides the Lapps, the *Hämeans*, or Tavastians, of the hinterland also belonged to the aboriginal population of the country, whereas the *Suomalaiset*—the name now applied in the Finnish language to all people who speak Finnish as their mother tongue—would seem to have occupied a narrow coastal strip in the regions now known as Varsinais-Suomi ("Finland Proper") and Ala-Satakunta. It is these *Suomalaiset* (literally, "Finns") who introduced the culture of the Iron Age into Finland.

During the epoch of barbarian invasions after the fall of Rome, between the years 400 and 800, relations between the Finns and the peoples to the south weakened, while contacts westward, with the Scandinavians, grew correspondingly stronger. Finland's Iron Age culture now triumphantly shed its Baltic features and definitely took on an independent character. The latter phase of the period of barbarian invasions (550—800) coincided with the culmination of Iron Age culture in Finland, as well as in Scandinavia.

Ancient Finnish society became differentiated late during the period of barbarian invasions, and, in its midst, a ruling class of chiefs arose. The Finnish boat tombs were of the same type as those of the Scandinavians, and they were used for the burial of chiefs. However, there was one essential difference: in Finland the vessel was burned before being buried. A description of such a fiery burial "in a boat of bronze" survives in some veres from a Finnish folk poem. Certain other verser describe in deail contemporary spearhead ornamentation. It has been concluded from these records that the oldest stratum of ancient Finnish poetry dates back to that remote heroic era, or about the same time the Anglo-Saxon *Beowulf* was born.

Does folklore reveal even more about that distant past of which no written records have been preserved? This is one of the most fascinating questions confronting Finnish historians—but also one of the hardest to answer. The ancient folklore of the Finnish people is among the richest in the world. It is often referred to as "Kalevalan," after the national epic *Kalevala,* published early in the nineteenth century by Elias Lönnrot; but the *Kalevala* contains only a fraction of even the narrative poetry into which t at revered compiler delved, and of which he shaped his epic poem. Including variants, the printed collection of folk poetry in the ancient Finnish meter comprises thirtythree thick volumes, containing 1.200.000 lines of verse. The greatest part was written down as late as the nineteenth century in areas east of Finland's political boundary, but researchers have been able to demonstrate that the poems had been transplanted there from western Finland.

There are relatively few poems that have sure temporal points of contact with, for instance, ancient or medieval times. Several scholars gave sought to identify the mighty and mysterious *Pohjola* (Northland) of folklore, against which certain of the heroes of Finnish antiquity waged war, with the ancient Scandinavian-type culture that once flourished in South Ostrobothnia (South *Pohjanmaa*), on the coast of the Gulf of Bothnia, but vanished totally in the ninth century of the Christian era. The *Pohjola* of folklore, however, was blended with distinct mythological elements, which many people have associated with the unknown Far North, the land of frost and interminable winter nights where no human foot has ever trod.

The rise of ancient Finnish society and the spread of settlement were based on the parallel exploitation of arable land and forests, just as was the Finnish economy of later times. A subsistence was obtained by cultivating the soil, but the forest was the source of wealth. Permanently established farms were very small and accounted for only a small part of the agricultural production. The biggest crops were reaped from fields that were cleared out of the wilderness one year and burned over the following year. The soil was worked with a light plow, and the seeds were sown among the stumps, roots, and ashes. Virgin land thus cleared yielded two or three good harvests, after which it was again abandoned to revert to forest.

Agriculture required labor only during the summer, while, during the spring and fall, the men went off on long expeditions into the wilderness to hunt and fish. The lake system of the Finnish interior made the goint easy for such expeditions, since it was possible to row up the lakes for scores of miles, after which other waterways could be reached by dragging the boats across narrow necks of land. The wilderness provided additional sustenance, but, above all, it yielded furs, which could be bartered for goods from foreign lands. It is significant that the Finnish word for money, *raha,* originally meant "fur." The wide range of the wilderness expeditions is evidenced by the fire-making implements, oblong pieces of flint, lost by huntsmen and later found all over Finland.

Finland on the Edge of the Vikings' Eastern Trade Route

During the early Iron Age, the stable settlements of Finland were concentrated chiefly on the western coast. The situation changed in the ninth century, when the Gulf of Finland became the main fairway of an important international trade route.

The Vikings of Denmark and Norway, at the end of the eighth century, started their plundering expeditions westward, whereas the Vikings of Sweden turned east, hoping to establish contact with the wealthy Arabian sphere. The Swedish expeditions were inspired by a desire for trade, but trade in those times easily turned into plundering. The traders who traveled over the great eastern route, called Varangians in Russia, founded colonies of their own along the way and formed the ruling class among the Slavic and the Finno-Ugrian peoples. The enterprise of the Varangian chiefs led to the founding of a Russian state in, according to tradition, the year 862 A.D.

The important trade route to the east crossed the Baltic via the Aland Islands and then followed the northern shore of the Gulf of Finland, which was sheltered by islands, to the Neva, and up that river to Lake Ladoga. From there, streams led to the upper course of the Dnieper, and by following that river it was possible to reach the Black Sea, Constantinople, and Arabian lands. The southern coast of Finland thus was brought into direct contact with the great international trade route. At first, when fabulous riches could be gained far in the east, this did not mean very much; but when the Varangian communities began to gain an independent status and the eastern route became blocked, the areas along the way took on more significance, principally as sources of furs. The influence of the eastern trade route can be seen in the progress of settlement in Finland. The Ostrobothnian center of population became desolate after having been bypassed commercially; and the settled zone along the southern coast, which became dangerously exposed to raiders because of its proximity to the eastern route and the lack of protective islands, was likewise deserted. By contrast, the settlements in the interior, situated at a safe distance beyond the twin Salpausselkä ridges, spread eastward parallel to the eastern

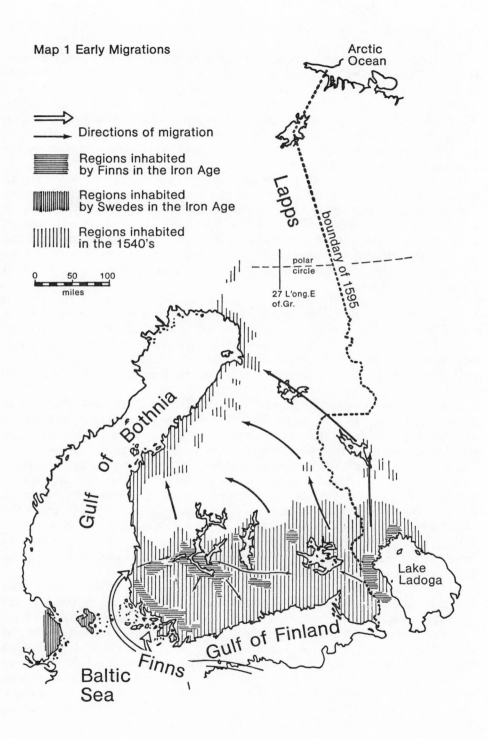

Map 1 Early Migrations

Directions of migration

Regions inhabited
by Finns in the Iron Age

Regions inhabited
by Swedes in the Iron Age

Regions inhabited
in the 1540's

0   50   100
miles

Arctic
Ocean

Lapps

boundary of 1595

polar
circle

27 L'ong.E
of.Gr.

Gulf of Bothnia

Gulf of Finland

Lake
Ladoga

Finns

Baltic
Sea

trade route and, by a bold leap, reached the shore of Lake Ladoga in Karelia as early as the 800's (see map 1).

The oldest Iron Age archaeological finds in Karelia are quite western Finnish in type. Nevertheless, conspicuous differences between eastern and western Finland already existed during the Iron Age; and these differences persisted to a late date in the material and intellectual folk culture as well as in the dialects. Therefore, it is hard to imagine Karelia as merely a colony of the western Finns. Presumably, the region had had earlier inhabitants whose culture was characterized by the utilization of wood and bone, and who were absorbed by the migrants from western Finland.

Karelia enjoyed a favorable position because it was located near the Varangian colonies of the East and could also maintain contact along the Gulf of Finland with the trade centers of the West. As a supplier of furs, it rapidly flourished. And, in spite of eastern influences, the Karelian culture remained basically western in character. A clear boundary, which appears also in burial customs, among other things, separates the Karelians living on the western side of Lake Ladoga from the population on the eastern side, which also was doubtless of Baltic Finnish stock.

The influence of the eastern expeditions of the Vikings on Finland was indirect, for the Finns did not take part themselves. The only exception was the Aland Islands, which were colonized by Swedes as long ago as the sixth century. Some 1,400 Arabian coins have been found in these islands, which evidently were brought back by islanders who accompanied their kinsmen on expeditions to distant lands in the East. Very few such coins have been found on the Finnish mainland.

The growing demand for furs that resulted from trade with the Vikings caused the Finns to extend their wilderness treks into remote Lapland and as far as the Arctic coast. The salmon-rich streams of northern Finland also served as a lure. The Finnish fur-trappers benefited not only by bagging their own game but also by compelling the Lapps to pay tribute, or by seizing the pelts collected by alien rivals. The furtrading center of western Finland was established very early at Pirkkala, which was probably named after Sweden's most ancient town, Birca. Pirkkala was advantageously situated along the upper course of the Kokemäki River, whence other waterways led northward. Relics of the early Viking period that have been found in Finland testify to the commercial influence of Birca rather than to expeditions which happened to skirt the Finnish coast on quests of the wealth of distant lands.

Armed trading associations were formed in Finland, too, to procure furs and collect tribute from the Lapps. They could, in a way, be compared with the Varangian traders. The earliest record of them appears in an Anglo-Saxon source, the celebrated geography produced at the end of the ninth century by King Alfred the Great. He received data concerning remote hyperborean regions from, among others, the Norseman Ottar, who could tell about Kainuu (Cwenland), which was located beyond the *fjelds,* over which the Kainuans (Cwenas) dragged their boats to carry out surprise raids along the Arctic coast. The Kainuans are also depicted (under the name of "Kvenir") in the Scandinavian sagas, where, in addition to the Karelians, they appear as rivals of the Norsemen in Lapland.

The Kainuans apparently were not a tribe but actually a western Finnish organization of backwoods trappers. Similar organizations also operated in the eastern parts of the Varangian sphere of influence, including the "Beormas", mentioned by Alfred the Great and in the sagas, who roamed along the White Sea coast and spoke a language related to Finnish. The bases of the Beormas seem to have been located south of Lake Ladoga. The Karelians of Finland likewise roamed the wilds of Lapland from as early as the eleventh century. By using the excellent waterways, they reached the far end of the Gulf of Bothnia (see map 1), on one side, and, on the other, the shores of the White Sea, where they established Finnish colonies.

The end of the Viking period in the eleventh century was a time of unrest in Finland, as indicated by the numerous hiding places or "ground banks," that have been unearthed, yielding thousands of Anglo-Saxon and German coins buried by apprehensive people. Further evidence of those embattled times is found in Swedish runic stones, which mention the names of warriors who fell in combat in Tavastia and Viipuri. Canon Adam of Bremen, whose chronicle is one of the main eleventh-century sources for the history of the Nordic countries, tells about the unsuccessful expedition of conquest made by the Swedish prince Anund to the land of Kainuu. These Swedish expeditions were simply raids for the purpose of collecting spoils and tribute, and they did not lead to any conquests of long duration. On the contrary, the influence of the centers of Swedish political life appears to have weakened after the fall of Birca. Its commercial position in Finland was inherited in the eleventh century by the island of Gotland, which was the great trade center in the Baltic Sea and, starting in the twelfth century, came under strong German influence. Gotland maintained its commercial hold on Finland even during the crusades, when the Church strove, by threatening to inflict its ban, to prevent the sale of arms to infidels who obstinately clung to heathen beliefs.

Except for the Aland Islands, there were no permanent Swedish colonies in Finland at the end of the pagan period. Trading colonies were established from time to time in that country, first by the Goths and then by the Swedes; finally, there may have been some Russian and, also, some German colonies. But the few inhabitants of such communities either were absorbed by the main population or migrated back to their native country when the opportunities for economic gain declined.

At the end of the pagan period, there were three fairly uniform areas of settlement on the Finnish mainland (see map 1). In the southwest were the *Suomalaiset,* or Finns proper, who eventually gave their name to the whole country, *Suomi.* The western lake district of the interior, comprising the areas drained by the Kokemäki and the Kymi river systems, was held by the Tavastians (or, in Finnish, *Hämäläiset*). The Tavastians held the coast of the Gulf of Finland as an uninhabited economic domain, where they practiced fishing and, at certain market places, dealt with traders who were using the eastern route. To the east lived the Karelians, whose most thriving centers were situated on the western shore of Lake Ladoga, while the coast of the Gulf of Finland — the main artery of traffic over the eastern trade route — seems to have been uninhabited even in that part of the country.

The material culture of the Finns was approximately on the same level as that of their neighbors to the west. Active cultural relations in that direction had given Finnish culture a Scandinavian stamp, although its origin was different, deriving chiefly from the Baltic regions to the south.

On the other hand, in respect to social organization, the Finns lagged behind their western neighbors. It was in the eleventh century, at the latest, that the Scandinavian peoples formed into three kingdoms. No unified state evolved among the Finnish tribes. Within the framework of smaller areas, however, measures of social organization were taken for the supervision of religious rites, the administration of justice, and defense against aggressors. Evidence of such defense measures are the ancient fortresses, numbering about ninety, which consisted of rocky slopes reinforced by constructions of stone and wood without masonry. With the possible exception of the fortress of Rapola, in Tavastia, they were not permanently manned but were used as places of refuge when there was the threat of an enemy attack. Fires lit by sentries on top of the fortified hills swiftly spread the alarm to all the men of the region to take up arms against an approaching foe. The unbroken system of signal stations formed by the fortifield hills of Tavastia testifies to the fact that the tribal region represented the degree of political and military organization to which ancient Finnish society attained.

The weakness of the political organization that prevailed among the Finns was due to the sparseness of their settlements. Between them lay vast stretches of wilderness. The northern boundary of the inhabited area did not extend beyond the 62nd degree of latitude. No farther inland than 125 miles from the coast, the wilderness began. The Finns had enough manpower to utilize their vast hunting grounds — *erämaat*, the Finns called them — all the way to the shores of the Arctic Ocean and the White Sea. On the other hand, they were not numerically strong enough to repel the organized invasions of their more numerous eastern and western neighbors. Thus, sparsely settled Finland, with her wealth of natural resources, soon became a coveted prize of aggressive foreign powers.

2

Finland Is Drawn into the Western Cultural Sphere

The Western Church and Sweden Capture a Beachhead in Finland

Finland drew the interest of its neighbors when those leading commercial powers decided to acquire permanent control of their sources of raw materials, as competition between them intensified. During the twelfth century, this competition began to develop into a conflict between West and East. One reason was the Slavification of the Varangian centers and their alienation from their mother country, Sweden. Mighty Novgorod emerged as the custodian of the interests of the East in the northwestern parts of Russia. At first, it carried on an active trading policy: For instance, a Novgorodian trading post appears to have been situated in southwestern Finland, near Turku. The trading center of Turku (Aboa) is mentioned for the first time in an Arabian geography that was published in 1154, whose learned author evidently had received his information via the eastern trade route.

The contrast between East and West was heightened by the religious breach between them. The conversion of the Swedes to the Roman Catholic faith began as early as the 800's and was completed in the eleventh century. The Russians were converted to the Greek Orthodox faith at the end of the tenth century. At first, the opposition between the two churches was not great. But it became intensified by the influence of the aggressive crusading ideology of western Christendom, and by the beginning of the thirteenth century it had reached the point of open hostility.

The first Christian influences to which the Finns were exposed apparently came from the East, judging by the fact that a number of key Finnish words belonging to the Christian sphere of ideas are loans mediated by Slavic languages. Soon, however, the western form of Christianity, which arrived peacefully in the wake of international trade, rose to greater prominence. The success that was achieved by promulgators of the Christian faith is disclosed by archaeological material: burial customs changed. At first, the heathen custom of burying goods with the body was adhered to, but the orientation of the graves was changed to east and west, as in Christian burial grounds; and a typical Christian token, such as a necklace with a cross, was likely to accompany the deceased on his last journey. The final phase was the abandonment of burials in pagan village graveyards altogether and the adoption of Christian cemeteries, in which the dead were buried without the heathen tomb furniture.

In some cases, a Christian church was erected in the middle of a pagan graveyard, as if to symbolize the triumph of the new religion. The shift to Christian burials (which meant both the exhaustion of archaeological finds and the end of the prehistoric epoch) took place in the Aland Islands and, in a limited area, in the northern parts of Finland Proper at about the year 1050. Throughout the rest of Finland Proper and Tavastia, it occurred in approximately 1150, but in Karelia as late as about 1300. That change in burial customs indicates the advent of the Christian church, but the victory of Christianity in a social sense did not necessarily mean success in winning the hearts and minds of the people, for pagan practices and magic persisted to some extent into modern times.

The description of the conversion of the Finns to Christianity that is provided by historical sources generally agrees with the picture that can be reconstructed from archaeological material. Finland is mentioned along with Estonia (*Findia* and *Hestia*) in a list of Swedish provinces drawn up for the Pope as early as 1120. Evidently, the provinces had been designated as missionary areas under the jurisdiction of some Swedish diocese, though it probably was only an assertion rather than the documentation of an actual conquest.

The earliest reliable information about the outbreak of hostilities from the direction of Finland dates from 1142, when, according to a Russian chronicle, the king of Sweden and a certain bishop launched an attack on some ships that were bound for Novgorod. In the same year, Tavastians made a devastating raid on the southern coast of Lake Ladoga, after which the Karelians retaliated by raiding Tavastia. The Tavastians thus appeared, even at that early date, as an enemy of the Novgorodians, whereas the Karelians allied themselves with their eastern trading partners.

A serious attempt to draw Finland into the sphere of western Christendom and, simultaneously, under Swedish political domination was not made until a quarter-century later. Present-day knowledge of these events, which were glorified by posterity as the First Crusade, is quite poor. Information about them is derived from a couple of sources dating from at least a century later: a liturgical legend that originated in Sweden, and a Finnish folk poem. Such narrative sources may serve as historical evidence insofar as the things told appear to agree with otherwise known facts of the same period.

In 1153, a cardinal legate of the Pope arrived in Sweden. He was the English-born Nicholas Breakspear, who was destined to become Pope Hadrianus IV. If the information contained in the aforementioned Russian chronicle is to be trusted, the King of Sweden—then named Sverker—had made an expedition to the East with his bishops even earlier. The Pope's legate could scarcely have been able to incite the Swedes to action merely for the sake of spreading the Catholic religion; but, of course, he would have met no opposition to his offering the blessing of the Church to any expedition that they might have been planning for economic or political reasons.

The connection between Nicholas Breakspear's mission to the North and the Swedish crusade to Finland is suggested by a report (dating back no farther than late medieval times) that St. Henry, the apostle of Finland, accompanied the legate to Sweden. According to tradition, Henry, who also was an Englishman by birth, served two years as bishop of Uppsala before joining the crusade to Finland that was organized by King Eric, Jedvard's son. Judging from this, the date of the crusade has been recorded as 1155. However, Eric was forced to fight a more legitimate pretender to the throne in his own country before he could make good his crusader's pledge. Accordingly, the date of the crusade should perhaps be set a couple of years later, about 1157. King Eric landed with his troops somewhere on the coast of southwestern Finland and easily defeated the Finns.

Bishop Henry was left behind, after the king's forces withdrew, to organize the ecclesiastical establishment. But he was slain with an ax the following winter on frozen Lake Köyliö, in the province of Satakunta, by a Finnish yeoman named Lalli. The bishop's body was buried in Nousiainen, north of Turku, and by the end of the 1100's he already was beginning to be revered as a saint. Subsequently he became the patron saint of the diocese of Turku and also of the whole medieval population of Finland. St. Henry symbolized the intellectual and spiritual unity of the country. He also was recognized as one of the patron saints of the kingdom of Sweden.

It is impossible to tell how much truth is contained in the many stories about King Eric's crusades and about Bishop Henry. But there is no reason to doubt the historical existence of that apostle of the Finns: Bishop Henry's violent death, at least—the date of which (January 20) caused special provisions to be made in the calendar of saints of the diocese of Turku—appears to be a reliable historical fact.

An interesting explanation of Lalli's motives for taking the bishop's life is provided by a folk poem that differs from the saint's legend. According to the legend, Lalli was a murderer who had been censured by the bishop and disciplined by the Church. However, the bishop had provoked Lalli's anger by taking provisions and fodder from his farm without permission, although he left payment for them. Furthermore, the organization of the Church, which called for the establishment of the bishop's office, the creation of a network of parishes, and the building of churches imposed new burdens on the people. In addition to material contributions, they were required to entertain representatives of the Church. A violent reaction to these impositions from Finnish proselytes may well have led to the bishop's murder.

In assessing the underlying political and economic motives of the crusade, we might disregard the Finnish attacks reported in the legend insofar as the Western Finns are concerned; for, in the twelfth century, the Western Finns tended to show a desire for cooperation rather than for war with their Swedish neighbors. With the Karelians, the situation was perhaps different; there is a story about their attack all the way to Lake Mälart, in Sweden, a few decades later.

Militarily, the first crusade need not be imagined as having been on a larger scale than certain other expeditions made by the Swedes to eastern parts earlier and again somewhat later. For ventures of this kind, the Swedes had at their disposal, at least for a few weeks in the summer, the so-called *ledung* fleet, fiitted out by the coastal and island provinces on the Baltic side. With such forces, it would not be easy to make permanent conquests—if such, indeed, were the aim. But the aim was rather to exact tribute and, perhaps, to bring about some sort of loose relationship, either of dependency or of alliance, that could be secured, for example, by taking hostages.

Finland's relations with Sweden and the position of the Christian church among the Finns after the first crusade are revealed in a Papal bull that was sent to a Swedish political leader in 1171 or 1172. The Pope had been informed that the Finns gladly acknowledged themselves to be Christians and welcomed priests when they were threatened by an enemy army, but renounced their faith and persecuted the priests as soon as the foe had withdrawn. From data provided by Russion chronicles, it appears to be certain that the unnamed enemies were the Novgorodians and their allies, the Karelians. The Pope advised the Swedes to alter their relationship with the Finns: Instead of treating them as allies, the Swedes should force them into a state of submission by permanently manning the fortresses of Finland. This was easier said than done.

Since Finland and Sweden are separated by a sea, the Swedes could aid their Finnish allies only with their naval forces. Some evidence exists to indicate that the southwestern Finns were in some way bound to Sweden's compulsory naval service. The Finnish name for Sweden is *Ruotsi,* which is derived from *Roden* or *Roslagen,* as the part of Sweden that is located nearest to Finland was called. It was in that region that conscription for the Swedish navy was organized. Thus, at a very early date, the Finns learned to know the Swedes as a militarily organized nation of seafarers.

An ancient souvenir of the adoption of Swedish organizational measures in Finland is the name *Satakunta,* which is applied to the province that runs along both sides of the Kokemäki River and forms the borderland between Tavastia and Finland proper (see map 2).

Satakunta is a Finnish translation of an administrative and juridical term that is applied in central Sweden to a regional division, *hundare* (compare the English country division, "hundred"). The ties binding southwestern Finland to Sweden evidently antedate the so-called first crusade. This comparatively modest undertaking need not have signified the creation of the first Swedish beachhead in Finland, but rather the reinforcement of an earlier sphere of influence during a period of crisis. On the other hand, it should be noted that archaeological material testifies only to the commercial dominance of Gotland—but not to the political power of the Swedish sovereign.

The exiguous source material, therefore, seems to indicate that between southwestern Finland and Sweden there had existed ancient political and economic ties that can be traced back to the early twelfth century. The first crusade strengthened these ties, mostly, perhaps, by the subsequent reorganization of the Church of Finland along lines laid down in Sweden. At least, bishops serving as missionaries were sent to Finland from time to time; but, when the Church of Sweden received her own archbishop in 1164, Finland was not included among his dioceses. The political ties were reinforced when, perhaps through the action of the bishops, the castles in Finland were ordered renovated, with a view toward having them manned permanently.

Map 2 Finnish Boundaries: 1323, 1595, 1617

The domain of the missionary bishop of Finland (i.e., that part of Finland that had been Christian and politically oriented toward Sweden the longest) consisted only of the southwestern part of the geographical entity that is present-day Finland. It included "Finland Proper," presumably the western-most part of the province of Nyland, the province of Satakunta, and, in a narrow strip, a portion of the Bothnian coast. The center of gravity of this area was in the west, on the coast of the Gulf of Bothnia, where communications with Sweden were, for geographical reasons, most natural. Of the Tavastians, only those settled farthest west, in Upper Satakunta, had organizationally joined the diocese of Finland.

The main task of the Swedish régime in Finland during the following decades was to pressure Tavastia into joining the ecclesiastical system. The accomplish-ment of this task also settled the question of control over the northern coast of the Gulf of Finland, which the Tavastians had utilized as their special preserve.

The Conversion of Tavastia; the Birth of Pioneer Swedish Colonies

The end of the twelfth century witnessed the beginning of new competition on the Gulf of Finland. German traders had been maintaining regular contact with Novgorod via Gotland. Concerned about the success of their rivals, the Danes also sought to establish bases on the coast of the Gulf of Finland.

Now the procedure was different from what it had been before. Crusades were reduced to highly organized military expeditions for permanent conquest. This objective was attained by building fortresses in the conquered areas and also, in many cases, by moving in reliable settlers. On the southern side of the gulf, where the Germans were striving to expand the mission area they had established at the mouth of the Düna River toward the north, the aim was to achieve a direct land connection to Russia and to capture the mouth of the Neva. This would have brought both of the main arteries of eastern trade under German control. Conquest of the northern shore of the Gulf of Finland also was motivated by a desire to control the sources of the fur supply and to secure the maritime traffic off the Finnish coast.

During the final decade of the twelfth century, many crusading expeditions were made to both shores of the Gulf of Finland. The Danes, who appeared on the scene as rivals of the Swedes, are reported to have invaded Finland in 1191 and 1202. Possibly operating from bases established on the southern coast of the country, they seem to have had considerable success. In 1209, the Pope, who had been informed that the Finns had lately been converted by the nobility, authorized the head of the Danish Church, the archbishop of Lund, to appoint a preacher who was stationed in Finland to take over the vacant bishop's seat.

The Swedes saw the fruits of their efforts slipping out of their hands, so they proceeded to take countermeasures. In 1216, the King of Sweden obtained from the Pope confirmation of his title to the lands conquered by his predecessors from heathens, as well as to any additional territory he himself might capture. In that mission territory of Finland, he was authorized to establish a seat for one or two bishops who would have to answer to the head of the Church of Sweden, the archbishop of Uppsala. The mission territory was recognized by the Pope to be expressly under the suzerainty of the Swedish monarch and to belong to the Church of Sweden.

The destiny of Finland, however, was not decided by the bulls issued by the Pope in Rome, but by the evolution of power politics in the Baltic sphere. The Germans gained great successes at the end of the first decade of the thirteenth century in the mission territory of Livonia and pressed forward into Estonia. The Danes challenged their advance, after taking possession of northern Estonia, including the trading center of Tallinn. The Swedes tried to share in the division of spoils, too, but their efforts ended in gory defeat. The geographical spheres of interest now became stabilized so that the northern coast of the Gulf of Finland remained Swedish mission territory, while the Danes concentrated on securing their positions on the opposite shore.

The strenuous rivalry on the crusading front in Estonia, which led, among other things, to enforced mass conversions, also stirred up the eastern neighbors of the Finns. evidence of this development is the Papal ban, issued in 1221, on selling arms to heathens—presumably the Karelians, who threatened to crush the fresh buds of Christianity in Finland. The crusading front of the West in the Finnish sector was thus in a defensive position, but Novgorod became active and adopted the coercive tactics of the westerners in making conversions. In 1227, Duke Jaroslav put into effect a program of forced baptisms on a mass scale among the Karelian population. "It was only by a narrow margin that we missed baptizing all the people," boasted the chronicler of Novgorod. The purpose of this program was to tighten the bonds that joined Karelia to Novgorod.

Around the same time, the Novgorodians carried out a military expedition to Tavastia, which, according to the chronicler's boastful claim, was almost totally conquered. The invaders' success, however, could not have been very great, for, as early as 1228, the Tavastians again were strong enough to counterattack.

The situation was viewed in Finland as extremely menacing. The organizational activities of the Church had produced good results in Tavastia during the previous years. Christian churches had been erected to replace the pagan sacrificial groves. The gains that had been made now appeared to be slipping away. And even the ancient beachhead of western Christendom seemed to be threatened. An urgent appeal for aid was sent to the Pope, seeking his support of the creation of a common crusading front. In 1229, the Pope reinvoked the commercial blockade, now specifically aimed against the Russians. Moreover, the bishop, clergy, and people of Finland were taken under apostolic protection. The aim of these acts was to prevent every measure that was liable to hamper operations on the crusading front in Finland against the Russians and the pagans from being taken.

The bishop of Finland around that time was Thomas, an energetic character of English birth who, according to the chronicle, had previously served as canon at Uppsala. He evidently deserves great credit for bending the Tavastians to the Christian yoke, and it probably was he who also procured the important letters of the Pope in 1229. I has been supposed that the intent of the Pope's pledge of protection was to create a Papal protectorate out of Finland. This sort of procedure was being tried out around that time in the mission territories of

Prussia and Livonia. Such a new approach, however, tended to create friction with the secular authorities behind the crusading program. In Finland, the direct guidance of the Pope became manifest in 1232, when Balduin of Aulne was appointed papal legate to both Livonia and Finland. It was forbidden to negotiate a peace or a truce with the Russians or heathens without his consent.

The Teutonic Knights of the Sword were summoned to support the hard-pressed crusading cause in Finland. If these plans had been realized, the leadership of the crusading forces there could easily have been lost by the Swedes. However, the plans fell through, and the protective policy on the southern side of the Gulf of Finland was soon abandoned. As applied to Finland, such a policy can scarcely be given serious consideration. There was nothing in Bishop Thomas's conduct of office to indicate a desire to cut the bonds between the diocese of Finland and the mother country of Sweden, but, in his predicament, he naturally appealed for assistance wherever it promised to yield results.

Bishop Thomas's treatment of the Tavastians was evidently too rough. They rose up in 1236—1237 in fierce rebellion. As a consequence, the Pope gave his permission for the crusading cause to be preached throughout the Swedish realm and in neighboring countries. Exactly what effect the exhortations had, however, is not known. The theory has been advanced that the second crusade was made to crush this rebellion and should be dated, therefore, at about 1238. But this view is opposed by the argument that Earl Birger, who appears in the annals as the leader of the crusade, had not yet been elevated to the rank of arl in 1238. Indeed, there is good reason to believe that the supression of the Tavastian rebellion and the crusade into Tavastia are not necessarily one and the same. It was impossible to achieve lasting success by local pacification measures. Behind the unrest lurked powerful Novgorod. Only a direct blow to its most vital areas of interest was likely to bring about a decisive success in proselyting activities plus control of the Neva trade route. An opportunity seemed to arise early in the 1240's, when Russia was weakened by an invasion of Tatar hordes.

The Pope's legate, Wilhelm of Modena, strove to rally the Western forces into joint action, but he was not altogether successful. The Novgorodians were fortunate in gaining the opportunity of meeting the forces advancing on each side of the Gulf of Finland in separate engagements. In the summer of 1240, Duke Alexander Jaroslavovic defeated the northern force at the Neva. The force included the *ledung* fleet, with its bishops, led by a Swedish earl, contingents of Finns from "Finland Proper" and Tavastia, and, presumably, numerous crusaders arriving from m quarters as volunteers. The Western Finns fought on this occasion against Novgorod, but the Eastern Finns fought as its allies.

According to an old Russian account, it was an Ingrian (Finnish) tribal chieftain from the mouth of the Neva who had brought the first warning of the aggressor's approach. Duke Alexander, who, in the winter of 1242, consummated his triumph by repulsing a German offensive on frozen Lake Peipus, had the honorary title of Nevski conferred upon him in Russia. The battle of the Neva proved to be a turning point, for it halted the advances of the Western forces toward the heartlands of Russia and the Eastern Orthodox Church and, in addition, sealed the division of the Finnish people.

Bishop Thomas certainly did not take any prominent part in the Neva adventure, as was long supposed in Finland; but he did throw all the resources of his diocese into the battle. The defeat was probably one reason why he quit his office in 1245. Thereafter, the mission territory of Finland remained for some years without competent administration. Then, to the rescue came Western Christendom's new spiritual fighting organization, the Dominican order. In 1249, it founded a convent at Turku, which, during Thomas's term, had become the center of the diocese. The Dominican order had a lasting influence on the ecclesiastical culture of medieval Finland.

Politico-military assistance also arrived before long. The situation had deteriorated to the extent that the sporadic forays of Swedish naval forces and crusading volunteers nh ger sufficed to maintain and expand the bridgehead of Christendom. The firm intervention of Swedish governmental power was needed. Sweden's most powerful political figure, Earl Birger, the king's brother-in-law, led an expeditionary force, in 1249, into Tavastia. Our knowledge of this expedition is based on a swedish chronicle that appeared a couple of generations later. In the light of its internal chronology, the year of the expedition was 1249. A papal letter issued at the end of the same year, whereby the clergy and the people of Finland were onn gain taken under the protection of the Pope, indicates that the undertaking was known even at the seat of Western Christendom. This second crusade was aimed more to pacify the province and consolidate Swedish control there than to conquer and baptize the inhabitantsm on th s epehition, the earl built a castle in Tavastia and, available evidence indicates, some minor fortifications on the southern Finnish coast.

The most notable measure taken during that crusade was the transportation on swedish colonists to an ar hn e finnish coast that soon began to be known as Nyland (Finnish *Uusimaa,* meaning "New Land"). Probably as early as the eleventh century, Swedish settlers had moved to the northern coast of Finland prophn here the Christian faith gl o first took root. Starting in the decade of the 1250's, the colonization activity grew to the proportions of a mass movement.

Somewhat later, the eastern coast of the Gulf of Bothnia also began to attract Swedish settlers. As a result of the Swedish colonizing activity o early Middle Ages, there became established—besides the Aland Islands, which had been anciently inhabited by Swedes—a Swedish zone of settlement in the province of Nyland, in Finland proper, and along the bothnian coast. This Swedish zone, which nowhere extends more than thirty kilometers inland from the seaboard, remained practically unchanged in its boundaries until recent decades: only solitary islets of settlement surrounded by people speaking the other language of the country were from time to time linguistically absorbed by the local majority.

When the Swedish migratory movement started, the coastal regions were nearly uninhabited, through their natural resources were exploited by the Finns who lived in the interior. Of course, the loss of these reserves was felt by the Finnish inhabitants, but no really vital interests were at stake. The relations between the two nationalities that comprised the population of Finland therefore developed from the very beginning along peaceful lines.

The Conquest of West Karelia

The Swedish chronicle considered the result of the Tavastian crusade a defeat for the "Russian king." This judgment seems to be correct. The coast od the Gulf of Finland was now securely held by the Swedes all the way to the Kymi river in the east, and the influence of the west began to extend even beyond that point.

Tavastia had become firmly attached to the kingdom of Sweden and the diocese of Finland. During the following decades, the question of Karelia's position became dominant.

Karelia was successful in those times in preserving a considerable degre of independence in its relations with Novgorod also. In trade pact concluded with the Germans in c. 1262 and 1269, the Novgorodians agreed to accept responsibility for securing peaceful commercial conditions only to the extent that it was practicable in operating from the island of Kotlingen (later Kronstadt), at the far eastern end of the gulf, but they refused to commit themselves to any pledges concerning the region of Karelia, farther west. On the latter occasion, the Germans specifically asked that the Novgorodians for the area between Kronstad and the island of Koivisto (east of Viipuri), as well, but the request was turned down.

The coastal stretch between Koivisto and the Kymi River was no longer under the domination of Novgorod even in the Germans' viewpoint. Colonists from Finland Proper, and some Swedes, too, probably moved into the region around that time. Before the crusade into Karelia, the Swedes controlled the coast of the Gulf of Finland, perhaps past the eastern side of Viipuri. The Russians endeavored to strengthen their hold on the western shore of Lake Ladoga, which long ago had been colonized by the Karelians. Mention was made in 1270 of Karelia as a *volost* under the jurisdiction of Novgorod; but the bond connecting the region to the Novgorod government was evidently quite loose. In 1278, feeling that its interests were being jeopardized by the Karelians' collaboration with Western traders, Novgorod sent a punitive expedition to Karelia.

After Novgorod had once more been weakened by a Tatar invasion, Marshal Tyrgils Knutsson, the political leader of Sweden, launched, for the second time, an excursion that had failed half a century earlier. In 1293, he organized an expeditionary force for action in Karelia, and he built the Castle of Viipuri on the site of an old trading post on the coast, at the mouth of the older outlet of the Vuoksi River, which in those times was still navigable. From this base, the Swedes sought to conquer all Karelia. They did manage to capture, at an early stage, the Castle of Käkisalmi, which dominated the heart of Ladoga Karelia, which stood on the shore of Lake Ladoga, at the mouth of the Vuoksi's newer outlet. But the Swedes failed to gain permanent possession of the castle. In the year 1300, Swedish forces, under the personal command of the marshal, sailed to the Neva and built a fortress near the site of the present city of Leningrad. However, this base likewise had to be surrendered a couple of years later under enemy harassment and the ravages of scurvy.

The second Swedish attempt to seize control of the Neva route thus miscarried. During these operations, it became obvious that the Swedish strategy of conquest and the interests of international commerce did not run parallel. The German traders did not want the trade route leading to Russia to be brought under outside domination.

After the collapse of the Neva Expedition, the strength of the Swedish attackers waned, giving Novgorod time to consolidate its positions in Ladoga Karelia, which it valued for the readily accessible natural resources there.

The almost ceaseless succession of battles that lasted thirty years brought no change in the situation. Viipuri, as the new outpost of the West, remained. But every attempt to penetrate deeper, to Ladoga and the Neva, failed. With the German traders acting as mediators, peace was established at last in 1323, in the Russians' new border fortress at Pähkinäsaari (Orekhov, later Schlüsselburg).

The peace treaty confirmed the division of Karelia between Sweden and Novgorod, and in a formal sense, too, ended the independence of the province. Novgorod surrendered to the Swedes the three westernmost Karelian areas, Savo, Jääski and Äyräpää, i.e., territory already in actual Swedish possession. The boundary started at Siestarjoki (later named Rajajoki, meaning "border river") and ran through precisely marked points across the Karelian Isthmus to Lake Saimaa. Only two or three local points were mentioned in the lake district of Savo, which in those times was still uninhabited. The border terminated in the northern part of the Gulf of Bothnia (see map 1). The northern coast of the Gulf of Finland was thus acknowledged to be under Swedish rule.

But Novgorod retained its grip on the true heart of Karelia, the territory bordering on Lake Ladoga, whose traditional rights to the salmon waters of North Ostrobothnia were recognized by the way the new border was drawn. It was in the interest of the German mediators that unobstructed passage to the Neva was expressly guaranteed by the peace treaty. Several provisions, including a ban on building new fortresses in Karelia, were designed to secure a lasting peace.

The Peace Treaty of Pähkinäsaari is the first written document drawn up between Sweden and Russia in which the eastern border of Finland is defined. It remained formally in effect until the signing of the Peace of Täyssinä (1595); every time a recurrence of hostilities ended, that treaty was acknowledged to be the legal basis of neighborly relations.

The boundary line that was drawn at Pähkinäsaari established Finland's now historical eastern border in the southern part of the Karelian Isthmus, until 1940. In the interior and in northern Finland, the spheres of interest were very roughly divided by the peace negotiators, because their main attention was riveted on the commerce in the Gulf of Finland. Thus, the border of the territory that belonged to Novgorod, extending from the Gulf of Bothnia to Sweden proper, was ignored. In fact, it was not until three years later that Norway, then linked to Sweden in a personal union, was forced to settle border relations with Novgorod alone. The northernmost regions remained undivided by the three states, and title to the territory was held jointly.

In Finland, the period of the Crusades ended with the signing of the Peace of Pähkinäsaari. During that period, the bridgehead of Christendom in southwestern Finland, comprising the original diocese of Finland, had expanded to the far end of the Gulf of Finland, into the boundless wilds of the Finnish interior, and up to the far northern shores of the Gulf of Bothnia. In short, the bridgehead had expanded into the Finland of the Middle Ages. Also during the Crusades, the loose alliance of the Finns and the Swedes had become transformed into a firm political bond. Finland became attached organically to the kingdom of Sweden—but part of the Karelian branch of the Finnish people had been taken under the wing of Novgorod on the other side of the line dividing Western and Eastern Christendom.

Society in the Early Middle Ages

The organization of ancient Finnish society into more compact forms, resulting in the medieval social stratification according to estates, was carried out largely by the Church. The Church built on an old foundation in doing so. The areal communities of pagan times served as the framework for the ecclesiastical parish division. The yeomen were pressured into erecting churches and paying tribute, partly, perhaps, on a system derived from the ancient sacrificial impositions.

A conspicuous change took place after Earl Birger's expedition to Tavastia. The Swedish Crown no longer merely gave occasional military support but undertook to establish permanent bases of its own in Finland. The episcopal administration was replaced by secular rule. Bishop Thomas's immediate successor, Bero, let the king take over the collection of tribute from Finland in the middle of the thirteenth century. By the end of the century, the Crown had set up a firm administrative apparatus in Finland, for the support of which three large, centrally located castles had been built, in Turku, Hämeenlinna and Viipuri (see map 2). The labor performed in building the castles, the assessments paid for their upkeep, and the duty of entertaining members of their garrisons—who traveled about the respective provinces and were characteristically called *ruokaruotsi* (Food Swedes)—placed additional burdens on the Finnish population. When the military expenditure was not particularly heavy, the surplus revenue collected from Finland could be delivered to Sweden. At first, these payments probably consisted chiefly of expensive furs and, later, also of grain and money.

The Folkungs, the royal dynasty of Sweden founded by Earl Birger, set a high value on the dominion of Finland and endeavored to keep a firm hold on the country. In the division of the royal inheritance, Finland was twice handed over as a duchy to the king's younger brother: in 1284 to Benedict, and in 1302, to Valdemar. On the latter occasion, however, the king shortly afterward laid personal claim on the fief of Viipuri. Owing to the squabbles within the royal family, the ducal system of government did not last long.

The partitioning of Finland for administrative purposes varied, but the firmest unifying tie was ecclesiastical. The whole of Finland, including, right from the beginning, the Swedish-settled island of Aland, composed the unified diocese of Turku. Accordingly, the provinces incorporated at a later date also began to be regarded as belonging to the oldest Christian province, Finland (Proper). At first, the designation used was *Finlandia et partes orientales* (Finland

and the eastern regions). Later on, the name Finland—or, as viewed from Sweden, "Eastland(s)" (*Österlanden, Österlandia*)—covered the entire diocese of Turku, comprising the territory on the eastern side of the Gulf of Bothnia that had been annexed to the kingdom of Sweden.

The new political system brought about major changes throughout Finnish society. Two new estates, the nobility and the clergy, evolved, partly out of the native population and partly by transplantation from abroad. Among Finland's oldest noble families, the Swedish element was quite notable. Later, it received fresh blood from Germany and Denmark. The native stock contributed a small portion. The founder of the Kurki family was, according to folklore, the chief of the Lapland fur traders from Pirkkala. Later, however, the class lines were not so rigid that a Finnish yeoman capable of performing cavalry service could not be raised to the status of nobleman. In frontier districts and along the coast, whole groups of estates formed, which were exempted from land dues in return for various services to the Crown.

Among the clergy, the native element was conspicuously represented from the very start. In order to act as confessors and teachers, the clergy had to know the vernacular. As early as the second decade of the thirteenth century, missionaries could be sent from Finland to Estonia. In 1291, a native Finn, Magnus I, was appointed to the office of bishop of Turku for the first time.

In spite of the transfusions of alien blood, Finnish society continued to develop on a native basis. The local administration of justice and political affairs took place within the framework of the ecclesiastical parishes. At first, the law was administered according to the unwritten native code, which was rooted in custom. But, the Swedish commandants and magistrates naturally adhered to the principles of provincial justice they knew from Sweden. The first example of the extension to Finland of Swedish general law, which was then only in the process of development, was King Birger's letter of 1319, in which the regulations governing "women's peace," were declared applicable in Karelia, still a theater of war. It was not until the fourteenth century that the general law of King Magnus Erik's son was applied in Finland; but, since it failed to live up to local needs, the customs of the land continued to serve.

More extensive areas of local administration were the provinces, which were partly drawn along the lines of the tribal regions of pagan times and partly on the basis of the new partition of the country into large fiefs, each dominated by a castle.

An excellent picture of the early medieval Finnish society and its economy is provided by the system of Church assessments that was set up in the thirteenth and fourteenth centuries through agreements made between the ecclesiastical authorities and the inhabitants of the provinces. In the ancient Finnish districts of southwestern Finland, agriculture (evidently consisting of field cultivation) had made such progress that full canonical tithes could be collected there in crops and livestock, in addition to which an extra portion of rye was claimed by the local priest. The pioneer Swedish settlements along the coast practiced dairy farming to a greater extent, so only two-thirds of the canonical tithes were paid by them in grain, with the balance made up by various payments in butter.

The demarcation line between the Finns and the Swedes was not particularly rigid, for the pioneer Finnish settlements in the interior of southwestern Finland were brought under the same system as the Swedish colonies. The Swedish system of Church dues spread throughout all the coastal provinces. Fishing and sealing were important means of livelihood, besides agriculture, for the coastal population, and they likewise were subject to levies. It was not possible, however, to introduce canonical tithes into the interior of the country—that is, Upper Satakunta, Tavastia, and Finnish Ostrobothnia. Instead, the farms were required to pay various kinds of dues to the bishop, priest and Church, according to agreement.

Agriculture was quite advanced in the interior, too. This is indicated by the fact that, besides the farm, or household, the unit of assessment applied was the *aratrum* (plowland), which was scaled in ratio to the size of an holding. It was known in many European countries. In Finland, however, the *aratrum* included not only arable land but also, as its natural complement, an extensive *erämaa,* or wilderness reserve—and that is why the owner of an *aratrum* made payments in both grain and furs. A tax was also levied on fish caught in the wilds. An individual assessment unit that was applied in addition to farms and *aratra* was the "bow", meaning every man capable of joining a hunt and drawing a bow.

A similar system of Church dues based on mutual agreement with the farmers was applied in eastern Finland; but, because of the nature of the local economy, characterized by the large-scale practice of raising crops on burnt-over clearings, which had to be abandoned after two or three seasons, considerable modifications had to be made in the system. The farmes of Savo kept shifting their cultivations from forest to forest. Their holdings could not be divided into fixed units of land; their clearings had to be assessed all over again each year. In Karelia, a further step was taken. There, the source of wealth was not land, of which there was a sufficiency on every side, byt rather the manpower capable of cutting the clearings out of the forest. The most important unit of assessment, accordingly, became the "bow." The dues paid in kind, furs and grain, were largely interchangeable. Toward the end of the Middle Ages, furs played a declining role, while grain took on greater importance.

In northern Ostrobothnia, where both the western Finnish principle of tithes and the system based on the joint agreement that was applied in the interior were observed, the ancient wilderness economy still prevailed. Agriculture yielded only small barley crops and some butter, but the wealth yielded by the wilds was much greater: marten and squirrel skins, bear meat and venison, and fish—pike, whitefish, and especially, that prized denizen of large rivers, the salmon.

The coexistence of Finnish and Swedish customs, most clearly manifest in the collection of Church dues and in the administration of justice, was particularly characteristic of medieval Finland. In this respect, conditions were altogether different from those prevailing south of the Gulf of Finland, where the German proselytizers and conquerors forced the natives into submission and, finally, into serfdom. The Swedes were not a very much larger nation than the Finns. They managed to impose their rule on the Finns, but they could not enslave them.

The Finnish yeomen retained their freedom and managed their local affairs pretty much as they pleased. Of course, the creation of the new social order caused tension and friction, and the new economic burdens the Finns were obliged to bear were liable to be resented. Still, the Finnish farmer was not bound to the soil or to any narrow local sphere of life, like his central European fellows. Whoever got fed up with the exactions of organized society and the mores imposed by the ruling class could always withdraw into the virgin wilds. Out there, church bells could never be heard ringing and the bailiff's watchful eye could not see the smoke rising from the backwoodsman's cabin chimney. It took a long time for government authority to catch up with him. Thus, pioneer settlers had an important part of their own to play in both the internal development of the country and its external vicissitudes.

Finland's Borders Become Established

Either party could scarcely have entertained the illusion that the Treaty of Pähkinäsaari would establish "everlasting peace." It remained unbroken for only fourteen years. The spark that ignited new hostilities was unrest in Karelia.

After the treaty had been signed, Novgorod endeavored to tighten its grip on the part of Karelia that was left in its possession. In order to nourish the Eastern Orthodox faith, a monastery was founded, in 1329, on the island of Valamo (Valaam in Russian) in Lake Ladoga. The border regions were given as fiefs to a Lithuanian prince. When he drew the leash too tight, there was a reaction. In 1337 the Karelian commandant of Käkisalmi, a man named Vallittu, invited the Westerners from Viipuri over to his castle. Thus, the border peace was broken. After a couple of years of fighting, peace was restored on the former terms. The lord of Viipuri castle was branded guilty of starting the war.

In conjunction with the peace negotiations, King Magnus Erik's son (who also ruled Norway) had an opportunity to acquaint himself more thoroughly with the problems of Eastern policy. Among his close advisers were numerous advocates of an energetic line of action. Presumably prompted by information volunteered by Bishop Hemming of Turku, the great Swedish woman prophet, St. Birgitta, began to spread propaganda for a crusade. She proclaimed that Christ had now chosen a new portal which he wished to enter, namely, the portal into the souls of the Karelians and the heathens. For the last time, a genuine crusading zeal flared up in Scandinavia.

After careful preparations, an attack aimed straight at the Neva was launched in 1348. Participating in the campaign, in addition to the Swedes and Finns, were German mercenaries (whose hiring St. Birgitta considered to be a betrayal of the crusading ideal), as well as a number of Norwegian nobles. The offensive was directed not only against the Neva area but also far beyond the border, past the northern shore of Lake Ladoga. Military operations were paralyzed, however, by the outbreak of the plague—known as the Black Death—which wreaked havoc amog both forces.

Peace was reaffirmed in 1351 at Tartu (Dorpat) on the same terms as before. A *status quo* after the heavy losses was tantamount to defeat. Crusading zeal was extinguished forever in Scandinavia, and, along with it, the active Neva policy was buried for centuries. Throughout the later Middle Ages, the Swedish-

Finnish authorities were content to defend the old border on the Karelian Isthmus and to reinforce the walls of Viipuri.

The situation was different on the coast of the Gulf of Bothnia, where the salmon-rich waters held by the Karelians of Novgorod were thrust like a wedge between territories involving the interest of their Western Finnish kinsmen. These interests were looked after by the organization of trappers who roamed Lapland known as *Pirkkalaiset (bircarli* in Latin), apparently named after the parish of Pirkkala. They followed the chain of lakes emptying into the Kokemäki River system northward, and, after dragging their boats over the narrow necks of land in between, they rowed down the rivers of Ostrobothnia to the coast of the Gulf of Bothnia just south of the Karelians' zone of interest. In return for the payment of a small tax in squirrel skins, the king of Sweden, in 1277, ratified the rights of the *Pirkkalaiset* to exact tribute from the Lapps and to fish in the far northern rivers. These Finnish trappers were the only ones in those times who were in a position to look after the interests of the Swedish Crown in the vast Arctic wilds.

After the Treaty of Pähkinäsaari, there was a wild rush to the rivers of northern Ostrobothnia and their rich yield of salmon. Swedes were colonizing the western coastal areas along the Gulf of Bothnia around that period, and were bent on claiming the territory on the opposite side, too. Bishop Benedict of Turku, however, took brisk countermeasures. He incorporated into his diocese the entire Karelian coast of the Gulf of Bothnia under the dominion of Novgorod, which, in the north, extended up to the Kemi River. The archbishop of Uppsala hastened to baptize the few Karelians and Lapps who inhabited the seaboard, but he was too late. At a meeting of the archbishop of Uppsala and Bishop Hemming of Turku in 1346, it was agreed that the easternmost salmon-fishing river of the *Pirkkalaiset,* the Tornio, was under the jurisdiction of the archibishopric of Uppsala and that the northernmost salmon river emptying on the Karelian coast, the Kemi, belonged to the diocese of Turku. When the Swedes repeated their demand, the boundary between the two dioceses was definitely ratified in 1374. This boundary, which ran slightly west of the Kemi River, remained the ecclesiastical and administrative border of Finland against Sweden proper until the year 1809 (see map 2).

The annexation of the Karelian coast of the Gulf of Bothnia to Finland had taken place without consulting Novgorod, which by no means relinquished its political claims. Nor did the Karelians of Novgorod abandon their economic and commercial interests. They made frequent destructive raids to revenge themselves on their kinsmen of an alien faith who had colonized the Bothnian coast; and also they clung to their rights in Lapland, where Norwegians intruded as a third contending party.

The dispute over the Bothnian coast and the far northern wilds was a constant cause of friction with Finland's eastern neighbors. The fighting in the far North consisted of unorganized tribal warfare, which was not directly in keeping with the official policies of the states concerned. The inhabitants of Ostrobothnia often complained that the Karelians of Novgorod made treacherous attacks after the reaffirmation of peace. From the standpoint of Novgorod, such aggressive action was quite natural, since the Karelians were simply exercising their right to utilize the sector of the Ostrobothnian seaboard which had been awarded to them by treaty.

Lapland proper, where Norwegians took a hand as a third party, in addition to the Western Finns and the Karelians, remained undivided, commonly held territory for a long time after the opening of the modern era. The right to levy taxes did not relate there to areas of land but to families of Lapps leading a nomadic existence. This by no means did away with the injustice that the same Lapps were liable to pay tribute to more than one crown.

The Stabilization of Finland's Status

King Magnus Erik's son strove to keep Finland as securely as possible in his grasp and to utilize her resources in the royal struggle against the Swedish nobility, which was steadily groving stronger. Finland had been firmly linked to the royal dynasty of old, but the poweful Swedish aristocracy had no secure foothold in the country outside the province of Viipuri. The monarch took pains to develop the administration of Finland and to increase her revenue yield. He decreed, for instance, that lands, including burnt-over clearings in the forests, which could not be farmed by their owners, should be divided among settlers. King Magnus was the first Swedish sovereign who personally acquainted himself with conditions in Finland in his travels.

War with Russia began a new phase in the king's internal administration. An acute shortage of money forced him to put up a stiff front against the aristocratic opposition. One act that most deeply offended the Swedish nobility was his awarding Finland and other territories, in 1353, as a duchy to Bengt Algot's son, who was a nobleman but not a member of the royal family. This incited a rebellion, during which the Swedish nobility reaised the king's sons, Eric, and, later, Haakon, to the position of sovereign alongside the king. Although the Swedish throne was elective, the king's eldest son was usually the logical candidate. Entitled to take part in the elections at this period were the yeomen of the different provinces, under the leadership of their highest magistrates, or *lagman* ("law men"), and representatives of the Church. Especially significant from the standpoint of the status of Finland was the election of King Haakon on the 15th of February in 1362. At that time, the real ruler of Finland was a rebel leader named Niles Ture's son, Bielke, who participated in the election as the *lagman* of Finland. On this occasion, the youthful king drew up a letter in which, "by virtue of the loyalty and love that our parents always were accorded in Finland," he recognized Finland's right to participate in the elections of Swedish sovereigns, which the dioceses and provinces of Sweden had enjoyed since ancient times. The bishop was entitled to attend the election in the company of a few clergymen, and the chief justice was accorded equal status with the other parts of the kingdom, whose inhabitants were privileged, in line with the traditional Swedish forms of provincial selfgovernment, to participate also in the highest affairs of state.

King Haakon's letter gained considerable significance in its relation to political law. It is notable that the date of the election of the president of the independent republic of Finland coincides with the date on which the letter was drafted. However, its contemporary significance was not equally great. Because of its ice-locked sea, Finland was isolated from the main part of the realm for nearly six months out of each year. Consequently, she could not effectively influence the affairs of state within the framework of the aristocratic constitutional system that was characteristic of medieval Sweden. Finland needed her own administrative authorities, who could act with relative independence of the Swedish organs of state. They might be either loyal lieutenants of the king or semi-independent holders of large fiefs, who asked advice from no quarter. Both kinds of administrators were known in medieval Finland.

A couple of years after the election of King Haakon, the national dynasty of Sweden was overthrown and the upper nobility invited the German Albert of Mecklenburg to accept the Swedish throne. In Finland, the old dynasty continued to have staunch support. The Castle of Turku surrendered to the Germans in 1365, the last of the major castles of the realm to do so.

The initial phase of the Mecklenburgian period was a restless and violent occupation, which weighed heavily on the nation. The Germans built a number of new castles to consolidate their power. Compulsory labor service and the maintenance of the castles proved to be a strain on the population. A folk poem of the period complains of the high cost of living: One loaf of bread cost a cow, while to purchase just a slice, a bull-calf was needed. The German sovereign did not have the same kind of personal relationship with the Finns that his Swedish predecessor had. Once, in financial straits, he even planned to sell the whole country of Finland to the Teutonic Order of Knights.

Conditions were stabilized once more by the Swedish nobleman Bo Jon's son, Grip, who, through shrewd political maneuvers and skillfull financial manipulations, acquired, mainly as security for loans, one province after anothet, both in Finland and in Sweden. By the year 1374, he had gained title to all of Finland. In addition, he took over the office of *lagman*. He was the first Swedish nobleman to use Finland as a springboard for an attempt to gain control of the whole realm. Finland was not an independent objective for him, but he was obliged to consider her welfare for the sake of his own personal interests. Accordingly, he defended the rights of the Finns at the far end of the Gulf of Bothnia against both the archbishop of Uppsala and the Novgorodians. He continued the German project of building castles. Since, in addition to their defensive function, the castles also served as administrative centers, administration became mor effective—which, in turn, necessitated heavier taxes.

The Mecklenburgian period at first appeared to be forcing into new channels the evolutionary trend of the preceding couple of centuries, which had made Finland a geographical entity, a Christian community founded on Scandinavian principles of justice, and, in spite of her union with Sweden, a country with a unique national character.

Bo Jon's son, Grip's power restored the old trend, but, more than ever, it underscored Finland's relative detachment from the political organs of Sweden. When Grip died in 1386, he left behind him a testament intended to secure the preservation of the provinces he held by right of lien—among them, all of Finland—in the hands of the Swedish national aristocracy, irrespective of the king's will. Such an arrangement was essential from the standpoint of the interests of the aristocracy, because, contrary to the situation in continental Europe, there was no hereditary feudalism in the kingdom of Sweden during the Middle Ages.

3

Finland in the Scandinavian Union

The Finns Are Drawn into the Union

Under political tension, usually all that is needed to set the machinery of major events into motion is a slight shift of forces in a limited area. Such was the situation that prevailed in Sweden at the time of Bo Jon's son, Grip's death. The man who confounded the Swedish nobleman's neatly drawn-up plans was his former subordinate, Jakob Abraham's son, Diekn, the lord of Turku Castle.

In providing for the future of the realm, Grip had forgotten to reward his own retainers. It was not difficult for discontented Jakob Abraham's son to convene the provincial assizes of Finland Proper and convince the members that he knew the customs, burdens, and poverty of the land better than any stranger could, and that he was eminently qualified to serve as the chief justice of Finland. King Albert of Mecklenburg, who was petitioned to ratify the election of the chief justice, saw his chance. In addition to the office of *lagman*, he gave Diekn authority over three provinces in western Finland. Thus, the testament of Bo Jon's son, Grip, was nullified.

In their struggle with the German king, the Swedish nobility could see no way out except to appeal to the old, deposed Swedish royal family. But, at that point, Fate intervened with a cruel stroke: The last male heir to the Swedish throne died. Only his mothet, Margaret, Queen of Denmark and Norway, survived. However, the queen agreed to come to the aid of the Swedish nobles, provided that she would be recognized as the sovereign ruler of the realm and would be awarded almost all of Grip's legacy, including all the fiefs of Finland except Viipuri Province. After her forces had defeated Albert of Mecklenburg, Queen Margaret, in 1389, demanded that the lords of the castles in Finland also acknowledge her sovereignty.

However, a transitional period followed that was marked by confusion and lasted for the next ten years. German power appeared to gain the ascendancy in Finland once more when Diekn, fearing displacement a second time, handed his provinces over to Grip's son, Knut, who, under the influence of his German-born mother, leaned on the Mecklenburgians for support. The latter equipped pirates, so-called Vitalians, for operations on the Baltic. The result was the dislocation of maritime commerce. The pirates finally were driven away from every area except the Finnish coast. There, they even gained possession of the castle of Korsholm in Ostrobothnia. It was not until 1399 that the last strongholds of the Vitalians and also of Mecklenburgian power were surrendered to Margaret, and a Danish commandant took over Turku Castle.

The events leading to the Scandinavian Union originally had been set in motion in Finland, but the principal decisions had been made elsewhere. Only a few of the Finnish political leaders were present at Kalmar in 1397 to take part in the negotiations to decide the conditions for the political union of the Northern countries. To Finland, the constitutional conditions of the Union were not as important as they were to the Scandinavian countries, since Finland was not a separate state which required the safeguarding of her freedom even within the framework of the Union.

The establishment of supreme administrative headquarters in Copenhagen rather than i Stockholm could scarcely give the Finns cause for complaint. More important was the external security afforded by the Union. Its creation was further motivated by factors of foreign policy: the economic and political pressure exerted by the Germans forced the nations of the North to pool their resources in order to protect their freedom. The lifting of the German yoke, which the Union effected, was a great relief to the Finns, too, but they could hardly help wishing that membership in the great Union might also mean added security against the constant threat that lurked behind the eastern border.

The Autocratic Rule of Eric of Pomerania

Two centuries had passed since the Danish attempt to gain a permanent foothold on Finnish soil. After selling Estonia to the Teutonic Knights in 1346, the Danes had faded from sight. The Scandinavian Union signified their return. Denmark emerged as the leading power of the combination. Discontent was aroused in Scandinavia because the rulers of the Union dealt with it as a single totality, disregarding the constitutional rights of the separate states. The Finns could scarcely regard it as tyranny when, in addition to Swedish nobles, Danish and German representatives of the sovereign also took over castles as commandants and were appointed to other high offices in Finland. It was in this way, for instance, that the Fleming family, which was destined to influence the fortunes of Finland for generations, became established in that country, its original representative having been chief justice of Finland.

Although, on the whole, Queen Margaret held the reins of government throughout the Union firmly in her grip until her death in 1412, Finland—like Norway, to some extent—was in an exceptional position. The queen apparently entrusted Finland as an experimental domain to her young foster son, Eric of Pomerania, whom she had chosen as co-ruler and successor. The young king made two trips to Finland during the lifetime of his foster mother, and all the royal dicisions relating to that country were made in his name. Once again, Finland became a royal domain that was independent of Sweden's constitutional organs of state, as she had been during the heyday of Earl Birger's family.

For the Union monarchy, it was important to increase the revenue from taxes in Finland. The first measure calculated to further this end was a revision of the exemptions from dues to the Crown. This revision was aimed primarily at those who had risen to the nobility during the Mecklenburgian regime. A clear line was drawn between rent-exempt land and taxable property held by yeomen, and those families who were exempt from paying land rents were required to render cavalry service. After the revision, the king alleviated its effects during his second sojourn in Finland by distributing quite a large number of certificates of nobility.

Now, the taxable land, from which the rent-exempt property had been separated, could be partitioned into appropriate assessment units and administrative areas so that the general tax burden might be redistributed more equably. Toward expanding the area of taxable land and increasing Crown revenue, the government authorities began to promote the colonization of the wilderness. The narrow southwestern coastal strip paid 60 per cent of all Finland's taxes, because the adventorous inland farmers who cultivated remote, burnt-out clearings in the forests, and the hunters and trappers generally managed to dodge the tax-collectors.

Since the taxes were levied on arable land, the government authorities viewed the wilderness as unproductive and untaxable. Not so the farmers, for whom the *erämaa* (hunting ground) was a vital concomitant to their farming income. Without the yield of his wilderness reserve, the Finnish tiller of the soil was doomed to poverty. So, when the Grown began to parcel out land, mainly in the backwoods areas between parishes, for colonization by families who were willing to pay taxes in return for homesteads, the differing conceptions of justice held by the Grown and by the established village farmers were bound to clash.

The utilization of the tax yield also required special arrangements. Finland had been one of Stockholm's sources of food supplies, but predominantly agricultural Denmark did not need Finnish grain and butter. The supply of furs was already beginning to be exhausted. In order to place tax revenue at the disposal of the central government, payments in kind had to be converted into cash. Seeking to establish a sound monetary economy, the Finns began to use their own money, which was not linked to the monetary unit of Sweden but to Finland's closest trading partner, Tallinn, on the Estonian coast, just across the narrow Gulf of Finland. Since there was not yet much actual money in circulation, fixed rates were places on the produce that the working population continued to deliver as tax payments in lieu of cash, in order to prevent bailiffs from misappropriating taxes.

Considerable attention was paid to controls on administration and justice. The judiciary was reorganized on all three levels of the courts. The aforementioned reorganization of the assessment areas, or rentpaying communities, was of particular importance to administration and justice. It resulted in the detachment of the administrative and judicial division of the country from the ecclesiastical system. The circuit in which the lowest courts—roughly corresponding to the circuit courts of the United States or the assizes of England —held their sessions, no longer kept to the traditional bounds of the ancient ecclesiastical parish but formed a new, artificial unit of local government, the civil parish. In this new circuit, it was easier for a judge who belonged to the nobility to carry the written Swedish code into effect in order to supersede the unwritten local law, which consisted of the "custom of the land," even though a twelve-man yeomen's jury continued to interpret the opinions of the local citizens on law and justice.

The most important measure, to the Finns, was the establishment of a Finnish supreme court to replace the old King's Court. The supreme court was composed of the bishop, a few members of the chapter, all the members of the Council of the Realm who resided in Finland, plus the judges of the higher and lower courts. It was assisted by a jury of half nobles and half peasants. Although this supreme court of the land was primarily a court of justice, it also was called upon to decide many administrative questions, including, for instance, complaints that had been filed against bailiffs. The very fact that it held regular sessions was significant in itself, for it afforded the leading men of Finland a practical forum in which to discuss all topical problems. Thanks to its tremendous distance from the central government in Denmark, Finland enjoyed a high degree of autonomy.

The extra security against foreign aggression was not so great as had been hoped for in Finland. Early in the second decade of the 1400's, the Russians attacked and burned down Viipuri, among other places, and, toward the end of Eric's reign, they presented demands for sweeping border revisions. The power of membership in the Scandinavian Union was reflected, however, in the self-assurance with which Krister Nils' son, Vase, lord of Viipuri Castle, waged his trade war against Tallinn and demanded the surrender of a Western trading office that was located i Novgorod, to the citizens of Viipuri. On the strength of the support from the king of the united North, Viipuri aspired to gain a position of parity with the Hanse towns in mediating Russian trade.

The Swedish Revolutionary Movement

King Eric pursued an active foreign policy, aimed at achieving mastery of the Baltic. It involved him in a long-drawn-out war along the southern frontier of Denmark and also lined up the chief Hanse towns on the side of his enemies. The strains caused by these hostilities, not least of which was a commercial blockade, aroused discontent with the autocratic king of the Scandinavian Union in all the countries under his scepter. In Sweden, the common people rose up in violent protest in 1434, and, soon, the very foundations of the mighty Union monarchy were shaking.

In the beginning, the Swedish mutiny spread only across the western seaboard of Finland. The bailiff of Ostrobothnia, Erik Puke, joined the rebels and captured the fortress of Kastelholm in the Aland Islands. At first, the rest of the Finnish leaders, including such prominent figures as Krister Nils' son, Vase, and Bishop Magnus II Tavast, took no action, but cautiously awaited developments. Their sympathies apparently remained with the monarch, so it was not until 1436 that they finally joined the revolutionary Swedish Council of the Realm, which was afraid that the Finns might set off on an independent course. Even after joining the Council, they tried to iron out the differences and pave the way for the deposed king's return to power. But their efforts as mediators did not lead to complete success, for King Eric's own obstinacy had lost him his crown. However, the Scandinavian Union was saved—which, to the political leaders of Finland, was the most important thing.

Furthermore, during the negotiations on the fate of the Union, Finland obtained new legal safeguards for her special political status. In the revised Swedish general law, which took effect in 1442 and was confirmed by the new king of Sweden, Christopher of Bavaria, Finland's right to take part in elections of the king was specifically guaranteed. Since Finland had now been divided into two *lagman* territories, she was entitled to double representation at the elections. In principle, the "king's jorney" (*eriksgata*), during which the sovereign-elect received the recognition of the inhabitants of the different provinces, and mutual oaths were sworn, was supposed to extend to Finland as well. If the weather or other circumstances prevented the voyage across the gulf, a special royal electoral meeting was held in Turku for the swearing of the required oaths. This became customary during the later phases of the Union.

Although the authorities in Finland had promptly granted the same tax reductions as had been obtained by the Swedes through their rebellion, the spread of social agitation to that country could not be halted. During the years 1438—1439, when the government lacked firm direction and the foundations of society trembled, popular mutinies broke out in Satakunta, Tavastia and Karelia. The Finnish rebel leaders, David in Satakunta and Philippus in Karelia, undoubtedly had been stirred by the uprising in Sweden; but heavy taxes and the measures imposed in conjunction with the colonization of the wilderness reserves gave ample cause for local discontent. Bishop Magnus Tavast, a skilled negotiator, succeeded in pacifying the Satakunta rebels, and representatives of the different parishes swore to forsake their ringleader, who was branded a madman. The mutinous movement in Karelia was supported by Krister Nils' son Vase's rival, Regent Karl Knut's son, Bonde, who had joined the rebels in a bid for personal power. His efforts to secure a foothold in Finland failed on this occasion, but he succeeded shortly afterward.

Finland as a Base of Operations for Karl Knut's Son

The reformers of the Union wanted to do away with the autocratic rule of King Eric of Pomerania and set up a constitutional monarchy based on the ideals of the aristocratic Council of the Realm. However, an evenly balanced system of government by the estates proved to be impossible. The result was a keen rivalry for positions of authority and, before long, increasing decentralization. It led to a drastic weakening of Finland's ties to the central government in Sweden.

Having been thrust onto the sidelines by the election of King Christopher, Karl Knut's son, Bonde, hastened to secure for himself a position of power in Finland to effect its withdrawal from the Union. At first, the new king promised Bonde the whole of Finland as his province; but the monarch would not countenance the creation of the sort of provincial power, involving the enfeoffment of all Finland under one lord, that had been held by Bo Jon's son, Grip. Taking advantage of the rivalry between Bonde and Krister Nils' son, Vase, the king reneged and offered Bonde only half of Finland. Bonde accepted and chose the eastern half. Then, in 1442, his rival's unexpected death opened the gates of Viipuri for him. This type of bipartition occurred frequently during the period of the Scandinavian Union.

Western Finland was an important source of supply to Stockholm, and, therefore, the central government was unwilling to loosen its grip on Turku and the western Finnish provinces. On the other hand, Viipuri was usually ruled over by one of the powerful aristocrats after the fashion of a semi-independent feudal lord. It was his responsibility to maintain relations with the neighboring power to the east, to cope with the problems of international trade, and to manage the defense of the eastern border primarily through the resources of his own fiefs. Since external security was a matter of vital concern to the whole of Finland, there was a tendency for the political center of gravity of the entire country to shift to the east, especially in times of danger. The bishop of Turku, who served as Finland's permanent representative in the Swedish Council of the Realm, was obliged to collaborate closely with the lord of Viipuri Castle. Thus, the exigencies of foreign policy and the episcopal association created by the Church brought together again the two parts of Finland that had been administratively divided for reasons of domestic politics.

Bonde's judgment of coming events had been correct when he chose Viipuri as his stronghold. The years he had spent developing eastern Finland and reinforcing its defenses were by no means wasted, even from the standpoint of his personal prestige and power. When King Christopher died in 1448, Bonde sailed to Stockholm, where he was elected king of Sweden. The troops he brought along with him from Viipuri undoubtedly helped tip the scales for him.

Bonde, now King Charles VIII, knew Finland better than any of his royal predecessors, and even after being crowned, he took a deep interest in her welfare. However, his potential was limited by wars and a confusing political situation. The election of a Swedish aristocrat to the throne in Stockholm meant the break-up of the Scandinavian Union. The new king of Denmark was disinclined to resign himself to his development, so Union politics underwent a drastic change. In place of amicable negotiations among the member states, solutions to political problems began to be sought in armed combat. The fratricidal strife between Denmark and Sweden, which gradually developed into national hatred, drained the resources of Finland, too, and robbed her of the external security that the Union previously had brought her.

The struggle waged by King Charles VIII was doomed to defeat in the long run. But his resistance was strong. And he retained substantial support in Finland. But, in 1457, he was forced to abdicate and surrender his crown to Christian I of Oldenburg, who then reigned over the Union. King Charles VIII was twice returned to the throne. Then, after his second abdication in 1465, he took refuge in Finland and, for the next couple of years, he governed his pensionary fiefs from Raseborg Castle, until another turn in the wheel of politics opened the way for his third reascension to the throne.

During that era of party strife, the political climate in Finland was by no means tranquil, either. The earlier pro-Union sentiment was represented by the sternly belligerent Bishop Konrad Bitz, whereas the supporters of Charles VIII formed the nucleus of the political faction that subsequently rallied around the national regents of Sweden.

The Totts Rise to Power

After Christian I had established his position in Sweden as king of the Scandinavian Union, he dispatched an armed force to subdue Finland. While Turku Castle was still under siege, the Danish nobleman, Erik Axel's son, Tott, called a meeting, at which the representatives of the different estates of Finland were forced to acknowledge Christian I as king of the Union. Tott, who, as a former retainer of King Charles VIII, was already known to the Finns, remained in Finland to assume command of Viipuri Castle. During the troubled decade of the 1460's, he used the castle as a base of operations from which to create for himself the same position of power that Karl Knut's son had held in his time. His power at times extended as far as Turku, and for a short while he was even regent of Sweden. His position was materially bolstered by the support given him by his brothers.

It was the family coalition of Totts that returned Charles VIII to the throne for the third time. Afterward, Laurens, one of the Tott brothers, received the castle of Raseborg, which had been vacated by the king. The eldest brother, Ivar, who ruled over Gotland as a powerful liege lord, had married the king's daughter and had received the castle of Korsholm in Ostrobothnia as a dowry. The family sway of the Totts is a typical example of the power combinations that existed during the era of the Scandinavian Union. The brothers controlled the trade routes in the eastern Baltic in splendid disregard of national boundaries. King Charles, on his death in 1470, held personal title only to Turku and a couple of southwestern provinces out of the total territory comprising Finland. These possessions were inherited by his kinsman, Sten Sture, who was elected regent of Sweden. The major part of Finland remained under the rule of the sons of Axel Tott, almost independently of the central government.

It was a boon to Finland to have her economic and military resources concentrated in the hands of Erik Axel's son at a time when menacing storm clouds were gathering over the eastern horizon. One of his dreams was to develop Viipuri into a center of eastern and western trade, but its realization would have required peaceful intercourse. Instead, tension increased in the 1460's, and the situation took a critical turn in the next decade. During that period, the grand duchy of Moscow forced the commercial republic of Novgorod into its sphere of interest and finally absorbed it entirely. In place of a Novgorod that sought trade with the West, Finland now had as her immediate neighbor an expanding, power-charged Moscow, which, having just shaken off the hegemony of the Tatars for good, was pushing toward the sea.

There was no lack of cause for friction between the neighbors. The Novgorodians had never abandoned their claims to the Karelian stretch of the Bothnian coast. Moreover, Finnish pioneers who settled the lake-strewn wilds of

Savo had crossed the disputed boundary at some points in the east to establish homesteads. Erik Axel's son, Tott, now took a bold step. In territory which the Russians claimed as theirs, he erected a new castle to protect the settlers. Called Olof's Castle (*Olavinlinna*), it still stands intact on an island within the city limits of Savonlinna, reputedly the best-preserved medieval fortress in the North. The city of Viipuri was surrounded by sturdy turreted walls. Since Tott could spend the revenue of his domain to meet its own local needs, he had the means to support such large-scale projects.

The enemy's attacks were still in progress when Tott died in 1481. But his brother, Laurens, managed to restore peace the following year.

Tott's remarkable career is the most conspicuous example of how a foreign official could, upon assuming chief responsibility for the fortunes of a country (which lasted, in this case, for decades on end), identify himself with the native environment in his capacity of governing authority and do his utmost to advance its welfare. The walls of Olavinlinna that Tott built tower over the skyline of the idyllic little town of Savonlinna to this day as a monument to the military culture and fighting spirit of the Finns of the late Middle Ages.

The Heyday of Ten Sture; War with Russia

After Tott's death, Regent Sten Sture laid claim to the Danish nobleman's fiefs. Laurens followed his brother to the grave shortly afterward, and Ivar Axel's son was unable to maintain the dominion of his family in Finland alone. Under military pressure from Sten Sture, he was compelled to relinquish Viipuri and the other eastern Finnish provinces to him in 1483. That year marks the beginning of Sten Sture's hegemony over Finland, although it was no until 1487 that Raseborg, the last stronghold held by the sons of Axel Tott, fell into the hands of the regent after armed combat.

Now, for the first time since the reign of Charles VIII, a head of state was in possession of the most important castles in Finland. Sten Sture maintained a tight grip on the reins of government. He refused to bestow the castles upon the high and mighty aristocrats of the realm but, instead, appointed bailiffs of humbler birth—who turned over the surplus revenue to him—to maintain them. His ascendancy in Sweden rested largely on the revenue he drew from Finland.

Later, the opposition contended that Sten Sture had neglected the defense of Finland. There were considerable grounds for this charge, for, at that time, the regent was forced to keep a constant watch on the internal political situation in Sweden and on the threat of danger from Denmark. Therefore, he was unable to make sacrifices, as Tott had done, for the defense of Finland. When the situation along the eastern frontier grew critical, he was prepared to bestow Viipuri upon some powerful nobleman as a fief once more. But the defense of the border against the East was no longer manageable on the resources of a single province or, in the final analysis, even on those of the entire country without help.

In the late Middle Ages, relations with Finland's neighbor to the east were conducted in such a way that the Peace Treaty of Pähkinasaari was extended for a few years at a time and disagreements were smoothed out at meetings held at the border at stipulated intervals. At these meetings, the Russians put forward demands regarding border surveys in accordance with the terms of the peace treaty. The Finns were reluctant to comply, because the old boundary marked down in the treaty no longer corresponded to the realities.

Sten Sture tried at first to win time and steer relations into a pacific channel by luring the Dutch, who around that time were competing with the Hanseatic traders in the Baltic, to enter into commercial dealings with the Russians while using Viipuri as a base of operations. Moscow, though, was out for more. It wanted to open wider the narrow vent it had at the far end of the Gulf of Finland and to engage in active trade with the Western nations. The political leaders of Finland, Dean, later Bishop, Magnus III Särkilahti and Commandant Knut Posse, already convinced that the disagreement would lead to war, sought allies among the other powers on Russia's border, including the Teutonic Knights who held the Baltic province of Livonia, and the kingdom of Poland.

In the spirit of the crusades, Magnus III Särkilahti relied on the Pope's exhortation to the Western nations to join forces against a common peril. Times, however, had changed. The foreign policy of the European states was just then metamorphosing into modern cabinet politics, which resorted quite as much to surprise moves in drafting treaties of alliance as to armed force. Russia also was drawn into this political game. In 1493, King Hans of Denmark concluded a treaty of alliance with the grand duke of Moscow. Thus, Regent Sten Sture was confronted by the threat of a two-front war.

This prospect was extremely alarming to Finland. King Hans had endorsed the boundary that had been drawn in the old treaties though he could scarcely have been aware of its geography. However, war would threaten Finland, not only with the loss of her frontier regions, but with total occupation by the enemy. It was under such circumstances that the lords of the castles of Finland and Bishop Magnus Särkilahti found themselves left to their own resources in preparing for defense.

After large-scale preparations, the Russians launched their invasion in the fall of 1495. But Commandant Knut Posse repulsed the invaders at the walls of Viipuri on November 30—St. Andrew's Day. Thus foiled the enemy withdrew, and the successful defense of Viipuri was hailed as a miracle. The astonishing military feat gave rise to a host of fantastic stories. Reports spread about the appearance on the scene of battle of a marvelous light, which led to the belief that St. Andrew had personally intervened to aid the defenders (though the Russians revered the saint much more than the Finns did). Later, incredible tales circulated about Knut Posse's magic tricks and the mighty "explosion of Viipuri" that he had engineered. (Probably, a tower that had been used as a powder magazine had blown up.)

However, the following year, in the winter of 1496, the Russians devastated wide areas in Karelia, Savo, and the interior of Finland as far as the province of Tavastia. Because help from Sweden had been delayed by disputes between Regent Sten Sture and the political opposition, it arrived too late to be of any use to Finnish defense. But, by the following summer, the means were at hand to launch a counterattack under the command of Svante Nils' son, who later became regent. Although the commander was also named Sture, he was not related to his namesake. The counterattack led only to a tactical success: The destruction of the new fortress, Ivangorod, which had been built by the Russians on the coast of the Gulf of Finland opposite the Livonian city of Narva. Sten Sture, worried by the opposition at home, felt compelled to make peace without delay. An agreement was reached in March, 1497, which held that the Peace Treaty of Pähkinäsaari would remain in effect.

The danger of a Russian conquest of Finland had been removed; but the cessation of hostilities did not insure a lasting peace, for the threat of war was present at the border meeting which was to be held shortly, where disagreement could easily lead to armed combat.

However, the authorities in Finland then resorted to an expedient that was characteristic of the Renaissance period. Evidently on the initiative of Regent Sture, a new copy of the peace treaty was forged in Viipuri Castle to validate the border that had been arbitrarily established during the fifteenth century. The Russians could not be fooled, of course, but, fortunately, their expansionist aims turned farther south in the succeeding years. Nevertheless, at all the negotiations with the Russians for nearly a century afterward, the representatives of the kingdom of Sweden continued to uphold the fake treaty.

Finland as a Separate Military Government During the Final Conflicts of the Scandinavian Union

King Hans of Denmark did not join the Russian attack on Finland in 1495, but preferred to await developments. Then, later, Regent Sten Sture's opposition in Sweden made him the scapegoat of the mismanaged war. Toward the end of 1497, he was deposed, and Hans was hailed as king of the Scandinavian Union. Sten Sture received Finland as his retirement domain. The old regent still enjoyed considerable support among the Finns. They regarded the charge against him by the opposition of Swedish nobles as immoderate. King Hans, however, did not relish the idea of having all of Finland under the rule of a single powerful individual any more than Christopher of Bavaria had in 1442. As early as 1499, Sten Sture was pressed to give up the most important of his castles in Finland.

When King Hans became sovereign ruler of the Union, his four-year-old alliance with the grand duke of Moscow proved to be a liability. The Russians hastened to demand territorial concessions, which they insisted had been promised to them. The king's consequent loss of confidence was one reason for the shortened life of the Union. In 1501, Sten Sture was invited to take over the regency once more. Since the Danish monarch would not voluntarily relinquish his hold on Sweden, an almost uninterrupted series of wars within the Union were fought during the next two decades. The effects, both direct and indirect, told on Finland, too.

After the alliance between Denmark and Moscow, it would have been silly to expect continued support for the Union ideal from the Finns. Instead, they pledged their allegiance to the national regents of Sweden.

However, the horrors of the Russian incursions of 1496 had left ineradicable scars on the Finnish mind, and the Finns now took to viewing their own problems, more and more, as separate from those of Sweden. The most urgent problem was the security of the eastern border, and they endeavored to concentrate the resources of the land on coping with it. The decentralizing tendency that typified the period of the Union nourished this spirit. Thus, each councillor of the realm insisted on having a say in the appointment of the commandants of the castles in his native province. Since the attitude of the Finns was particularistic and not nationalistic, they could rely on the support of the high-ranking Swedish aristocrats who had become permanently established in Finland.

The lord of Viipuri Castle, Erik Ture's son, Bielke, who was primarily responsible for the defense of the country, supported the people of western Finland when they ran into difficulties with the Swedish bailiffs who had been sent over by the regent. Bielke openly demanded that public offices and other posts of authority be entrusted to sensible men of native birth. The conflict was aggravated when the new regent, Svante Nils' son, Sture, also sought recognition of his ascendancy in Finland, in 1504. The Finns wanted authority over the military and economic resources of the land concentrated in the same hands. In the end, an agreement was reached whereby the economic bipartition of the country was preserved, with Bielke recognized as the "plenipotentiary and powerful chief," i.e., military governor, of all Finland.

Bielke proved to be quite a modern administrator. It was he, for instance, who made the first attempt to dig a canal between Lake Saimaa and Viipuri. His signal achievement, though, was to restore peace along the eastern frontier. When the Teutonic Knights of Livonia became involved in hostilities with Russia, he remained unconditionally neutral. Nor did he collaborate in the commercial blockade declared by the Hanseatic League. Instead, he tried to acquire the rights of the abandoned Hanse office in Novgorod for Viipuri. He indignantly denied charges of secret collaboration with the Russians as an insult to his Christianity; but when Tallinn insisted that the burghers of Viipuri be required to swear an oath that merchandise imported by that city would not be resold to the Russians, he responded that such poor men could not submit to such a heavy sacrifice. He thereby gained the confidence of the Russians and succeeded in renewing the peace treaty for a period of sixty years. The border issue remained unsettled, however, and the frequent border conferences always held the threat of war.

When Danish naval raids began to extend all the way to the Finnish coast, peace on the eastern frontier became even more imperative. Bielke, along with the bishop of Turku, resisted the regent's demands that the Finns send ships to Sweden. Bielke wanted to concentrate Finland's forces on the defense of her own shores. Even so, grievous surprises could not be avoided. The Danes captured the Aland Islands and held on to them for a time; and in the year 1509, they made a destructive raid on Turku, even committing sacrilege on the cathedral. The period of fighting that marked the closing phase of the Union was a heavy strain on Finland, which still was impoverished from the destruction wrought by the Russians in 1496.

Bielke's death in 1511 left Finland without a political leader of his caliber. When, a year later, Sten Sture, the younger, succeeded his father, Svante Nils' son, Sture, as regent, the aristocratic opposition in Sweden attempted to take over Viipuri; but brisk countermeasures taken by the youthful regent foiled the plot. The post of commandant of Viipuri Castle went to Erik Ture's son's nephew, Tönne Erik's son, Tott, who, by continuing to pursue the policy of his predecessor, managed to keep the peace, notwithstanding the renewal of the Russo-Danish alliance. In the face of growing tension in foreign affairs, the regent entrusted the lord of Hämeenlinna, Ake Göran's son, Tott, with the same authority as military governor that had been held by Bielke. Sten Sture won greater Finnish support than had his father. When the national regency of Sweden fell in 1520 before the onslaught of King Christian II of Denmark, Finland remained as the last stronghold of the Stures' party. In the treaty of capitulation signed in Stockholm, provision even was made for the widow of the fallen regent to use Finland as a retreat.

Christian II's treachery caused the plan to fall through. The Finns opened the gates of their castles to the Danes in good faith, especially since they were urged to do so by the prelate Hemming Gadh, former confidant of the regent. Soon afterward, horrifying news arrived from Stockholm: the king of the Union had, in conjunction with the coronation celebration, ordered the execution of the adherents of the Sture party, who had been accused of imprisoning the archbishop during Union disputes, and therefore had been proclaimed heretics. Resistance was now too late, and the pronouncement of heresy had stunned the victims. The most prominent lords of the Finnish castles, including both Totts, who had not gone to Stockholm, also had their heads chopped off. The executioner's axe did not spare even the gray head of the prelate Hemming Gadh.

The hard defensive fight of the final phase of the Union had culminated in defeat. Finland had fallen under Danish occupation. However, there was some consolation in the country's misfortune: the Russions did not intervene even after the struggle for freedom led by Gustavus Vasa spread to Finland in 1521.

Without sufficient power, however, the Finns failed in their efforts to drive out the Danish occupation forces. Only after a decisive victory had been achieved in Sweden, in 1523, could Finland throw off the Danish yoke. The occupation thus had lasted for only a few years. But since the lords of the chief castles had lost their heads and the last Catholic bishop, Arvid Kurki, had drowned in the Gulf of Bothnia during the war of liberation, the element that had controlled Finnish politics up to that time was gone. Now, new men could take the helm. This proved to be the most far-reaching effect of the period of Danish occupation.

The Culture of the Late Medieval Era

The late Middle Ages have been referred to in continental Europe as the "autumn" of the medieval era. In Finland, where Christianity was introduced at a comparatively late stage, that period represented only the blossoming of medieval culture to full flower. During that period, the Finns wholeheartedly embraced the medieval Catholic culture, and the Renaissance currents undermining its foundations were felt only weakly at peripheral points like Finland. The Church patronized all the higher cultural pursuits, and it was likewise responsible for maintaining public education as well as for the care of the sick and the poor—services that took on semi-municipal features in urban communities.

A total of some eighty stone churches were built by the close of the Middle Ages, many of which were decorated with murals. To this day, their gray granite walls bear witness to the peaceful works and high spiritual aspirations of those times. Art, too, was patronized by the Church. It was sensitive to influences from neighboring countries, notably Germany and Sweden, but, toward the end of the medieval era, native stylistic trends and original modes of expression began to appear.

Some remnants of the medieval literature in Latin and, partly, Swedish, have been salvaged. Foreign literature, particularly in a religious vein, was well known in Finland; but there was little original creative activity in this field, which produced a few saint's legends in Latin and some translations into Swedish. Priests evidently composed some Finnish folk poems, including, for example, the ballad about the slaying of St. Henry, but they were preserved only as oral traditions and written down at a later date.

No literary records in the Finnish language from the Middle Ages have been found. However, the language was used to preach sermons and for religious instruction. Thus, Finnish cultural vocabulary developed during medieval times as a basis for literature. In requiring the clergy to have a knowledge of the vernacular, the Church barred aliens from the priesthood in the diocese of Turku and nourished the budding national spirit. All the medieval bishops after 1370 were of Finnish birth, and nearly all of them were members of native noble families. Moreover, nearly all the appointments to the chapter went to Finnish-born candidates. University studies abroad taught them skillful ecclesiastical diplomacy and made them capable of competing for office with foreign rivals.

Finnish students were particularly attracted to the University of Paris, where, for example, nearly all the bishops of Turku, as well as many of the rural parish priests, had earned their Master of Arts degrees. The Finnish students joined the English (later German) *nation* of the University of Paris. Two Finns were even elected rector of the University. For instance, during the Franco-English War of the 1430's, Olavus Magni, subsequently consecrated as bishop, gained this distinction. At the end of the late Middle Ages, most of the students were sent to the nearer German universities. The weakening of the influence of the Romanic culture, which was mainly superseded by that of northern Germany, foreshadowed the change in cultural life brought about by the Reformation.

The Church was also an exceedingly important political and social factor. The bishop of Turku, who had a castle fo his own and, in many cases, a Crown fief besides, was the peer of laymen of power and an ex officio member of the Swedish Council of the Realm. His duties often included emphasizing the Finnish point of view at meetings of the Council. Even in political matters, he had the assistance of the canons of the chapter: for example, they were frequently present as delegates in negotiations with the Russians. It was expressly among the leading ecclesiastics that the line of action that was characteristic of the Finns was most clearly drawn, the line that primarily underscored the external security of the country. The issues of internal dissension, including, in a way, the fate of the Scandinavian Union, were, by comparison, of secondary importance.

Like the leadership of the Church, the lay estate of the nobility became rooted in the local soil and became a homogeneous class during the course of the Middle Ages. The Finnish nobility was not, however, a rigidly exclusive caste but constantly received fresh blood through both immigration and marriage, especially from Sweden. The lords of the castles were, in most cases, members of the upper nobility of Sweden and sometimes aristocrats from Denmark or Germany. Finland's own nobles were appointed to less exalted administrative and military posts: As bailiffs and, in particular, as various types of magistrates, whose duties called for a knowledge of the vernacular.

The economic position of the nobility was primarily based on ownership of land. But although many nobles held a great deal of land, they did not farm large estates. The land they owned consisted of numerous small farms, from which they collected an annual rent. The Church also owned land. However, compared to most of the other European countries, there were very few farmers in Finland who did not own the land they tilled. Only in certain parishes located near Turku were half the farms held by the nobility or the Church. Most of the estates that belonged to the nobility were located in the southwestern and southern provinces, although there were quite a few of them in the province of Tavastia, also. But there were none at all in Savo or Ostrobothnia.

By the end of the Middle Ages, Finland boasted six towns, of which Turku and Viipuri were the largest. The role of the urban population in the structure of society was small, but the cultural contribution of the towns was conspicuous. According to the law, Turku alone had the right to engage in foreign trade, but this restriction was not observed in practice. Viipuri was a major center of trade with Russia; and the farmers of the southern coastal regions engaged in lively commercial intercourse with Tallin, the nearest trading town in the Hanseatic League, which dominated Finnish trade—as well as trade with other Scandinavian countries—up to the end of the medieval era. As late as the fourteenth century, the majority of the merchants in the towns were Germans; but in the following century, the native element among them, both Finnish and Swedish, increased. At least, in Turku, men of native birth superseded the Germans in the municipal administration also. Foreign trade was no longer exclusively under the control of German commercial agents stationed in the towns of Finland. The burghers of Turku and Viipuri carried on trade with Baltic ports, using their own ships, although piracy, commercial blockades, and naval warfare often interfered with freedom of trade.

The basic element of the medieval economic structure in the North was the yeomanry, whose rent payments ran the machinery of society. Finland was extremely important to the economy of the Swedish realm, since there were not many freehold estates that were exempt from dues there, and nearly all the yeomen paid land rents to the Crown. In contrast to the peasants of continental Europe, the farmers of Sweden-Finland were free men, but their political influence was slight compared with their share of the economic burden of society.

As members of boards, and by attending various meetings, the Finnish yeomen could bring some influence to bear on local affairs, the processes of law, administration, and the activities of church parishes. It also was possible for the yeomen to participate in political decisions, and their representatives were even included among the electors of the kings; but the roles they played were usually those of supernumeraries. It was during the conflicts of the period of the Scandinavian Union that the Swedish parliamentary system was born, and the Finns also were represented in the Diet of Four Estates. In the long view, the creation of the Diet ranks among the most notable achievements of the era. It did not, however, clear the way for the common man's emergence to political power. Nor did it directly improve social conditions.

4

From the Middle Ages to the Modern Era

The Grip of the Central Government Tightens

The regents had laid a serviceable foundation for the internal policy of Gustavus Vasa (1523—60). And he enjoyed further advantages that his predecessors had lacked. He had been crowned King of Sweden. Mutual hostility prevented either Denmark or her exiled ruler, Christian II, from seriously threatening Sweden. And, except for two short wars, King Gustavus was able to manage the affairs of state under conditions of external peace. But he failed to preserve internal peace.

King Gustavus had won his crown as a leader in the national fight for freedom, a fight that amounted to a rebellion against the prevailing system. And he had ascended the Swedish throne at a time when traditions were being shattered and medieval society was disintegrating throughout Europe. These parallel background factors, national and universal, laid their stamp on his reign.

The new king ruthlessly violated the rights that had been enjoyed by the people of Sweden since early times whenever he felt that the interest of the state —which he completely identified with his personal interests—required it. He was chronically suspicious, even of his closest associates. And, due to his extraordinary memory and his incredible capacity for work, he was able to manage his realm like a colossal private enterprise. Indeed, Gustavus Vasa has often been compared to the proprietor of a great estate or to a modern business tycoon. However, in addition to the business executive's power to hire and fire employees, he also had the power to hang them.

Striving to grab all the reins of government, Gustavus Vasa fought particularism in both the forms in which it had developed during medieval times: One, the provincial self-government that was partly under the leadership of the yeomanry, and, two, the independent status enjoyed by the lords of the castles. On the Swedish side of the Gulf of Bothnia, a series of local insurrections organized by peasants or nobles broke out. But they were violently crushed. On the Finnish side, however, peace reigned—except for two minor episodes. First, the Germanborn lord of Viipuri Castle, John, Count of Hoya, threw in his lot with the enemy while the king was at war with Lübeck, with the result that the castle had to be taken into royal possession by force, and his large fief in eastern Finland was confiscated. Then, there was some friction with the peasantry in Karelia, but a couple of executions prevented its developing into a local rebellion.

Previously, the regents had planned to convert the fiefs which were under the independent rule of the commandants of the royal castles into bailiwicks to be managed by obedient bailiffs who would deliver the revenue collected to them. Gustavus Vasa pursued the same course. However, during the period following the Diet of Västerås, he needed the help of the nobility—primarily to oppose the Church, which drew its strength from the support of the commonalty; indeed, there was an expansion of the fiefs at the expense of the bailiwicks.

In Sweden, this change started slowly about the year 1540, but in Finland, it took place earlier and faster. The last lord of a castle of the medieval type in Finland was Erik Fleming, who was at the same time a loyal deputy of the king: Gustavus Vasa had assigned him administrative duties throughout Finland. By 1540, however, even Fleming's fief had been confiscated, after which the country was divided up into eight bailiwicks, roughly corresponding to the ancient Finnish provinces. However, this division did not become permanent, for the more duties were heaped on the shoulders of the bailiffs, the more bailiffs were needed. In the end, there were some forty bailiffs in Finland to carry out the direct orders of the monarch in the administration of local affairs. And a royal demesne was established as the center of each bailiwick, the lands being confiscated from the Church of from the yeomen of some village.

The bailiffs collected the Crown rents in kind from the farms and rendered accounts of the revenue. Part of the goods collected was consumed by the officers of the Crown who were housed on the royal demesne or by the troops who were quartered in the castles, another part was sold by the bailiffs on behalf of the Crown, and the third part was shipped to Stockholm, where the king's tax collecting office took charge of the supplies that were accumulating there. The king's accounting office examined the accounts of the bailiffs, in which the alternate use of measuring units current in Stockholm and in provincial localities continues to bring confusion to historians who seek information from this source.

The tightening of the hold of the central authority thus called for organized bureaus and trained public functionaries, of whom there was a shortage. Around 1540, the king invited some German experts to Sweden to organize centralized administration, and he even promoted one of them to the post of chancellor. But the experiment failed: The Germans became unpopular, and Gustavus Vasa's rule became more personalized than before. The network of bailiwicks remained, but it did not evolve into the hierarchy that is characteristic of the modern bureaucratic system. The king, or his royal secretaries, usually transmitted orders straight to the bailiffs, but to perform broader tasks in Finland, King Gustavus employed a special representative as an assistant, notably (after the death of Erik Fleming) Henrik Klaus' son, Horn. Later, the monarch's representative in Finland was given the title of governor, though even then he did not serve in any regular capacity of supervision over the activities of the bailiffs. Accordingly, the administrative apparatus that was fabricated by Gustavus Vasa combined both medieval and modern features.

The most lucrative source of Crown revenue by far was the land rent exacted from the farms in kind. With that yield, the bailiffs and the king carried on a profitable trade. Trying to devise means of augmenting the profits from his grand national enterprise, Gustavus Vasa made arrangements to raise the land rents, but this met with strong opposition. It was easier to lure members of large farming households into clearing virgin farms for themselves, thereby creating new rentpaying units. Especially in Finland, the opportunities for pioneer farming were boundless—both to the north and to the south of the limit of settlement (see map I). In the south, the land indisputably belonged to the farms and villages, while to the north stretched the *erämaat*, the vast wilderness reserves which were exploited for fur trapping, hunting, and fishing, and which the yeomen claimed as their domain on the strength of immemorial prerogative. But, according to the principles expounded by King Gustavus, no ancient prerogative could be allowed to obstruct the interests of the state. Therefore, in 1542, he proclaimed the uninhabited wilds to be the property of God, the king, and the Crown.

Around the same time, the bailiff of Savonlinna, Klemet Krook, drew the king's attention to the fact that the settlement of northern Savo would secure the area lying between the border that was drawn in the Treaty of Pähkinäsaari (Orekhov) and the boundary line claimed by Sweden. Thus, in addition to the economic considerations, the program of systematic colonization was justified by the exigencies of foreign policy. The Savoans farmed by making clearings in the forests, burning the trees thus cut down, and sowing crops in the ashes. Such plots could be harvested only two or three times. Hence, this method of farming quickly exhausted the land and forced the farmers to move on. A spontaneous migratory movement from the settled southern part of the province to the unsettled north had begun at the end of the fifteenth century. It received additional momentum when the king and Krook placed their prestige behind it. After the Savoans had migrated northward to the Oulujoki watercourse, the regions in the northern parts of Tavastia and Satakunta formed a kind of vacuum between the East Finnish and Bothnian populations.

"And we have been informed," wrote King Gustavus to his Finnish representatives and bailiffs in 1550, "that this wilderness comprises an enormous forest, and that there is plenty of room in it for the creation of good farms, capable of supporting their settlers.... Wherefore, it is our will and our command... that part of the common nation undertake to clear and settle the said wilderness, particularly, that a number of them clear farmlands everywhere in the vicinity of the Russian border so that they would be on hand to resist the Russians should they desire to commit violence in this realm." The king thus continued to promote his colonization measures along the lines of foreign policy, for northern Savo still was sparsely populated and formed only a weak frontier bulwark. However, his command also included these words: "The wilderness in Finland must be cleared and settled in order to augment the revenue due the Crown of Sweden."

But when Gustavus Vasa commanded the Tavastians, Satakuntans, and Bothnians to push on into their *erämaat* preserves, they did not respond with anywhere near the zeal of the peasantry from the eastern regions, for the western Finns were bound to their old farms by cultivated fields. The impatient king did not wait long but granted the Savoans the right to colonize the wilderness reserve of the western Finns, and he issued outright orders to the bailiff of Savonlinna, Gustaf Fincke, to send colonists across the provincial boundary. The Tavastians however, laid waste to the first Savoan holdings on their side of the boundary. In retaliation, the king appointed Fincke to take charge of the colonizing activity in Tavastia, but he did grant the local inhabitants priority in settling their own *erämaat.*

Many Tavastians now declared themselves willing to avail themselves of this privilege, but, in most cases, the declaration was only a pretext toward retaining title to their hunting grounds and fishing waters. Thus, the final solution of the colonization problem was, at best, only postponed. In the end, primarily Savoans colonized the regions north of the limits of the settlement. Within about three decades, the government-directed colonization program resulted in the settlement of nearly as much territory as had been settled during the entire medieval era, when the establishment of pioneer holdings had taken place mainly on a spontaneous basis (see map I). And the peasants whose clearings blazed in the lonely depths of the trackless wilds, apparently removed from all organized society, actually were guided in their actions by the omnipresent hand of the Crown.

In 1552, consistent with the centralizing tendency, the right to collect taxes that was held by the trading company of *Pirkkalaiset,* the organization of trappers of old, was revoked. The Crown reserved for itself the exclusive power to levy taxes. Even though King Gustavus may not have been as accurately informed about the wealth collected by the *Pirkkalaiset* as present-day historians are, he did know enough to deem it to the Crown's advantage to take over the collection of fur taxes imposed on the Lapps.

The Reformation Begins

Near the end of the Middle Ages, the moral corruption that had infested the highest levels of the clerical hierarchy on the Continent had only lightly touched the Swedish realm, particularly Finland. Therefore, there was no reaction within the realm that was strong enough to produce a reform movement. The Reformation actually was transplanted to Sweden-Finland from Central Europe, and its doctrines, if not its actual spiritual content, were first embraced by the royalty. The head of the Swedish Church had supported Denmark in the conflict over the Scandinavian Union, thus working against his own national government. Also, the broad autonomy of the Church and the Pope's power of appointment did not coincide with the new political ideal, which presupposed the sovereignty of the king in every sphere. Friction with the Roman Catholic Church could not be avoided, chiefly because King Gustavus had no desire to avoid it. The Church was enormously rich, while the Crown was poor. So the king prepared to reverse these conditions.

At the Diet of Västerås, in 1527, King Gustavus dramatically threatened to resign in order to persuade the estates of the realm to pass measures that would radically change the status of the Church. The king's maneuver succeeded, and the Church was forced to forfeit nearly all of its power to administer justice, while the king was given the authority to fill the highest ecclesiastical offices. He used that authority to keep the offices of the various chapters vacant—except the offices of the bishops. By that action, the Church lost an influential medium of its autonomy. The bishops had to surrender their castles, and the episcopal castle of Kuusisto was destroyed, because the Crown did not need it. Then the Crown appropriated the "superfluous" portion of the Church income. The nobility was rewarded by the return of many estates that formerly had been bequeathed to the Church.

The expression "superfluous income" was given a broad interpretation that left practically nothing to be desired. For a while, the Church was permitted to collect its own dues and retain its remaining property. But it was obliged to pay the Crown such huge annual sums that, in effect, it was reduced to the role of tax collector and caretaker of landed estates for the Crown. Later, in the 1540's and 1550's, with the exception of the small share claimed by the parish priests, ecclesiastical taxes began to be paid directly to the Crown, which also expropriated all the landed estates still belonging to the Church. The valuables of the churches, even including the bronze church bells, were confiscated; and the chasubles of the Finnish priests were converted into clothing for the numerous children of the royal family. The private property of the clergymen also was seized so unscrupulously that when the will of one of the deans of Turku was opened, an extra clause was surreptitiously inserted for the amortization of debts of the realm.

In Finland, the Church was not excessively wealthy. Its revenue from taxes was modest and the land in its possession was not extraordinary. According to one, somewhat deficient, estimate, the Church held, in addition to the parsonages—which remained Church property—800 landed estates. Since it had spent the income derived from land rents to maintain schools, hospitals, and welfare services, as well as on grants for academic study abroad, the Church had possessed no superfluous funds. In Sweden, on the other hand, the Church had owned more than one-fifth of the land, so the contrast between the rich, rent-exempt Church and the impoverished Crown was most extreme. When the Swedish Church collapsed, it apparently pulled the Finnish Church down with it. For the reversion program was carried out in both parts of the kingdom with the same thoroughness, even though there was no urgent need for a transfer of revenue in Finland.

Since the Crown assumed little responsibility even for the lay duties of the Church, both the schools and the institutions for the care of the sick and the poor went to rack and ruin. The confiscation of church property, especially bells and objects figuring in divine services, provoked resentment and contributed to the outbreak of the popular uprisings on the Swedish side of the Gulf of Bothnia. But in Finland, the people tolerated the plundering of the churches.

The Diet of Västerås opened the gates of the realm for the Reformation—without prescribing what cloth the newcomer should wear. The assembled estates of the realm were content to ask that the Word of God be preached throughout the realm in its "purity". The Protestant doctrine had been introduced into Sweden by an ardent pupil of Luther, Olaus Petri, whose religious zeal led to many a collision with the king's realistic politics. As early as the 1520's, sermons were preached in Finland for a short period in the spirit of Luther by the uncompromising Petrus Särkilahti. The helpless chapter looked upon his teachings as "very strange," but Särkilahti died young.

A year after the Diet of Västeras, in 1528, the king appointed a member of the Finnish nobility, the Dominican friar Martinus Skytte, as Bishop of Turku. During Skytte's tenure of office, sermons in the vernacular replaced the mass to dominate divine services; the worship of saints was eschewed, though their sculptured images were not removed from the churches; and gifted youths aspiring to don the cloth traveled to Wittenberg or other centers of the Reformation to study. Skytte's stand has given historians ample cause to wonder: Had he not, after all, received his training at the Dominican college situated in Naples, whence originated the demand for the restoration of the strict monastical discipline of old? And had not his truly Catholic personal piety been acknowledged by his contemporaries? However, he had also apparently been influenced by Erasmus of Rotterdam, and he belonged to the generation that still believed in the possibility of reconciliation between Protestantism and the Holy See. He himself was prepared for conciliatory action along lines that, in his mind, were of secondary importance. And, pressured by the king, he was obliged, in fact, to go further in making concessions than he would have liked. In sending students abroad, the Church had to provide the funds but yield the management of the study program to the government.

Among the students chosen by Skytte to go to Wittenberg was Mikael Agricola, who later became rector of the Cathedral School of Turku and eventually Bishop of Turku. The bishops of Finland had been national political leaders, too, during medieval times, and, after Skytte's death, King Gustavus apparently feared the rise of Agricola, who was considered heir apparent to the bishop's chair, to such a position of influence. That is why, after first keeping the office vacant for four years, the king divided Finland into two dioceses, with the other seat located in Viipuri. During the three years that Agricola served as bishop, the Church of Finland took its decisive step toward Lutheranism. But even that step was by no means a leap across a chasm: instead it was in the nature of an organic continuation of a course already started out upon.

Agricola was an amiable and moderate man, and he got along with the monarch better than had the stubborn Olaus Petri. Moderation likewise marked his activities as a religious reformer, though, perhaps, a contributing factor was the circumstance that during his period of study in Germany, Lutheranism had already left behind its *Sturm und Drang*. Agricola also left the images of the saints in the churches and he preserved the Latin masses and Catholic liturgical rites, such as the raising of the chalice, as part of the divine services. Furthermore, the institutions of confession and absolution were retained, and fasts were observed. Nothing, in fact, was to be altered, Agricola declared, that was not "downright blasphemous." Such outward forms of the old rituals as were still highly revered by the masses, who little understood the inner meaning of the Reformation, remained unchanged, while they were being educated to understand the new doctrine. For this purpose, a religious literature in the vernacular was created. At first, it could reach parishioners only through the clergy. Yet, Agricola's ABC-Book indicates that he planned to spread the ability to read throughout the nation, so that every member of the Church should have direct personal access to the Holy Bible and devotional literature.

Although some religious texts had been translated into Finnish back in the Middle Ages, and apparently there was a fairly abundant vocabulary of religious terms even in those remote times, Agricola is nevertheless celebrated as the father of Finnish as a language of literature. At any rate, Agricola's books were the first to be printed in the Finnish language. And, whereas the Turku dialect had been used in earlier translations, Agricola (who had been born on the southern coast and attended school in Viipuri) availed himself of material from all the dialects, although, like his predecessors, he constructed his language primarily on a southwestern Finnish basis. Agricola's highest literary goal was to produce a Finnish version of the Holy Bible, but he lived only long enough to complete the New Testament (1548) and certain books from the Old Testament.

Finland's Eastern Border Remains Vague

Novgorod had become resigned to the fact that Finnish farmers who paid taxes to the Swedish Crown were crossing the boundary that was established by the Peace of Pähkinäsaari to settle new areas. But Moscow, Sweden's new and much stronger neighbour to the east, vigorously opposed such penetration. That was why the lord of the castle of Viipuri had drawn up the fake peace treaty. It was during the reign of Gustavus Vasa that the previously almost static situation along the frontier underwent a violent change.

Whereas early Finnish colonization had advanced only a few miles in a whole generation, it expanded in the fifth and sixth decades of the sixteenth century to more than a hundred miles. Meanwhile, when Novgorod fell under the power of Moscow, it raised an issue of prestige, which in the minds of people in the sixteenth century loomed larger than it would today. The Czar of all Russias—the Eastern heir of the emperors of Rome, claimant to the splendours of Byzantium—regarded himself as being of higher rank than the king of Sweden, especially since the Swedish throne was occupied by a mere upstart from an obscure, though noble, family. Therefore, the czars were unwilling to stoop to negotiations with the Swedish rulers, but insisted that the latter accept the governor-general of Novgorod as their opposite number at the conference table. Gustavus Vasa tended to respond to such demands by authorizing Finnish members of the Council of the Realm, whom he considered experts on the Eastern question, to act as his deputies. But there were occasions when the exigencies of power politics forced him to compromise with considerations of prestige.

At these negotiations, the Finns hypocritically spread before the Russians the forged document that was alleged to contain the Peace Treaty of Pähkinäsaari, of which, to make doubly sure, Russian and Latin copies had also been made during King Gustavus's reign. The boundary survey was continually postponed, to the distinct annoyance of the Finns, who found it distressing to have an ever-increasing part of their population living in a region that an alien power claimed as its own, especially when that power was considered to be a traditionally hostile and heretical neighbour.

The hostility between the peasants who paid taxes to the Russian Czar and the farmers who owed allegiance to the Swedish king was vented in frequent border skirmishes. Although the same Finnish language was spoken in opposing villages, perhaps with slightly different accents, religious differences formed a formidable barrier. Gradually, the Finnish nobles became convinced that the problem could be solved only by war.

King Gustavus was moved to reinforce the defences of Finland, and he even sent troops over from Sweden. It was also around this period, the middle of the sixteenth century, that the king displayed his zeal for the settlement of the Finnish interior. When the border skirmishes developed into ever larger forays of destruction on both sides, the king ordered the armed forces of Finland to assemble in Viipuri and appointed Henrik Klaus' son, Horn, as their commander-in-chief. This gave the Finnish nobility an opportunity to enter negotiations, and a more active policy than ever was adopted: a deputy was sent to Stockholm to tell the king that the Tatars were tying down the Russian armies and to recommend an attack the following summer.

In the winter of 1555, Finnish confidence was bolstered by the battle of Joutselkä, which was fought on the Karelian Isthmus right by the border. There, Finnish frontiersmen, moving swiftly through the wooded terrain on skis, wiped out a considerable Russian force that was advancing up an icy road. Thus, open warfare actually had begun, and the Finnish nobility was more certain of victory than ever.

After long hesitation, King Gustavus apparently accepted the war policy of the Finnish nobles. He traveled to Turku in the spring of 1555, and during the hostilities some twelve thousand troops were shipped over to Finland from Sweden—nearly all her available military forces. An equal number of Finns were mobilized, but the majority of them were common peasants who had been armed for the emergency. Never before had the question of the kingdom's eastern border been so dominant a factor in Swedish policy as during Gustavus Vasa's war—nor did it have comparable importance for the next couple of centuries.

The Finnish offensive was launched the next autumn. Its objective was the Neva line. But the attack failed, and the cautious old monarch soon gave orders to retreat. Meanwhile, the Russians advanced to the gates of Viipuri, and King Gustavus fled to the Aland Islands, where he immediately sued for peace.

At the peace conference, the king suggested that the simplest solution to the border dispute would be to recognize the territories that actually were held by each side, since the place names along the frontier that were mentioned in the Peace Treaty of Pähkinäsaari had changed during the course of centuries. The Russians, however, could not be persuaded to give *de jure* recognition on such a pretext to the more eastern boundary claimed by King Gustavus. The peace treaty that was signed in 1557 provided that the border survey should be carried out on the basis of "the Peace Treaty of Grand Duke Yuri and King Magnus"—though the wording did not make clear which document was meant, the one endorsed by the Swedes or the one the Russians adhered to (if either). And, once more, the execution of the survey was put off. Both sides secretly wished to avoid a settlement.

The Baltic Question Comes to the Fore

In his war, Gustavus Vasa had hoped to gain as allies the Teutonic Knights who ruled over the southern coast of the Gulf of Finland. However, that religious order had been disintegrating ever since Lutheranism had spread over the territories under its control. A political vacuum was developing in Livonia and Estonia, through which a considerable part of the Russian trade passed. The king earlier had considered plans to divert this trade to some port on the Finnish coast; and, after conferring with Erik Fleming, he had concluded that a seaport should be founded opposite Tallinn, across the gulf. That is how, in 1550, Helsinki came into existence.

The Finnish nobility also showed a lively interest in this manifestation of a dynamic eastern policy. As typically indifferent to the rights of his subjects as Gustavus Vasa seemed to be in commanding the inhabitants of some small towns to move to Helsinki, the initiative in this matter was actually taken by the political leaders of Finland. This also was true of various other decrees and prohibitions connected with the founding of the city, for the king accepted the proposals laid before him with little hesitation.

After its founding, however, Helsinki basked in the favor of the Crown continuously, though for two and a half centuries the city failed to attain any position of prominence in either domestic or international trade.

More realistic was the bid made by Klaus Krister's son, Horn, lord of Viipuri Castle, after peace was established, to lure part of the Russian trade to Viipuri. The volume of commerce of this easternmost of Finnish cities grew tenfold in the first two years after the war. And when the merchants of Tallinn started to harass ships bound for Viipuri, Horn arranged convoys to guard them. But, in his greed, aging King Gustavus imposed crushing customs duties on merchandise passing through Viipuri. Horn resigned in protest, and the Swedish Crown lost another round in the competition for Russian trade.

Meanwhile, in 1558, the Czar's forces had launched an attack on territory held by the Teutonic Knights and captured the city of Narva, near where the waterway that extends deep into northwestern Russia swerves away from the Gulf of Finland. For a time, Narva became an important staple town in Russian trade, and when Sweden tried to block maritime traffic to the Baltic city, the action served only to earn the displeasure of the other states and cities with commercial interests in the Baltic area.

The terrible devastation wrought by the invading Russians in Livonia, together with the helplessness of the crumbling order of Teutonic Knights, forced the inhabitants of the Baltic countries to look for security wherever it could be found. And help was proffered from many sides, for even under slighter inducement the princes of the Baltic sphere could have been expected to act: It required no special perspicacity to see the opportunities for territorial aggrandizement. Besides, that which one holds is, at least, out of the hands of the enemy, whether real or imagined.

Particularly in Finland, the penetration of Russia into the Baltic area was viewed as no small threat. In 1558, Henrik Klaus' son, Horn, traveled to Estonia as the representative of Duke John of Finland, but King Gustavus, now doddering with age, restricted his activity. The Teutonic Knights retained those castles which Horn had attempted to acquire for Sweden and Finland. Before long, however, the knightly order was compelled to place itself wholly under the protection of Poland. Meanwhile, Denmark seized Saaremaa, the largest island in the Baltic Sea.

Swedish politics underwent an immediate change when the young Renaissance prince Eric XIV succeeded to the throne upon the death of his father, Gustavus Vasa, in 1560. He sought control of the Baltic countries not so much out of fear of Russia as to be able to watch over Russian trade from both shores of the Gulf of Finland and direct it to ports that were held by the Swedish Crown. Already, as Crown Prince, Eric had sent his brother, Duke John, to court Elizabeth of England in order to bolster the English-Swedish commercial supremacy in the Baltic that he was dreaming of with the bonds of marriage. The courtship failed, as did the rest of Eric's princely bids for brides of royal blood. And, gradually, the brothers became estranged. Still, as king, Eric held to his policy of expansion in the Baltic. Evidently, he had absorbed the influence of the Horns of Finland as well as that of his brother, John. Klaus Krister's son, Horn, was dispatched to Estonia, where he succeeded in winning over part of the Polish mercenary troops in Tallinn and defeating the rest of them. The chief commercial center of Estonia thus fell into Swedish possession in 1561, and the Crown had a beachhead in the Baltic countries. The program of Duke John of Finland was on the way toward realization, although he himself was left empty-handed.

In taking under its wing the disintegrating Order of Teutonic Knights, Poland inherited from them their war against Russia. Since trade cannot be conducted without peaceful relations, Eric tried to avoid hostilities with the Russians in the Baltic area and attempted to concentrate his aggressive activities on the castles that had been presented to the Poles by the Teutonic Knights. Duke John again adopted the anti-Russian outlook of the Finnish political leaders; and, because he saw in Poland the Russians' strongest opponent, he began to seek collaboration with the Poles. Just as fighting broke out in Estonia between Poland and Sweden, Duke John married the Polish king's sister, Catherine Jagellonica, lent his new brother-in-law a sum of money, and received from him as security a number of castles in Livonia, together with their lands. In the division of the estate left by the Teutonic Knights, a fifth heir had unexpectedly appeared on the scene, in addition to the Czar and the kings of Poland, Denmark, and Sweden, to stake his claim—the Duke of Finland!

The Duchy of Finland

King Gustavus spent most of his life in working to concentrate power in the hands of the monarch. But even monarchs are mortal, and the king had to make sure that this power was not removed from his successor by the people after his death. Besides, Gustavus was only a usurper and not of royal lineage; and, since there had been many rival pretenders to the throne during his reign, he knew there would be many more as soon as he was dead. Therefore, he proposed that the throne become the hereditary property of his family. The Diet accepted this proposal in 1544, and thus Sweden joined the majority of the kingdoms of Europe as a hereditary monarchy.

However, the logical consequences of this change led to inconsistencies in the rest of the king's program. Since the realm of a hereditary monarch was understood to be his private property, King Gustavus decided to bestow part of it to each of his sons so that the brothers of the royal heir would retain their status as princes, thus establishing the new dynasty. Accordingly, each of the king's younger sons received a dukedom with extremely broad and vaguely defined authority. This simply meant a reversion to particularism, and only a credulous old parental mind would assume that the brothers would not quarrel among themselves and jeopardize the unity of the realm.

In 1556, King Gustavus conferred on his son John the most important and most thickly populated, southwestern parts of Finland as a duchy and also appointed him governor of the rest of the country. The decision to set up a Duchy of Finland was prompted not only by the general situation but also by special considerations. First, Sweden was empowered to create an office corresponding to that of the governor-general of Novgorod to deal politically with Russia, whereupon the Swedish king's rank automatically rose to Czar's level. Second, Gustavus Vasa had recently undergone the experience of having the Finnish nobility provoke a war with Russia almost against his royal will, so he decided that a member of the royal family who resided in Finland would help to restrain the overactive nobles.

The establishment of the Duchy of Finland introduced a brilliant chapter into the lackluster annals of the land. Duke John surrounded himself with a council of Finnish nobles, and founded a chancery and exchequer, like the king. The Castle of Turku, which had been built for defense, was repaired, enlarged, and furnished in a style fit to serve as the court of a Renaissance prince. And, as lady of the castle, the duke brought over his wife, the Polish princess Catherine Jagellonica.

John was aware of the special character of his duchy and is reported even to have learned the Finnish language. Still, it would be anachronistic to look upon him as an advocate of Finnish nationalism, as did the poet Eino Leino of the romantic nationalist period some decades ago, who put into John's mouth these spirited words:

The court would speak the native Finnish tongue,
And love of native soil would there be sung.

King Eric XIV viewed particularism as pernicious. Immediately after ascending the throne, he prevailed upon the Diet to ratify the Articles of Arboga, which precisely and narrowly defined the powers of the dukes. It was expressly stated that the dukes had no right to pursue an independent line of foreign policy.

When Duke John helped himself to territory in Livonia, he violated the Articles of Arboga. He compared himself to the petty princes of Germany, who formally recognized the overlordship of the emperor but did not obey him. As differences became greatly aggravated, violence was committed by both sides; but the duke was in a weaker position, since he could be impeached by the Diet, whereas the king had no fear of being forced to face a tribunal.

The Finns now were confronted with a tragic dilemma. The duke's pro-Polish policy suited their convictions, but they did not want to sever relations with Sweden. They wished to remain loyal to the realm and to the king. In the end, the population of the duchy became politically divided, with many of the leading Finnish nobles, including Henrik Klaus' son Horn, openly siding with King Eric.

The Diet that met in 1563, which was attended by a number of deputies from the duchy as well, obeyed the will of the king and his influential adviser, Göran Persson, and sentenced Duke John to death. Of course, the judgment included a reference to the king's power of pardon. Yet, it was obvious that the days of the Duchy of Finland were numbered. At around that same time, the duke delivered a speech to the Finns who had come to Turku for the summer fair. It was the custom in the sixteenth century to use fairs as occasions for political agitation, and John won an ovation from the crowds. Moreover, the clergy of the dukedom swore a fresh oath of loyalty to the duke.

Then, Swedish forces sent by the king landed in Finland to carry out the sentence passed by the Diet. The punitive army was reinforced by Finnish supporters of the king. The besieged Castle of Turku was able to hold out for only a few weeks. Some thirty nobles who remained faithful to their duke to the end were executed. John and his wife were imprisoned in the Castle of Gripsholm in Sweden.

The settling of differences with the duke had been hastened by the war that broke out the same year, 1563, with Denmark. The formal cause of hostilities was the dispute over the Scandinavian Union and the king's titles, but the fundamental cause was the incipient struggle for mastery of the Baltic Sea. The Finns took part in the fighting both along the border between Sweden and Denmark and at sea where the Hanseatic town of Lübeck in north Germany also was treated as an enemy, and the forces commanded by Klaus Krister's son Horn gained such a total upper hand over the foe that the Swedish-Finnish fleet was able to collect tariffs from the Danes in the Sound within the very boundaries of their realm.

A Finnish army also simultaneously occupied Estonia, which had gradually fallen under the sway of Sweden while it was being threatened by Poland. Henrik Klaus' son Horn was appointed to be the first governor-general of Estonia for the Swedish Crown. Such was the decisive contribution made by the Finns to the wars being waged by Sweden both in the West and in the South. For, along the border to the East, peace reigned: The Tatars were harassing Russia and, hence, Czar Ivan the Terrible was compelled for a time to forget the question of prestige and send his own envoy, and not that of his governor-general at Novgorod, to Stockholm. Actually, the Czar's envoy was on a very personal mission: To demand the imprisoned duchess of Finland, Catherine Jagellonica, as a bride for his master. Eric, though he was a typical Renaissance prince, nevertheless had moral scruples enough to temporize in order to avoid the shameful surrender of his sister-in-law.

However, King Eric's domestic administration became ever more arbitrary during the war. Deeply aware of his position as hereditary monarch and at the same time morbidly suspicious, the king began to accuse many nobles of treason and, with his own hand, slew some of the accused who were being held prisoners for trial. After committing these murders, he was possessed by his latent insanity. During this attack of madness, he freed Duke John and Catherine.

The outraged nobles revolted, under the leadership of Duke John and Duke Charles of Södermanland, and deposed Eric, replacing him on the throne with John. The change of ruler, in 1568, nearly caused the loss of Estonia, where the positions of power were held by Finns who had been disloyal to John when the Duchy of Finland collapsed and who therefore feared the vengeance of their erstwhile lord. But a reconciliation was reached, and the rise of John III to the throne ended hostilities between Sweden and Poland.

The war against Denmark and Lübeck terminated in the Peace of Stettin in 1570. The boundaries remained unchanged, but Sweden had to redeem Elfsborg from Denmark, for it was the kingdom's only means of direct access to the North Sea and therefore of vital importance. The Danes had captured Elfsborg at the very beginning of the war.

After he was dethroned, Eric spent nine years in prison, part of the term in the selfsame Castle of Turku from which he had banished his brother. John issued detailed instructions for the deposed king's execution by poisoning in case of a plot to free him—and plots were reported. After the death of Eric, the fortunes of the late king's family were wedded to Finland. Following his fit of insanity, Eric had legalized his liaison with Karin, the Daughter of Magnus, a soldier from Stockholm, and John presented the widow with the royal manor of Liuksiala in the Finnish province of Satakunta. Karin moved to the manor with her retinue and servants, and thus, in the interior of Finland, a miniature royal court was established, for the length of the unhappy queen's widowhood, which lasted half a century. The daughter of Eric and Karin married a Finnish nobleman, but their son Gustaf had to flee to Russia, where the Czars supported him in case he might prove useful in some future plot against Sweden. For a neighbour Karin Magnus' daughter had Karin Hans' daughter, who had been Duke John's mistress before his Polish marriage. John had given her the royal manor of Vääksy, and he married the daughter she bore him to the French general Pontus de la Gardie, who had joined the Swedish military service.

The Long Wrath

Even if it had not been followed by a rapprochement with Poland, the *coup d'état* of John III would have precipitated a crisis in relations with Russia. The Czar's attempt to force Catherine Jagellonica into marrying him was an act of infamy that the royal couple of Sweden could never forget. Nor could the Czar ever forgive the thrashing given to the Russians sent to fetch her by the citizens of Stockholm—as soon as Catherine had ascended the throne. The exchange of letters between John and Ivan that followed, for sheer virulence, is probably unmatched in the annals of quarrels between crowned heads of state. Further friction was caused by the persistent issue of rank. John insisted that Finland, as part of the Swedish realm, corresponded to Novgorod, which since ancient times had been a grand duchy, as part of Russia. In 1581, he added to his string of royal titles that of "Grand Duke of Finland and Karelia." This appendage was retained by all the Swedish monarchs until defeat in the Great Northern War compelled the Crown to practice restraint in all matters liable to offend the kingdom's formidable eastern neighbour.

When, immediately after John had seized the throne, the Czar threatened war, the new Swedish king sent to Russia a delegation headed by Paulus Juusten, Bishop of Viipuri—just as Gustavus Vasa, in suing for peace with Russia, had called on the services of Agricola as an expert. Lasting for three long years, the mission of Juusten and his party evolved into one of the strangest adventures in the history of diplomacy. Because they refused to negotiate with the governor-general of Novgorod, the poor men were kept waiting with calculating deliberateness from day to day, month after month, before being suffered, after many an insult and humiliation, an audience with the Czar. By that time, the Russians had already started war. The hostilities that broke out in 1570 lasted for twenty-five years. In Finnish history, the war is called the "Long Wrath."

Ivan the Terrible had timed his attack to coincide with the period when all the available resources of the Swedish realm were being mobilized to pay off the ransom demanded by Denmark for Elfsborg. The wages of the mercenaries could not be paid, military operations lacked punch, and the Russians were able to occupy almost the whole of Estonia. Destructive thrusts were also made by the enemy deep into southern Finland. The Finns retaliated. However, until the ransom for Elfsborg had been paid off, at the end of the decade, and Poland—with which Sweden-Finland was not allied, though it was acting as a co-belligerent—had captured many fortresses in western Russia, thereby weakening the Czar, John III did not deem the time ripe for taking the offensive. Indeed, he was even ready for new territorial conquests.

On the other hand, the Finnish nobility, which till then had been in charge of the campaign and knew the war-weariness and discontent of the population, advocated making peace. But such a move was frowned upon by the king, who then handed the post of commander-in-chief to the alien Pontus de la Gardie. However, the French general managed to reach an understanding with the experienced Finish military leaders, and, in short order, two notable victories were won: the Russian fortress of Käkisalmi, which dominated a province that was inhabited by Karelians on the western shore of Lake Ladoga, was captured in 1580, and the town of Narva, which controlled a key East European trade route, was captured the year after. The Russians withdrew from Estonia altogether and several fortresses in Ingrian territory fell into the hands of the Swedish-Finnish army. At this point, the Czar concluded a peace treaty with Poland which recognized the Polish conquests in Livonia. The exhaustive warfare between Sweden-Finland and Russia continued, however, though it was interrupted by prolonged truces, without a decisive victory on either side.

During the closing stages of the war, the command of the Swedish-Finnish army was assumed by Klaus Erik's son, Fleming, who was shortly to make his mark also as a political leader. The war was finally brought to a close by the Peace of Täyssinä in 1595, whereby Sweden-Finland gained two objectives. First, the Czar recognized the Swedish conquests in Estonia and even dropped his claim to Narva; and, second—of prime importance to the Finns—the eastern boundary of the Swedish realm was drawn up to Varanger Fjord on the Arctic coast instead of the earlier line, which had run to the northern end of the Gulf of Bothnia (see map 1). Thus, the settlements that had been established since the Peace of Pähkinäsaari and had originally belonged to Sweden on a *de facto* basis, then became a legal possession. Now, boundless wilds in the far North, where only nomadic Lapps roamed, opened up for the Finns to settle, too.

The fortress of Käkisalmi, which was situated on the eastern side of the new boundary, remained a pawn in the hands of the Swedish-Finnish troops until the border survey had been carried out. However, disputes arose over particulars along the boundary and, weakened by civil strife, Sweden-Finland returned Käkisalmi to the Russians. The border was never extended farther north than the heights of Iivaara, 500 kilometers south of the Arctic coast. Therefore, Russian bailiffs continued to collect tribute from Lapp villages that were located west of the theoretical boundary which ran northward from Iivaara.

The battles of the Long Wrath were fought either in the shadow of the eastern Finnish border or across the gulf in Baltic territory. Finland served as the base of operations for the king's troops, which were commanded chiefly by Finnish officers. The importance of Finland during that war and its aftermath would apparently have grown even without the personal attachment of John III to his former duchy. More than ever before, the governors of Finland gave direct orders to the Finnish bailiffs; and, though the unity of the country was weakened by the installation of a separate governor's office in Viipuri, an exchequer which combined both an accounting bureau and a bureau in charge of taxes to be paid in kind was operating in Turku for all of Finland.

During the twenty-five years' war, the special system of recruiting men for military service that had been introduced by Gustavus Vasa became definitely established, and was subsequently maintained throughout the realm for a century. The mercenaries that at the beginning of the modern era generally provided the manpower of the armed forces all over Europe were not unknown in Sweden and Finland either, but they were costly and sometimes proved to be unreliable. Therefore, King Gustavus had begun to impose a kind of conscription on his subjects.

When needed, all the able-bodied men of the common people, between the ages of fifteen and fifty, were summoned in each parish to report for selective recruitment. From the assembled group, the bailiff and the commander of the unit that required reinforcements selected as large a number for infantry service as the king, with the subsequent consent of the Diet, had decreed. Usually, one man out of every ten was drafted. The frequency of these conscriptions depended on the army's need for reinforcements at any given time, and those who were recorded in the army rolls of the seventeenth century were subject to almost lifetime military service.

The farther away from home that campaigns were being waged, the less willing peasants were to submit to conscription. But the attempt to escape recruitment by running away was rarely successful; it was much wiser to try bribing the bailiff or recruiting officer. It was a legitimate practice for nine men to pool their funds and hire a tenth to go off to war on their behalf. By reporting himself or some other member of his household for service as a cavalryman, a prosperous yeoman who was capable of equipping a mount could free his farm from the land rents and gain for himself—later on for the rest of his household, as well—exemption from the draft. Between campaigns, the part of the infantry that did not have to garrison fortresses was scattered all over the country and billeted on farms and in the homes of burghers. And soldiers—particularly foreign mercenaries, who were still employed in addition to the con-scripts—hardly made the most congenial house guests.

The generation of the Long Wrath could remember periods of peace during their youth. But the succeeding generations of Finns and Swedes again became so accustomed to ceaseless warfare that war must have seemed to be the normal condition of the world. The difficulties of adjustment to a permanent state of war were most acute during the Long Wrath, and the insolent behavior of the troops billeted in villages at times caused the bitterness damned up by extra taxes and repeated conscriptions to erupt into violence. However, in the frontier regions, especially northern Ostrobothnia, the farmers themselves organized military units under their own leaders for defense against plundering Russian expeditions and to set forth on expeditions of revenge far beyond the border. It was total war, in which all the inhabitants of enemy communities, regardless of age or sex, were slain. But, farther from the frontier, the peasantry had not yet learned to accept the inexorable strains imposed by war, and thus there gathered in the soul of the people a ferment that was soon to boil over, marking the first outbreak of civil strife in the history of Finland.

The Victory of the Reformation

King John III reigned during an era when the Catholic Church, which was undergoing an internal purge, embarked on a program to regain those nations that had been lost to Protestantism. John's queen was a Roman Catholic, and he himself, with his esthetic leanings, felt drawn to the solemn ceremoniousness of Roman church services. During his long imprisonment, he had delved into the issues of theological controversy, and he had become sincerely grieved by religious wars. The king took it upon himself to draw up a new liturgy, entitled the "Red Book," which brought the divine services held in the churches of Sweden-Finland closer to the ritual of Roman Catholicism; and he pressured the Diet to vote in favor of it. Perhaps political calculations influenced him to go even further: He proposed to the Pope the subordination of the Church of Sweden-Finland to the Holy See.

Since, however, John had sided with the Protestants in some ecclesiastical controversies (championing the right of the clergy to marry and the right of the laity to partake of sacramental wine), he was repudiated by the Pope.

In Sweden, John's religious policy provoked fierce opposition, and it was during this very struggle, and partly as a result of it, that the Lutheran doctrine became deeply rooted in the Swedish mind. In Finland, on the other hand, Lutheranism had not sunk such firm roots, nor had Bishop Agricola's reforms been so sweeping as those of Luther's pupil, Olaus Petri. In some cases, the Finnish clergy worked with outright enthusiasm to promote the new liturgy. And Erik Sorolainen, who was appointed bishop of Turku by the king in 1583, and who later achieved fame by composing the first book of homilies in the Finnish language, considered the forms of worship optional. It subsequently became clear that the opposition between Catholicism and Protestantism in Finland was not so intense as it was in Sweden.

Refusing to accept a partial return to the bosom of Rome, the Catholic Church extended its missionary activity to Sweden-Finland, also. When Crown Prince Sigismund, who had been reared in the Catholic faith, was elected king of Poland, his mother's native land, in 1587, there developed the prospect of a personal union with a Catholic country after John's death.

Throughout almost the entire reign of John III, there was conflict between the king and the upper nobility who were represented in the Council of the Realm. It was not so sharp as it had been during his late brother's reign but none the less irreconcilable. The feud halted plans that had been under consideration since Gustavus Vasa's reign for the creation of central bureaus to be organized along statutory lines. The nobility would not yield to pressure to serve the king, and the king did not dare to give the nobles independent status at the head of various branches of administration. The aristocrats calculated that the union with Poland would force the king to invest the Council of the Realm with the powers of a veritable regency. This, it appeared, would be the most painless means of settling the conflict between royal and aristocratic authority in favor of the latter. The union cause could further count on army support, for the officers were to a large extent Finns, who favored practically anything that was likely to promote collaboration between Sweden and Russia's other powerful neighbour, Poland. At this stage, the hostility between the churches did not yet have an appreciable effect on the various political positions. At John's death in 1592, however, there arose the question of the guarantees to be demanded of Sigismund in behalf of the Lutheran Church before he was crowned king of Sweden.

Yet, religion was only one thread in the tangled political skein of the following years, although, for propaganda reasons, it was profitable to make it an issue even when the real objective was mundane power. Four centers of authority existed: first, King Sigismund; second, Gustavus Vasa's youngest son, Charles, whose domain was the duchy of Södermanland in central Sweden and who resembled his father in his gift for demagogic speech and surpassed him in sheer unscrupulousness; third, the Swedish upper nobility which was represented in the Council; and, finally, the rough, granite-willed Finnish Councillor Klaus Fleming, nicknamed by his Swedish associates "Sootnose" because of his untidy appearance. However, because of his royalist sentiment, he was favored by John to the extent of being appointed Admiral of the Realm, Marshal of the

Realm and commander-in-chief for the Russian war. Fleming's influence among the Finnish nobility was considerable.

Before Sigismund arrived in Sweden from Poland for his coronation, a synod met, in 1593, at Uppsala. It was attended, according to Protestant principles, not only by the clergy but also by a certain number of representatives of the laity, and it rejected the "superstitious" Red Book and assailed the churchmen, like Bishop Sorolainen, who had accepted it. The synod at last laid a firm foundation for Lutheranism by deciding to have the Church of Sweden-Finland abide by the Augsburg Confession. All religious teachings that deviated from it were condemned as "horrifying heresies," and it was decided to ban public church services of other denominations. Lutheranism thereby bolstered its internal front and rallied its ranks. Still, the synod was given a political twist by the fact that the initiative had been taken by Duke Charles of Södermanland, who was using his stern Protestant attitude to pave the way toward the peak of power.

Because of the long journey, only a few Finns could attend the synod. Admiral Fleming, meanwhile, had summoned the Finnish nobility and officer corps to Turku for the purpose of taking an oath of fealty to Sigismund, in spite of the fact that he was a Catholic. Accepting the oath, the king's ambassador agreed to the Finns' reservation: religion had to be maintained in the form it had existed during the final years of King Gustavus's reign. The Red Book was not mentioned. And the nobility, in taking the oath of allegiance to a Catholic sovereign, were no less Lutheran than the Finnish peasants in certain parishes who drove away clergymen bent on "purging" church services of rituals prescribed by the Red Book.

Duke Charles, who, during the period of changing political combinations right after John's death, had for a time acted in collaboration with Admiral Fleming, now considered him to be an adversary. He started openly to incite the Finnish farmers to delay paying their taxes and the army to insubordination toward the Commander-in-Chief. The fleet was ordered to sail back to Sweden in order to prevent the admiral from bringing Sigismund from Poland to be crowned before the king had given the desired religious and political pledges. But the Finnish nobility, including Fleming's personal opponents, unanimously supported the admiral, because it was feared that otherwise the union with Poland would be jeopardized.

Admiral Fleming was thus able to transport the king to Sweden without broaching the subject of pledges. But after he arrived on Swedish soil, Sigismund was exposed to heavy pressure. Against Fleming's advice, he finally yielded and confirmed the decisions of the synod of Uppsala. Lutheranism was accordingly juridically established in Sweden and Finland as the State Church. Sigismund nonetheless handed his father-confessor a secret protest, in which he declared that he would not act against the interests of the Church of Rome; and the officially banned Catholic Masses continued to be held publicly.

The king was also compelled to invest the Council of the Realm with the powers of a regency and to appoint Duke Charles as its head. However, he did manage to retain for himself the right to nominate governors for the various provinces and to claim their obedience to him, instead of to the home government. Both solutions reached at the coronation inevitably led to worse discord than ever.

Klaus Fleming was appointed governor of all Finland, thereby concentrating more power than ever in the hands of this dynamic leader. At that point in Finnish history, the Peace of Täysinä was concluded.

Finland and Sweden at Odds

Political leadership had been the original ambition of Duke Charles, but the recent birth of a male heir inspired him to reach out also for that symbol of power, the crown, with its insurance of continuity. He convoked the Diet of Söderköping in 1595 and, exercising his demagogic powers, he succeeded in getting himself installed as regent—after a pattern borrowed from the period of the Scandinavian Union. It was further resolved to give no heed to the king's commands unless they were approved by the duke and the Council of the Realm. The threat was made that anybody who violated these rulings would be treated as a rebel.

Admonished by Fleming, the Finns had, with rare exceptions, stayed away from Söderköping. The duke's henchman, Karl Horn, was therefore dispatched to Finland to obtain ratification of the revolutionary measures passed by the Diet. Fleming summoned the Finnish nobility to Turku. Reaching a decision was difficult, because the Finns did not want to break with either Sweden or Poland. Many of the nobles were at first inclined to accept the resolutions of the Diet, Karl Horn reported, "but just as soon as they had been taken to task by Lord Klaus...., they came to think differently, that is, the same way he did." The majority signed a document pledging Finland to abide by the rulings of the Diet, but only provided that the king endorsed them!

It was obvious that Sigismund could not countenance a shift of power approaching a *coup d'état*. This meant that relations between Finland and Sweden had been severed. The Finns and the Swedes now became adversaries. And the old conflict is still reflected in modern historical research: the Swedes look upon Duke Charles as a champion of unity in the realm, whereas many Finnish research scholars do not see in him anything more than a usurper.

Fleming and his supporters did not, however, seek even partial independence for Finland, as certain Finnish fiction writers have fancied. But they did pursue a pro-Finnish policy, the cornerstone of which, since the Baltic crisis, had been collaboration with Poland. This policy rested on a narrow basis, upheld only by the nobility, among whose ranks there was also an opposition, including the influential Horn family. The Finnish farmers did not oppose Fleming's conciliatory church policy. But after the Peace of Täysinä, they did not appreciate the need to maintain the army and looked upon the rugged Marshal of the Realm as a despot, who taxed them excessively and forced them to billet troops.

When the embittered farmers of South Ostrobothnia failed to prevail upon Fleming to lessen his demands for the billeting of troops, they turned to Duke Charles, who advised them to take the dispensation of justice into their own hands. "There are, at least, so many of you that you ought to be able to shake those [soldiers] off, even if armed only with fence posts and clubs."

The duke's advice did not mean that the farmers' distress moved him to pity. On the contrary, the tax burden only grew heavier after his accession, and the billeting demands that he made were harsher than before. Nor, in exploiting the farmers to weaken Fleming's position, did he feel any concern for the fate awaiting those who took part in the rebellion. Duke Charles made use of propaganda so skillfully, however, that almost to this day histories have referred to him as the "peasant prince." This appellation, notes one Swedish scholar, applies more fittingly to the means used by him, however, rather than to his political ends.

The farmers lacked firearms, but they equipped themselves with bows and arrows and spears as well as the spiked clubs recommended by the duke. The rebellion thus became known as the Club War (1596—97). The violence broke out in South Ostrobothnia, which maintained the liveliest contact with Sweden and was accordingly particularly susceptible to the agitation of Duke Charles, but fighting spread over a large part of the country. The rebel leader was Jaakko Ilkka, a yeoman who was rich enough to have delivered a fully equipped cavalryman to the army. He had previously been imprisoned by Fleming as a rebel but managed to escape from the Castle of Turku. Perhaps Ilkka had more bitterness than skill as a leader. He is described in a folk poem in terms of ridicule: "The snake knew not how to wage war, nor the toad how to fight; but he drank in every house, in the manor of every squire." Reference is thus made to the plundering of estates belonging to the gentry by the club-wielding warriors. It reflects the social aspect of the conflict, which in other respects, too, merged with the political: by egging on the farmers, Duke Charles drove his few supporters among the Finnish nobility and even the clergy into Marshal Fleming's camp.

Fleming's experienced and disciplined troops easily gained the upper hand over the rebels, who lost all the open battles. Passions were so inflamed also on the nobles' side that a couple of large units of peasant warriors who had surrendered were put to death, in violation of promises, to the last man. After retreating to Ostrobothnia, Ilkka and certain other leaders were taken prisoner and slaughtered.

Scarcely had peace been restored, when, suddenly, in April 1597, Fleming died. To succeed him as royal governor of Finland, Sigismund named, on the recommendation of Fleming's widow and closest associates, the commandant of Narva, Arvid Stålarm. Into the vacancy left by the iron marshal stepped a man devoted to compromise to the point of opportunism. Yet, he found himself working under even more difficult circumstances than his predecessor, for Duke Charles was at last in a position to carry out in full the threat contained in the resolutions of the Söderköping Diet.

The Council, whose relations with the duke were by no means smooth, had contrived to stave off his planned attack on Finland. Consequently, at the beginning of 1597, the duke, defying the king's orders, had convened a new Diet at Arboga. The Council, which had of old served as the core of the Diet, regarded the convocation as illegal and, with the exception of a single member, failed to attend. Relations between the duke and the upper nobility of Sweden were thereby definitively broken.

Charles persuaded the abbreviated Diet to authorize him to subdue Finland by force. He led the punitive expedition himself. Aided by a traitor, he captured the Castle of Turku and took its commanding officers prisoner. In the chapel of the fortress, Fleming's still unburied body lay in its coffin. The duke ordered Widow Ebba to open the coffin. He pulled the deceased by the beard, and, according to an old legend, declared: "If you were alive now, your head would not be very secure." To this, Widow Ebba Fleming retorted bravely: "If my master and late husband were alive, your princely grace would never have entered this chamber."

The duke's insecure position in Sweden forced him to return before confronting the main Finnish troops. On his departure, he left the Castle of Turku in the hands of Klaus Herman's son, Fleming, who, despite his kinship to the late marshal, had belonged to the opposition. Charles's limited invasion served only to stiffen the Finnish front. Perceiving the weakness of the departed duke's position, Fleming and the other officers who were left in command joined Governor Stålarm, who once more took charge at the Castle. With their ranks united, the Finns set sail for Sweden to lend support to their king after Sigismund had landed at Kalmar in an attempt to regain the throne from which he had been gradually deposed. But the Finns landed too late: Duke Charles's troops already had decisively beaten Sigismund, compelling him to withdraw to Poland (1598).

The union of Sweden and Poland was thus *de facto* dissolved. Since the abiding motivation of the policy pursued by the Finnish nobility was security against the East, and since such security called for collaboration with both Sweden and Poland, Finnish policy likewise sustained a crippling setback. And, finally, even Sigismund forsook the Finns. In fact, he went so far as to order the Finnish fleet to a Polish port. That, of course, was demanding too much.

When, in the summer of 1599, the duke landed in Finland with his army and defeated the main Finnish forces at Marttila, the battle did not last long. Stålarm surrendered the Castle of Turku on the express condition that the charges against the Finns would be submitted to the Diet for investigation. Before that, however, Charles had started to execute his prisoners, nor did he keep the pledges he had made to the officers in command of the castle. This ruthlessness must be attributed primarily to calculating intimidation; but, apparently, it was also due, in part, to impatience—as displayed by the duke in wreaking vengeance on Fleming's two sons, one of whom was hardly more than a boy.

Only three Finnish nobles—who were joined in the dock by the Swedish aristocrats who had remained loyal to Sigismund—were tried by the Diet. Among them was Stålarm, who was sentenced to death but pardoned on the scaffold. The rest of Sigismund's Finnish followers were thrown into prison, where they were kept for years, uncertain of their ultimate fate. Among the prisoners were not only noblemen but also clergymen, including no less a personage than Bishop Sorolainen, in spite of his having worked sincerely to carry out the resolutions of the synod of Uppsala. The manors of the nobles were plundered by the duke's mercenaries, and a large part of the landed property of the nobility was confiscated. The Finnish nobles lost their offices and were replaced by henchmen of the duke from Sweden.

Charles experienced no trouble the next year in taking possession of Estonia, whose Finnish-born governor-general, Göran Boije, had till then been known to be a cautious supporter of Sigismund. Some of the Finnish nobles who had fled to that country moved on to Poland, where many a highborn Swede, too, had sought refuge and where the fugitives then proceeded to compose impotent lampoons about the "butcher's bench" of Duke Charles.

The butchery indulged in by the duke was not on a scale sufficient to bleed the nobility of Finland white, and its impoverishment was only temporary. Nevertheless, the consequences of the catastrophe were passed on to later generations. The sixteenth-century Finnish political leadership, comprising the nobility, had not thought along nationalistic lines in the sense of nineteenth century romantics; but these men had felt that they were in the same boat, they had looked at things from a Finnish point of view, and they had thus formed a group separate from the political leaders of Sweden. After the duke's victory, the subdued Finnish nobility never again formed such a unified body of leaders.

Arbitrary action and violence practiced on individuals who held different views could not, however, be kept up indefinitely. Every usurper aspires sooner or later to restore normal conditions and, after consolidating his position, he is likely to consider it expedient to avail himself of the services even of those against whom he had fought. That was the line taken by Duke Charles. Finnish nobles once more received lucrative appointments, and confiscated estates were soon returned—even to the families of executed men—so that in the end the net losses suffered by the Finnish nobility amounted to less than one-tenth of its landed property.

At first, reconciliation proceeded stiffly. When, in 1602, at a provincial meeting in Turku, the duke for the first time entered into negotiations with the Finnish nobility, he turned down requests for the liberation of the Finns still held prisoner and for the reinstallation of Bishop Sorolainen. Later, however, the policy of reconciliation was given impetus by reverses sustained by the duke in the war he had started against Poland. Stålarm was summoned from prison to assume the duties of commander-in-chief of the Finnish army; and his position was so strong that he was practically able to dictate the wording of the oath of allegiance which he had to give the duke.

Loyalty under the circumstances of anti-Polish politics, alien to the Finnish nobility, proved in practice to be a touchstone. A specialist on the period, Professor P. Renvall, points out that the Finnish nobility had to accept the authority of Duke Charles "in order to preserve some kind of economic and social position, regardless of how distasteful it was in view of his personality, his domestic politics and his foreign policy, which was opposed to the fundamental political outlook thitherto maintained by the Finns."

Charles conclusively established himself in power in the year 1604, when the Diet acknowledged the crown to be the hereditary property of his branch of the family. Thereafter, he could use the title of King Charles IX—and as such he is known to history.

Toward the Arctic and the White Sea Coast

After Charles had taken exclusive possession of the entire realm of his late brothers, Eric and John, no reasons of ambition or military exigency should have compelled him to continue his offensive into Livonia, which Poland had inherited from the estate left behind by the Teutonic Knights. However, Livonia looked like easy prey. The powerful Polish nobility, after all, had viewed Sigismund's ill-starred trips to Sweden as private politics and had refused to give him military support, even to maintain his grip on Estonia—though, in desperation, the king had ceremoniously made a "gift" of Estonia to Poland.

The Poles were therefore caught off guard when the Swedish-Finnish army crossed the border. As a result, nearly all Livonia, with the exception of its capital, Riga, fell into the hands of the invaders from the North in a short time. But when the Poles counterattacked, the Swedish-Finnish troops were unable to cope with the enemy cavalry and suffered one setback after another. At the same time, Finland was prostrated by the crop failure of 1601, one of the worst ever experienced. Historians have discovered more about the secret negotiations conducted with the Poles by the commander-in-chief of the Finnish forces, Stålarm, and certain other Finnish officers than Charles ever learned. But this collusion with the enemy hardly had time to affect the course of the war before Charles's suspicions awoke and Stålarm was again incarcerated. Final judgment on his guilt was never passed, and death at last intervened to release the old soldier after fifteen years behind bars. Lacking faith in his commanding officers, the king now set forth to direct military operations himself.

But at Kirkholm, in 1605, the Poles inflicted a crushing defeat on the numerically superior Swedish-Finnish forces. By a whim of fate, Charles IX was saved from capture by two officers, one of them a Finn who had once fled to Poland but returned home and been pardoned, the other a Baltic German who was the founder of a subsequently well-known Finnish noble family. And both men paid with their lives for their self-sacrificing efforts to serve the king.

The hostilities between Sweden and Poland abated after that, for the struggle over the succession to the Russian throne began to have a decisive effect on the politics of the countries bordering on the Czarist realm. The authority of the boyar Vasili Shuisky, who had been crowned Czar, was challenged by an adventurer who claimed to be Dmitri, the last scion of the royal line of Rurik, and he was backed by the Poles.

When the false Dmitri penetrated ever deeper into Russia at the head of his troops and began to threaten Moscow itself, Vasili Shuisky agreed to accept the assistance proffered by Charles IX. The Swedish king, in offering to support Shuisky, was motivated by the desire to prevent his chief foe, Poland, from gaining control of the vast country of Russia through the pretender, Dmitri. Furthermore, he expected to receive a reward for his aid, since the internal weakness of Russia presented an opportunity to expand Sweden-Finland eastward.

In 1609, by the terms of an agreement signed in Viipuri, Charles IX sent an army of 5.000 men into Russia to oppose Dmitri, and, in return, he received the province of Käkisalmi. John III had striven, in his time, to seize this territory and, after capturing the Castle of Käkisalmi had added to his title the name of the broader Russian administrative area *(Votskaja pjatina)*, part of which was Käkisalmi province. The acquisition of Käkisalmi province by Sweden-Finland shifted the eastern border of the realm to the great Lake Ladoga, and this border was easier to defend.

Although, to the king, the road to Moscow signified primarily a roundabout route toward an attack on Poland, the Viipuri treaty was in line with the traditional political program of the Finns and helped to close the gap between Charles IX and the Finnish nobility. The leadership of the Russian expedition was entrusted to Jakob de la Gardie, son of Pontus de la Gardie and John III's daughter. He had been brought up in his grandmother's manor in the Finnish interior, and he gave the other important commissions to Finns, with the result that, among the commanding officers, there were almost all the former opponents of Charles who were still alive.

Since De la Gardie marched into Russian territory as an ally of the Czar's, he did not meet with serious resistance until he had reached the Tver region (now Kaliningrad), where followers of the false Dmitri put up a fight. More than by the enemy, the advance was slowed down by the fact that the Finnish troops obstinately refused to march ever deeper into a strangeland that for generations had been regarded as hostile. When this psychological obstacle had at last been overcome, De la Gardie entered Moscow in 1610 at the head of his army.

Shuisky paid dearly for Swedish-Finnish aid, as it provoked Poland into starting open war against Russia, which precipitated the Czar's overthrow. For several years, Russia was in a state of utter chaos, and the main task of the foreign troops there was no longer to support heirs to the throne but to conquer new territory for their own country, either Sweden-Finland or Poland.

When it set forth on the Moscow adventure, supporting Shuisky was such a predominant aim of the Swedish-Finnish army, and confidence in the Viipuri agreement so implicit, that it was not even considered necessary to demand the fortress of Käkisalmi as a pawn. Instead, it had to be captured by force, and it surrendered only after a long siege. The city of Novgorod and the fortresses of Ingria were captured in the same way, resulting in the occupation of extensive areas of north-western Russia by the Swedish-Finnish troops.

Leaning on his military strength, De la Gardie even tried to steer an independent political course: Sweden must be content with the acquisition of Käkisalmi province, but the younger of Charles IX's sons, Charles Philip, must be made Czar, and an alliance bolstered by this dynastic bond must be concluded between Sweden and Russia against Poland. This plan at first won support, expecially in Novgorod; but Charles IX had a more ambitious program for expansion in mind, and his death, in 1611, produced a new constellation.

During the latter half of the sixteenth century, the port of Archangel had been establishe on the coast of the White Sea. Used by the Dutch and the English in trading with Russia, it had served the Czar during the Long Wrath by importing arms from England. In his day, John III, in initiating peace negotiations with Russia, had demanded the cession to Sweden-Finland of the western coast of the White Sea. Apparently, his object was to obtain a base from which to harass this commerce in weapons. Charles IX aspired to block both of

Russia's northern trade routes, the one passing via the Gulf of Finland and the one via the White Sea. Military expeditions made up of peasants from northern Finland were sent to the White Sea and Murmansk coasts, but the permanent occupation of those remote regions proved impossible.

Charles IX's activity extended also to the portion of the Arctic coast that lay west of the boundary drawn in the Peace of Täysinä. The Russian sovereign had given up his rights to tax the Lapps in this area in favor of the Swedish Crown. And since the latter had acquired, during the reign of Gustavus Vasa, the ancient rights of the *Pirkkalaiset*, the Swedish Crown held, in a sense, two parts of the Arctic coast of Scandinavia, while the Danish Crown held only on part. Charles encouraged Finnish pioneers to settle Lapland, had churches built for the native Lapps, and situated bailiffs in the province known as Finnmark.

It was much harder, however, for the Swedish bailiffs to travel across the barren fells to the Arctic coast than for Danish officials to sail there along the Norwegian coast. Moreover, King Christian IV of Denmark responded to the aggressiveness of Charles IX by ordering his bailiffs to collect taxes not only from the Lapps living along the seaboard but also from the reindeer herdsmen roaming the Arctic mountains farther south. The conflict became aggravated to the point of warfare between Sweden and Denmark. Hostilities broke out shortly before Charles IX died.

Youthful King Gustavus II Adolphus thus inherited war with all three of his neighbours. The Danes succeeded again, as they had during the previous war, in taking the fortress of Elfsborg. Otherwise. they scored no noteworthy successes, so Christian IV agreed to an end of hostilities, and peace was formally concluded at Knäred in 1613. Sweden simply could not afford to lose Elfsborg, her only harbour opening on the North Sea, and therefore she was ready to pay virtually any price at all to regain possession of it. The price demanded by the Danes for its return was such a tremendous war indemnity that they were certain that it would be beyond Sweden's capacity to pay. Hence, they expected the fortress, which was left in their hands as a security against the indemnity, to become a permanent possession. However, to the disappointment of the Danes, the debt was paid.

Despite the reparations burden, the balance of foreign trade was maintained by greatly increasing the volume of copper exports. Copper was mined from deposits in Sweden. But the Finns also participated in paying the extra taxes that were imposed on the population in order to help extricate the kingdom from its economic dilemma. The second indemnity that Sweden was forced to pay for Elfsborg was such a heavy burden on her economy that extra taxes were collected for a period of six years, requiring the surrender of a ninth part of the harvest, or almost all of the total national product.

Although the Finns carried their full share of the indemnity burden in order to safeguard the western Swedish border at a strategically and commercially vital point, the territorial conditions of the Peace Treaty of Knäred were especially damaging to Finnish interests. Sweden surrendered to Denmark her rights to collect taxes from the coastal Lapps. Thus, the whole seaboard went to Norway, while the interior was s still held in common. It was on the basis of that treaty that, in the following century, the national boundary was drawn: Finland extended northward to within a few miles of the Arctic Ocean without reaching the shore at a single point. The Peace Treaty of Knärenevertheless accorded with seventeenth-century geographic and traffic conditions in that it was difficult to maintain contact with Finnmark overland from Sweden-Finland.

As for Russian policy, the youthful monarch faced the alternatives handed down to him by his father: he would have to look after either dynastic or national interests. After Gustavus II Adolphus had ascended the throne of Sweden, his younger brother was at first recognized in northwestern Russia as Czar. But, in 1613, the Russians at last rallied behind a single candidate for the throne, the native boyar Michael Romanov, whose dynasty was destined to rule Russia until the revolution of 1917. The era of chaos was over.

The military position of the Swedish Crown was still quite strong. It held the city of Novgorod and a considerable part of the land belonging to this ancient grand duchy. Accordingly, as the war went on, though reverses were sustained, victories were also won. It was necessary to abandon the dynastic alternative, even in the diluted form of having Novgorod organized into a separate state under the rule of Charles Philip. Yet, there remained the possibility of annexing some lesser, perhaps even substantial, Russian areas.

For some time, the permanent abandonment of Elfsborg to Denmark was considered, in order to concentrate all the resources of the realm against the East. But this unrealistic plan, which would have forced Sweden to establish another port on the remote coast of the White Sea to replace Elfsborg, was soon rejected.

The peace talks with Russia were begun during the period when the Swedes and Finns were struggling to pay the indemnity for Elfsborg. The cunning Russians, who by then were recovering from the ravages of war and therefore had nothing to lose by temporizing, deliberately kept delaying the negotiations.

The Dutch and the English acted as mediators in the peace negotiations. They were themselves engaged in strenuous rivalry over Russian trade. So, when the Dutch sided with the Swedes, the English, of course, threw their weight on the opposite side.

During the internal strife in Russia, England had striven even to take under her administrative wing the trade route running down from Archangel to the Caspian Sea. But when the Englishman John Merick arrived to negotiate such ambitious demands, Michael Romanov had just been elected Czar and Russia could no longer be treated like a non-European colony. For the purpose of maintaining good relations with the Russians and eliminating the Dutch, the king of England ordered Merick to stay on in Russia and serve the Czar. Before long, Czar Michael began to rely on the Englishman, as the Council of Boyars testified, "exactly as if he were a subject of Boyar blood." Whereas the Russian-born peace negotiators got to know only what was meant for the ears of the Swedes, Merick learned even the concessions that the Czar was secretly prepared to make in a pinch. However, he played a crafty game, which made it unnecessary to resort to the secret concessions.

During the election of the Czar, Gustavus II Adolphus had come out with his great Eastern program: territories were to be acquired on the northeastern side of Lake Ladoga as far as the White Sea coast and a large area south of the lake, too—and even, if all went well, Novgorod itself. The Russians were now so badly beaten, explained Count Axel Oxenstierna, the Swedish chancellor, to the king's negotiators that "the greatest and best part of their land is now under enemy occupation or devastated and useless, besides which the major part of their best manpower has recently been killed off, so that scarcely anybody is left except forest bandits. To let them loose now, even to help them to their feet without plucking some feathers off them and weakening their position, at the same time strengthening ourselves a bit, would appear to be both harmful and blame-worthy."

Yet, from the very beginning of the peace negotiations, restraint had to be practiced in plucking feathers. And, in the end, Sweden-Finland secured, in the Peace of Stolbova, signed in 1617, the cession only of Ingria, in addition to the province of Käkisalmi, as promised by Vasil Shuisky, and the payment of a trifling war indemnity.

"Nobody would have believed," Merick, the Englishman, was complimented in Moscow, " that the king of Sweden could be induced to give back Great Novgorod for such a tiny sum of money."

5

Finland as Part of a Great Power

The Eastern Border of Sweden-Finland

Historians have been challenged by the problem of why King Gustavus II Adolphus, who had dreamed of mastery of the Arctic Ocean, should have been content to accept such small territorial concessions that even the Russians apparently were surprised by the mild peace terms.

Part of the answer may lie in the fact that the territories sought by Sweden-Finland during the first stage of the negotiations and those that finally were acquired were not well known. Thus, on account of erroneously drawn maps, it was not realized that west of Ingria a Russian wedge of land remained that ran deep into the zone bordering the Gulf of Finland and that, consequently, the land connection obtained through the treaty with the Baltic part of the realm was extremely narrow. Mistakenly, Gustavus II Adolphus thought that Ingria was buttressed by bodies of water on three sides. Similarly, he imagined the terrain just north of Lake Ladoga to consist of barren moors, "where no army can march."

Another partial otion to the problem is that the door to an active Eastern policy was still thought to have been left ajar. Certain statements by the king and by the Council emphasized the strategic advantages of the new border in the event of a new attack by Sweden-Finland. Furthermore, at that time, Poland was considered to b the chief enemy. After all, the military expedition into Russia had been aimed primarily against Poland. Even as hostilities were drawing to a close, the Diet in Sweden expressed the fear that the Poles, after first defeating the Russians, "would seize us harder than ever by the throat."

The king probably did not really believe that Poland was capable of conquering Russia, any more than he believed the Swedes to be capable of it. Informing the Diet of the Peace of Stolbova, Gustavus II Adolphus proved himself to be a statesman with a much more realistic view of Russia than Charles XII, Napoleon, or Hitler. Resorting to flovery language, the king described to the estates the boundless expanses of the Russian realm, its riches and its navigable streams which facilitated its power to mobilize men for warfare. It was wise, he told them, to maintain good relations with Russia and to "reinforce" one's own kingdom in other directions.

Moreover, King Gustavus II Adolphus was also able to uphold the thesis that the new border would be easy to defend if, in spite of peaceful intentions, war did break out: Lake Peipus protected Estonia, and Ladoga was as broad as the sea that divided the Baltic lands from Sweden. "Across that puddle it will not be easy for the Russian to leap," he declared. Finland's forward terrain, Ingria, was separated from Russia by boggy stretches; and after these were crossed, the Finnish shores were safeguarded, for the domain of the Czar had no access whatsoever "without our leave" to the Baltic Sea.

The stress that the king laid on strategic advantages was by no means empty boasting, for during the next nine decades, Finland was incomparably less exposed to military action than during the previous two centuries or during the following century.

In the Peace of Stolbova, the Czar had ceded to the Swedish king the province of Käkisalmi as well as Ingria, "with all its provinces, lands and people ... just as the great lords of Russia, the Czars and grand dukes, have previously owned it." The Ingrian boundary ran through inhabited territory and there could be no dispute about its course, whereas the question as to what areas belonged to the province of Käkisalmi was left to the boundary survey to resolve.

Documents had been seized by the Finns at Novgorod that revealed what villages had paid taxes to the lords of Käkisalmi Castle in ancient times. The Russian border commissioners, however, paid no heed to the evidence produced by the Finns, but systematically, by means of cunning delaying tactics, kept prolonging the execution of their task. As time passed, sentiment mounted in Sweden for setting the forces of the kingdom against Poland. In 1621, the king decided that it was not worth postponing a major military campaign for a slice of Karelian wilderness: The border commissioners were ordered to draw the boundary quickly along the line claimed by Russia.

Käkisalmi Province and Ingria—like Estonia and the regions that later were conquered across the Baltic—failed to gain the status in the realm that was enjoyed by Sweden proper and the Finnish provinces that had been united with her for centuries. They were governed as conquered territory, and their inhabitants were never granted the right to be represented in the Swedish-Finnish Diet, nor was conscription ever introduced there.

The natives of Käkisalmi Province were Karelians, while those of Ingria were Karelians (so-called Ingrians) and other peoples related to the Finns in addition to some Russians. Therefore, no essential differences of nationality existed between the inhabitants of the old Finnish part of the kingdom and those of Käkisalmi. However, there was one difference that in the seventeenth century was far more significant than differing nationalities: religious difference. For, the populations of both conquered territories were of the Greek Orthodox faith.

In Sweden-Finland, where only a short time earlier a ban haden issued against joining the Roman Catholic Church which carried a penalty of death, the absorption of tens of thousands of new subjects who belonged to the Eastern Orthodox Church raised a challenge to the policy of religious integration. The problem had political connotations, because the Czar had also been head of the Russian Church since olden times; hence, the inhabitants of Ingria and Käkisalmi were considered to be bound to their former ruler by ties of loyalty and allegiance through the Church.

Efforts were made to solve the problem in various ways. King Gustavus II Adolphus was prepared to forgo categorical demands for religus conformity, provided the priests of the conquered regions accepted the Patriarch of Constantinople as their supreme spiritual leader instead of the Patriarch of Moscow. But during the reigns of his successors, the stand taken by native conformists stiffened, and the idea of reorganizing the Eastern Orthodox Church in Finland lost support. Instead, the native opposition became bent upon destroying the alien faith. Every parish was forced to support a Lutheran minister, and every inhabitant had to attend Lutheran church services, while no new Orthodox priests were appointed to replace those who died. This harsh policy drove Orthodox worshippers across the boundary to the Russian side to attend church, and many eventually chose to stay. If the inhabitants of the conquered regions had not been politically unreliable before, they were soon made that way by religious persecution.

During the next war with Russia, which was fought in the 1650's these harassed people sided with the Russians, and when the Russians retreated, they fled in large numbers over the border to escape punishment. Extensive areas in Käkisalmi and Ingria were deserted, to be settled by newcomers of the Lutheran faith from different parts of Finland, who were lured by the freedom from conscription that was enjoyed by the population of the conquered territories.

At the close of the century, the province of Käkisalmi was almost totally Lutheran, and it has been estimated that, by that time, fully three-quarters of the Ingrian inhabitants also were Lutheran. The change in religious beliefs was due only to a small extent to forcible conversions. Mainly, it was the result of mass migrations into and out of the conquered regions. For Finland, these successive migratory movements eastward signified a heavy loss of manpower: Karelians by the thousands moved to Russia, and they were replaced by western Finns— partly in areas that later fell into Russian hand.

The Birth of a Modern State

King Gustavus II Adolphus (1611—32) was a ruler with versatile talents who knew how to manipulate people by the sheer force of his personality, without resorting to direct pressure tactics.

The vigorous and conscientious Chancellor, of State Axel Oxenstierna who rose to his high office as a young man and stayed there for nearly half a century (1612—54), acquired unique administrative and diplomatic experience as a faithful servant of the Crown. The accession of Gustavus II Adolphus produced the conditions required to terminate the struggle that had been going on between the upper nobility and royalty—represented by kings who were bent on gaining absolute power—for half a century. The fact that the young king had not yet reached the age when, according to the rules of royal inheritance, he would be entitled to take charge of the government, made conciliation easier. The Diet invested him with full rights at the tender age of seventeen, but he was required to give a pledge which was tantamount to the ratification of a constitutional law.

He pledged tt he would not start war or make peace, demand new taxes or a new conscription, or enact new laws without the approval of the Council and the Diet. Accordingly, the Council was no longer considered a mere advisory body, and, for the first time, the Diet was recognized as an authoritative organ of the state. The upper nobility had scored a victory, but it had also accepted the duty of serving the realm as permanent members of the Council or as holders of high administrative offices. The Diet, on the other hand, proved in practice to be only a sounding board, which echoed the voices of the king gd the Council; but care was taken to assure that this echo reached foreign ears, too, and that the foreign policy of the king and the Council was understood abroad to be the foreign policy of the whole Swedish nation. The roughly drawn regulations which the king issued to govern the functions of the Diet did not make it nearly so modern an institution as the administrative and juridical branches of the Swedish-Finnish government evolved during the reign of King Gustavus II Adolphus.

Even though Gustavus II Adolphus spent one-half of his reign beyond the borders o his kingdom, personally leading military operations, he did manage, in collaboration with his chancellor, to carry out a colossal program of internal organization. The king's protracted absence obliged him to leave the handling of routine matters to the Council of the Realm, which, starting in 1621, became established as a permanent organ of administration. As much as the Council of the Realm differed in many respects from a modern Cabinet, the resemblance between them is heightened by the fact that certain of the councillors simultaneously served as chiefs of central bureaus, or collegia, and thereby had charge of affairs in a special sector of government. The men who served in those new central bureaus were state officials, whereas the secretaries, accounting officers, and clerks who previously had functioned at the royal court had been private servants of the king. Their duties and range of authority were defined by regulations: they could not be dismissed and they were entitled to a stipulated salary (which, however, was seldom paid on time). The superior functionaries issued orders to subordinate ones, and the central bureaus to local ones, whereas previously there had existed no clear scale of ranks, and the king and his trusted lieutenants had issued all the orders. In this centralized system, the office of governor-general, which could be established for special reasons in certain parts of the realm, represented an abnormal intermediary level. The governors-general were deputies of the king, and Finland was under the authority of such an officer several times.

For a long time, justice had been administered by lower courts, vested with inferior authority, and higher courts, vested with perior authority. Now, these courts of justice were organized in a hierarchical order that culminated in the Royal Court of Appeals, thus introducing the system of appealing verdicts of lower courts to higher ones. Finland received her own "Royal" Court of Appeals in 1623. However, in spite of their name, these courts were no longer he supreme arbiters of justice, for their verdicts could be referred to the sovereign, i.e., the Council of the Realm, for review.

The recruitment of soldiers was conducted as before: infantry was raised by conscription and farmers volunteered for service in the cavalry in return for relief from land rents. A new feature of the recruiting policy provided for detacments which previously had been maintained on a provisional basis to become permanent units.

Finland's quota of recruits was set at nine infantry regiments and three cavalry regiments, or a relatively larger share of the armed forces of the realm than her population would have presupposed. However, there was no deliberate intention to place a heavier military burden on Finland than on the mother country. This is indicated, for instance, by the fact that the Finnish quota was disproportional chiefly in respct to cavalry, which was based on voluntary service. The real eason was that the nobility owned much more land in Sweden than they did in Finland. The landed estates of the nobles were required to supply one infantryman from twice the number of men on them as on the freeholds of yeomen. Moreover, a tenant farmer was never expected to report for cavalry service because he had no land rent to pay to the Crown.

The economic policy of King Gustavus II Adolphus and Oxenstierna solidly established the mercantile system in Sweden-Finland. The target of regulatory measures was foreign trade, in particular, and the aim was to prevent competition among exporters and importers in markets abroad. Consequently, only a few towns—so-called staple towns—were permitted to carry on foreign trade. Not a single town on the Gulf of Bothnia was granted staple rights.

To Finnish maritime commerce, such regulations proved detrimental, even ruinous. The country's chief export was tar, which was to an ever-increasing extent produced by burning wood. And tar production was concentrated along the Bothnian coast. But the small towns founded there by government decree were allowed to ship the tar only as far as Stockholm. In order to prevent the merchants of staple towns from competing for foreign buyers or sellers, the export or import of profitable commodities, like tar, was placed in the hands of some trading company as a monopolistic right. This restrictive policy also helped to strengthen the economic position of Stockholm.

Mercantilism patronized the capitals of other European states likewise. Thus, Copenhagen, for instance, controlled Norway's trade even more completely than Stockholm controlled Finland's. And, since their commodity was guaranteed a steady market at a stipulated price, the actual producers—the farmers, in the case of tar—were perhaps the winners rather than the losers in the system.

Mercantilistic principles led to the founding of a colony on the Delaware River in North America by the Swedish government in 1638. But it was soon lost to the Dutch. The settlers included many Finns.

The only sphere in which no reform could be effected during the first half of seventeenth century, despite every progressive effort, was public finance. The farmers, who humbly referred to themselves as "taxpaying peasantry," were coerced by the Diet to accept one tax after another; and, since these taxes had an innate tendency to become permanent fixtures, they became stratified on top of the old land rents. But the new taxes, like the old, were mostly paid in kind, whereas the Crown needed cash.

The wars now were shifting far afield, beyond the eastern and southern shores of the Baltic, and the wages of both the foreign mercenaries and native conscripts were paid in cash. Cash was also required for the purchase of provisions in the areas of military operations, whenever plundering failed to keep the troops adequately fed. A certain amount of money also was needed to pay the salaries of the functionaries who staffed the new bureaus, though they were not so liable to quit as foreign soldiers were if they were unpaid for many months, or even years. Sweden's status as a great power would have called for the establishment of a money economy. But, since it was thoroughly agrarian, the country's finances still depended on payments in kind, and overcoming this discrepancy would have been too much to ask even of the most ingenius administrator.

The development of the Swedish kingdom into a modern state deeply affected the position of Finland. Although there was no systematic plan, before 1680, to make Finland Swedish, it seems that the government aimed at a strict uniformity between Swedish and Finnish institutions; and, in any case, Finland lost her special status as the administrative order became more and more centralized, and she gradually became transformed into a group of provinces among the other provinces that comprised the realm. The royal governors or lords-lieutenant of old were, to be sure, compensated for by the governors-general. But only on exceptional occasions was a governor-general appointed to serve in Finland and especially the first governors-general, Nils Bielke and Gabriel gt's son, Oxenstierna, worked vigorously to achieve uniformity between the administrative systems of Finland and Sweden. And even if the Finns had gained a royal court of appeals for themselves, corresponding high courts of justice had been established in other parts of the kingdom as well. Furthermore, centralized administration attracted to its service the most talented of Finnish nobles: thus, many members of the leading Finnish families of Horns and Flemings moved over to Stockholm.

The modernized structure of government bureaus everywhere required the conduct of business in writing, whereas, earlier, the affairs of state and judicial proceedings had been managed orally, with written summaries being briefly drawn up only of decisions and orders. This change, again, affected the status of the Finnish language. Orally, Finnish had been used and was still used (it was, for example, also used in commanding Finnish military units), even if the written language of official documents had been Swedish for centuries. The more documents that had to be written, the more important the Swedish tongue became in Finland and the more necessary it became for officeholders to have a complete mastery of it. Judging from the fact that, in semi-official correspondence between some military officers, Finnish phrases occur here and there in the main Swedish body of the text, the Finnish nobility still had a command of the vernacular. Finnish, which in secondary schools had been used to supplement Latin, was replaced by Swedish when the school regulations of 1649 took effect, and the clergy began to adopt Greek, Latin or Swedish surnames.

More functionaries than ever began to arrive in Finland from Sweden as relations became more firmly established. And after the death if Bishop Sorolainen (1625) the king took to appointing only Swedish-orn candidates to the bishop's seat in Turku. The first of these, Isaac Rothovius, tried to enforce in Finland strict ecclesiastical discipline in general, and the statutes of the Swedish bishoprics in particular. In the middle of the century, complaints were heard in Finland about the great number of Swedish officials in the country. But the peasantry expressed their indignation only when language difficulties caused trouble. And the educated classes, for their part, were bitter only because, owing to the increased competition, their own opportunities to gain office had narrowed. Finnish complaints were inspired by no nationalistic ideology. Nor did nationalistic considerations determine the administrative policy of the Swedish government in regard to Finland.

Besides, many of the newcomers from Sweden became quickly acclimatized. This was true also of the bishops who arrived in Turku from the other side of the Bothnian gulf after Rothovius. One of the Swedish-born bishops, Eskil Petraeus, became so proficient in the language of his new homeland that he wrote the first Finnish grammar.

The War That Spawned New Wars

During the war with Russia, and afterwards, too, the chief enemy, to the Swedes, still was Poland. Sigismund, the king of Poland, for his part had hopes of gaining the Swedish throne, and thus dynastic reasons in themselves kept Polish policy in the forefront. Poland was a Roman Catholic country, and during the fiercest stage of the conflict between the "papists" and the Lutherans, religious differences played a prominent role in international politics. In propaganda addresses to the simple masses, religion could easily be blown up into the dominant issue.

Swedish foreign policy remained active, but the spearhead of activity now turned from the East, where, except for brief intervals, it had been aimed ever since olden times. Gradually, it turned toward the South and, finally, the West. In the Eastern sector, not only did the Crown refrain from conquest but, to Finland's misfortune, both the navy and the artillery were removed after the conclusion of the Pace of Stolbova, while the fortifications of the country fell into negle.

The primary target of tack was thus consistently in the east-southeast. Operations were concentrated against Riga, which was one of the most strongly fortified points on the Baltic coast and, since it was situated at the mouth of the River Dvina, it commanded the trade of extensive regions in eastern Europe. The city of Riga capitulated to Sweden in 1621, and its conquest conclusively decided Swedish possession of Livonia. But Poland would not accept peace, so the fighting went on.

Year after year, havoc was wrought on Livonia, which had often suffered the ravages of war in the past. In the battle of Wallhof, in 1626, King Gustavus II Adolphus personally took charge, and his cavalry, half of which consisted of Finnish troops, for the first time gained the upper hand completely over the Polish cavalry. Since the heart of Poland could not be assailed from Riga because of the long supply lines, the king decided to shift the campaign to East Prussia, a province under Polish domination and ruled over by his brother-in-law, George Wilhelm, the elector of Brandenburg.

The Swedish troops made a successful landing, and the maritime cities of East Prussia were taken, after which they were forced to pay customs to the Swedish

Crown. Danzig (Gdansk), the most important grain export harbour of Poland and all Europe, was surrounded but resisted capture. Meanwhile, the dislocation of the Polish grain trade irritated the Protestant maritime powers, Holland and England. The campaign was waged in the sector to the south and southeast for more than three years.

At the same time, hostilities were going on in Germany which were part of what eventually came to be known as the Thirty Years' War, although then they were primarily an inernal struggle of the native Protestants and small states against the Catholics and the emperor. Now and then, the Swedish-Polish front appeared to be linked to the German firing lines, and at other times to be quite separate. Rather than the petty German princes in the danger zone, it was the foreign foes of the Habsburgs that inveigled the Swedes to abandon their war with Poland and to join the struggle in Germany with all their might.

Through the mediation of France, England, and the Netherlands, the Pole, whose nobility did not want to let their grain rot for the sake of King Sigismund's dynastic dreams, were persuaded, in 1629, to agree to asix-year truce. The Treaty of Altmark left the issue of succession tothe Swedish throne unresolved, bit Poland ceded Livonia and the ports of East Prussia. When, in the same year, the Council of the Realm took up the question of joining the war in Germany, the king declared pessimistically that it inevitably would lead to new wars. And, in regard to his own future, he painted an even gloomier picture: "I see that I can no longer look forward to rest of any kind, except eternal rest."

Both prophecies came true. But was Sweden actually so entangled in overseas politics that she had no means of extricating herself? The question has a particular relevancy to the history the Finnish half of the Swedish kingdom, because the war only brought to the Finns colossal losses in human life, heartbreak, and hunger, without any direct benefits. Historical research in Finland has taken a far more critical view than in Sweden of the Swedish intervention in Germany.

Although King Sigismund's claims to the Swedish throne could be exploited as an effective propaganda weapon to maintain the country's fighting spirit, there gs no real reason for taking the threat of a Polish invasion seriously. It hgsbeen said that the attack that led to the fall of Riga was the first rgressive war that was initiated by Sweden without the excuse of preventve action. In modern terms, it was the first step on the path to outright imerialism. But it cannot be denied that the spoils that were won gave satisfaction for a long time.

But, in the summer of 1630, when a Swedish-Finnish army of 40,000 men was transported to Pomerania, in north Prussia, to fight in the German war, the rationale was far more obscure.

The emperor's forces had advanced to Denmark on the Baltic coast. The Danes—disdaining collaboration with Sweden—had resisted singlehanded, were beaten, and had made peace. With such a mighty army standing on the opposite shore the alarmists in Sweden could perhaps raise a hue and cry about the need to set forth on a preventive war, and the Diet could proclaim that it was better to tie one's horse to a neighbour's fencepost than to one's own. But to cross the sea to tie the horse was a gamble which could result in the loss of a whole army, and Gustavus II Adolphus was fully cognizant of the risks involved. However, the

Council affirmed that if worse came to worst, the home front could be defended. And this secret estimate of the situation reveals that the poltical leadership in Sweden did not believe in the existence of any genuine military threat.

Idealistic historical writing used to depict the intervention of Gustavus II Adolphus in the Thirty Years' War as an unselfish act to help the Protestants of the German empire. The truth is, however, that by the time Sweden entered the war, it had already lost much of its character as an armed conflict between rival churches; and some of the German Protestants, among them the Swedish king's brother-in-law, the elector of Brandenburg, accepted the proffered aid only under pressure.

However, apparently King Gustavus II Adolphus, himself, also felt that he was fighting for the cause of the true faith. Still, in making almost a martyr out of him, posterity overestimated the religious motives behind the king's actions. The roots of this idealization extend to the decade of the 1620's, and during that whole period, popular sentiment in Sweden was systematically aroused. Propaganda is like a stone that keeps rolling downhill even after those who sent it on its way have left the scene. And before Gustavus II Adophus and Chancellor Axel Oxenstierna could persuade the peoples of Sweden and Finland to join the fighting in the heart of the continent for the first time, a veritable boulder had to be rolled down a mountainside. Purposeful and skillfully directed propaganda was primarily disseminated from pulpits and thus incorporated into the fulminations of orthodox preachers against papism. Year after year, it was expounded in ever stronger terms how the German Protestants were being persecuted and how the oppressor, the emperor, was gradually closing in on the kingdom of Sweden.

If propaganda did not produce the desired effect, then, on occasions when one of the estates represented in the Diet faced the task of underwriting some grandiloquent declaration of foreign policy or of approving new taxes and conscriptions, the government reproached the deputies for having hearkened to enemies of the realm in reaching their decision. Hints were at the same time let out to the docile opposition that the wages of discord were death.

Yet, the successes scored in both Poland and Germany cannot be explained merely on the basis of national and religious zeal stirred up by ceaseless agitation, for such zeal does not last long in the everyday routine of army life. The fundamental factor of success was the circumstance that the backbone and, at first even the numerical majority of Gustavus Adolphus's army consisted of native conscripts, whereas his adversaries used mostly mercenaries.

"These infantrymen have not been recruited with money," Gustavus Adolphus pointed out, when he was describing his army to the Dutch. "Nor have they been assembled in ignorance of the perils of war by the persuasive powers of tavern keepers. For they have been drafted into the service by careful selection from among the rural population. They are in their prime, accustomed to doing work, to carrying burdens and to enduring cold, heat, hunger and lack of sleep, but not to the gratification of their appetites."

Since the mercenaries had entered military service only to earn a living and since the foe of today was likely to be the comrade-in-arms of tomorrow, the idea of fighting to destroy the opposing forces was utterly alien to them. Although warfare in central Europe had not yet become refined into the large-scale game of chess that it evolved into during the eighteenth century, the commanders of mercenaries generally aspired to gain only limited objectives. The Swedish-Finnish troops—notably the Finns, in fighting along their eastern frontier—had become accustomed to battles in which tournament rules did not apply, and their unrestrained fighting tactics resembled the total warfare of modern times more than did those of their adversaries. During one exchange of prisoners, a Polish officer of high rank asked the Swedes to refrain in the future from hacking to death all the enemy troops who fell into their hands. "After all, we Poles are Christians, too," he added. Later on, during the war in Germany, the Finnish cavalry earned the nickname of "Hakkapelis," from their battle cry, *"Hakkaa päälle!"* (meaning to chop down the enemy).

The bold and reckless fighting methods of the Finns were best employed in the cavalry. But Gustavus Adolphus greatly increased the mobility of the other branches of the army, too, by eliminating the deep, clumsy, square formations of the infantry, increasing fire power, and replacing the heavy artillery with light field cannon that could be drawn even by a single horse. The nobility, which previously had claimed the prerogative of fighting only on horseback, agreed to lead the infantry as officers. The king was not only a skillful organizer of the military establishment and a field commander of genius, but, after the fashion of medieval princes, he personally took part in battle, thereby inspiring his men to greater effort—and it was on the field of battle that he met his death.

The contribution of the Finns to the Thirty Years' War was more than just the ferocious fighters and officers. There also were Finns in the highest command, such as Gustaf Horn, who later became Marshal of the Realm and Count of Pori, and who, after being taken prisoner, was exchanged for no less than three of the emperor's generals; Field Marshal Ake Tott, grandson of Queen Karin, Magnus' daughter; Cavalry General Torsten Stålhandske, commander of the Hakkapelis; and, a less conspicuous though extremely important figure in the army supply service, Commissioner-General of War Erik Trana.

Among the preconditions for expansion southward the left flank had to be secured by a policy that was friendly to Russia. That was one of King Gustavus Adolphus's ideas, and he succeeded in implementing it so well that hundreds of church bells in Moscow were rung in celebration of the conquest of Breitenfeld, the greatest victory won by the Swedish-Finnish army. The Czar even gave Sweden economic support, hoping that she would turn against Poland.

The Thirty Years' War stands out as one of the crucial events of world history, but for the sake of unity, even in a chronicle of Finland, the broad outlines of the war from the point at which the Swedes and Finns entered it must be included.

When Gustavus II Adolphus landed in Germany with his troops, his allies held him in contempt, since he came from a small and little-known country in the far North, and his foes saw no reason to fear him. A year and a half later, following the victorious battle of Breitenfeld, he established his headquarters in the richest district in southern Germany, the Catholic valley of the Main. There, the political threads of Europe were joined together, and the Swedish king attained the position of leader of the German Protestants.

On November 6, 1632, a date which the Swedes of Finland still celebrate as a national holiday in memory of Gustavus II Adolphus, the great king fell in battle at Lützen. But, nevertheless, that battle ended in defeat for the imperial troops. However, now that the cohesive force of the Swedish monarch's personality was gone, the war failed to bring the Protestants any decisive success for a long time. On the contrary, at Nördlingen, in 1634, a crushing defeat was sustained. A contributing factor to that defeat was the disagreement between the commander-in-chief of the Swedish-Finnish forces, Gustaf Horn, and the commanderin-chief of the German Protestants. It was in this battle that Horn was taken prisoner. Three years later, the Swedish-Finnish army held only a small strip of Pomerania.

Meanwhile, in 1635, the truce of Altmark had lapsed. In order to extend it for twenty-six years, Sweden was obliged, because of her difficult military position, to give up the harbours of East Prussia, along with the revenue they yielded from customs duties.

The emperor's hereditary foe, Catholic France, with which Gustavus II Adolphus had made an alliance in his time and which had given his campaign economic support, took up the cause of the petty Protestant princes, and the leadership in the war slipped more and more into French hands. The hostilities, which brought devastation to Germany, as the battleground, and exhaustion to all the belligerents, dragged on for more than another decade before ending in that landmark of world history, the Peace of Westphalen, in 1648.

During the course of the great war, Sweden-Finland had had the time and the resources to wage a private war on the side with Denmark, an ancient, fraternal enemy (1643—45). The Danes' capture of the fortress of Elfsborg on two occasions had taught the Swedes to appreciate the importance of their connections with the ocean, and they had started to toy with the idea of occupying a more extensive stretch of the coast. Another objective was the destruction of Danish dominance in the Baltic Sea. When a favorable opportunity presented itself, the Swedish army attacked the Danish mainland from German soil without a declaration of war. Admiral Klaus Fleming, a Finn by birth, took charge of naval operations to destroy a major part of the Danish fleet. Old King Christian IV submitted to the terms of the Peace of Brömsebro, which gave Sweden part of her objectives: Denmark ceded to her the great Baltic islands of Gotland and Saaremaa, certain provinces along the Norwegian border, and an area which widened the Swedish territorial wedge that extended into the western seas.

Then, in the Peace of Westphalen, Sweden gained territory on the German coast and her king thus obtained a voice in the assembly of princes, known as parliament, which was a feature of the loosely composed empire. Sweden became bound by three-fold ties to European power politics during this most warlike period in the history of the continent: she had territory in Germany to defend; she was entrusted, along with France, with the right and the duty to maintain the status quo in Germany; and she had become so powerful that any foreign state in Europe was likely to court her as an ally. The large army she had to maintain—at heavy cost in peacetime—in her position as a major power was a constant temptation to engage in military adventures, for during offensive wars it could be supported at the expense of the invaded country. Participation in the

Thirty Years' War did lead to new wars, with no end in sight. Ceaseless warfare and an apparent decline in the standard of living at home were the price Sweden had to pay for becoming a great power and for her place in world history.

Finnish soldiers had fought for more than two decades on the battlefields of central Europe. They had been summoned for military service from forest clearings and rude, chimneyless log cabins with only a vent in the roof or wall to emit smoke. Some of them had never even had a glimpse of any of the drab little towns of their own country before being transported far across strange seas. And then they had exchanged their daily beverage of buttermilk for wine, and, in a single day, they were likely to see more splendour than existed in the whole of poor, remote Finland.

The surviving soldiers returned home carrying a new stimulant in their knapsacks: tobacco. Their officers brouhgt back books and tapestries. And they all returned with a new self-esteem, a proud realization that, thanks to the exploits of the widely feared Hakkapelis, the fame of the Finnish people had for the first time spread throughout Europe.

"The Era of the Count"—and of the Counts

King Gustavus II Adolphus, having died in his prime, left behind a six-year-old daughter, named Christina, and for the duration of her minority, the royal prerogatives were entrusted to a regency of five nobles. Before the king's death, Chancellor Axel Oxenstierna had drafted a Form of Government that was designed to establish the administrative organization that hdeen gradually built up by the king in conjunction with his chancellor. It also provided for the establishment of a regency to rule in the event of the monarch's absence, serious illness, or minority.

Gustavus Adolphus had approved the main features of the draft, and the principles embodied in it were applied to the formation of the regency, which was to include the chiefs of five branches of the administration (who today would be called ministers), to be headed by the chancellor of the realm. After the Diet had studied the proposal and had voiced some complaints about its aristocratic character, it was published in 1634 as a Form of Government, which actually, if not formally, may be regarded as the first Constitution of Sweden-Finland.

The aristocratic nature of the system was apparent in the provision for the monarch's replacement during the regency, not by any individual member of the royal house, but by a group of leading nobles. The numerous and, at times, divided body of regents, which lacked the mystical authority exercised by a king over the populace, was incapable of managing the estates with the sovereign majesty of a king, let alone the spellbinding power of a Gustavus Adolphus. Collaboration with the estates was facilitated, however, by the regulations that had been issued by Gustavus Adolphus in respect to the Diet, which placed the decisive authority of that organ of the government also in the hands of the upper nobility, i.e., the same social class that controlled the regency and the Council. Moreover, the Diet was not always convened in full to make decisions in the sphere of foreign policy. Sometimes, only selected nobles and clergymen were called. However, if all four estates did meet—namely, the nobles, representatives of the clergy, the burghers (merchants and master craftsmen), and the yeomanry—the Parliamentary Act of Gustavus Adolphus did not explain how decisions should be made when differences arose between the estates.

The nobles insisted that no decisions could be made against their will. In contrast to this confusing feature, there were regulations relating to the House of Nobles, which were open only to a single interpretation and which reposed the power of decision of this first chamber of the Diet in the hands of just a few men. The small number of families that formed the upper nobility were divided into two so-called classes, with the numerous lower nobility forming a third class; and if differences of opinion occurred in the House of Nobles, the voting took place on a class basis, with each class being credited with one vote in the final count.

Accordingly, Sweden-Finland was ruled during Christina's minority in a somewhat sovereign fashion by a tight knot of aristocratic families. Above the others were the Oxenstiernas, who were represented by three of the five regents. The opponents of the Oxenstiernas included Count Per Brahe, a member of the Council. In this vigorous personality, the conservatism of an aristocratic country gentleman and an uncompromisingly original character were combined with a will to govern. The Oxenstiernas conveniently took advantage of a provision in the Form of Government to establish Finland on a provisional basis as a governor-generalship, and to ship Brahe across the gulf to expend his energy in administrative chores. Brahe served as governor-general from 1637 to 1640 and, for a second term, from 1648 to 1654. He assumed that Finland was, in a sense, his own principality. Remarkably, this Swedish aristocrat became a representative of Finnish nationalism during an era when nothing like Finnish nationalism in its modern form had ever been known.

Brahe was not content to emphasize knowledge of Finnish as a requirement for holding offices in Finland; he even demanded that Swedish nobles and Prince Charles XI, himself, should study Finnish. The governor-general's nationalistic zeal was evident in his presentation of a Finnish Bible that was inscribed with a Finnish dedication in his own hand to a Swedish-speaking congregation in Finland. Brahe was the first statesman to draw attention to the fact that beoynd the eastern border of Finland there lived peoples who "spoke Finnish" (actually, languages that were closely related to Finnish), and he laid a nationalistic foundation for the expansionist policy of the realm toward the East. This policy was not really an ideological one, but a matter of practical politics: If all the areas that were populated by "Finns" in Russia were annexed to the kingdom of Sweden, then the migration of members of the Orthodox Church across the border would considerably diminish, for they naturally preferred to settle among their kinsmen rather than among alien Slavs.

On Brahe's initiative, the entire Holy Bible was translated into Finnish. And he also supported the project of Bishop Petraeus when he composed his Finnish grammar expressly to help Swedish officials who were transferred to Finland to learn Finnish. The governor-general's administrative and economic measures were many, but his most enduring gift to Finland was the university that was founded in Turku in 1640.

The University of Turku received the land rent from hundreds of estates and was granted considerable autonomy, including jurisdiction over the whole teaching staff and other employees, as well as their families, and over the student body. This autonomy was reduced in the very same century, but certain significant features of still survive. To the office of chancellor of the University, the king usually appointed some influential noble who was recommended by the professors. Brahe, himself, served as chancellor for more than thirty years.

Methods of instruction and patterns of student life were borrowed chiefly from Germany, where Finnish scholars had been accustomed to pursue their studies during the Reformation. At the close of the first academic year, the student enrollment totaled 249, many of whom had come from Sweden. But the number rose slowly. Standards of instruction and examination remained low, with some rare exceptions. In theology, the department that enjoyed the highest prestige, the staff was content to quibble in defense of the Lutheran doctrine; and the natural sciences were taught by depending on the authorities of antiquity. Nevertheless, the foundation for the pursuit of higher learning in Finland had been laid.

Leaving his post as governor-general of Finland for the second time, Count Brahe himself declared, ''I was highly satisfied with this country and the country with me.'' This frankly egoistic declaration was quite true. The period of Per Brahe's governor-generalship has been labeled in Finnish history as ''the Era of the Count,'' with apparent honor and affection for the Swedish official.

The second and third quarters of the seventeenth century might also be designated as the ''era of Counts'' in Finland, but the plural version contains mixed and predominantly negative connotations.

The nobility of Sweden-Finland took advantage of its undisputed position of power to transfer into its own possession a substantial part of the Crown lands and of the land rents that were paid by the freeholding farmers. The system of taking over the right to levy taxes due the Crown dated back to the end of the preceding century, but it grew to enormous proportions during Queen Christina's reign (1644—54).

The victorious commanders in the European war and the skillful diplomats of the young Great Power had to be rewarded with an open hand. To the right to collect the land rents were added many other feudal prerogatives. Since the property rights of the freeholders were not regarded as unqualified, the noblemen became their landlords. Per Brahe, for example, believed that the peasants were primarily subjects of their lords and only indirectly of the king. In the most extensive of the alienated areas, the baronies and earldoms, the administrative and even juridical power shifted from the Crown to private hands. In one case, a count, on the pretext of conscripting men for the army, recruited manpower from his Finnish earldom for his manors in Sweden. Just as it was considered more advantageous in maritime states to surrender to trading companies the administration of overseas colonies than to have the government maintain direct control, so in the kingdom of Sweden it was believed that administrative affairs and the levying of taxes were managed more efficiently

—especially in remote communities—when left in the hands of private persons. For this reason, the provinces of Ostrobothnia and Käkisalmi teemed with earldoms and baronies. Elsewhere in Finland, only smaller areas, consisting of a village or two, were generally alienated; but, precisely by virtue of their small size, they fell neatly into the feudal society that was characteristic of the lands lying along the southern and eastern coasts of the Baltic Sea. All told, nearly half the lands or land rents in Finland (exclusive of Käkisalmi province) were alienated.

Charles IX had started to make such endowments in Finland to Baltic Germans, who had served as officers in the Swedish army. Back in their native country, they had been accustomed to the institution of serfdom and to farming on a large scale. In Finland, they attempted to establish the same type of manorial estates and demanded that the peasants who lived on the alienated farms do work days on them. However, unless these foreign nobles had acquired the legal rights, the courts of law generally rendered impartial judgments and prevented them from carrying out their high-handed plans. The status of the farmer varied greatly on feudal estates, depending on the personal character of the landlord; but, at least in baronies and earldoms, their material lot was no worse than it was on farm which paid taxes to the Crown. As cogs in the bureaucratic machine, the Crown bailiffs had to insist on the payment of taxes regardless of crop failures and the inability of farmers to pay, whereas the counts and barons could be flexible—less for humane reasons, of course, than on grounds of expediency. But as the tax burden grew heavier on both the farms taxed by the Crown and those taxed by the nobles, and as curbs were imposed on local self-government everywhere, the bitterness of the rural population turned with double potency against the landlords, who lacked the glitter of the royal crown over their heads.

An aristocratic society is like the two sides of a medal, one bearing an enslaved rural population and the other a high material and intellectual culture developed by the nobility. In the seventeenth-century society of Finland, the brighter side of the medal had little to show, for the leading native families of the nobility had moved to Sweden and most alienated Crown lands or rents had also gone to old Swedish families. With their ships, the landlords carried off their surplus tax revenue from Finland—and also from Estonia and Livonia—to the vicinity of Stockholm, where they built themselves baroque-style castles by the score. In Finland, there are only a few counterparts of these architectural monuments: the majority of the dwellings of the local nobility—both of native and Baltic origin—were built of wood and have since vanished.

The Height of Swedish Power

Queen Christina, one of the most remarkable women in world history, was more interested in brilliant festivities, intellectual conversation and religious meditation than in politics. Even after she had come of age, the reins of government remained in the hands of the upper nobility, principally those of old Chancellor Axel Oxenstierna. The queen rejected all plans for her marriage, bringing the issue of the succession to a head. In settling the question, she displayed both enterprise and political craft. She persuaded the Diet to elect her German-born cousin, Charles Gustavus, as her successor. In 1654, Christina unexpectedly abdicated. Later, she became a Roman Catholic and settled in Rome.

Axel Oxenstierna died that same year, and one year later King Charles X Gustavus attacked Poland, setting into motion another chain reaction of wars.

The truce with Poland had still been formally in effect and, having grown steadily weaker, Poland was by no means interested in breaking it. Therefore, Sweden was guilty of a wholly unprovoked aggression. One of her objectives was the conquest of Polish-held shores, to make the Baltic a Swedish sea. Yet, oddly enough, the attack was also largely motivated by the need to engage in preventive war, because Russia, regaining her strength after a period of chaos, now aspired to expand westward. Some Russian leaders advocated expansion at the expense of Sweden, but the Czar favored recovering Russian territory that had been annexed by Poland. When war broke out between these two powers, Sweden entered the fray in order to prevent the balance of power in eastern Europe from being upset. The alternative course would have been direct action against Russia in collaboratin with Poland, but this was precluded by the antagonism of the Polish monarch, in whose veins flowed the blood of Vasa. This impelled the Swedes to strike for the Baltic coast of Poland before the Russians could get there. The king reasoned that it would be better for the Swedes to annex a section of Poland than to have some foreign power take the whole of it.

In less than half a century, the situation had been completely reversed: during the reign of Charles IX, an army had been ordered to march to Moscow to fight the Poles; now the Swedish army was sent to Warsaw to oppose the Russians.

King Charles X Gustavus was more alert to the problems of eastern Europe than Oxenstierna had been. The chancellor had underrated the power of Russia. It was Brahe, the governor-general of Finland, who sounded the most vigorous warning about the danger of Russia: in his opinion the czardom was now "more formidable than ever before." And the Finnish-born Marshal of the Realm, Count Gustaf Horn, understood the king's decision to attack Poland to mean that he intended to settle his differences with her first and then "engage in a bigger undertaking."

The settling of differences appeared to proceed rapidly: within a few months both Polish capitals, Warsaw and Krakow, had been occupied by Swedish forces. Charles X Gustavus advanced in a series of swift marches from one side of the kingdom to the other. But he soon perceived that he was able to maintain control of only that part of Poland over which he was moving at any given time. Poland was like the surface of a sea, on which the wake of a ship—in this case, the Swedish-Finnish army—lasted only a short while. When Charles X Gustavus had advanced so far over this Polish "sea" that every familiar landmark had vanished below the horizon, the Russians went into action.

In the summer of 1656, the Russians penetrated into Livonia, and marched across Ingria, which proved to be only a weak obstruction, to the Karelian Isthmus. A force of 1500 men attacked around the northern shore of Lake Ladoga, where King Gustavus II Adolphus had claimed no military force could operate. Logically enough, Russia made a truce with Poland. The Greek Catholics in the Ingrian and Karelian areas occupied by the Russians now joined the invaders and assaulted the local Lutheran civilian inhabitants.

Almost to the last man, the Finnish military forces had been recklessly transported to Poland so that only a few hundred men were left; no wonder the Russian attack sent shock waves all the way to the Bothnian coast. A force of irregulars stopped the Russian advance. The peasantry consented to extraordinary conscription measures, and a discussion concerning the employment of the reinforcements ensued between the king and the governor-general in Livonia, Count Magnus de la Gardie, on the one side, and Baron Gustaf Evert's son, Horn, who had been appointed governor-general of Finland, on the other. The king weighed the question on the basis of the total military situation and wanted to send the men to the Baltic provinces, where the threat was most conspicuous; that certain parts of Finland might be overrun by the enemy again was of little concern to him. Horn, as a Finn, wanted to keep the reinforcements in Finland. He managed to keep the best troops, and the Finns took to the offensive, carrying out a punitive raid across the border. Contemporary observers failed to see, however, that the defense of Finland succeeded only because of the small size of the Russian forces.

While measures were being taken to repulse the peril from the East, a new threat appeared in the West when Denmark declared war. Taking advantage of the absence of the Swedish army, the Danes sought to avenge their defeat of the preceding decade. However, a swift march of his army from Poland to Jutland enabled Charles X Gustavus to forestall a Danish invasion of Sweden. But, as before, the Danes lulled themselves into a false sense of security on their islands—until the severe winter of 1658 froze the straits. Then the Swedish forces were able to advance, almost without resistance, to the very gates of Copenhagen. At Roskilde, the Swedes dictated the peace terms to the Danes. All the Danish provinces on the Scandinavian peninsula were to be ceded to Sweden, so that the previous natural forest boundary would be replaced by the sea boundary, which later came to be regarded as the natural one. Sweden also took certain other Danish and Norwegian territories, and even established a Swedish corridor across Norway to the Atlantic coast.

The unexpected victory in the West also strengthened Sweden's position in the East, and, furthermore, the strange triangular drama in eastern Europe had taken such a turn that Sweden's enemies, Poland and Russia, were once more locked in combat. In the same year of 1658, the Russians agreed, through the Treaty of Vallisaari, to a three-year truce, during which time they could hold on to the Livonian districts they had captured.

Sweden had now attained her greatest geographical expansion, but her position was menaced, for, although a truce had been concluded with Russia, a state of open war prevailed with Poland, Austria, and Brandenburg, and Denmark was waiting for her hour of revenge. It had been a military gamble to cross the thin ice to the Danish islands, but the situation had left no choice except to take this chance, and it had paid off. It was a political gamble to break the peace that had been concluded with Denmark half a year before and to start an unprovoked aggression to destroy the Danish kingdom. But the Dutch, on guard to preserve the balance of power in the Baltic, joined the Danes, and their combined navies inflicted a crushing defeat on the Swedes in the Sound. Copenhagen was saved by the patriotic zeal of the Danes.

In 1660, King Charles X Gustavus succumbed to a sudden illness. His heir, Charles XI, was only four years old, so it was necessary to establish a regency. The regents took vigorous measures to restore peace. Some of the areas that had been lost by Denmark in the Treaty of Roskilde, including the Swedish corridor through Norway, were returned to her. Poland and the Central European states readily agreed to make peace, and the Vasa dynasty of Poland now definitively abandoned its theoretical claims to the Swedish throne.

The only remaining problem was peace with Russia. Negotiations for a peace treaty had been started while Charles X Gustavus was still alive, and, indeed, at the peak of his power. Although the great eastern program of Gustavus II Adolphus was not brought forward as such, even as a point of departure for bargaining, demands were made for Russian Karelia, Russian Lapland—consisting mainly of the Kola peninsula—and certain regions farther to the south, such as the Russian wedge between Ingria and Estonia. However, perceiving that Poland's value as an ally against Russia was very slight, the regency was prepared to relent and, as a last resort, even settle for the old boundaries. Actually, the recognition of those boundaries amounted to a concession on the part of the Russians, who held some small areas on the Swedish side.

Count Per Brahe worked with his usual obstinacy in favor of expansion eastward, and through his influence new instructions cancelling the concessions were sent to the Swedish peace delegates. But the delegation disregarded the revised instructions and signed a treaty at Kardis in 1661 that left the boundaries unchanged. When an opportunity arose to nullify the peace treaty because of differences in the interpretation of provisions concerning the repatriation of fugitives, the Count's renewed efforts toward that end failed. In fact, he was forced to admit before the estates that the annexation of East Karelia and the Kola peninsula would not establish security in the East unless territory in Pskov and Novgorod were also captured. That, of course, would require a "powerful attack."

The series of wars that had lasted for six years finally had ended. The main reason for Sweden's original attack on Poland had been her fear of Russian expansion. After peace had finally been restored between Russia and Poland, Sweden saw that the status quo in Eastern Europe, which she had set out to preserve, had been upset—to her disadvantage. On the other hand, she had gained populous areas on the Scandinavian peninsula at the expense of Denmark, her old western rival, over which she now had the undisputed upper hand. So, although Sweden had failed to expand in the East, she had made concrete gains in the West.

From the standpoint of Finland, the most important thing was what happened in the East; accordingly, the closing of accounts at this juncture signified a deficit. Also internally, the balance of power had become upset in favor of the mother country. The populous provinces that Sweden won from Denmark were not ruled as conquered territory but were incorporated into the old main body of the realm and an energetic Swedification program was introduced there. At the end of the century, the population of Sweden proper was considerably over a million, while that of Finland, including the province of Käkisalmi, was not quite half a million.

The shift in the center of political gravity was a logical consequence of the fact that the arrow indicating the activity of Sweden in the field of foreign policy had turned an angle of nearly 180 degrees. When Gustavus II Adolphus had ascended the throne, it had pointed eastward toward Russia; during his reign, it turned first east by southeast (Livonia), then toward the south-southeast (East Prussia) and, finally, south (Germany); and during the reign of Charles X Gustavus, it shifted to the southwest (Denmark)—and even turned temporarily due West, toward the Atlantic coast of Norway.

From Aristocratic to Autocratic Rule

The crown that Queen Christina had bestowed upon her cousin, Charles X Gustavus, was no light burden to carry: the finances of the State were in such a hopeless muddle because of the alienation of Crown lands and land rents that officeholders were given not even the hope of receiving their salaries regularly. Even many among the upper nobility, which had profited most from the institution of fiefs, felt that part of the land rents should revert to the Crown, for those same men were responsible for the functioning of the machinery of state. Nevertheless, they felt that the price of such a concession should be an acnowledgment that the right to collect the rest of the rents would remain a prerogative of the nobility forever. The problem could not be solved without serious diagreement.

The lower nobility argued that the difficulties the state economy had to cope with stemmed from the fact that the rents from vast areas of land had been endowed to only a few families. But the upper nobility complained that knighthood had been conferred with a prodigal hand and that the advantages enjoyed by this estate had consequently become a burden to society. Among the upper nobility, the overly modern opinion had gained headway in seventeenth-century Sweden-Finland that state finances ought to be sustained by cash revenue so that land rents paid in kind could still be collected by the nobility, provided that this estate then paid taxes in cash to the Crown. As the alternative to a far-reaching revocation of the endowments, it was proposed that the nobility be taxed, which further exasperated the lower nobility. "If we are not exempt from taxes, we are not nobles," declared one Finnish member of the Diet.

The nobility of Finland favored revocation for a number of reasons: Its members were conservative in their economic outlook, the Finnish nobles held only small fiefs, and in Finland it was the negative aspects of the system that were mostly in evidence. The lower estates were agitated again by the proposal of guarantees that the rest of the endowments would remain permanently in the possession of the aristocracy. Down to the yeomanry, they had begun to experience a political awakening, which was developing a social friction in internal politics. The resolution that was passed at the Diet of 1655, after numerous adjustments, revoking certain of the alienations, left the question of guarantees open, along with numerous other outstanding issues. Still, in any event, the reversion of endowed Crown lands and rents had started. To execute this so-called "reduction," a special central bureau was established under the direction of Baron Herman Fleming, a Finn.

Following the death of Charles X Gustavus, a regency was again needed. In accordance with the Form of Government, the king in his testament had appointed as regents the heads of the five administrative branches, and named Herman Fleming as the head of the exchequer. He also named his widow as a member of the regency. But the nobility, which this time was unanimous, pressured the lower estates in the Diet to annul the king's will, for its members could not stomach the thought that Fleming, favorably disposed as he was toward the "reduction," was to be entrusted with the administration of financial affairs. One of the most violent opponents of the testament was Brahe, and one of its stoutest defenders was Terserus, Bishop of Turku. The changes made in the testament also brought about an amendment of the Form of Government (1660). The Council of the Realm as a whole was to render a decision in matters where the regents had failed to reach unanimity.

The shift of royal power from the five-man regency to a council of about forty members of the upper nobility emphasized, in more bold relief than ever before, the aristocratic features of the social order. At the same time, however, the position of the Diet grew stronger: It elected a head of the exchequer to replace Fleming, it began to fill other vacancies in the regency as they occured, and, for the first time, the Constitution included a stipulation — as part of the amendment to the Form of Government — that the Diet was to be convened regularly, or at least once every three years.

The "reduction" was almost totally suspended. New fiefs were distributed, and the regents helped themselves. Chancellor Magnus Gabriel de la Gardie, the son of Jakob de la Gardie, was not a leader of the caliber of Axel Oxenstierna, and the diverse currents of opinion represented in the government caused vacillations in foreign policy. De la Gardie himself pursued a pro-French policy and concluded a treaty of alliance for Sweden with Louis XIV just before the latter, in 1672, attacked the Netherlands. A broad anti-French front was formed by powers anxious to maintain equilibrium in Europe, but the French envoy in Stockholm succeeded so craftily in pulling Sweden into open warfare on the side of his monarch that he himself wrote back home that the Swedes were flabbergasted over the course they were steering. Sweden became involved in hostilities with Prussia and Denmark, and the peasantry in the provinces that had been ceded by Denmark in the Peace of Roskilde revolted. The Swedes suffered numerous defeats, but they also scored a number of victories. Still, it was only the political support of France that saved them from sustaining heavy losses in the ensuing peace treaties (1679).

The war did not directly affect Finland, but Finnish units participated in the defense of the mother country. In the biggest battle of all, at Lund, a full third of the Swedish army consisted of Finnish troops. It was during that war, in 1676, that the Finnish estates met locally for the last time to agree to extra conscriptions. Once more, as during the reign of Charles X Gustavus, the Finns strove to keep the reinforcements on home soil as security against the potential danger of a Russian attack. This time, they did not succeed, but, fortunately, peace prevailed along the eastern border. For a new Czar had ascended to the throne and Russia was in a condition of internal weakness.

Even before the outbreak of war, in 1672, Prince Charles had been declared of age. In spite of his tender years, Charles XI took charge in both military and political arenas. His most influential adviser, Johan Gyllenstierna, condemned the foreign policy that on four occasions in three decades had led to hostilities with Denmark. If the Scandinavian countries would collaborate, he argued, the issue of the Baltic Sea could be "confined to the crowned heads of the North, and the two of them could keep their neighbours in check: the king of Denmark the Germans, and the king of Sweden the Muscovites, whereupon it would be easy to acquire one thing and another from them."

The hostility between Denmark and Sweden was not in accord with the interests of at least the eastern half of the realm, Finland. This pro-Nordic policy brought a Danish princess to Sweden as queen, but Gyllenstierna soon died, and King Charles XI began to seek collaboration with the duchy of Holstein-Gottorp, situated on the southern border of Denmark, by means of which he would be in the position, in a way, of encircling Denmark. On the other hand, he did not continue the traditional orientation toward France, for it bore the stamp of the regency, which was being more and more called to account for having plunged the country into an ill-fated war. Other demands were put forward, too. Of course, the "reduction" decree of 1655 had been issued after Charles XI's investment with full powers: but the war had proved that an army corresponding to the country's status as a Great Power could not be maintained unless incomparably more tax revenue reverted to the Crown.

Clouds had gathered in the aristocratic sky when the Diet of 1680, one of the most notable in the annals of Sweden-Finland, convened. But royal lightning was not seen to flash nor was thunder heard at the Diet. Yet, both the social order and the system of government underwent an upheaval within the space of a few weeks. The Council of the Realm was shoved aside. It had only its own irresolution and lack of enterprise to blame. While the Council sank into insignificance, the Diet laid down the basis of autocratic rule by the king. No sign of any attempt at a violent usurpation of power is evident, and in view of the undeveloped and unregulated forms marking the activity of the Diet, there apparently was no lawless procedure. The king did not step out onto the stage himself or issue orders to the estates, but he did expect members of the Diet to turn to him for support against other members and to give assurances that the power of decision rested with His Royal Majesty. Nor did he publicly make any proposals for the settlement of burning issues of the day. Nevertheless, the proposals that were brought up before the Diet directly reflected the king's wishes.

Among the yeomen's estate, which in this Diet demonstrated extraordinary enterprise and capacity for action, the post of chairman was for some time held by a Finnish yeoman named Henrik Henrik's son, Vaanila. He seems to have been one of the agents that the king had cultivated in the various estates, judging from the fact that, at the next Diet, complaints were made that he had blurted everything that the yeomen's delegates discussed among themselves to the king.

The Diet set up the commission that the king wanted to investigate and judge the members of the regency, who, together with the members of the Council in office during the period of the regency, were sentenced to pay huge reparations to the Crown. When the aristocracy was again confronted with the alternatives, reversion of the Crown lands and rents or submission to taxes, the third class, backed by the king, forced the first and second class at a chaotic session to submit to a resolution restoring to the Crown all the earldoms and baronies and other large fiefs. In regard to the authority of the king, the Diet proclaimed that in his decisions he was not obliged to follow the advice of the Council and that he was bound to neither the Form of Government of 1634 nor the amendment to that document. Administrative power, including the management of foreign policy, had thus been wholly placed in the hands of the monarch.

At the next Diet, convened in 1682, the very forces that two years before had supported the king fell prey to the encroaching autocracy, namely, the lower nobility and the entire parliamentary system. The Crown needed ever more revenue, and the unprivileged estates clamored for an extension of "reduction" measures; and when the king relentlessly tightened the pressure screw on the aristocracy, it at last agreed to leave the execution of reversion measures entirely in the hands of the monarch. King Charles XI thus gained the right to restore to the Crown all the alienated Crown lands and rents, if he should so decide. And when he voiced his displeasure over a speech that had been given in the House of Nobles, wherein it had been remarked in passing that the legislative power belonged to the Diet, the estates were like wax in the king's hands. They signed a document which decreed that the sovereign could enact laws without the consent of the Diet. All they asked for, in their humbled state, was to be allowed to express an opinion regarding legislative proposals. Later on, they even granted the king the power to levy new taxes — only in times of war, of course, but, in the 1600's, war was the normal state of affairs. Thus Sweden-Finland became an absolute monarchy.

A seventeenth-century European autocracy actually was not exactly like a twentieth-century totalitarian system. In the first place, political theory held that the power of the monarch must be limited in numerous ways. For instance, he was "responsible to God" for his realm, which was given to him by God as a hereditary fief, and this responsibility was more than a rhetorical phrase to the rulers of that era. And the king himself was obliged, in particular cases, to obey the law, although, of course, he was empowered to amend it. Furthermore, he had no right to violate the person or property of any of his subjects. By virtue of these restrictions, Western monarchy, even in its absolute form, was viewed as diametrically opposed to Eastern despotism.

Charles XI exercised his authority with care, as if intuitively aware that the autocratic ideology of Sweden-Finland was an alien loan rather than a native development. He summoned the Diet to meet several times for negotiations, and in all essential respects he adhered to the administrative organization created during the reign of Gustavus II Adolphus and crystallized in the Form of Government of 1634.

In Sweden-Finland, as in the other Lutheran countries, the power of the autocratic ruler was enhanced by the circumstance that the Church also owed him obedience. The Ecclesiastical Act of 1686, issued by Charles XI, firmly established the status of the Lutheran Church in Sweden-Finland as a State Church in two ways: one, no inhabitant of the realm was allowed to acknowledge any other faith; and, two, the king was regarded as the "supreme bishop," who not only appointed the bishops and the majority of the lesser ecclesiastics but also supervised the administration of the Church. The king weakened a clause which had been included in the draft of the law relating to parish meetings, at which the members of the congregation decided on the affairs of the parish under the chairmanship of their minister. These were almost the only organs that, after the centralization and administrative authority, had been left to function as a survival of the previously flourishing system of local self-government, which had been chiefly in the hands of the yeomanry. But the king did not wish to grant legal validity to the decisions of even these agencies, because the source of all power had to be on high. In practice, however, the parish meetings continued to function during the autocratic era.

The Church, orthodox in its outlook and dominated by the authority of the sovereign, considered one of its prime duties to be the training of the masses to lead a Godly life and to be obedient to the laws of the land. According to the ecclesiastical law, the clergymen were required to make the rounds of their parishes to test the Christianity of their parishioners; nuptial banns were not allowed to be published unless the bridal couple had been confirmed; and nobody could be confirmed who had not passed a catechism test. In order that the examinees might "see with their own eyes what God commands and demands in His sacred word," and not merely parrot what had been driven into their heads by dictation, the Church began to carry out its great program of reform: to make the whole nation literate. Under the influence of the two energetic Bishops Johannes Gezelius, father and son, the diocese of Turku became a forerunner in spreading literacy among all the dioceses of the Swedish realm. But the diocese of Viipuri lagged far behind.

Having been given a free hand, King Charles XI revoked the greatest part of the Crown lands and rents. The work of restitution was led for the longest period of time by Baron Fabian Wrede, a Finn. This "reduction" did not necessarily bring about any improvement in the status of the farmers, but sometimes actually increased their poverty. Still, in the long run, it stopped the process that had gradually been transforming the freeholders who lived in enfeoffed areas into tenants of aristocratic landlords. Yet, it was not the condition of the farmers that concerned the king. He was not bent on salvaging their independent status. He was merely acting to bolster the exchequer.

Closely tied to the reversion program was King Charles XI's largescale reorganization of the military establishment. He created a system that survived in Sweden and Finland for two centuries—almost unchanged, even in minor details—although economically it was more backward than the systems that had preceded it.

During the early part of the seventeenth century, plans to organize public finance on a monetary basis had constantly run into difficulties caused by the predominating system of payments in kind. Accordingly, a solution had to be found for dealing with the state's biggest item of expenditure, which was to maintain the soldiers during times of peace. The plan called for all the farms in the realm to be grouped into units, each one of which would be directly charged with the maintenance of one common soldier, for whose enlistment it was responsible. Weary of conscriptions, the farmers who paid rent to the Crown perhaps might earlier have been prevailed upon to agree to the permanent maintenance of soldiers. However, the nobility demanded exemption from this imposition for the men who lived on its own estates and its enfeoffed lands, or, at least, some basic relief. And since these two categories of estates comprised half the land in Finland and over two-thirds of the land area of Sweden, it would have been possible under these conditions to maintain only a very small army. It was not until after the reversion measures had been put into effect and the nobility was so humbled that it did not dare to cling even to the special privileges accorded to its own landed property that the Diet, in 1682, could be persuaded to pass a resolution endorsing, in principle, the system of maintaining soldiers on farms on a permanent basis. The detailed arrangements were left to be worked out in the contracts drawn up in each province by the landed proprietors—the yeomen and nobles—together with the governor.

Since the negotiations failed to produce results in Ostrobothnia, the implementation of the new system there was deferred until the following period. Although he was an absolute monarch, King Charles XI wanted to honor the traditions of local self-government and to advance on a basis of negotiation rather than coercion. The number of infantry regiments recruited from Finland was now reduced from nine to seven.

The smaller farms were grouped by twos, threes, or fours as units of the military tenure establishment, each unit being obliged to maintain one foot soldier, or, in the case of certain coastal districts, one naval seaman. Larger farms each maintained a cavalryman and his horse, and, in return, enjoyed exemption from rents. Non-coms and officers were settled on Crown estates in the same districts where the men of their detachments lived. The yield of these estates provided part of their salary, while part was paid them in kind: this was done by awarding them, as a prerogative of their office, the land rent of certain farms. Thus was created the relation of taxpayer and taxcollector between farmer and officer — sometimes also between farmer and civil functionary. It was feudalism in a new guise.

The system devised by Charles XI has been severely criticized from the military standpoint; it has been asserted that he founded a military establishment that went bankrupt as soon as it was needed. This criticism is, to say the least, exaggerated. Mobilization was, it cannot be denied, extraordinarily slow, for the army was scattered evenly throughout the entire realm, and the reserves were untrained. However, mercenary detachments were still maintained as security forces along the borders and in other garrisons, as well. Furthermore, critics of the system should bear in mind that the conscripts called to colors under the earlier system also had lacked the benefits of training.

When the farmers accepted the new burden of the permanent maintenance of soldiers on their farms, they received a solemn pledge granting them perpetual exemption from the dreaded conscriptions. Although formal conscriptions were no longer carried out thereafter in the Finnish part of the realm, the promised exemption proved to be rather illusory. During wartime, it was difficult for a unit in the military tenure establishment to enlist a stranger to replace a fallen soldier. When nothing else availed, some man in the group of farms would be obliged to go off to war himself. Besides, the Crown was not content with replacements, which Charles XI probably reckoned would suffice: As soon as the next war broke out, it was demanded that the soldiery maintained by the landholding population be doubled in strength.

Finland and Absolutism

Chares XI traveled widely and, although, because of his blunt manner, he was incapable of charming his subjects like Gustavus II Adolphus, he nevertheless became a popular ruler in Sweden. He never visited Finland, which probably meant no more to him than a cluster of provinces among other provinces. The decline of Finland's special status had imperceptibly progressed during the early part of the century as a by-product of the centralization of authority. With the establishment of autocratic rule, the merging of Finland with the mother country became an ideological objective. *Una religio, una lingua, una lex, iidem mores* (one religion, one language, one law, identical customs) was the political ideal of the age, and even though a common language could not be achieved immediately in the Swedish realm, work nevertheless was begun toward that end. The inhabitants of the former Danish provinces, which had revolted as late as the war of the 1670's, were taught to speak Swedish in an incredibly short time. As for Finland, it was not necessary to undertake any systematic integration measures as long as there could be no doubt about the loyalty of the Finns.

But even Finnish soldiers began to be taught military commands in Swedish, and non-commissioned officers who were unable to speak Swedish were discharged. When the Finns complained about the practical difficulties caused by the appointment of only Swedish-speaking persons to civil offices in Finland, the government rejected such protests by asserting that nobody was entitled to hold office by virtue of linguistic ability alone. The new ecclesiastical law, however, required that the ministers in charge of Finnish-speaking congregations have a command of the Finnish language, and research has revealed that functionaries sent over from Sweden who knew only Swedish remained a rarity in the civil offices in Finland. There perhaps were more of them among the officers who were scattered around the country as a consequence of the new military system, and all Finnish-speaking congregations were ordered to hold church services in Swedish every third Sunday—in addition to the Finnish services—for the benefit of those officers. The aim of this measure was not merely to serve the few Swedish members of the congregation, but it also was calculated to instil a gradual knowledge of Swedish in the native population.

Thus, once in a while during that period of absolutism, the idea of Swedifying the Finns arose on the theory that a universal language would unify the kingdom, just as practically the entire population of the realm was then united by the same faith. A Swedish-born professor at the University of Turku, named

Israel Nesselius, agitated for virtually a total abandonment of the Finnish language. He advocated that it be preserved only in a couple of backwoods districts as a kind of relic of ancient times. The means he proposed to achieve that aim were quite radical: Finnish speech should not be recognized by courts of law, church sermons should gradually be changed to Swedish, and the learning of Swedish should be accelerated by exchanging hired hands and soldiers between Finland and Sweden. He further propounded that, since the political ideal also included uniform customs, the native Finnish steambath, or *sauna*, should be banned.

Nesselius was not hostile to Finland, as is shown by his numerous proposals for the improvement of the Finnish economy. But he had fallen under the spell of the ideology of national integration, which became still more intensified in his mind when, misinterpreting certain developments of the next war period, he branded the Finns as politically untrustworthy.

"In the past, Finland used to beat the Russians back," he wrote in 1710, "but she is no longer the same country now ... If these people, whom the sea separates from the mother country and who speak a different tongue (would that God had made them all use Swedish long ago), and observe almost different customs, were one day to get some crazy idea in their heads (may God, however, forbid), I cannot see how they could be trusted, especially some of them."

It was probably Nesselius to whom Bishop Gezelius the younger retorted in a celebrated debate: "All tongues doth God acknowledge." That debate was recorded for posterity by a witness, young Daniel Juslenius, who later became a professor and a bishop. Probably there were others who disparaged the Finns, for Juslenius directed against this trend a book boldly titled *Vindiciae Fennorum* ("In Vindication of the Finns"). But the learned professor's chief contribution to the cultural history of Finland was his publication, in 1700, of the historical tome, *Aboa vetus et nova* ("Turku, Old and New").

In Sweden, there arose a desire to claim a historical precedent for the position that the country had achieved as a major power by depicting her as one of the world's oldest and mightiest kingdoms. The loose critical standards of the seventeenth century for the evaluation of historical sources presented no obstacle to such legendary treatment of history. And the prestige of Sweden was bound to be enhanced if Finland, which, in addition to Svealand and Götaland, was looked upon as the third integral part of the realm, also could be furnished with an ancient and illustrious past.

In Finland, learned individuals volunteered to fabricate, for the greater glory of their fatherland, catalogues of kings dating back before the Christian era. Just as that naively nationalistic type of historical writing culminated in Sweden with the publication of Rudbeck's *Atlantica,* it reached its peak in Finland with Juslenius's *Aboa vetus et nova.* In the latter work, Finnish is ranked among the basic languages of the world that originated during the building of the Tower of Babel, and Turku is claimed to have been founded by the descendants of Japhet, third son of Noah, soon after the flood. Everything Finnish is described as better and worthier than its foreign counterpart. The rise of Juslenius and other Fennophiles shows that the spirit of nationalism had begun to grow in the academic circles of Finland. This trend was partly animated by Sweden's great-power status and partly was a reaction to the pressures toward integration forced by an autocratic regime. This nationalistic sentiment was wholly non-political, and there was hardly any connection between it and the separatist political movement which appeared in Finland nearly a century later.

The loyalty of the Finns to the Swedish realm and, particularly, to the king was not shaken even by the ineffectiveness of the aid given to Finland by the mother country during the unique catastrophe that befell her at the close of the century. In 1696, an early frost in Finland ruined most of the crops, and seed for the new sowing was taken from the small rye crop that had ripened previously, with a self-restraint which evidenced a confidence in the swift arrival of government assistance. In the laconic official reports we can read descriptions like this: "Except for a bushel of rye, no harvest was reaped in the village. It was sown in common, but it did not germinate." When real bread gave out and the cattle had been butchered, people were forced to resort to emergency fare, usually bread made of pine bark—and even this was hard to obtain, for removing the bark from trees was difficult, owing to the severe cold in winter. As a last resort, people ate chaff, the roots of the bog herb, water arum, or the carcasses of farm animals. Before the next harvest could be reaped, about one-third of the Finnish population starved to death or died from diseases spread by wandering hordes of beggars. Probably in no other country and at no other time in Europe has death ever taken so heavy a toll proportionately; not even the ravages of the Black Death seem to have been of the same magnitude.

During the entire seventeenth century, a continental climatic phase in the meteorological history of Europe brought severe winters in the North, followed by the late arrival of the spring season. The growth of vegetation, having fallen behind schedule in the spring, was bound to collide with the advancing front of autumn frost, dooming the grain crops before they had time to ripen. And since agriculture in Finland was primitive, the resistance of the growing crops was weaker than if the soil had been more deeply plowed and properly fertilized. A perfect rationing of grain among self-sufficient farm households is impossible in practice. Also, there were few ships, and for half a year, after the sea had frozen over, no grain could be shipped to Finnish ports. Nevertheless, it must be stated that more could have been done than the bureaucratic government of the autocratic king did to help the starving country.

A bad harvest had been reaped in central and northern Sweden, but the bread shortage in those regions had not reached a catastrophic scale, and grain was shipped abroad from southern Sweden. The major European grain harbours along the southern coast of the Baltic were not far. But the guiding principle of the government was to save the Crown from forfeiting a single penny or distributing gratuitously a single bushel of grain to stricken Finland.

The small grain supply on hand and the shipments that were brought in after spring had broken the ice in 1697 were sold at prices inflated by the crop failure, or were loaned against security. Human distress did not move the government, so the only basis on which the peasants could appeal for relief was that death was robbing the king of his subjects on a mass scale. Having become aware of the appalling extent of the calamity, the Crown finally was moved to compromise a little. But during the following summer, bailiffs were sent to every farm to collect debts for His Majesty.

Without the havoc wrought by the great famine, Finland would have been incomparably stronger, both in manpower and material, and better able to endure the hardships awaiting her and to resist the peril that was soon to threaten her.

The Collapse of a Great Power

In the spring of 1697, when beggars, emaciated like living skeletons or swollen from poor nourishment, were staggering down the muddy roads of Finland, which were lined with the corpses of those who had succumbed to starvation or disease, King Charles XI had already died. His heir, Charles XII, was fifteen, and the old king's will called for the establishment of a regency until the prince became of age.In line with tradition, the regency was to consist of the five heads of the different branches of the government and the queen mother. However, absolute monarchy and the fate of the previous regents had made high officials wary of assuming responsibility. Hence, the members of the appointed regency wanted to be released from their duties as soon as possible. The Diet was convened, and it proclaimed the prince to be invested with full sovereignty.

At the coronation, Charles XII placed the crown on his own head and took no oath whatsoever. For a headstrong character, it hardly was wholesome training to become accustomed at such an early age to act as God's deputy on earth. The autocratic regime of Sweden-Finland underwent a transformation. During the whole of Charles XII's reign, the Diet was convened only once. Even on that occasion, the king himself was far from home, and the initiative was taken by the Council. This body, which during the period of absolutism was referred to as the Royal Council, also remained on the sidelines at first. When Charles XII set forth on his warlike expeditions, he did not follow the example of Gustavus II Adolphus, who left the administration of internal affairs to the Council, but endeavored to manage them himself from his office in the field; or else he concentrated vast powers in the hands of certain favorites.

This signified a partial reversion to the primitive, personal method of administration which had been reformed in Sweden by the skillful organization carried out by Gustavus II Adolphus and Axel Oxenstierna less than a hundred years before. But, unlike the situation in the 1500's, the administrative structure was now centralized and the king's commands were distributed automatically to all parts of the realm where they were passed on to all its institutions. Discipline was preserved and the cult of the king was maintained, but nobody bore responsibility. And when the realm was confronted by great difficulties, it was weaker than during the reign of Gustavus II Adolphus, when, at least, the upper strata of society acknowledged the prevailing policies of the State to be their own.

These trying times began when the neighbouring countries, at whose expense Sweden had expanded, joined forces, after prolonged negotiations, in a league against the great Baltic power. Russia, ruled by its reformer, Peter I, aspired to gain access to the Baltic coast. In population, it was in those days probably six times as large as the kingdom of Sweden, but it was more difficult for the Russians to concentrate their forces and they did not dare to launch an attack alone. The most ardent champion of the alliance was Augustus II, elector of Saxony, who ascended the Polish throne in 1697 and whose court Czar Peter visited on his return trip from his celebrated tour of Western Europe to study its culture. Augustus's share of the spoils was to be Livonia, whose nobility, discontented because of the reversion of Crown lands and land rents, was plotting against Sweden.

Meanwhile, Sweden disturbed Denmark by marrying the king's sister to Duke Frederick of Holstein-Gottorp and maintaining Swedish military forces behind the Danes' backs in Holstein. Denmark also had a change of sovereign, in 1699. Her new youthful king decided to ally his country with Poland and Russia. Western Europe awaited the death of the sick, childless king of Spain, which, it was calculated (quite correctly, as subsequent events proved), would lead to a general war for the mastery of Spain and her colonies. Accordingly, the rest of Europe could not intervene in the conflict in the North for the honorable purpose of safeguarding the balance of power. Hence, its outcome was to be determined by the superior odds pitted against Sweden by the Russian-Polish-Danish coalition. Ever since the Thirty Years' War, all the general wars fought in Europe have, in one way or another, affected the fortunes of remote Finland.

The hostilities known in history as the Great Northern War started in February, 1700, with the invasion of Livonia by the forces of Augustus II. But when part of the Finnish army advanced in rapid marches on Riga, the Saxons took to headlong flight. The Swedish king landed at Zealand, and with a lightning attack he forced the Danes to cease their harassment of the duchy of Holstein-Gottorp. Denmark agreed to conclude a peace treaty and promised not to support the foes of Sweden; but international pacts are honored only so long as their violation is not expected to yield any advantages.

Scarcely had the peace treaty with Denmark been signed when, in September, the Russians stormed across the border at the point where only a narrow corridor joined Ingria and Estonia, and laid siege to Narva. The poor condition of the fortress at Narva had already been pointed out by the governor-general of Livonia, Erik Dahlberg, Sweden's foremost expert on building fortifications; but the new naval base, Karlskrona, which had been built in southern Sweden during the reign of Charles XI, had exhausted all the funds available for fortification works. Charles XII sailed with the forces released from action against the Danes to the western coast of Estonia. He wanted to attack the army of Augustus, which, at that time, represented no threat whatsoever. However, his generals managed to convince him that the situation on the Russian border was more critical. After he had decided to march to Narva, he obstinately stuck to this decision, despite the grim realities that demanded a change of plan.

The Russians outnumbered the Swedes at a ratio of four to one, not counting the minor Swedish detachments besieged at Narva. The troops under Charles XII had provisions for only four days, and the march to the gates of Narva took seven days. The road ran through a region that had been laid waste by the Russians, and the men had to sleep in sleety rain in open fields. Unless a miracle happened at Narva, the exhausted army could expect only total annihilation.

The plan was a wild gamble—but that was hardly surprising since it came from the stubborn mind of an eighteen-year-old boy.

Czar Peter could not believe that such a mad scheme could actually be seriously considered. He therefore accepted exaggerated reports of his adversary's strength as true. And since he felt that defeat would be a heavy blow to his prestige, he left the camp and, through a document drawn up in confused terms, appointed Duke de Croy, an adviser dispatched by Augustus, to lead the battle.

The army of Charles XII, nearly half of which consisted of Finnish troops, arrived on November 20th in front of the strongly fortified postions of the Russians. The king gave the order to attack without delay straight at the center of the enemy lines. Under the cover of a driving snowstorm, the Swedes and Finns climbed up the ramparts and unleashed on the enemy their pent-up fury, aroused by the hunger and cold which they had suffered during their long march. The Russian lines cracked, the troops were thrown into chaos, and the rank-and-file soldiers began to kill their alien officers, whom the Czar had hired to teach his men how to fight. Duke de Croy himself was forced to seek refuge on the Swedish side. The Russian cavalry retreated in wild disorder across the swiftly flowing waters of the Narva River, where many men and horses drowned in the torrent. The infantry attempted to flee over the pontoon bridge farther downstream; but the bridge fell to pieces from the overloading and the pressure of the carcasses of cavalry horses swept down by the raging current.

The victory won by the Swedish-Finnish army was entirely conclusive, and the battle of Narva has gone down in the military annals of the North as one of the most glorious battles in history. The booty included 145 cannons, and the Russian losses in men reached ten thousand, or about the same number as the attackers' total strength. But no one besides the tight-lipped king, except for a few of his officers, realized how colossal a risk had been taken.

After the massacre at Narva, Czar Peter made a prediction: "The Swedes are destined to inflict many a defeat on us yet, but they will gradually teach us how to win."

Charles XII, whose heroic fame had spread all over Europe, began to hold his most powerful adversaries, the Russians, in greater contempt than ever, and the following spring (1701), he shifted the scene of conflict to Poland. The Polish nobility insisted that it would not support their sovereign in his private war unless Charles XII invaded the country. And the Swedish king, filled with hatred for Augustus and deaf to the warnings of his advisers, accepted the Poles' challenge. He conquered Poland, dethroned Augustus, and installed Stanislaus Leszczynski, who had the backing of a Polish party, as a puppet ruler. As a byproduct, he gained freedom of worship for the Protestant subjects of the Habsburgs in Silesia. Reaching Augustus's hereditary realm, Saxony, he exacted of Augustus, in the Peace of Altranstädt (1706), the same pledge that had been previously extracted from the Danish sovereign: He must stay out of the war. But on weak and loosely knit Poland, Charles XII failed to get any better a hold than Charles X Gustavus had before him; nor did Poland have the value as an ally against his last unvanquished enemy, Russia, that apparently was imagined by the Swedish monarch. For a stretch of nearly a hundred years, there had been no other experience of the Russians besides the war of 1656—58, when the weak militia in Finland had repulsed the invaders—and Charles XII probably viewed the situation he was confronted with as analogous with the earlier one.

Russia had by no means been reduced to passivity by the battle of Narva. During the six-year period, the main Swedish-Finnish army marched back and forth across Poland, with only small forces left to defend the long eastern border of the Swedish realm. Hence, the initiative was in the hands of the Russians, who, with the exception of a few unsuccessful sallies, advanced slowly but steadily. No modern bastions had been built in either Finland or the province of Ingria, and what fortifications did exist were in a neglected condition. Year by year, one town after another, one fortress after another, fell into the possession of the Russians.

In 1703, the Czar captured the minor fortress of Nevanlinna at the mouth of the Neva River. And on this boggy site he began to build a harbour and naval base, which he named St. Petersburg. The following year, the ancient fortress of Narva, which had witnessed the glorious victory of Swedish arms, surrendered to the Russians, and in 1706, the Czar reached the gates of Viipuri at the head of an army of 20,000 men. The city was under the protection of the Swedish fleet, however, and because of a lack of provisions and artillery, the Czar was unable to undertake a serious siege.

The Russian occupation of Swedish territory was followed by plundering, destruction, and the deportation of large numbers of people as slaves to Russia. This brutal advance of the enemy terrified the people of both the Baltic countries and Finland. On the other hand, no political upheaval was feared.

"So these forsaken provinces have been left to the enemy for looting, if not for acquisition," wrote H. R. Horn, officer in command at Narva, when the Baltic garrisons were being sucked dry for the sake of the king's adventures in Poland. Czar Peter would have been ready for peace after the Treaty of Altranstädt was councluded, if he could only have been allowed to keep Ingria. Charles XII maintained that he would discuss peace terms only after reaching Moscow—and he prepared to set forth on the road that Gustavus II Adolphus had avoided—the same road that Napoleon and Hitler later followed.

After the Treaty of Altranstädt, it would still, perhaps, have been possible to drive the Czar out of the Baltic countries and Ingria. A proposal to this effect was, in fact, made by the king's influential councillor, Count C. Piper. Charles XII refused to consider it, however. Instead, he ordered the march on Moscow to dictate the terms of peace to the Czar. He failed to understand that peace terms could not be dictated to the Russians even if he succeeded in reaching Moscow.

The expedition into Russia, which started in the spring of 1708, proved to be a series of miscalculations and blunders. The Russians practiced scorched-earth tactics, which forced the Swedes to swing down ever father south, and their communications to the rear fell apart. The slight assistance that Poland was able to send was prevented by the Russians from getting through. The expected revolt of Ivan Mazepa, hetman of the Dnieperian Cossacks, which was included in Charles XII's plan of war, did not occur. The army, under the command of General A. L. Lewenhaupt, which was supposed to deliver to the main forces a large baggage train (the loss of which had further weakened the defence of the Baltic countries), was defeated by the Russians at Lesnaya. Part of it managed, however, to join the king's forces, but those men gave little cause for cheer after the loss of essential supplies. The winter of 1708—09 was extraordinarily harsh, and disease combined with frost to wreak havoc in the Swedish camp. When spring arrived, the strength of the army had shrunk from its original 40,000 to nearly half that number.

The decisive battle was fought at Poltava on the 28th of June, 1709. The Swedish troops were dispirited by the knowledge that their sovereign, who had seemed to possess a supernatural ability to lead men into battle, had been wounded and could not direct operations personally. After suffering heavy losses, the Swedish army was forced to retreat toward the Dnieper River. At the junction of the Dnieper and Vorskla Rivers, the main forces, led by Lewenhaupt, surrendered to the numerically weaker and poorly armed Russians. The king had by that time crossed the Dnieper with more than a thousand men. He fled to Turkey.

Thus, the main army of the Swedish realm was destroyed and the border against Russia, difficult as it was to defend, was only weakly manned. "Now are the foundations of St. Petersburg unshakable," declared the Czar. And, absolutely confident of his final triumph, he proclaimed this city, which nominally still belonged to the kingdom of Sweden, to be the capital of his vast empire. In addition to Ingria, he decided to demand of Sweden the cession of Estonia, Livonia, and southeastern Finland, in order to acquire bases for his navy and to push the border farther from St. Petersburg.

During the year 1710, the Livonian capital, Riga, the Estonian capital, Tallinn, and Finland's key defensive stronghold against the East, Viipuri, surrendered, each after a severe siege. Denmark and Augustus II, the elector of Saxony, rose, up in arms once more against Sweden; the latter easily drove the puppet ruler, Leszczynski, out of Poland, and the communication line that Charles XII had still been able to maintain with his own army from Turkey was thereby completely broken. The Danes' attempt to reconquer the provinces that they had lost half a century before was foiled, but the foreign trade of Sweden-Finland was hampered because of the hostilities with Denmark. Furthermore, Charles XII angered The Netherlands and England by declaring a commercial blockade of the Baltic ports. The number of his open enemies grew by two when Prussia and Hanover joined in the division of spoils. The influence of the Council of the Realm was bound to grow under the circumstances. Its Finnish-born president, Count Arvid Horn, was convinced that Sweden had already lost the war and therefore started to take action toward keeping the army as weak as possible in order to compel the king to make peace. Disagreement about objectives and methods sapped the vitality of Sweden during the most critical phase of her history.

Charles XII tarried year after year in Turkey while his kingdom was in extreme distress. He was by no means idle there, however, for he strove to further the interests of Sweden by luring the Turks into war with the Czar. He succeeded in instigating as many as three wars, or at least declarations of war, and they prevented the Russians from continuing their offensive operations against Finnish territory for some time. At last, however, the protracted stay of the foreign sovereign and his military force began to disturb his Turkish hosts. In 1714, having worn out his welcome, the Swedish king rode in disguise across the continent to the German part of his realm. He never returned to his own capital. And he abandoned Finland, across which Russian invaders had already swept, to shift for herself while he set forth on his last adventure, the attempt to conquer Norway.

The Great Wrath

For thirteen years, Finland fought on before she was overrun by the enemy— with the exception of her southeastern corner. With a population of between three and four hundred thousand, she had nevertheless given the Crown nearly 60,000 men, of whom only ten thousand were left the fighting ranks. The rest had perished or had been taken prisoner in Ingria, the Baltic countries, Poland, White Russia, the Ukraine, and finally, even Viipuri. Conscriptions failed to yield more manpower for simple reason that the supply of able-bodied men had been almost totally depleted. The small number of men that could still be rounded up by combing the whole population was trained to serve as irregulars for use only in an extreme emergency, but the only weapons available to equip them with were hatchets, spiked clubs, bear-hunters' spears, and scythes. There was also a shortage of horses, following the butchery of thousands of these animals during an unsuccessful campaign that was waged deep in Ingrian territory in 1708.

The responsibility for that military expedition belonged mainly to Georg Lybecker, commander-in-chief of the Finnish army, and it can hardly be denied that the operations were conducted without distinction. But if the other acts and omissions of this Swedish-born officer aroused the ire of the Finns, it was partly because the person of the absolute monarch was sacred and the bitterness of the people needed an outlet, so they vented it on his highest subordinates.

After the fall of Viipuri, the Council ventured to relieve Lybecker of his duties and to replace him with old but vigorous K. G. Nieroth. During his period in command, the Finns took the initiative in the hostilities with Russia, endeavoring even to encircle Viipuri. However, Nieroth died shortly after his appointment. Because he was still in the king's favor, Lybecker once more took command in Finland, even though the Council had already assigned the post to another man.

In the spring of 1713, the Czar ordered his troops to advance from South Karelia deeper into Finland. His intention was not to seize the country but only, by occupying it and threatening Stockholm, to gain a more favorable position for peace negotiations. Even if the Czar's true intentions had been known to the Finns, the opening of the offensive campaign would nevertheless have brought fear to their hearts. In the wars between Finland and Russia, neither side had been accustomed to show any mercy to the civilian population; but for over two hundred years the parts of Finland west of Viipuri had not been drawn into the theater of actual hostilities, except for a couple of destructive raids made by the Russians to the coastal area of Uusimaa and eastern Savo. The fate of Viipuri gave a foretaste of what could be expected: in violation of the treaty of surrender, the survivors of the garrison as well as many women and children were dragged off to Russia as captives.

Right after the loss of Viipuri, socially prominent people in Finland began to move to Sweden or failed to return home from trips to the mother country. The bishop of the eastern diocese, defending his own flight, said with naïve frankness: "When the danger grows too great and death cannot be avoided, it is only natural for a person to try to save his life while it is possible, especially in view of the fact that even the churchgoers presumably are taking to hiding." The Council prohibited leaving any congregation without a single minister, but the members of the clergy felt that they were in special danger of falling victim to the violence of the "heretical" Russians, and the king actually urged the civil functionaries to flee.

When the Russian attack began, the burghers and, in some places, even the farmers, panicked and followed the army with their loads of belongings if they did not succeed in escaping by ship to Sweden; others withdrew to log cabins that were hidden in trackless wilderness. After confidence in the government and in the army had been shaken, people went over to local Russian commanding officers to beg for mercy, and many were driven to betray the partisans of their own army. This treacherous conduct was by no means inspired by a feeling that Russian rule would be better than Sweden's, as some Swedes suspected, but simply by sheer uncontrollable fright.

With their fleet of galleys, the Russians made a landing on the coast of Helsinki. The Swedish fleet was late and Lybecker marched the Finnish army to and fro or let it stand by and watch as the enemy advanced up the main coastal highway. Apparently, Lybecker wanted to save the armed forces even at the price of losing Finland, and in this strategy he was a faithful lackey of the king.

But again the fumbling tactics of the general were too much for the Council. Lybecker was ordered to report to Stockholm for an accounting of his plan of action. The duties of commander-in-chief then passed to a subordinate of Lybecker's, K. G. Armfelt, a popular figure in Finland. The Finns charged Lybecker with having betrayed their country to the Russians. He was sentenced to death, but before the execution was carried out, he died in prison. At the Diet held that year, where the criticism aimed (from Swedish quarters, too) at the politics of Charles XII was so violent that it even took the Council by surprise, Bishop Gezelius the younger of Turku demanded that, regardless of the king's orders, an army be sent to Finland.

Having assumed command of the military forces in Finland, Armfelt strove to salvage all that was humanly possible, but the entire southern coast right up to Turku had to be abandoned. He stationed his main forces in defensive positions in southern Tavastia behind the short stream known as Kostia, which joined the waters of two lakes. The enemy had penetrated so deep into the interior that the Finns were obliged to scatter their forces along many roadsides, whereas the Russians, who had no need to fear the initiation of any action by their adversary, ventured to concentrate nearly all their forces at the stream of Kostia, where they enjoyed a fivefold numerical superiority.

For many days, however, the Finns kept repulsing the invaders' efforts to cross the river. But then, on the foggy morning of October 6th, after building five hundred rafts, the Russian troops made the crossing over the lakes. Armfelt was forced to issue orders to retreat. But, weary of retreating and caught up by the battle, his men failed to obey. Consequently, the disengagement took place too late, resulting in heavy casualties. The Finnish army withdrew across the wilderness between the provinces to Ostrobothnia, where the Russians followed only after the roads became fit for sleighing.

Commander Armfelt deemed it better to engage the enemy in decisive combat in the southern part of Ostrobothnia. From the populous valley of the Kyrö River he was able to raise a sizable force of irregulars, which would scarcely have attached itself to the army after the conquest of its native region by the invader, and it was easier to supply the troops there than in the poorer districts to the north. Counting the irregulars enlisted on the spot, the Finnish force numbered 5,500 men, as against 16,000 Russians.

Armfelt deployed his troops in the village of Napue on each side of the Kyrö River, so that the front extended from the edge of one forest to the edge of the forest on the opposite shore. And there, for three days, the men waited for the Russians to advance, in driving snow and bitter cold. On the 19th of February, 1714, the enemy approached along the river bed. But only a minor detachment kept to this route, in order to mislead Armfelt. The main body of the Russian troops made a detour through the wooded zone farther north to the open bogs, which the severe cold had frozen to a sufficient depth to carry men and horses. From there, the Russians appeared directly in front of the Finns.

The surprise tactic did not succeed; on the contrary, Armfelt maintained the initiative. For a while, it looked as if the Russian front would fall apart. The Finns captured six cannon. But the Russians had plentiful reserves, and large Cossack detachments were dispatched to encircle the Finns through the forests on both southern and northern sides. The cavalry led by Major-General De la Barre, which was stationed along the right flank of the Finnish lines, first noticed the encircling movement from its elevated position, and it managed to break through. For this, it earned the (principally groundless) criticism of contemporaries and of students of military history. The further participation of the cavalry in the battle could not have changed its course, though it might, perhaps, have secured an avenue of escape for part of the infantry. As events turned out, escape was blocked.

The surrounded infantry fought with the fury of a wounded beast, for it realized that the only alternatives were death and imprisonment. Of the 500 men who could not avoid capture, only seven survived the journey to St. Petersburg; the rest perished of their wounds, the cold, and harsh treatment. Commander Armfelt himself succeeded in escaping over to his own side only after wandering three days in the wilds. The Russian commander-in-chief, Prince Golitsyn, declared that, since Poltava, the Russians had not taken part in such hard fighting, and their losses in dead and wounded rose, despite the heavy odds in their favor, to nearly 2,000 men.

With the remnant of the Finnish army, Armfelt withdrew, after the calamitous battle of Napue, around the Gulf of Bothnia to the Swedish side. A couple of weakly manned fortresses capitulated to besiegers, and in July, 1714, the

Russians inflicted a defeat on the Swedish naval forces off the peninsula of Hanko, compelling them to withdraw from Finnish waters. The enemy now was enabled to push forward into the southwestern archipelago, too, and then all Finland was conquered.

The Russian occupation lasted about eight years. That period is called the "Great Wrath," an expression that in traditional Finnish historical writing has become a symbol of all the terrifying things that can befall a nation. However, recent research has revealed that the picture was somewhat exaggerated. It is now known that the population of the country did not decrease in those years, but it actually expanded a little, if war casualties are discounted. A considerable part of the arable land continued to be tilled, so apparently the inhabitants did not generally stay in hiding in wilderness cabins. And even courts of law continued to administer justice, albeit irregularly, and to render impartial verdicts.

Reproducing an overall picture of the period of the Great Wrath is exceedingly difficult, because conditions varied greatly in the different parts of the country and in different years. Much depended on the conduct of individuals. For instance, under the Russian commander-in-chief, Prince Golitsyn, the occupied country received fairly humane treatment, but before long Russian civil authorities took charge.

Numerous factors for which the alien rulers cannot be blamed added to the trials and hardships suffered by the Finns. For one thing, foreign trade, which under normal circumstances was wholly oriented westward, had become paralyzed. In the second place, because of the enormous casualties that were sustained in the war, labour resources were extremely limited. Since the horses had also been expropriated for military service, farmers' widows had to team up to plow the fields; as related by contemporaries, one woman would guide the plow while two others pulled it. In the third place, the flight of the public functionaries and the clergy had deprived Finland of her spiritual and civil leaders. And, finally, it is important to note that the Czar had no intention of annexing Finland (except her southeastern corner) and that Russian interests did not, therefore, necessitate the safeguarding of material values in the occupied territory. Laying waste to the entire country was not in line with the Czar's interests, either, for Finland was a potential base of operations for an offensive against Sweden.

For strategic reasons, the Russians totally devastated those areas which for a long time might be the objectives of possible Swedish military action: The portions of Karelia lying west of Viipuri, parts of southern and central Ostrobothnia, and the Aland Islands. Individual acts of violence against the civilian population were frequently committed, particularly in connection with military operations, but those occurred without the knowledge of the higher commanding officers, or, at least, without their official consent.

A cruel fate awaited those who assisted the partisans, of course. Partisan activities had been started back in the days when Ingria was occupied; there, the Finnish peasantry was exempt from conscription but wanted, nonetheless, to fight the invader. The commander of the forces stationed in Ingria, A. Cronhiort, opposed partisan action, because he feared, with ample reason, that it would provoke terrible reprisals. But Charles XII sanctioned it, and it continued throughout the whole war, rendering services to the Swedish-Finnish army and bringing suffering to the Finnish civilian population. Many partisan bands took no orders from the Swedish military headquarters but waged their own private war and lived by plundering.

To punish the Ostrobothnian peasants for their participation in the fighting as irregulars in such great numbers, the Russians abducted whole families in that region—totaling nearly 5,000 people—and deported them to Russia. Käkisalmi province had been the victim of a similar fate during an earlier stage of the occupation. After military operations had ceased, the traffic in human beings became unsystematic and evidently only half compulsory: Now carpenters were demanded to work on the construction of St. Petersburg, now "maidens and pretty servant girls" were sought to serve boyars. When several age groups had reached adulthood during the occupation, so that Finland once more had men fit for military service, a conscription was proclaimed by the Russian army, in 1720. One-third of the number called up avoided conscription by going into hiding, while the rest revolted and were killed or imprisoned.

For lack of public functionaries, the administrative machinery broke down as the Russians advanced. At first, the military handled all civil matters, but a civil administration was set up in the western parts of Finland in 1717, and in the eastern regions in 1719. Although to some extent the forms were in Russian, some knowledge of the native tongues and local conditions was required for administration of both civil affairs and justice. Some officials were appointed from among the local inhabitants, but when they showed a lack of normal competence, Baltic Germans and Swedish prisoners of war hired, also. Among the latter, G. O. Douglas was appointed governor-general of Western Finland.

Since the Swedish officers were expected to demonstrate their loyalty to their new master, the Czar, in the performance of their duties, there was a strong temptation for them to show a special disregard for the Finnish point of view. Therefore, according to contemporaries, the conscription was undertaken on the initiative of Douglas. Moreover, the provisional officeholders took up the custom prevalent under the Czars, and accepted bribes.

A few schools were opened. The stubborn will of the nation to pass on to posterity the ability to read that had been achieved by preceding generations was dramatically revealed by a famous ABC-Book that was carved into a tree trunk. This desperate measure was engendered by the lack of printed books during the Great Wrath.

The Peace of Uusikaupunki

The final seven years of the Great Northern War were poor in military events but rich in zealous activity in the sphere of foreign policy. King Charles XII—or, rather, his minister of foreign affairs and finance, Baron von Görtz, who enjoyed the boundless confidence of the king—played for high stakes; and his game was not lacking in enterprise or hampered by prejudice, although it was only slightly based on realities. As a native of Holstein, von Görtz hated

Denmark and wanted the war on both armed and diplomatic fronts to be concentrated against Sweden's western neighbour; it was he who urged Charles XII to attempt the conquest of Norway. He did not grasp, or want to grasp, the fact that the chief foe of Sweden-Finland was Russia, but he was ready to yield before pressure from that direction. In his private political scheming, he went so far as to give the king false information about the demands put forward by the Russians—just as he gave the Czar false information about the extent to which Charles XII was prepared to make concessions. His scheme was to enlist Russia's aid in a Swedish effort to seize Norway, and then to convert that country into a base of operations for the Stuarts to gain the English throne. Engineered from Norway, a rebellion and coup d'état were to be staged in England, after which the English would help Sweden recapture the territories lost to Russia.

After feelers had been out for a long time, peace talks were started in the Aland Islands between von Görtz and the Czar's delegate, Ostermann, in the spring of 1718. Attention was focused on the establishment of a new eastern boundary for the realm: the line comtemplated would have left Viipuri and the Karelian Isthmus on the Russian side but would have joined considerable territory in East Karelia to Finland.

Among the constantly changing plans, only the one calling for the conquest of Norway was actually attempted. The king himself led the army that invaded the country from the south, while, simultaneously, Commander Armfelt advanced into the Trondheim region with the remnants of the Finnish army, reinforced by Swedish troops. Armfelt's army perished on New Years's night, in 1719, in a snowstorm in the barren mountains while attempting a withdrawal after word of the king's death had arrived.

It was on the last day of November, 1718, that a bullet struck Charles XII in the temple as he stood in a trench in the shadow of the fortress of Frederickssten. There is strong evidence to indicate that the bullet was fired at close range. Moreover, a critical analysis of the official notices about the king's death will also support the theory of an assassination, behind which was Charles' brother-in-law, Frederick, landgrave of Hessen-Kassel. He sought the crown, as did the king's nephew, Karl Frederick, who, at the time of the shooting, was at the front, dangerously close to the king, so that suspicion could easily fall on him.

Following the violent death of the autocrat, his subjects behaved "like flies awakened from their winter's hibernation," and, as the symbol of the disliked regime, von Görtz was executed. The system of absolutism was blamed for all the losses suffered by the kingdom. When it was convened, the Diet offered the crown to Charles XII's sister, Ulrica Eleonora—Frederick's wife—but only on condition that she renounce the sovereign's autocratic powers and sign the Form of Government of 1719, which fundamentally limited the authority of the ruler.

Very shortly after his death, Charles XII became, in Sweden, the object of hero worship, which in varying degree and manner had continued to the present day. The Finns, on the other hand, have not been inclined to bless his memory.

"His kingdom he cast adrift," the Swedish-language Finnish historian

Hornborg has written as his final estimate of Charles XII, "but he demanded that it none the less blindly place all its resources at his disposal. His troops he treated without mercy but expected that they follow him wherever he might lead with machine-like lack of feeling. Poland he trampled underfoot—yet he believed that it would become a trustworthy ally against Russia. To Czar Peter he gave a free hand for eight years—yet he believed that his own military power would stay on the same level that it had been during the days of the Battle of Narva." Charles XII, Hornborg goes on, " sacrificed Riga, Tallinn, and Viipuri for houses of cards fabricated by him in Poland and Turkey. He sacrificed even more, for he sacrificed Finland's faith in Sweden."

Hornborg's verdict reflects the prevailing view held in Finland, though it disregards the fact that Russia's emergence as a Baltic power sooner or later was inevitable.

After the deaths of Charles XII and von Görtz, peace was discussed along realistic lines, and it was achieved at the price of minor concessions during 1719 and 1720 with all the enemies of Sweden except Russia. Count Johan Lillienstedt, a Finn, carried on negotiations with the Czar's representative, but they failed to reach a compromise and the congress that was held in the Aland Islands broke up. Russia bolstered the position of its peace negotiators by trying to effect a landing near Stockholm and having its naval forces devastate the Swedish coast during three summers. On the other hand, Sweden's hopes of receiving aid from England proved futile, for that island kingdom was little concerned about the balance of power in the Baltic sphere.

In 1721, peace negotiations were resumed at Uusikaupunki, and Sweden was compelled to submit, to the conditions laid down by Russia: Livonia, Estonia, Ingria, and southeastern Finland were surrendered (see map 3). According to his original plan, the Czar, at any rate, gave back to Sweden the biggest part of Finland, and he even paid considerable war reparations. When Lillienstedt once pointed out during the discussions that he was not authorized to cede Viipuri, Ostermann told him to take a closer look at his instructions. Obviously, the Swedish delegates had been indiscreet, and the Russian spies had done a skillful job. Still, it is not necessary to refer to this anecdote to explain the peace treaty. History was moving along its inexorable course.

6

Sweden or Russia?

The Changed Status of the Swedish Realm and Its Finnish Part

Sweden had irretrievably forfeited her claim to being a Great Power, and her resources no longer sufficed to enable her to take an active part in continental politics. Her remaining German possessions still provided her with a pretext for a couple of military adventures toward the south; but the pressure of realities at last turned the attention of her political leaders to the East, which at times held a threat to the very survival of the kingdom as an independent state.

Now opposed to Sweden-Finland along the eastern border was an incomparably stronger neighbour than during the heyday of Swedish power. The possession of Estonia and Livonia enabled Russia, for the first time in history, to vie for mastery of the Baltic and, in the event of war, to threaten the maritime communications between Finland and Sweden. However, only a broad corridor of the Czarist domain extended to the Baltic coast, for, farther south, the land masses held by Poland spread deep into the interior toward Moscow. So it was most important to Russia to retain its grip on that corridor, especially since the establishment of St. Petersburg as the Russian capital and its development into a military stronghold had shifted the center of gravity of the empire to its northwestern corner.

In the opinion of many Russians, the border had been drawn too near St. Petersburg. The new capital would not be safe, declared the Russian politician Mihail Bestuzev, until the "natural boundary," formed by the Gulf of Bothnia, had been reached. As an alternative to the capture of Finland, however, control of the policies of the kingdom of Sweden as a whole was suggested by the remarkable Section 7 of the Peace Treaty of Uusikaupunki. In that section, His Imperial Majesty, the Czar, pledged that he would not meddle in the domestic affairs of Sweden, such as the Form of Government, "but rather, toward demonstrating sincere and neighbourly friendship, would endeavour in every way to prevent and forestall every move aimed against it." The equivocal wording of the section implied a threat of danger to Sweden-Finland, for its second half afforded the Russians an opportunity for action that was denied them by the first half—namely, interfering with the internal politics of its neighbour. And such interference could easily be just as serious a violation of sovereignty whether the internal threat to the Swedish Form of Government was fancied or real.

Sweden-Finland was confronted with several choices of policy in her new situation. By taking advantage of changes in international political conditions, she might try to push the national boundary back once more so far east that the balance of power in the Baltic sphere would be restored. Or else, she might try, by leaning on western European—namely, French—support to observe a firm and independent policy in her relations with Russia, thus at least preventing future Russian expansion in the north as well as resisting Russian influence on domestic affairs. The political party formed during the 1730's, known as the "Hats," tried to travel along both these paths in turn, first the former and, after failure, the latter. The third path, taken by the opponents of the Hats, who were known as the "Caps," was an attempt to achieve security by pursuing a pro-Russian policy. The eastward orientation of the Caps and the Russians' alternative of controlling all Sweden provided ground on which the two neighbours could meet. Fearing the devastation of war, most Finns at the beginning of the period backed the Caps. The fourth choice, previously perceived by Charles XII, was to seek compensation in the west for territory lost in the east.

Both the Hats and the Caps accepted bribes from abroad, the former from France, the latter mostly from Russia; and, in the fierce conflict between the two parties, neither one tried to avoid employing foreign policy as an instrument of internal politics. To France, too, Sweden was only a pawn in the game of power politics: her object was to keep the right flank of the Russian front engaged in return for French silver. But distant France was no threat to the independence of Sweden.

The French had become familiar allies in the 1600's and agreements with them did not humiliate the kingdom of Sweden in the same way as espousing the interests of Russia did, since the latter was regarded as a "hereditary foe" that strove to annex the eastern part of the realm. Therefore, with the exception of extremists, the Caps also viewed the pro-Russian policy as only a temporary and emergency expedient; in their hearts, they disliked it. According to a program drawn up in 1727, reflecting the position taken by Arvid Horn, adjustments and concessions were to be used to keep Russia, "this dangerous neighbour, in good spirits... until time and conditions might permit a different approach." And when, thirty years later, a politician, who was a member of the Caps, opposed the fortification of Finland, he argued: "A time must be awaited when the current period in the fortunes of the Russian people will change and the Lord God... will mercifully deign to provide circumstances favorable to Sweden."

If the military-political status of the realm as a whole had fundamentally changed, that of Finland had been completely dislocated. Finland had lost her buffer territory, Ingria, the easily defended, narrow Karelian Isthmus, and her main fortified stronghold, Viipuri. Her new, strategically unfavorable border was totally unfortified. Compared to the mother country, she was tremendously weakened; populous areas that once had belonged to her had been taken away from her, whereas Sweden had regained possession of the southern provinces that had been conquered by Charles X Gustavus and, along with them, a secure maritime boundary. The population of Sweden after the war was 1,440,000, while Finland's was only between 330,000 and 340,000. While Sweden had been spared, Finland had been badly devastated by the war. Indeed in some Finnish districts, colonization had to be started all over again.

The proportional strengthening of the mother country also had the effect of bolstering the dominant position of the Swedish language on the eastern side of the Gulf of Bothnia. Almost the entire office-holding class of Finland had fled to Sweden and had become accustomed to speaking Swedish exclusively there; but many of the officials never returned home and were replaced by newcomers from Sweden. After the restoration of peace, the Swedification of the educated strata of the population continued at a rapid pace. "As late as the beginning of this century," wrote Prof. Henrik Gabriel Porthan at the end of the 1700's, "the clergy, the majority of the gentlefolk in the country, and a large part of the merchants and bourgeoisie of the towns mostly used the Finnish language in intercourse among themselves. But how greatly has all that now changed and is daily changing more and more; and no compulsion whatsoever has been needed to bring this about." The common people and the public functionaries now no longer were able to understand each other, and the question of the officials' knowledge of Finnish became of prime importance.

The worst shock to the Finnish people, however, was the collapse of Sweden as a major power and the first conquest of Finland by the Russians. Sweden's prestige fell to an all-time low, and the sense of security that had been enjoyed by the Finns during the period when Sweden was a Great Power was replaced by the fear that the occupation might be repeated and that Finland might eventually be annexed by Russia. The military commander-in-chief for Finland, who was appointed right after peace was restored, described the attitude of the Finns as so defeatist that, of the peace were threatened again, they "would let their courage and their hands drop" and surrender to the enemy.

During the eighteenth century, however, the Swedish government turned its attention to Finland to a degree unprecedented in past history. Without Finland, "Sweden would not be Sweden," declared Crown Prince Adolphus Frederick. And one Swedish parliamentary spokesman praised the Finns for having remained just as loyal to the Swedish Crown as the inhabitants of any of the provinces west of the Gulf of Bothnia, even though "all the thrusts received by Sweden from her worst enemy have gone right through Finland's heart." The basic object of this attention was to persuade the Finns to be contented subjects and, moreover, to emphasize the fact that the mother country fully intended to defend them and was entirely capable of doing so.

The foregoing citations are from the records of the Diet of 1747, up to which time very little had been done to enhance the contentment of the Finnish population. When, in the 1730's, Finnish yeomen petitioned Sweden for the establishment of her own central administrative bureaus in Finland, or, at least, for the appointment of public functionaries with a knowledge of Finnish, they were accused of separatism. The resolution that was passed by the government concerning linguistic ability was couched in ambiguous language: Offices in Finland were to be awarded to persons who knew Finnish "as far as the circumstances as well as the skill and years of service of the individuals concerned make it practicable."

The defenses of the eastern border had not been bolstered, either. To be sure, immediately after the end of the Great Northern War, Major-General A. Löwen had drawn up a plan that called for the erection of two fortresses on the coast of the Gulf of Finland, one in the frontier area and the other in Helsinki. He did not think any large fortifications were needed in the nearly roadless interior. However, that program was neglected in favor of fortifications that were constructed mainly in the archipelago of Stockholm.

To some degree, the neglect of the Finnish defenses was influenced by a fear that the Russians might regard such construction as a hostile act, despite its defensive nature. Swedish dreams of revenge were another factor that made the fortification of the "provisional" boundary seem unnecessary. The decisive factor, however, was Sweden's refusal to consider the defense of Finland as an end in itself. From a purely Swedish standpoint, it was sensible to build permanent fortifications or station naval units in Finland only if the most favorable defensive lines of the mother country appeared to be situated there. But the prevailing attitude toward the chances of defending Finland remained one of hopelessness.

It was in the 1740's, at a time when public sentiment in Finland also became a force to be reckoned with, that a change in Swedish strategic thinking finally took place.

The Parliamentarism of the "Age of Freedom"

In 1719, Ulrica Eleonora had to pay for the crown by affixing her signature to the Constitution. When, a year later the crown was handed over to her consort, Frederick, the Constitution was amended to limit the authority of the monarch even more. The Forms of Government thus created in those two years were not based on any system of political science; and their provisions represented compromises between differing points of view to such an extent that they did not form any cohesive whole. Absolutism was categorically condemned by both documents, and a greater burden of sins was heaped on it than it deserved on any reasonable grounds; it was branded as a "disease" that had killed the power and prosperity of the kingdom and had brought success and profit to its foes.

The abolition of absolute monarchy had restored "freedom" to the realm, and, even to this day, the period is referred to in history as the "Age of Freedom." Hence, the primary purpose of the Form of Government was to fix rigid limits to the authority of the monarch, and, in practice, this authority was destined not to extend even as far as these limits. There was something contradictory about the circumstance that a king who was accorded the same ceremonious worship as the absolute monarchs of the continent was not even allowed to choose a tutor for his own children without the sanction of the estates, and that his queen (as in the case of the proud Prussian princess, Lovisa Ulrica) was constrained to submit to scolding by the clergy like a naughty schoolgirl.

A genuine conflict between the Form of Government and practical administration arose in deciding the role of the Council of the Realm. The conservative circles had aspired to restore, through the Constitution, the distribution of power that prevailed before the establisment of autocratic rule. This would have meant putting the Council back into political authority and the upper nobility back into social preeminence. But progressive groups, which gradually gained more and more influence, strove to augment the authority of the Diet and, along with it, the power of the lower nobility and the other estates.

According to the Form of Government, the Council of the Realm was the highest department of the government. Its members were irremovable office-holders who were appointed by the king in the basis of nominations made by the Diet. But, in practice, a rudimentary parliamentarism evolved in respect to the forms observed. First, the king's power of choice in the appointment of councilors was reduced to almost nothing. Second (and even more significant), the Diet began to force governments out of office. Of course, it could not get rid of disagreeable councilors by a vote of non-confidence; but if it decided to look for errors in the discharge of their duties, it was a foregone conclusion that some ground for censure would be found in order to have the guilty councilors impeached. Councilors who were afraid of possible impeachment proceedings were likely to consent to voluntary retirement, especially since they were granted the right to retain their titles of office. Vacancies in the Council were thereby created for the Diet to fill with more congenial officers.

However, the Diet was not content merely to rule through governments that enjoyed its confidence, but it also exercised direct administrative authority. Its secret committee held the strings of foreign policy in its hands and occasionally acted as the real GHQ of the armed forces. The Diet established its own bureaus, especially for economic branches of administration; it even took upon itself the management of petty administrative affairs that should have been the concern of bureaus on a lower level; and it served as the supreme court of the realm, to which controversial cases were appealed. The Estates considered themselves entitled to all this by very loosely interpreting a number of obscure provisions of the Form of Government, and, as often happens in history, political theory was developed to defend powers already acquired.

Bishop of Turku J. Browallius declared in his report of 1751, which reflected a generally accepted viewpoint, that the Diet was infallible and that the executive government, instead of being an independent organ of state, possessed only such powers as were delegated by the Estates. According to Browallius's conception, a member of the Diet, on the other hand, was not either morally or legally responsible to his constituents. The "people" had, once and for all, surrendered their power to the four Estates—the nobles, clergy, burghers, and yeomen—which exercised this power in the Diet.

Of the four Estates, the yeomen ranked lowest. Ordinarily, they were excluded from the secret committee and from certain other politically significant bodies. The upper nobility had lost its predominant position, for the division of the classes had been abolished, and the numerically large lower nobility thus decided the results of the voting in the House of Nobles. Successful rivals of the lower nobility were the clergy and the burghers, who together tended to dictate, for instance, the decisions of the secret committee. The predominant position of the Diet caused more detailed regulations than ever to be drawn up to govern its activities and the election of representatives of the different Estates. In parliamentary history, the Age of Freedom therefore signified a long step toward modern forms. Inasmuch as the number of members of the Diet rose to a thousand, and even more, interest in statecraft and knowledge of politics spread to ever wider circles. Outside the Diet, however, the "Age of Freedom" did not tolerate free political discussion.

The War of the Hats

The first two decades of the Age of Freedom were dominated by the figure of one man to such an extent that the period is often named after him in historical works. That man was Count Arvid Horn, the Finnish-born aristocrat who aspired to restore the Council of the Realm and the upper nobility to the position of power that they had held before the absolute monarchy was established. It was his downfall, in 1738, from the post of President of the Council, which he had held continuously since 1720, that spelled the death of the system that reflected the political ideals of the conservative faction; and the supreme authority of the Diet, which is regarded as characteristic of the Age of Freedom, started at the time when he retired.

In the management of foreign relations, Horn was a realistic and skillful politician who knew the weakness of his country and prudently avoided offending the Russians—but he did not submit to their bullying, either. When the Czar tried to force one of his kinsmen on Sweden as heir to the throne, the Diet frankly declared that the Swedish succession was not the affair of Russia any more than Russia's succession was an affair of Sweden's, and the government asked the English fleet to make an appearance in the Gulf of Finland. Sweden was simultaneously allied with Russia and France, Russia's opponent in western Europe. Finally, France refused to remain in this political triangle and left the renewal of the treaty of alliance unratified.

The loss of the traditional friendship of France aroused resentment against Horn in high, pro-French Swedish quarters. Moreover, the war that broke out between Turkey and Russia at that time seemed to lay bare the hereditary foe's right flank, thus offering an opportunity for revenge. Horn's adversaries organized themselves into a party, which adopted the name of Hats. In the Diet of 1738, the Hats gained the support of the majority among both the nobility and the burghers, who were attracted by the radical mercantilistic economic program of the new faction. Horn and his supporters were forced to quit the Council, and their ministerial seats were taken over by the Hats.

The policy of revenge was now begun on the basis of a program drawn up in advance, with a total indifference to the prevailing realities. Turkey and Russia concluded peace, and thus it was necessary to eliminate a fundamental factor from the calculations, which even earlier had been immediately optimistic. But, slightly later, a Czar who was only a few weeks old was seated on the Russian throne, and it was known that Elizabeth, the daughter of Peter the Great, was conspiring to have the child deposed. The Swedish Diet assumed that Elizabeth would welcome her neighbour's assistance in carrying out her palace revolution and that she would repay Sweden by restoring to her the provinces that had been ceded by the Swedes in the Peace of Uusikaupunki. France, which was just then preparing to attack Austria, wanted to keep Russia out of the Central European war and therefore promised Sweden abundant funds.

At this stage, Swedish foreign policy was for the first time exploited as a mere tool of internal politics. The most fanatic Caps were not above collusion with foreign agents. They proposed to the Czarist envoy that Russia force Sweden, by assuming a threatening attitude, to mobilize her army, which would mean the imposition of heavy taxes and the spread of popular discontent; and if these means did not succeed in unseating the government, Russia should occupy Finland.

One of the men who were arrested on suspicion of treason was the government's Finnish translator, J. Mathesius. His point of departure appears to have been the fear that was prevalent in Finnish circles that a war with Russia inevitably would end in crushing defeat, with the recurrence in Finland of the sufferings of the Great Wrath, and that, consequently, it should be prevented by all means, fair or foul. As a matter of fact, the country had recently had a foretaste of war, for, two years before, considerable Swedish military forces had been transferred to Finland—something that during the heyday of Sweden's power had never happened, even in a time of danger. The billeting of the troops had inflicted economic hardships and contagious diseases on the Finnish population.

The exposure of the treasonable activities of the Caps stirred the Hats to action against the country with which their internal adversaries were conspiring. In July, 1741, the secret committee of the Diet decided on a ceremonious declaration of war on Russia. Under the same momentum, it even drafted instructions for the peace negotiations: under the most favorable circumstances, all the provinces lost in the Great Northern War should be demanded, as well as the territory situated between Lake Ladoga and the White Sea, and under the worst circumstances the restoration of southeastern Finland and a slice of Ingria.

The first big battle of the war was fought in the vicinity of Lappeenranta, on the Swedish-Finnish side of the border—and it also proved to be the last genuine battle of the war. The Russians, with the odds heavily in their favor, were the attackers, and they forced the Swedish-Finnish troops into chaotic retreat. The fleeing troops lost half their strength, but the Russians lacked the resources to maintain the offensive. A short while later, Elizabeth, acting without the benefit of Swedish aid, had the infant Czar imprisoned and herself proclaimed Empress. A truce was signed, and when the deadline for its termination drew nigh, Commander-in-Chief C. E. Lewenhaupt dispatched one of his officers, Col. C. O. Lagercrantz, to Russia to petition for an extension of the truce. From the perspective of two hundred years, a mission of this kind appears quite insignificant; yet, Lagercrantz's trip is one of the many epochal missions to Moscow that have been recorded in Finnish history.

Lagercrantz brought back with him Elizabeth's Manifesto, dated March 8, 1742, in which, for the first time, the idea of Finnish independence was expressed. The Empress accused Sweden of having started the war, but she did not want to place the responsibility for this "wrong" on the Finnish people. Although she was compelled to permit her armed forces to advance into Finnish territory, she entertained no ambition to annex even a "foot's-breadth" of it. On the contrary, she was prepared to offer her assistance to the Finns if the "Duchy of Finland" (the Empress thereby transferred into the realm of reality this conception based on the titulary assumed by Swedish kings of the past) desired to be a "free country under the dominion of no power." The Empress had deemed it useful to add a threat to the enticements: if the Finns supported the Swedish army, she would lay their land waste "by the agency of fire and the sword's edge." To what extent Elizabeth meant what she said in her declaration was to be revealed subsequently. The Swedish attack had, at any rate, made timely the need to push this neighbour farther from the proximity of St. Petersburg, and this objective could also be attained by making a buffer state of Finland. The politicians of the Caps' faction had described the dissatisfaction of the Finns with Sweden to the Russian ambassador in Stockholm in exaggerated terms. How to explain the part played by Lagercrantz, who had been one of the most vociferous champions of conquest in the Diet, in producing the Manifesto has puzzled historians.

The lure held out by the Empress had the desired effect, although the wretchedness that followed the truce was contributed to by the witless leadership of the army and the previously existing poor morale of the officer corps. The naval forces and the land forces vied with each other in the rapidity of their retreat; in Helsinki, 16,000 men capitulated to an equally strong Russian army without a fight; the commandant of the fortress of Hämeenlinna ordered salutes fired when he surrendered the keys of the fortress to the victorious enemy. Only the peasants of North Karelia, heedless of the protests of military officers, waged fierce guerrilla warfare against the invaders.

Thus Finland fell into the hands of the Russians within a few months. A new occupation, known as the Lesser Wrath, started. This time the great majority of officials stayed at home and endeavoured to work out relations with the army of occupation, while the latter tried to avoid acts of violence. The Scottish-born Russian General James Keith, who directed the military and, at first, also the civil administration, left behind a favourable memory.

Czar Peter had not been interested in keeping Finland, which he had decided in advance to return to Sweden. Now, the future destiny of Finland was open, and Empress Elizabeth considered it all important to cultivate friendly feelings among the Finns. But since Finland had given up almost without a fight, the Russian court chose to ignore the offer of Finnish independence that was incorporated in the Manifesto. Still, even if they had considered the Manifesto to be primarily war propaganda, the Finns were forced to accustom themselves to the ideas that it presented, because the only alternative seemed to be a total annexation of their country by Russia.

At a provincial meeting held during the occupation in Ostrobothnia, reference was made to the promise of the Manifesto; and a provincial meeting held in Turku sent a deputation to the Empress to discuss, among other things, the election of her sister's son, Karl Peter Ulrik, Duke of Holstein, as Grand Duke of Finland. But this mission miscarried. Elizabeth had decided that "independent" Finland would not remain loyal to the Czarist régime unless strong Russian forces were stationed there.

During the war, the Swedish Diet had met and the usual number of delegates had come from Finland. The Hats were made to answer for the consequences of their reckless politics. But the party made scapegoats of the military leadership —in part, for valid reasons, in part, groundlessly—and Lewenhaupt and another general were executed. It further managed to turn the attention of the Estates to the question of the succession to the throne, which the advanced age and childlessness of King Frederick made a timely issue. Finland could be regained, it was argued, by electing Karl Peter Ulrik as future king of Sweden. But Russia announced that it demanded both the possession of Finland and the choice of an heir of its designation to the throne. The Empress's candidate was not the Duke of Holstein, whom she had already picked as her successor to the Russian throne, but another kinsman, Adolphus Frederick, the princely bishop of Lübeck. Russia's position was so strong that it ventured to press the demand, at least as the point of departure for negotiations, for simultaneous fulfillment of both its political objectives: advancing its border to the Gulf of Bothnia and taking over control of Swedish political affairs from within.

Other candidates for the Swedish throne appeared, among them Frederick, Prince of Denmark, who promised the aid of the Danish army to reconquer Finland from the Russians. But party lines were ignored as the Finns unanimously opposed his candidacy. They feared that the prince's plan would make Finland a theater of war and would bring suffering and devastation, with no certainty of the outcome. Instead, they felt that it would be better to court the Empress's favor by accepting her candidate and then trying through negotiations to salvage what they could of Finland.

When the Council of Russia met to discuss the peace terms, opinion was divided. Some of the Empress's advisers referred to the Manifesto that had been issued to the Finns and proposed that Finland actually be established as a buffer state, which, as was bluntly stated in one speech, would be "under the protection" of Russia. The majority, however, wanted Russia to keep all of Finland, although a number of those who maintained this stand were prepared to return parts of the country on condition that Adolphus Frederick be chosen as heir to the Swedish throne. The Empress shared the latter view and decided that the territory to be ceded to Russia should include the entire coast of the Gulf of Finland. After much bargaining, Elizabeth, doubtless influenced by rumors of an impending revolt in Finland, agreed to cede the province of Uusimaa (Nyland) as well; and when the Swedish Diet had chosen Adolphus Frederick as heir-apparent, the peace treaty was signed in Turku in August, 1743. It included an amnesty to all who, during the war, had "with arms or otherwise" given aid to the enemy; the condition was formally mutual but, in practice, it concerned only those Finns who had hastened the capitulation. The treaty accordingly afforded the Russians a pretext for supervising even the functioning of Swedish-Finnish courts of justice. The notorious Section 7 of the Peace of Uusikaupunki was not repeated; the Swedes interpreted the omission as cancelling it, but the Russians pointed out that the stipulation had not been specifically nullifield.

Finland had escaped the threatened fate of being divided equally between two hostile powers, but once more she had lost a slice of territory. Her population had been reduced by about ten percent, and the new boundary (see map 3) was defensively even more unfavorable than the one that was previously drawn. The connections of eastern Finland with the nearest seaport, which the Peace of Uusikaupunki had lengthened, were now totally cut, damaging the economic life of that extensive area.

Cold War and the Fortification of Finland

After the Peace of Turku, the kingdom of Sweden was at the lowest ebb of her fortunes. The war had revealed to both friend and foe the miserable state of her army. When Denmark threatened war, the government of the Hats was constrained to turn to Russia for naval aid and was forced to submit to the humiliation of having considerable Russian land forces stationed on Swedish soil for some time. The Russian ambassador in Stockholm constantly meddled in Sweden's internal affairs—expressly on the strength of the controversial Section 7 of the Peace of Uusikaupunki—and the newly elected heir to the throne, who had settled in Sweden, could be expected to support Russian policies. The leaders of the Caps were regular callers at the Russian embassy, where they made it their business to explain the weaknesses of the Swedish defense establishment and to demand more severe measures from their neighbour against their own country. "He hoped," wrote Ambassador von Korff about Dean J. Serenius, a leader of the Caps, "that ten thousand men would march into Finland bearing the tidings that they would remain there until the people had been released from bondage and French tyranny, and Swedish liberty had been saved. He was wholly convinced that all Finland would side with Your Imperial Majesty."

The final assertion, whether it be attributed to Serenius or the ambassador himself, was groundless. In Finland, Russian threats to start a new war understandably frightened people more than those on the western side of the Gulf of Bothnia, and the government of the Hats, which in its partisan zeal identified opposition with treason, suspected that a secret separatist movement had been organized in Finland. But neither G. F. von Rosen, the suspicious governor-general who was sent over by the Hats, nor later historians could find evidence of such activity in the Finland of the 1740's, in spite of painstaking study, if the doings of a few unbalanced individuals are discounted. A striking spirit of defense was demonstrated by the yeomanry, who generally agreed to maintain reserve troops by the permanent support of soldiers; and the farmers of the southwesternmost part of the country actually went so far as to petition for the right to use the time that they usually spent on destroying wild beasts in their home district for the building of fortifications along the eastern border. The further fortification work advanced in Finland, the more the feeling of insecurity faded, the insecurity that had accounted for the submissive mentality the government had condemned as Finnish separatism.

A resolution regarding these fortifications was passed during the sessions of

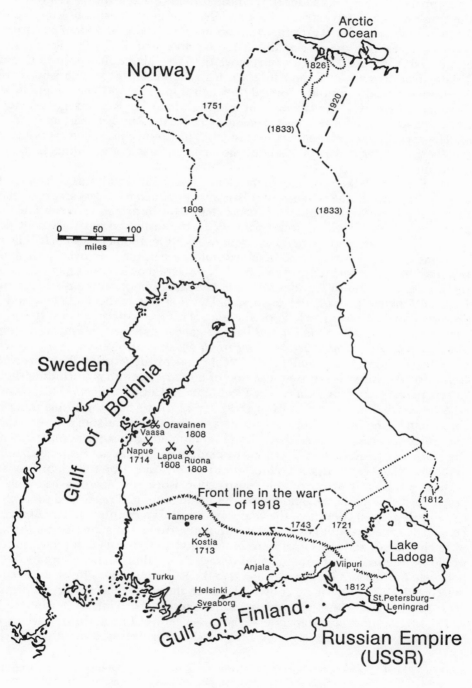

Map 3 Finland after the Peace Treaty of Turku, 1743

Arctic
Ocean

Norway

1826

1751

1920

(1833)

1809

(1833)

0   50   100
miles

Sweden

Gulf of Bothnia

Oravainen
Vaasa   1808

Napue   Lapua   Ruona
1714   1808   1808

Front line in the war
of 1918

1812

Tampere

Kostia
1713

1743   1721

Lake
Ladoga

Anjala   Viipuri

Turku

Helsinki
Sveaborg   1812

St.Petersburg–
Leningrad

Gulf of Finland

Russian Empire
(USSR)

the Diet of 1746—47, which also marked a turning point in political history. The heir-apparent, Adolphus Frederick, whose influence was growing as a result of the king's dullness, had extricated himself from the guardianship of Russia. The Empress had begun to regret the restoration of Finland to the Swedish Crown, but in her vexation she carried things too far and provoked a strong reaction. She urged Adolphus Frederick to remove the Hats, above all, Count C. G. von Tessin, from the Council, and to place his reliance on those who valued the Empress's friendly attitude toward the heir-apparent and the kingdom of Sweden. It was no coincidence, of course, that the Russian government simultaneously asked Sweden's permission to have the Russian fleet station itself off Helsinki if it was driven there by a storm. The Council preached caution; but the Diet proclaimed that the Swedish government was not accountable to any alien ruler.

Significantly, all the vacancies in the Council were filled with stiffnecked Hats, among them two Finns, while von Tessin was appointed to no less an office than that of President of the Council. To take charge of the armed forces in Finland as commander-in-chief and to keep an eye on the suspected separatist activities of the Finns, a governor-general was sent over—as had sometimes been done in previous centuries for reasons of a less military nature. Moreover, a gigantic program was approved to fortify Finland. It was based on Löwen's plan. Close to the border a system of fortifications was to be built, both on the islands in the Gulf of Finland and on the mainland. Helsinki was to be walled in and a powerful fortress was to be built on the islands off its coast, one that at the same time would serve as a base for the fleet of galleys stationed in Finnish waters. The fortress was named *Sveaborg*, meaning "Castle of Sweden",* and it was sometimes referred to proudly as the "Gibraltar of the North." The construction work was directed, during a period of a quarter-century—including slight interruptions caused by politics—by Field Marshal Count Augustin Ehrensvärd, who lies buried inside the walls of the fortress. In respect to the planning of some details, the fortress represented an antiquated system from the very start, but criticism aimed at Ehrensvärd always rebounded against his popularity with the Hats. His patriotic fervor cannot be denied, and it was not his fault that his ambitious plans could never be brought to a conclusion due to lack of funds.

During the early years of the construction work, the fortress had only a psychological significance, and although the kingdom had recovered somewhat from its depressed condition, the cold war with Russia continued. The Empress bombarded the Swedish government with notes, rumors of an impending attack were circulated, and the Finns were intimidated with threats that their country would be reduced to an uninhabited desert. A. Fredenstierna, a Finnish-born politician of the Caps faction, proposed to the Russian ambassador that a Diet of the Grand Duchy's own be convened under the protection of the Empress's army of occupation, and the ambassador suggested that Finland herself might issue a declaration of independence at this meeting. In the shifting winds of European power politics, Sweden-Finland slowly tacked into open water; she

* When Finland became independent, the official Finnish name of the fortress was changed to *Suomenlinna*, or "Castle of Finland." The fortress then no longer had any military significance.

received diplomatic backing from France and finally from Prussia, while Russia was supported by England and, at first, by Denmark.

The gradual improvement in the position of the Swedish realm was demonstrated by the government's response to three successive Russian notes. In the first, the Empress charged that Adolphus Frederick intended to revive absolutism when he ascended the throne, and she threatened to execute the measures sanctioned by Section 7 of the Peace of Uusikaupunki. Council President von Tessin replied that the Empress's suspicions of a planned change in the Form of Government were unfounded. In her second note, the Empress declared that she would send an army into Finland as soon as Frederick I died and keep the country under occupation until both the king and the people pledged to uphold the Form of Government and abide by Section 7 of the Peace of Uusikaupunki. Count von Tessin replied that Sweden would meet force with force. In the third note, Russia proposed an agreement to preserve the Swedish Form of Government. Sweden refused to accept the proposal and availed herself of the opportunity to give notice that the repeatedly cited Section 7 was no longer in effect.

The stiff language was backed by deeds. General Keith, the former Russian general who had entered the service of Prussia and whose expert knowledge could not be doubted, described to Frederick the Great how the Russians were capable of conquering Finland in six weeks. After obtaining this information, the Swedish government undertook the unprecedented measure of shipping a force of 8,000 men, in a time of peace and without any intention of attacking, to reinforce the defenses of Finland.

The foregoing exchange of notes showed how important it was to Russia to prevent the Swedish king from augmenting his authority at the expense of the quarrelsome Estates.

The long-awaited death of Frederick I occurred in 1751. The Empress took no military action; but she escaped the appearance of having lost the game, for Adolphus Frederick swore an oath of allegiance to the Form of Government. Besides, any increase in royal authority would by no means have pleased even the Hats. The cold war was over. By its refusal to compromise, the Hats' party had averted a peril to the realm. It now enjoyed general esteem and sat in power more firmly than ever before. It had bolstered the defenses of Finland, but it did not take a kindly view of the Finns for wishing to have their own countrymen appointed to administrative posts. However, an increasing number of Finnish members of the Diet supported the Hats.

The same year, neighbourly relations were stabilized in another direction, too, although Finland was forced to pay a price for the solution that was reached as a consequence of the Swedish Crown's weakness at the time. By the treaty of Strömstad, the common territory of Lapland was divided between Denmark-Norway and Sweden-Finland, with the result that Norway—according to a statement by the Norwegian border commissioner—received three times as much territory in Lapland as she was entitled to. Between the "arm" and "head" of Finland a deep curve was drawn in the boundary in Norway's favor. The border had little practical significance, however, as it was agreed that the Lapps remaining on the Finnish side could continue to fish in the Arctic Ocean during the summertime. It was not until the following century that Norway revoked that privilege.

Political and Social Criticism Aroused

The Hats' party remained in control of the political affairs of Sweden until 1765. It no longer pursued a policy of revenge against the East, but it did lead Sweden, as an ally of France and Russia, into the Seven Years' War. The aim was to conquer territory from Germany in order to prevent an upset of the balance of power, for Russia had the same objectives; but hostilities were waged feebly and without success.

The attention of the Hats began to be focused more and more on economic matters—on supporting industry in a mercantilistic manner by means of high tariffs, monopolistic grants and subsidies, none of which, however, benefited Finland to any appreciable degree, and on getting rid of the open field system through general field consolidation measures. The Hats were incapable of straightening out the financial situation. During the war against Russia, the Bank of the Estates had issued such an overabundance of paper money that it was obliged to cease redeeming notes with silver after the war. Also, when Sweden managed to extricate herself from the Seven Years' War, the amount of notes in circulation had doubled again. The exchange rates for foreign currency rose, along with prices, providing the Caps with favorable grounds for agitation. The opposition also obtained ammunition against the Hats from the subsidies distributed to business undertakings on a partisan basis.

The heyday of the mercantilistic ideology was by then drawing to a close in Europe, and one of the few men to raise his voice as early as the 1760's for unrestricted freedom of enterprise was the Finnish clergyman Anders Chydenius. He was more an original crusader than a theoretician, and, in the latter respect, he cannot be compared to the Englishman Adam Smith, who appeared on the scene slightly later and became much more famous. But Chydenius did mix social pathos with his economic liberalism in opposing the system, which included the mercantile policies of compelling all non-farmers and non-enterprisers to serve some employer—a system which, he argued, had the effect of legally enslaving the lower strata of society.

Chydenius served as rector of a parish in Ostrobothnia, where Finland's most important export, tar, war produced. But its marketing abroad had to be done through Stockholm. It was primarily through his efforts that the monopoly of the capital city was broken and one town after another on the Bothnian coast, starting in 1765, gained staple rights, i.e., the freedom to conduct direct trade with foreign lands. After that, the Ostrobothnians began to ship their tar directly to western Europe and they built themselves a considerable merchant fleet, although they continued to obtain their imports primarily from Stockholm. Otherwise, Chydenius's economic liberalism proved to be so far ahead of its time that no practical steps were taken toward realizing his program, and he never even became the spiritual father of any school of thought. On the other hand, Chydenius exerted an effective influence on another measure inspired by a liberalistic spirit: In 1766, censorship was abolished, except in respect to theological writings. Thus, Sweden-Finland became one of the first countries in the world to introduce freedom of the press.

In the Diet of 1765—66, the Caps held a majority in all four Estates, and the Hats were obliged to relinquish their posts in the Council of the Realm to them. After this change in the relative strength of the two parties, the secret committee of the Diet urged the government to "maintain and broaden the mutual friendship" with Russia. Although no alliance was made, fortification work in Finland was almost totally discontinued.

Against the advice of Chydenius, the Caps undertook a hapless experiment in financial policy: to raise the value of Swedish currency to what it had been before the inflation started. Deflationary policy is generally difficult to carry out, and the Caps badly bungled the job. A wave of bankruptcies resulted, and when government subsidies were abruptly withdrawn from industry at the same time, the productive life of the realm became disordered and unemployment followed.

In the opposition, the Hats did not sink into the same insignificance as the Caps had in the corresponding situation, for, during their long period in power, the party had filled the leading offices with adherents, who now practiced sabotage against the government of the Caps. They received powerful support from the king, who, in the end, refused to sign government resolutions unless new elections to the Diet were held.

The Council attempted, at first, to rule by means of a seal, which the Hats had fabricated during their term in order to keep obstinate Adolphus Frederick within bounds, but the public functionaries and military officers joined the king in his royal strike. In 1768, the Council was forced to submit to a summoning of the Diet. The election campaign was fiercely fought, and the effects of the freeing of the press appeared in the publication of numerous political pamphlets. The Caps showed little wisdom in appealing to Russia during such an internal struggle. "Our neighbour will teach the nation to dance," they warned, if the Caps did not win a majority in the Diet. The result was a victory for the Hats. But in the very next elections, in 1771, the Caps won again, though by so narrow a margin that, in order to secure their majority, they had to spend tremendous sums of money to buy the support of three clergymen in the Diet.

The surprisingly bold attack of the unprivileged classes against the nobility simultaneously brought to an end the state of social peace that had reigned throughout almost the entire Age of Freedom. The Finnish burgomaster A. Kepplerus published a tract that hailed the principle of human equality. This tract anticipated the declaration of human rights later formulated by the French Revolution.

In all spheres, new ideas clashed with the prevailing system. But, in those years, criticism was particularly aimed against the Form of Government. The French philosophy of enlightenment had spread, especially Montesquieu's doctrine of the separation of the legislative, executive and judicial branches of government; and it was obvious that this doctrine had not been realized in Swedish political life. The Diet took a hand in administrative details and it reversed verdicts of the courts of justice. And since the members of the Diet were to a large extent public functionaries, their political activities, as one Swedish historian has remarked, amounted to "an anarchy of official personnel, positions being turned upside down, subordinates giving orders to their superiors." The bureaucratic Swedish-Finnish Diet was loath to grant the Council of the Realm the same degree of independence that had been given to the English Cabinet by a Parliament under the control of the landed aristocracy. Reforms that were introduced during the 1760's increased the legal security of the citizenry only to a slight extent.

Political life in Sweden-Finland provided another target for criticism that involved practice less than principle. The weakness of the royal authority made the leading party the actual ruling power. The parties were upheld by foreign governments. Vote-buying involved such sums that, during the elections and session of the Diet of 1768, this money had a significant effect on the country's balance of payments. At the beginning of the 1760's, a court party had been active as a rather loosely knit organization whose political program aimed at augmenting the royal pover. It later drew closer and closer to the Hats, for it was in France's interest that Sweden be strong, whereas Russia's interest was to keep her immobilized, through internal dissension. "Without a majority in the Diet, it is impossible for the Swedes to move [i.e., start a war], no matter how large the subsidies paid them by foreign nations," it was noted in certain instructions dispatched by the Czarist government to Stockholm. Russia could then rely on "peace in the North," as its slogan ran, while it waged wars of conquest in other sectors.

Thus, the Czar's Grand Chancellor Panin described as the "most glorious triumph of his career" an act he succeeded—with the aid of the Caps—in pushing through the Diet of Sweden, whereby amending the Constitution—and, accordingly, increasing the royal authority—was made more difficult than earlier. And so important did the neighbours of Sweden-Finland consider the preservation of her "free" Form of Government that, in addition to the internal obstructions set up to prevent its being amended, they erected external ones. Russia, Denmark, and Prussia concluded an alliance aimed at upholding the Swedish Form of Government; and when the covenants were renewed in 1769, the high contracting parties stated that they would consider every change in the Swedish Constitution that increased the power of the monarch to be a warlike provocation. As a reward for military intervention, both Denmark and Prussia were promised Swedish territory. No mention was made of Russia's share of the spoils, but Grand Chancellor Panin hinted to a certain diplomat that Empress Catherine might, in such an eventuality, set up Finland as an "independent" state.

Thus the inhabitants of Sweden-Finland forfeited the power to make decisions regarding their own Constitution. A hint of the fate in store for her was given by the rulers of Russia, Prussia, and Austria when, in July, 1772, they carried out—in the name of the "Holy Trinity"—the first division of Poland.

The Bloodless Coup d'État

A year before the division of Poland, Adolphus Frederick died, and the throne of Sweden-Finland passed on to his son, Gustavus III. The new king, in contrast to his two immediate predecessors, had been born and raised in the land he ruled, and his popularity was enhanced by the superficial circumstance that his Christian name reminded his subjects of the glorious reigns of Gustavus I and II. Ever since childhood, Gustavus III had followed palace intrigues and had watched the court lean, now toward the Caps, now toward the Hats. He had learned that political skill included the ability to revise one's opinions whenever changes of circumstance made it expedient. His motivations were a mixture of personal ambition and a firm belief in the uncompromising demands of national interest, and the means he employed were decided just as much by the daring of an imaginative mind as by the refined cunning of a calculating and intelligent politician. His Prussian mother had taught him to esteem autocracy, and a stay at the French court had strengthened the French influence. He was aware that even his most royalistic subjects would not stomach absolute monarchy, to which he aspired. He had good reason to deplore the fact that Charles XI had "torn the veil that separated the prerogatives of the king from the rights of the people," i.e., had put an end to the old, undeveloped form of government, which permitted the king to rule with sovereign authority without the formal vestments of an absolute monarch. This confounding veil now had to be woven anew by putting into effect an obscure constitution open to diverse interpretations.

The Diet could be induced to approve the new constitution only under pressure, and the *coup d'état* had to be engineered swiftly and skillfully in order not to give the ill-disposed neighbouring powers time to act on the terms of their treaty of alliance. The plan was drawn up by a Finnish colonel, Jakob Magnus Sprengtporten. In executing his coup, the king could count on the support of his officer corps. It was strongly royalist, and the Diet of the Age of Freedom, in whose House of Nobles the officers played a very prominent role, had trained them more as politicians than as soldiers. As members of the nobility, they were frightened by the doctrines of social equality that had spread among the untitled Estates. The military revolt was to start in Helsinki, whence action was to be taken against Stockholm; and in the event of failure, another blow was to be struck in southern Sweden. The day that was selected for the revolt was August 12, 1772. Extra precautions were taken to guard the eastern frontier, using the plague that ravaged Russia as a pretext, in order to prevent the spread of intelligence from Finland to St. Petersburg. However, rumours about the plan leaked out and reached the ears of leading Caps, and it had to be revised at numerous points.

The revolt was initiated in the little Finnish town of Porvoo (Borgå), where Col. J. M. Sprengtporten and his half-borther, Georg Magnus, persuaded the company of dragoons stationed there to join them. From there, in a hailstorm and buffeted by hostile winds, the conspirators started out in rowboats toward Sveaborg. The fate of the Swedish kingdom seemed to depend on whether the burgomaster of Porvoo, who had been dispatched by his dumfounded citizens to

Helsinki, would reach the city in time to alert the strong garrisons before Sprengtporten's small force arrived at the fortress. The burgomaster failed. Three hours before the commanding general of Sveaborg, who belonged to the Caps, received official tidings of the revolt, Sprengtporten's men had penetrated the fortress, where unit after unit of the garrison joined them. For a week, Helsinki was, in a sense, the capital of an independent state, for Sprengtporten ruled Finland from there in his own name, not daring to associate the king with the undertaking while the issue was still uncertain. The country remained calm, and the confused nation pledged to forsake the Diet and serve the king. Only one politician who belonged to the Caps' faction was arrested.

Col. Sprengtporten was under orders to transport troops by ship to Stockholm, but they arrived late. In the capital of the realm, the Council, having received intelligence of the revolt carried out in southern Sweden ahead of schedule, had taken counteraction, and the king also was obliged to proceed in advance of the timetable. On August 19th, he had his bodyguards take the members of the Council prisoner along with certain other politicians who were known to be among the most vehement antiroyalists, and, on the 21st, he summoned the Estates to the royal palace. There, the members of the Diet, surrounded by troops and loaded cannons, listened to the new Form of Government as read to them by the king, and, without further ado, they approved it by shouts of "Yaa!" Not a single hand was raised in the whole realm to seize arms in defense of the Form of Government of the Age of Freedom. Also the surprised foreign powers, having placed their hope in a protracted civil war, failed to budge, though, of course, Russia and Denmark refused to recognize the amended Swedish Form of Government. Meanwhile, Russia was involved in a war with Turkey, and France declared that she would intervene if Sweden were attacked.

Gustavus III had saved the independence of his realm. Sweden-Finland had shown the world that she was determined to decide her own system of government. The Finnish subjects of the king had played a prominent part in the revolution, though it had turned out to be not quite so prominent as originally planned.

The Form of Government of 1772 was destined to have a much greater and more far-reaching significance to Finland than to Sweden, for the autonomous status of the Finnish nation was to depend on the interpretation of the confused provisions of that law, for more than a century. The executive power was placed exclusively in the hands of the king. Since the Council was so dependent on him, it hampered his movements very little, and the Diet not at all, for it ceased to intervene in executive matters. And there was no longer any relationship of confidence between the Council and the Diet. The Diet also ceased to convene at established intervals. But, in order to pass new laws and approve new taxes, the king found it necessary to convoke the Estates from time to time.

The Finnish Independence Movement

It has become customary for historians to paint the first decade of Gustavus III's reign in bright colors and the second decade in dark colors. This differentiation derives from the literature of aristocratic memoirs and, primarily, it reflects the attitude of the top-ranking social class toward the ruler. However, it also has a broader validity, since, until about 1780, the dissension did not reach disturbing proportions, whereas afterward, the friction between king and subjects increased. The unrest reached the point of rebellion, and the bitterness finally led to the assassination of the king.

The "happy" first decade of Gustavus III's reign was marked by many reforms. After the skillfully executed devaluation of 1776, the silver standard was re-introduced, but the old *thaler* notes were redeemed at only half the value that they had had when the country had shifted to the paper money standard thirty years before. On the initiative taken by Anders Chydenius, complete freedom of worship was granted to all christian foreigners settling in the country and to their descendants. In Finland, the Crown started a large-scale colonization program for the settlement of such common village lands as were deemed unnecessarily extensive when the village commons were enclosed; in reality, the program amounted to an expropriation of untilled lands, though the estates of the nobles were exempted from such action.

Finland received new local bureaus, and roads were built through her pathless interior. Since these new communication lines ran from the eastern frontier zone toward the Gulf of Bothnia, it was feared that they would help the enemy to invade the country and would thus tend to make it more difficult to defend Finland. Simultaneously, the army maintained by the farmers was reinforced and fortification works were continued. In training eastern Finnish detachments, Col. G. M. Sprengtporten took into account the demands of forest terrain: he abandoned the linear tactics of Central Europe and placed chief emphasis on mobility. During the period of these arrangements, the peasants of Finland demonstrated their old readiness to make sacrifices for the good of the defense establishment.

"How fortunate would the fatherland be, if all hearts were even a wee bit Finnish," wrote Sprengtporten to the king.

The attitude of the nobility toward the king was affected by numerous factors, some positive, some negative. Gustavus III consistently favored the upper nobility. Modern statistical surveys have proved that the increase in the number of official posts that were held by the unprivileged Estates during the Age of Freedom ended and that the hegemony of the nobility over high military offices remained almost complete. The king remembered the upper nobility by restoring the division of classes in the House of Nobles. The officer corps, in particular, was pleased with the growth in the military power of the realm and with the stress laid on independence. On the other hand, the nobility had been the strongest of the Estates represented in the Diet and to it belonged the element of the population that was most keenly interested in politics; now it was obliged to look on from the sidelines as the king, year after year, ever more autocratically, and soliciting the counsel of only a handful of men, directed the political affairs of the country.

Everything for the good of the nobility, but nothing through the efforts of the House of Nobles, appeared to be Gustavus III's motto—somewhat contrary to the enlightened autocrats of the continent. But the king's pets loved power more than social advantages. As is usual for the uppermost class of society, the nobility of Sweden-Finland was in the closest communication with foreign countries and adopted the freshest currents of thought. It was the period when minds in France were ripening for the great revolution. Absolutism was not in fashion and the negative factors gradually gained the upper hand among the Swedish nobility over those favouring the monarch. Also, the curve that indicated royalist sentiment among the untitled Estates sometimes dipped below zero. Gustavus III still managed the first Diet that was convened after his *coup d'état;* but the second Diet, in 1786, witnessed the emergence of such a united and uncompromising opposition that the king could get nothing done, but, on the contrary, was forced to give certain "explanations" concerning the Constitution that were distasteful to him.

Special influences worked on public sentiment in Finland, which during the period after the king's usurpation of power had been a contented and royalist part of the realm. For, during the second decade of his reign, intelligence regarding Gustavus III's adventurous aims in the field of foreign policy leaked out to the upper class of the population; and his secret defense plan must have become known to many Finnish officers because of the preliminary measures that it called for.

Empress Catherine's activity was directed against Poland and Turkey. She occupied the khanate of Crimea, which had been held by Turkey, first making it an "independent" state but soon afterward, annexing it outright. To Catherine, it was important not to be disturbed in these diversions of hers and not to be obliged to keep large military forces in northwestern Russia against the danger of a Swedish attack. In order to obtain the surest possible guarantees of "peace in the North", she invited Gustavus III, in 1783, to the town of Hamina, in the Russian-held part of Finland, for negotiations. Gustavus, for his part, was not content merely to listen to Catherine's proposals but asked her whether Russia would remain neutral if Sweden were to conquer Norway from Denmark. The talks ended without any practical results, and, afterward, the Empress once more started to seek the restoration of the Form of Government in effect in Sweden during the Age of Freedom.

In high Swedish military circles, there was gossip again about the possibility that Sweden might conquer Norway in spite of everything and offer Finland to Russia to appease it. The Russians cleverly sustained the rumours circulating in Finland about that sort of political speculation and added to them vague promises granting Finland her independence under the protection of the Empress. The rumors aroused anxiety in Finland. The caretaker of the frontier post office, who served the government as a kind of special observer to report on public sentiment, wrote: "Russian rule is feared like slavery, and the same outcome is apprehended of independence, for even in such a circumstance, as they say here, Finland would be no more than a mouthful for Russia to swallow whenever it might pop into its head."

These rumours also inspired dissatisfaction with Sweden, which, it was suspected, was prepared to abandon the loyal Finns and exchange the eastern half of the realm for Norway. As if to confirm the rumours, fortification activity ceased in Finland and the remaining funds were spent on building an ocean fleet for use in the conquest of Denmark. According to the defense plan endorsed by the king in 1785, the army was to withdraw, as soon as war broke out with Russia, as far as Helsinki, and in a pinch the whole of Finland—with the exception of Ostrobothnia—was to be surrendered to the enemy in order to spare the army for the protection of the mother country. It was precisely in the southeastern frontier district, which, therefore, even under the best of circumstances, was to be allowed to fall into enemy hands, that numerous noblemen in the officer corps had their homes and landed property; and these officers consequently strove, regardless of the means, to prevent the outbreak of hostilities. The educated class, having embraced the profiteering morals of the Age of Enlightenment, was not ready to display the same dutifulness toward government authority that had provided the backbone of the army and the community as a whole during the period of Swedish political power. Further seeds of discontent were sown by the policy of appointments to office, which favoured, or was believed to favour, native Swedes.

In the 1780's, when the Finns paused to survey their position, they could not help but notice that, year after year, Russia was growing steadily stronger in comparison with the kingdom of Sweden. They also knew from their own experience or from history that Russia had already declared its intention to conquer all Finland and that hints had come from Russian quarters about broader or narrower independence to be conferred upon Finland.

"Our destiny is, in any event, to fall under the domination of this power, but our position will be much worse if we do not voluntarily submit"—thus the outlook that evolved in Finland during that period was described a short time later. Even under the best of conditions, it was felt, Finland would be constantly reduced to a battlefield so long as she remained joined to Sweden. Hence, the Finns would have to take matters into their own hands and approach the Russian government directly. The English colonists of North America afforded an example of a people who had taken up arms against their mother country overseas and won freedom; nor had the world condemned this war of liberation as treason but had treated it with sympathy.

The same hopeless defeatism that had led to the collapse of national defense during the Lesser Wrath thus laid its stamp on the Finnish separatist movement of the 1780's. Fear of Russia caused people to throw themselves on her mercy. The movement expanded when Sweden appeared to be neglecting Finnish defense, and it declined when the king withdrew the defense orders of 1785.

On the other hand, the age-old suspicions of Russia persisted, and these suspicions were stirred to new life by the annexation of the Crimea. The failure of the separatist plan was subsequently explained on the ground of the "panicky terror" inspired by the fate of the Crimea. Although, to the champions of independence, Finland was not simply a part of the Swedish kingdom but was also understood to constitute a distinct entity, Finnish nationalist feeling played no part in this movement, as national-romantic historical writers once assumed, and its support was confined to narrow aristocratic quarters.

Perhaps underestimating the significance of the independence movement somewhat and immoderately misrepresenting its objectives, the leader of Finnish cultural life in those days, Prof. Henrik Gabriel Porthan, wrote about it:

141

"Maybe four or six aristocratic flibbertigibbets, who thereby have hoped to become the lords of their countrymen and, on Livonian soil, to make them serfs, are truly enamoured of such an undertaking... Our common people hate the Russian and his protection... so much from the bottom of their hearts that I should not advise anybody to propose such a plan to them."

The leader of the independence movement was Gustavus III's righthand man in his coup, Col. G. M. Sprengtporten. Describing this leader's ideological development is hampered by the fact that the available data was recorded as much as a quarter-century later or is contained in the contemporaneous writings of his enemies, which exaggerate the treacherous character of his activities, as viewed from the standpoint of Sweden.

Col. Sprengtporten was an officer of genius, but he was a difficult and suspicious person. He was disappointed when he was not honored according to what he considered to be his due for his part in the king's revolution; he was bitter because the king, who had just achieved tolerable relations with Empress Catherine, would not, for reasons of caution, accept all the measures toward reinforcing the army of Finland that he had recommended. Accordingly, he tendered his resignation from the army in 1777, and thereafter lived part of the time on his estate and part of the time abroad, also in Russia, where he was perceived to be a man likely to prove useful in furthering Russian political aims and where he was introduced to the Empress herself.

Personal indignation over loss of the king's favour was coupled with a hopeless view of his fatherland's defensive position. But it was far away, in the Netherlands, in 1785, that Sprengtporten began to follow the path laid out by politicians of the Caps' faction back in the Age of Freedom, which involved hatching plots with alien agents against his own country. He presented to the Russian ambassador at The Hague a plan for the separations of Finland from Sweden, and, subsequently, he continued negotiations with Morkov, the Russian ambassador in Stockholm.

Finland was situated so near the Russian capital, Sprengtporten argued, that, as long as she remained part of Sweden, she was bound to excite the suspicions of the Czarist regime, but she was also situated so far from Sweden that the mother country was incapable of giving her protection. The independence of Finland would remove both defects and make possible the fostering of relations on a basis of mutual confidence between Russia and Sweden. The Finns would have to start their revolt in the winter, when communications with Sweden were hardest to maintain, and the Empress should give the young state military and economic aid and guarantee her Form of Government. Sprengtporten seems not to have believed that Finland could achieve full independence under Russian protection. When the colonel compared Finland to the British colonies of North America, Ambassador Morkov responded by likening Russia to France, which had supported the colonies with arms in their fight for liberty.

Morkov reported to the Empress, however, that Sprengtporten was more dazzling than inspiring of confidence, and he did not seem to take the colonel's claims about the strength of the independence ideal in Finland seriously. Consequently, he was cool toward the scheme for staging a rebellion, and the

Empress, while conceding that Russia might profit thereby, would give no political pledges.

"It is the business of the Finns to shake the yoke off their shoulders, and when this has happened, everything else will follow as a matter of course," she responded cautiously, thrusting the initiative into the hands of the Finnish separatists. To Sprengtporten she sent an invitation to join her retinue. Realizing that his negotiations with the Russian envoy were bound to be found out by the king, the colonel decided, in 1786, that it would be safer to leave the country.

The Finnish Officers' Mutiny

After the hectic session of the Diet of 1786, Gustavus III conceived the daring idea of restoring his lost popularity by means of a victorious war, and awareness of the separatist movement in Finland only increased his eagerness to grapple with the alien power in whose support the separatists placed their hope. Foreign policy was thus exploited by the king, as it had been by the rival factions during the Age of Freedom, as an instrument of internal politics. But Gustavus III's activities had another motivation too: a successful war against the future peril threatening from the East.

Early preparations for war included the search for allies. Since France was approaching internal catastrophe, she could offer no assistance; and the king's visit to Copenhagen did not yield the hoped-for fruits of an alliance with Denmark. On the other hand, the pretended friendliness of the Danes lulled Gustavus into the false belief that their country would at any rate keep out of the war. Efforts were made to incite the German nobility of the Baltic provinces into mutiny; their discontent with Russian rule, however, was neutralized by an unwillingness to fight against overwhelming odds. The Poles also remained passive. But, partly incited by Sweden, the sultan of Turkey declared war on Russia. For the Swedes' own attack, a plan was drawn up that, though it was not new, was now to be put to the test for the first time: the naval forces of Russia were first to be thoroughly defeated, after which a landing was to be made at Oranienbaum, southwest of St. Petersburg, with the aim of capturing the Russian capital, in a sense, from the rear. "Or, if insurmountable obstacles occur, it should at least be bombed and shelled so heavily that the enemy would have no time to think of anything except surrendering." Simultaneously, an operation designed to lead the enemy astray was to be carried out from Finnish territory.

One of the few restrictions put on the royal authority was one denying the king the right to engage in offensive war without the consent of the Diet. But summoning the Diet would only have made Gustanus III's position more difficult. And, as even the king's military experts warned him, and, as the reluctance of the Finnish officers, in particular, to go to war was generally known, Russia must be provoked into appearing to be the aggressor. The Empress was humiliated, but she swallowed her humiliation; so there was nothing left to do but stage an incident along the Finnish border. Cossack uniforms were ordered from the opera tailor, and they were shipped to J. Hastfer, commanding officer of the Savo brigade, with instructions to have some of his own men don them and then run riot on some Finnish farm. The work of the opera tailor went to waste, however, for a Russian reconnaissance patrol accidentally crossed the frontier—as often happened in wilderness border zones—and this petty incident sufficed to brand Russia the aggressor.

Contriving a formal pretext for waging war was not, however, where the difficulty lay. It was in carrying out a mobilization under circumstances where even the highest officers had to be kept ignorant of the cause. Thus, the commander-in-chief of the forces in Finland, Lieutenant-General F. Posse, received official mobilization orders in a sealed letter which he was to open only if the Russians became active along the border; but by means of messages delivered unofficially, the king put pressure on Posse to break the seal on his orders. By such trickery, Gustavus III succeeded, in June of 1788, in concentrating the armed forces of the realm in Helsinki and along the eastern border of Finland. However, the king's young Finnish favorite, Baron G. M. Armfelt, reported the sentiment among the officers to be "devilish," and documents brought to light at a later date proved that there was a conspiracy afoot to take the king prisoner. But nothing happened when Gustavus III arrived in Helsinki and took command. A note was despatched to Russia demanding the restoration of the territories that had been ceded in the peace treaties of Uusikaupunki and Turku, and, simultaneously with the sending of the note, the army marched across the frontier. The formal declaration of war came from the Empress. At least, on this point, Gustavus had attained his objective.

The Russian army was fighting in Turkey and the fortifications of St. Petersburg were dilapidated. The Empress's court actually considered the situation to be so critical that it made preparations to evacuate to Moscow. The Russian Baltic fleet had also been preparing to sail to the Black Sea, but Gustavus made such haste to start shooting that only a small squadron had had time to weigh anchor. Impatience thus led to a gross strategic error, for the whole plan of war was based on the attainment of supremacy in the Baltic waters. The evenly matched naval forces of Sweden-Finland and Russia clashed off Suursaari on July 17th. For the first time since the triumphant early years of the Great Northern War, the military forces of Sweden-Finland held their own against the concentrated might of Russia; but the fact that the naval battle produced no decision wrecked the invasion plan.

The morale among the troops, who were wholly ignorant of the true state of affairs, was satisfactory, but the officers—notably the Finnish ones—were worried: "The old dame [Catherine] will never forget the mischief we have done to her." It was feared that Russia would demand another slicing up of Finnish territory. The officer corps began to grumble and to incite the rank and file troops to disobedience, too. In the wee hours of August 9, in the village of Liikkala, seven high Finnish officers signed a remarkable letter, addressed to the Empress of Russia. This "note" explained that it was the desire of "the whole nation, and particularly the people of Finland," to regain the peace which "a few restless souls" had broken, and the Empress was asked to restore the territory ceded in the Peace of Turku as a pledge of peace.

Chosen to deliver the "note" to St. Petersburg was the initiator of the scheme, Chief Adjutant J. A. Jägerhorn, a young idealist, who, during the period before the war, had wavered between royalism and separatism. In St. Petersburg, Jägerhorn reported that the forces of Sweden-Finland would fight only in the event they were attacked on their own side of the border. Thus betraying the weakness of his army, he doubtless correctly interpreted the thoughts of his associates and many other officers. But Jägerhorn's notes and the records taken of his interrogations include other material as well, and historical research has not fully ascertained what he proposed to the Empress on his own. Evidently, their discussions touched on the future political status of Finland. The response to the "note" returned by the Empress, which for reasons of caution she left unsigned, only contained a demand to withdraw from Russian soil and an exhortation to convene a Finnish Diet. At any rate, it was a disappointment to the inexperienced Jägerhorn.

When Gustavus got wind of the Liikkala "note," he deemed it necessary to demand a written pledge from his officers that they would fight to the last man. In response, 113 officers of Finnish military units gathered together at the estate of Anjala on August 12 to sign the so-called Covenant of Anjala, drawn up by Lieutenant K. H. Klick, in which they assumed co-responsibility for the Liikkala "note." They condemned the attack on Russia and described the military situation (contrary to the realities) as hopeless. They nevertheless promised to defend the fatherland unless the Empress consented to an honorable peace. Research has revealed that when the signatures had been collected, the Liikkala "note" had been represented to the officers in an abridged version, from which, among other things, the references to the special desire of the Finnish people for peace had been omitted.

Gustavus III was humiliated; and when he confessed to the President of the Council that he feared the outbreak of a civil war, his fear was laid at rest with the scornful observation that civil war called for two armies, one of which, however, was lacking. In order to maintain at least ostensible discipline, the king demanded an apology from the signers of the Anjala Covenant, promising favorable consideration in advance. This attempt at reconciliation fell through, and even the Swedish officers began to demand the convocation of the Diet.

Meanwhile, Jägerhorn had returned from St. Petersburg and reported to the inner circle of rebels the fruitless outcome of his mission. The signers of the "note" did not dare, however, to tell the truth to their fellow officers, but put into circulation rumors about the Czarina's disposition to make peace and restore to Finland the territory ceded to Russia in the Peace of Turku. The mutiny spread also to the loyal Savo brigade: Hastfer withdrew his troops of his own volition back across the border, betrayed to the Russians the scheme whereby Gustavus III had intended to provoke war, and pledged his forces to support the plan for establishing Finland as a separate state under Russian protection.

The king was disappointed not only in his own subjects but also in his neighbours, for the mobilization ordered in Denmark revealed an intention to launch an attack on Sweden's rear. The threat of a second front gave Gustavus

III at least the advantage that he could withdraw from Finland without giving the appearance of a fugitive afraid of being taken captive. He entrusted the post of commander-in-chief to his scheming brother, Duke Charles of Söderman-land, who went much further in negotiations with the Russians than he had been authorized to. In vain, he pulled his main forces back over the border: it proved that the Empress was not disposed to wiping the slate clean of what had happened and to agreeing to a truce. The pledge of the Finnish officers to fulfill their military duty as soon as the Russians crossed the frontier, however, prevented the enemy from attacking. New proposals regarding the future status of Finland were made and came to naught, and all the characters cast in the drama hatched plots of their own.

The tension was released by Sprengtporten, who had followed the developments from the Russian side of the border. He made the mistake of sending old General K. G. Armfelt, who enjoyed great prestige, a detailed program for action aimed at cutting Finland off from the mother country. Although Armfelt had signed the Liikkala "note", he had probably done so on the basis of misinformation, and his spirit of opposition, like that of the majority of the officers who participated in the Anjala League, was motivated on constitutional grounds or by defeatism, certainly not by separatism. The general was horrified by Sprengtporten's proposals and gave one of his letters to Duke Charles, who dreamed of one day gaining the Swedish throne and certainly desired no reduction in the size of his future domain. Since no attack from the Russian side was to be expected, the duke ordered the troops to disband to winter quarters, where the officers had no opportunity for scheming or conspiring. The troops obeyed.

The last flare-up of the independence movement was the "diet" that met in December at the frontier estate of Paaso. Consisting of certain of the gentry living in the border region, it declared the independence of Finland, requested armed assistance from the Empress, and elected Sprengtporten as leader.

Meanwhile, Gustavus III had succeeded in reviving Swedish memories of the glorious days of Gustavus Vasa and in building up a solid front against Denmark. The Danish attack was beaten back, and since even the Danes felt no joy over the prospect of Russia's growing too strong, they agreed to a truce.

Having thereby consolidated his position, the king dispatched orders to Finland for the imprisonment of a number of mutinous subjects. Jägerhorn, Klick, and several other officers had managed to flee to Russia, where the Empress lent anything but an enthusiastic ear to their Utopian plans: The separatist activities of the Finns unmistakably bored her. But the majority of the accused men continued to stick to their posts on the Finnish front. "One day they had to face a court martial and the next, or even the same, day risk their lives in battle against the enemy." After hearings that lasted two years, the supreme military court sentenced eighty-seven officers to die. The condemned men appealed to the king for mercy. Gustavus III released the majority from every penalty and ordered only one man to be executed, but even in decreeing royal pardons this whimsical monarch could not refrain from giving rein to his personal antipathies or sympathies. In any event, there were many who had to be given a scare and few who had to suffer actual punishment. Yet, from the moment the executioner chopped off the head of Colonel J. H. Hästesko, one of the signers of the Liikkala "note," extremists in the opposition began to plot the king's assassination.

The King's Counterattack

Before his violent end, Gustavus III achieved a series of the most brilliant triumphs of his life. The Finnish people did not stand behind the stiff-necked officers but behind their king, for the hereditary fear of Russia weighed far more in the balance than the indignation over Gustavus III's unlawful recourse to war. The government's proclamation citing the fate of Poland and the Crimea as a warning to Finns inclined to rely on the independence proffered by the Russians and the sermons of preachers describing the horrors of the Great Wrath were scarcely needed to fan royalist zeal among the rank and file of the Finnish population. In Sweden, again, the king placed his adversaries in a bad light by identifying the constitutional opposition with Finnish separatism.

Both in Finland and in Sweden this constitutional opposition had gained headway among the nobility. Favorably disposed as he had originally been toward the nobility, the king was therefore reluctantly obliged to come to closer terms with the untitled Estates. For this purpose, it was necessary to convene the Diet—which the opposition had desired, which the seditious officers had demanded, and which the Russian Czarina had considered as a means of achieving her ends. Now, at last, it happened by the free will of the Swedish king, and it was far from his intention to summon the Estates in order to confess his sins to them. On the contrary, in his eloquent opening address, he charged Russia with attempting to dictate to the people of Sweden "laws whereby he thinks he can best keep you under his yoke."

It was on February 17, 1789, that Gustavus III summoned all four Estates to a joint session, which culminated in perhaps the most dramatic episode in the long history of the Swedish-Finnish Diet. In his speech, he fiercely attacked the nobility and then ordered all the members of that Estate to leave the throne room. The moment that followed was one of those during which the destiny of a nation seems to perch on a razor's edge. Would the nobles obey the king's command? If not, it was to be feared that the conflict might become aggravated to the point of precipitating civil strife. But the nobles departed.

Having thus given vent to his feelings toward the nobles, the king urged the untitled Estates to choose representatives from their own ranks to confer with him on amendments to the Constitution. Delegates were picked, and they leveled some criticisms at the proposals advanced by the king: but, on disbanding, the delegation did not learn whether the taciturn monarch had taken notice of their remarks or not. On February 21, a proposal was read out to the Estates concerning the amendments to be made in the Form of Government. Once more, as on the occasion of the *coup d'état* seventeen years earlier, they were required to make their decision immediately, in joint session, without discussion, and while the leaders of the nobles were under arrest. When the vote was taken, the "Nays" were clearly in the majority among the nobles, whereas only cries of "Yaa!" could be heard among the non-nobles—but most of the clergymen appear to have remained silent.

Later, the nobles took up the law proposal in a private session and unanimously rejected it. Notwithstanding, the king signed the law, although, even according to the loosest juridical interpretation, at least some of the amendments introduced were of a type that required the acceptance of all four Estates. In that ugly manner, the Act of Union and Security took its place as the constitutional law of Sweden-Finland alongside the Form of Government of 1772, which remainded in force to the extent that it had not been amended.

In the very same year that absolute monarchy in France was overthrown by the revolution, the Act of Union and Security placed unrestricted executive power in the hands of the king of Sweden. It was now possible for Gustavus III to abolish the ancient, venerable Council of the Realm and, in making decisions, to solicit the counsel of "kitchen cabinets," which had no legal standing and therefore possessed no authority. Also, the rights of the Diet were curtailed. As a return gift, the king took steps to improve the social position of the yeomen. But the clergy and the burghers, who had demonstrated a comparable readiness to serve their sovereign, were disappointed in their hopes of a reward.

Gustavus III's War

The war with Russia had to be continued, for pride and ambition prevented Gustavus III from begging the Czarina for peace and forced him to show foreign governments that the Swedish army obeyed his orders. Although he planned an offensive, the initiative was taken by the Russians. The enemy penetrated into the province of Savo, where on June 13, 1789, at Porrassalmi, the Finns, under G. H. Jägerhorn, repulsed an attack by a Russian army that outnumbered them seven to one. Col. Sprengtporten, who fought on the side of the enemy, was wounded by a rifle bullet. After the Russians employed encircling tactics, however, the Finns were forced to withdraw from southern Savo. J. A. Jägerhorn, the former Finnish chief adjutant, followed the Russian troops in Finnish officer's uniform, and his mission was to incite the peasants of Savo to fight against the Swedish-Finnish army; the objectives now appeared to be a revision of the Swedish Form of Government and a more independent status for Finland under the hegemony of Sweden.

The politicizing ended abruptly when the Finns defeated the Russians at Parkumäki and compelled them to return the territory they had captured. It was the first offensive victory scored since the days of Charles XII, and thanksgiving services were held in all the churches of the realm. In a more important sector of the front, at Kymijoki, on the other hand, no gains could be made because one of the Swedish generals beat a retreat in defiance of orders, and the Russians inflicted a shattering defeat on the galley fleet. In the autumn, the positions were unchanged, after a summer during which internal dissension had paralyzed Finnish-Swedish military operations. Many a Finnish noble was reported to have awaited Sprengtporten as the "savior of the country" and to have kept a Russian flag on hand to be raised over the roof of his manor house, whereas the peasants believed that their rich harvest was a reward from God for their loyalty to the king.

Since no decision had been reached, the king went back to his original plan of war. All winter long, strenuous work was done to build up the galley fleet, and by spring it contained 350 units, equipped with a total of 3,000 cannon. Immediately after the sea had broken the winter ice block, the combined high seas and coastal fleets sailed, under the personal command of the king, into the eastern corner of the Gulf of Finland. There, the Russians shut them up in the Bay of Viipuri and a stubborn west wind made it impossible to attempt a breakthrough for several weeks. When the wind finally changed, Gustavus succeeded in opening up a path of escape, but he had to pay a heavy price in ships sunk and men lost, and the expedition, which had set forth with such soaring hopes, ended in another humiliating setback. Against the advice, therefore, of nearly all miliary experts, the king ordered his galley fleet, on July 9, to engage the Russian coastal fleet of approximately the same strength in the Ruotsinsalmi narrows. The gamble ended in one of the most spectacular victories in the military annals of Sweden-Finland: The Russians lost fifty-two vessels and 9,000 men, the Swedish-Finnish flotilla only six vessels and 300 men. The result of the Russian debacle was that the Czarina agreed to discuss peace.

At the negotiations held in the village of Värälä, Sweden-Finland was represented by G. M. Armfelt, who was a more experienced and skillful diplomat than his Russian counterpart. The boundaries were left unchanged in the treaty that was signed in August, 1790, although Russia did give vague (and subsequently forgotten) promises of minor revisions. The Empress at first demanded a pardon for the signers of the Anjala Covenant, whose fate had not yet been finally decided, but she yielded on this point. Section 7 of the Peace of Uusikaupunki was expressly cancelled, but it should be remembered that no provision entitling Russia to meddle in Sweden's internal affairs had been included even in the Peace of Turku. When, therefore, Gustavus III boasted, after the signing of the new peace treaty, that his domain had retrieved not only her honor but also "independence", he was certainly guilty of overstatement. Her honor alone had been at stake. And posterity could see that Gustavus III's war proved one thing: That Sweden-Finland was incapable of defeating Russia's northwestern army even when the main military forces of the Czarist empire were occupied in the south.

Finland at the Crossroads

In March, 1792, J. J. Anckarström, a member of the nobles' conspiracy, shot Gustavus III with a pistol. The mortally wounded king still had time to amend his testament, and he decreed that, in addition to Duke Charles, four of his confidants, among them the Finn G. M. Armfelt, serve as regents on behalf of his minor son, Gustavus Adolphus. But scarcely had the physician announced that the king's heart had stopped beating when Charles had the royal will opened and declared the amended version void. He became sole regent, and was guided by his ambitious friend G. A. Reuterholm. Baron Reuterholm paraded as a Jacobinite, but when he undertook to form an alliance with the France ruled by the National Convention, he could hardly have done it so much out of admiration for the revolution as out of a desire to cross the friends and advisers of Gustavus III, or so-called Gustavians, whom he violently hated. By this move, he angered Empress Catherine, who regarded it as her mission to protect Europe from contamination by revolutionary France. As often happens in history, the enraged Gustavians adopted the program of their erstwhile opponents: Baron Armfelt called upon the Czarina to demand that Duke Charles change his advisers. The advisers heard about the plans of the Gustavians and, although their innocuousness ought to have been revealed by the trunkful of letters that Reuterholm's spies stole from Armfelt, the duke staged a treason trial, blown up out of all proportions, in which the principals on both sides were Finns—for Reuterholm also had been born in Finland and owned estates there. Armfelt saved himself by fleeing to Russia.

The military peril threatening the kingdom was by no means averted by exposing the "conspiracy." On the contrary, Russia had just finished carrying out the latest division of Poland and was free to act on its northwestern boundary. A general mobilization had to be put into effect in Finland. But Empress Catherine died in 1796, and at about the same time, the regency in Sweden ended as the prince came of age.

Gustavus IV Adolphus is commonly portrayed as stupid but honest, though in reality he was neither. Surely, he was not the ridiculous dunce that the Finns, influenced by Runeberg's "Tales of Ensign Stål," think of him as having been; but he did lack his father's eloquence and, because he was dogmatic and obstinate, he was inflexible in his choice of methods. In the administration of internal affairs, he encountered incomparably less difficulty than his father, for he inherited the new constitutional laws drawn up through his father's efforts whereby the people and the Diet pledged their fealty, and nearly total authority was placed in the king's hands. In other words, the new king was in a position to do lawfully and without fear of criticism what Gustavus III had done unlawfully, thereby provoking opposition and, in the end, inviting an assassin's bullet. Moreover, the general European background of public opinion had undergone a change in favor of royalty during the years following the execution of the French king, when France had experienced the reign of terror under the National Convention. Gustavus IV Adolphus convened the Diet only once during his whole reign and, for all the noise it made, the opposition formed by the nobility remained insignificant.

Even though the administration of internal affairs was easy, foreign relations placed a heavy burden on the young king. Preserving the neutrality of the country during the wars and ceaseless changes of political constellations sweeping across the whole of Europe, which started in 1792 and lasted throughout the period of the French Revolution and Napoleon's time, would probably have proved beyond the capacity of a far more skillful statesman than Gustavus IV Adolphus. At first, the king tried to follow a middle course, but later, especially after Napoleon had crowned himself emperor, he made no serious effort to maintain neutrality. His personal antipathy toward the upstart ruler of France, whom some German augur persuaded him to believe to be the beast of the Apocalypse, bound Sweden absolutely, and in disregard of all the facts, to the opponents of Napoleon. That experienced and wise statesman, Baron Armfelt, who had returned from exile, explained to the king in vain that upholding the cause of righteousness was the business of God, whereas the duty of a temporal ruler was to look after the interests of his own subjects.

Sweden proved to be an acceptable ally to England, to which she was bound by commercial interests, and to Russia. In 1805, using as a base the remnants of Sweden's possessions in German territory, the king joined the war against Napoleon; but, before long, he was compelled to ship what was left of his expeditionary force from Pomerania to the safety of the mother country. When Russia and France made peace and became allies, and Sweden was thus threatened by war from the east, Gustavus IV Adolphus again demonstrated his dogmatic foreign policy by tactlessly returning the cross of the order of St. Anne, which he had received from Czar Alexander, because the Czar had bestowed the same decoration on Napoleon.

As the general European war raged, Finland was exposed to a constant threat of invasion. A program drawn up by General Klingspor, who was pretty much of a stranger to the Finns, had been accepted as the official plan of defense for Finland. Based on an avowal of weakness, it must have appeared downright cynical in Finnish eyes. The army was to be spared; therefore, it was to yield before superior odds. If the attack took place in winter, all Finland, with the exception of Svartholm (the island fortress at the border), Sveaborg, and Ostrobothnia, was to be surrendered, and only the next spring, when the Swedish fleet could bring aid, were measures to be taken toward reconquering the country.

The enlightened Finnish public, which followed events in Europe, saw how the map was changing year after year and how entire countries were vanishing. Finland had been occupied by the Russians twice, and for over six decades there had been talk in one connection or another about her being seized by Russia. Against this background, it is understandable that the Finnish educated classes should have become resigned to the idea that their country might become separated from Sweden.

Henrik Gabriel Porthan, professor of eloquence in the University of Turku, observed to the young poet F. M. Franzén: "We must pray to God that Russia will succeed in situating its capital in Constantinople. Then it might leave remote Finland in peace under the scepter of Sweden. But, now that its capital city is located so near, I am afraid that Finland will sooner or later fall under the power of Russia... I hope that I won't have to witness this misfortune, but you may live to see it, you, who are young."

Professor Porthan did not have to witness that "misfortune"; he died in 1804. Yet, as the most outstanding cultural personality of his nation, he had trained a generation that, in changed circumstances and under the hegemony of Russia, was to uphold and propagate the national tradition that he had initiated. Political separatism was alien and disagreeable to Porthan. He didn't even use Finnish as the chief language in his publications—notwithstanding the fact that he considered Finnish to be his mother tongue. Nevertheless, as the first critical student of Finnish history, the Finnish language, and Finnish folklore, he laid the foundation for the national awakening to come. His own interest in things Finnish was inherited from his mother's uncle, Daniel Juslenius, and stimulated by his youthful environment, which was peopled by early Fennophiles.

Thanks to Porthan and his pupils and colleagues, intellectual life in Turku attained an unprecedented vigor. The first literary society and the first newspapers in Finland were founded in that city, and the previously backward scientific research took such a leap forward that one English observer praised the University of Turku as being as much in advance of Uppsala as the latter was in advance of Lund.

The inhabitants of the different provinces of Finland and the members of the different Finnish estates had begun to be increasingly conscious during the latter half of the 1700's of their Finnish identity—in contrast to the Swedes living on the other side of the Gulf of Bothnia. The expansion of local spirit to love of country—meaning the Finnish part of the realm of Sweden—led to many a joint action in the Diet. The Finnish representatives were unswervingly loyal to their king, but they had to be reminded on occasion that Finland was joined to Sweden, and that Swedes were subjects of the selfsame king.

Thus, Finland braced herself for the great change, and even when she became politically joined to Russia, she kept her Western legal system and cultural heritage.

7

Finland Becomes an Autonomous State

The War for Possession of Finland

In June 1807, when almost the entire continent of Europe was under the thumb of either Napoleon or Alexander I, the two emperors met at Tilsit. At their momentous meeting, it was decided that Russia would undertake to mediate peace between France and England. If England refused to come to terms, Russia would declare war on her by a set date. Pressure also would be put on Portugal, Denmark, and Sweden, which formed wide gaps in Napoleon's continental blockade, to break off relations with England. If Sweden refused, she would be treated as an enemy by the Russians and subjected to punitive measures by the Danes, too. In the war then raging between Russia and Turkey, France would act as mediator; and if satisfactory results could not be achieved at the negotiations, the French and the Russians would divide the biggest part of the Balkan peninsula between themselves.

Czar Alexander was interested in expansion mainly toward the southwest, whereas the prospect of war with Sweden did not please him and hostilities with England appeared not only to involve a dangerous military risk but also could be economically ruinous.

The Czar at first hoped that the Danish navy would be capable of bottling up the Baltic Sea, thereby protecting Russia's most vulnerable shorelines from British naval action. But by a powerful surprise attack in September the British captured the entire Danish fleet. Yet, under heavy pressure from two sides, Denmark joined the Tilsit system—even though she had lost her naval forces. The threat of landings by hostile troops caused Russia to concentrate strong military units on the coast of the Gulf of Finland. Nor were the troop concentrations kept secret; on the contrary, exaggerated reports about them were spread abroad in order to intimidate Gustavus IV Adolphus and turn him away from England. The Swedish king, however, showed no sign of alarm. And, prodded by Napoleon's repeated reminders of the commitments of the Tilsit pact, Russia began in November to make preparations for an attack. Alexander's desire to avoid war as long as possible is borne out by the fact that delivery of the already prepared declaration of war was postponed for a month. Sweden still did not yield, so on February 21, 1808, Alexander ordered his troops to march across the Finnish border.

Russia thus instituted military sanctions against Sweden in order to fulfill its duty as an ally—not to wage a war of conquest. In a proclamation to the Finnish people, signed only by the commander-in-chief, it was stated that the Czar had decided to take possession of Finland "for the time being," or until the Swedish king agreed to come to terms with Napoleon. Moreover, the fact that at an early stage of operations Napoleon began to urge Alexander to carry his offensive against Sweden proper as well, indicates that the conquest of Finland was a secondary objective.

In accordance with the terms of the treaty of Tilsit, Sweden-Finland was simultaneously confronted by another foe, Denmark. And in the mother country, the southern front was regarded as the main one. Denmark did not amount to a serious threat, however, for the British fleet prevented Napoleon's troops from crossing the Sound. And the king's unrealistic estimation of the situation was probably influenced by the fact that several of his advisers happened to be natives of Skåne province. Whatever the reason, the defense of Finland was left wholly to her own forces. The total strength of the Finnish army was 22,000 men, and there had been plenty of time during the long period of the threat of hostilities to carry out the mobilization and troop concentrations. The Russians put 24,000 men into the field; hence their numerical superiority was very slight. But the reserve strength of the invaders was practically inexhaustible, whereas the Finns had only a few reserves to draw on and these dwindled to almost nothing during the long retreat.

The Russian commander-in-chief was the veteran Lieutenant-General F. W. von Buxhoevden. At the head of the Finnish forces, however, was General W. M. Klingspor, who had been active mainly in the supply service and whose portrait was later sketched by the poet Runeberg in one short line: "Two chins had he, one eye, and only half a heart." As a scapegoat, he has been made out to be worse than he actually was, for he was forced to bear the responsibility for a plan of war indifferent to the fate of the Finnish people and for the unsuccessful implementation of that plan. The truth is that an addition had been made—presumably on the king's initiative—to the secret orders that retreat was justified only in the face of absolute necessity. Both Klingspor and the majority of his officers employed pre-Napoleonic methodef warfare, aiming at the attainment of limited objectives and forgetting the lessons taught by Sprengtporten about making the terrain an ally. The higher officers in command of Finnish units had been trained along old-fashioned lines and they lacked vigour, whereas the Russian officers, fresh from campaigning in Central Europe, had a more modern conception of warfare. The attitude of the Finns toward the war revealed the same split in the ranks of the nation as during the reign of Gustavus III: The common people had a horror of the centuries-old enemy, and the soldiers were willing to fight, while a large part of the educated class felt that the wisest course was to reach a quick understanding with the invaders. The attitude of the educated class also prevailed among garrison officers, but it was not so strong among the officers in command of the troops that were maintained on the farms.

General Klingspor, who had been in Sweden when the Russian invasion started, hastened to the headquarters of the Finnish army and held a council of war. The reports about what took place are contradictory, but disagreement arose apparently only with regard to the timetable and route of retreat. The start was hastened by the withdrawal of the army in Savo, which was faster than expected: Oulu had to be reached before the enemy could march there from eastern Finland along the main roads. Since, moreover, reconnaissance was poor, the haste in fleeing the evenly matched enemy forces was such that hardly any contact between the opposing sides occurred. Eventually, however, after the Russians had spread out along the southern coast, they were outnumbered by the Finns. But Klingspor was simply bent on saving his army.

When the retreat ended at last in northern Ostrobothnia, credit for the successful operation went, not to Klingspor, but to his chief of staff, C. J. Adlercreutz. It was during a skirmish at Siikajoki between the advance Russian troops and the retreating Finns that Adlercreutz had delivered a counter-blow on his own responsibility. There was little to boast about in the victory scored, for the Finns outnumbered their pursuers three to one. However, it did raise the Finnish morale — and Klingspor then permitted his army to attempt an offensive, which succeeded. The Russians decided there was no alternative to withdrawing a long distance southward. At first, the Finns pursued the enemy slowly. Then, during the summer, they recaptured a large part of Savo province and all of Ostrobothnia.

It was at that stage of the war that many of the battles glorified by Runeberg in his "Tales of Ensign Stål" were fought, including the first full-scale battle in the field. That battle was fought at Lapua on the 14th of July, which is celebrated as a provincial holiday in southern Ostrobothnia to this day. Typically, the Finnish attack at Lapua was made by the troops on their own initiative, without consulting their officers. And after the enemy had been routed, the officers failed to follow up the advantage gained. Meanwhile, at the enemy's rear, the local peasants set fire to his provisions and carried out raids on his supply column.

It was during the summer campaign that the Swedish plan of war had called for the reconquest of the territory lost to the invader, with the assistance of the Swedish navy, while the sealanes were open. But it miscarried. From the southern coast, paralyzing news had reached the army: Sveaborg, the "Gibraltar of the North," had surrendered! Its garrison of seven thousand had outnumbered the besieging forces; its artillery had been many times stronger; it had had plenty of food and ammunition; its commandant had been the hero of the glorious naval victory at Ruotsinsalmi, Vice-Admiral C. O. Cronstedt. Even while the sea had been ice-locked, Alexander had not dared to risk an assault, which in all likelihood would have ended in disaster. And after the ice had broken up, conquest of the heavily fortified islands would have been an even more formidable task—especially if the Swedish fleet had, according to expectations, maintained contact between the home country and the garrison. After a few days of feeble artillery fire, Cronstedt nevertheless signed an agreement with the Russians on April 6 whereby the fortress and the fleet of galleys under its protection would surrender unless at least five Swedish ships of the line sailed into the harbour of Sveaborg by May 3. The agreement was almost tantamount to a capitulation that was postponed for a month, as Cronstedt must have known that the waters around Helsinki are not normally free of the icy grip of winter until the end of April. Moreover, nobody in Sweden realized the need of haste in getting the men-of-war under sail, for the Russians delayed the delivery of the message that was anticipated by the agreement; it did not reach the royal court in Stockholm until May 3!

Historians have done painstaking research to discover the reasons for Cronstedt's baffling conduct, but have failed to uncover any completely satisfactory explanation. The admiral took no bribe, neither did he receive any tokens of gratitude from the Russians later in his life.

On the contrary, one thing is known for sure: the one-time separatist Klick had been busy hatching plots in Helsinki. And officers' wives residing in the city had obtained permission from the Russians in occupation to visit their husbands who were stationed in the fortress. It was not hard for these women to influence the minds of their husbands, whose decisions were dictated by the utilitarian morality of the Age of Enlightenment. Expediency was the criterion of duty, as it applied to both citizen and soldier. So what was the sense in fighting mighty Russia—especially since its ally was Napoleon, who was looked upon almost as a superhuman military genius? It was evidently impossible for Cronstedt to resist the increasingly solid front formed by his subordinates, who demanded capitulation. And pessimism was not alien to Cronstedt's character, either. The admiral was not the demoniac traitor that he has been viewed as by many generations of Finns who were influenced by the ''Tales of Ensign Stål''*, but he was too weak for his task. A contrast to the calculating officers was presented by the uncorrupted soldiers, who, following the surrender, refused to be drafted into the Russian service and secretly made their way to the fighting ranks of the Finnish army hundreds of miles away.

In spite of the loss of Sveaborg, Swedish forces made a number of landings on the Finnish coast, but they did not succeed in forming any beachheads. These operations did, however, prolong the war, for they tied down Russian troops to guarding the long coastline. For some time, plans were entertained in St. Petersburg to set up winter quarters for the Russian army in southern Finland. But since, thanks to reinforcements, the Russians outnumbered the Finnish troops at least two to one by the end of August, Gen. von Buxhoevden decided to initiate an offensive. In doing so, he followed Napoleon's tactics of seeking to destroy the opposing forces with a series of rapid strikes. In the gory battle of Ruona on September 1, however, the Finns displayed unheard-of tenacity and might have been able to stabilize the front for the winter, in spite of everything, if Adlercreutz, misled by erroneous intelligence about the military situation, had

---

* ''Take all that's dismal in the tomb,
Take all in life that's base,
To form one name of guilt and gloom
For that one man's disgrace,
'Twill rouse less grief in Finland's men
Than his at Sveaborg did then.''
(Translated from the Swedish by Charles Wharton Stork)

not issued orders to retreat. After that, the Finnish forces suffered several defeats, the worst of them at Oravainen on September 14, where part of their main body of troops was driven to chaotic flight. The king at this point relieved Klingspor of his command. But the general had still had time to conclude a truce, the terms of which included withdrawals—even in Savo, where the lake-strewn terrain and Colonel J. A. Sandels' skillfully managed defense had hampered the enemy's advance. At the end of the truce, winter was on its way, supply difficulties on both sides were formidable, and many men had fallen sick. A new truce, which was signed in November, called for the withdrawal of the Finnish troops across the Swedish border. Toward the end of winter, the Russians marched over the ice and around the Gulf of Bothnia to Sweden, and there the remnants of Finland's loyal army continued to fight for the realm from which their own native land had already been severed.

From Occupation to Annexation

The royalistic and anti-Russian sentiment that prevailed among the Finnish peasantry was not unknown to Gustavus IV Adolphus; and, relying on it, he had exhorted the Finnish peasants, even before the outbreak of hostilities, to engage in guerrilla operations at the enemy's rear. Popular uprisings had caused unexpected difficulties to Napoleon in certain of the lands he had conquered. Therefore, during the very first days of the war, Gen. von Buxhoevden had asked permission of the Czar to extract an oath of fealty from the Finns, after which every person who was caught giving aid and comfort to his own army could be treated as an anti-Czarist rebel. Persuasion was to be used in addition to intimidation.

The proclamation issued at the beginning of hostilities pledged the Russians to honor the native Lutheran faith and the privileges of the various estates as well as, in accordance with the ancient laws of the land, to convene the Diet. Both in Finland and abroad, the proclamation gave rise to the assumption that Russia was determined, regardless of Sweden's conduct, to take permanent possession of the country; but, on the other hand, it pacified the compliant educated class of Finland, although no great hopes could be placed in a Diet that was convening under the scepter of an autocrat. To the officials who had been trained according to the rationalism of the Age of Enlightenment, it was of secondary importance under whose authority they lived and worked, so long as they could enjoy personal security and the established benefits. The stand taken in Finland was the same as in the Central European countries that had been subjugated without trouble by Napoleon. The Eastern Orthodoxy of the Russian authorities no longer appeared to represent the menace that had been feared during the era of religious intolerance. The bitterness that the foreign policy and strategy of Gustavus IV Adolphus had generated in Finland had uprooted all feelings of allegiance to the Crown, as was stated in one passage of a contemporary diary, and there were those who directed their bitterness against Sweden as a whole for abandoning Finland to her own resources.

Having embraced that type of reasoning, the corps of public functionaries remained at their posts during the enemy's advance. And when the Russians, led by a military band, marched into the open national capital, Turku, the supreme court was in session, a public academic examination was in progress at the University, and the theatrical season was in full swing. Bishop J. Tengström (who later accepted a decoration from the Czar while hostilities were still raging) bid von Buxhoevden welcome at the city gates. And another, subsequent, bishop, in a sermon later delivered in connection with taking an oath of allegiance, turned fatalist: "A defenseless country is like the sea; who is there to call it sin if its waves roll up the shore the wind has driven them to? God has given us a ruler, and we must hold him up in honor." In contrast, the enemy's exhortations to the soldiers of the Finnish army in the field to surrender their arms and go back home fell on deaf ears. In the army, orders were obeyed, whether the command was to retreat or to advance.

At first, the only orders were to retreat, and nearly the whole of Finland fell into Russian hands without serious opposition. Buxhoevden hastened to transform the occupation into annexation and succeeded in persuading the Czar to give his consent, on the 28th of March, to the issuance of a proclamation that joined Finland to the Russian empire and allowed the military commander-in-chief to require an oath of fealty from the Finns. The promised session of the Diet was now conceived to be only an occasion at which the Estates ceremoniously took the oath, and in the manifesto published a short time later in the name of the Ministry of Foreign Affairs, which promised Finland certain economic advantages, there was no reference to the Diet.

Copies of von Buxhoevden's proclamation were also delivered to foreign powers. According to the official account, which many historians have accepted as correct, the reason for the change in the Czar's plans was his resentment over the fact that Gustavus IV Adolphus had ordered the imprisonment of the Russian ambassador to Stockholm. Yet, as gross a violation of diplomatic etiquette as the king's singular act was, such things do not decide the policies of great powers; the true reason apparently was Alexander's realization that Napoleon would not tolerate a Russian advance into the Balkans, as a result of which he was obliged to seek territorial aggrandizement in the North. Simultaneously, it became clear that there was no longer time to march across the ice into Sweden—at least, not that winter—and that there was no likelihood of a penetration from Denmark, either, so that the chances of compelling Sweden to join the continental blockade were gone.

The proclamation that annexed Finland to the Czarist realm was re-issued in the name of the Czar himself in June at a time when the Finnish army was advancing on both the western and eastern ends of the front and the spirit of resistance among the civilian population was rising. In spite of every threat, there were those who refused to take the oath demanded by the Russians. No less a personage than the rector of the University of Turku, M. Calonius, boldly defended the citizens who would not yield, and Bishop Tengström had become so widely hated for his submissiveness that he went into hiding. Finnish resistance was a factor Alexander had to take into account, and he announced that, out of concern for the welfare of his Finnish subjects, he wished them to send a deputation representing all four Estates to St. Petersburg. The elections of the deputies were conducted obediently, but at many of the election meetings it was strongly emphasized that the deputation was not to act with the prerogatives of the Diet. Before the deputation had time to assemble in St. Petersburg in November, the Russians had conquered all of Finland and Alexander had met Napoleon again at Erfurt.

Owing to the military setbacks he had suffered and the threat of war with Austria, the French dictator's position was now weaker than it had been during the previous summit conference; and it was now that he really did what history textbooks for many generations have said he had done at Tilsit: he promised Finland to Russia. From that point on, Alexander had a free hand in every respect to decide on the future status of Finland. His interest had become focused on the organization of the internal affairs of his wide domain. It was Mihail Speransky, his most influential adviser at the time, who laid the plans for organizing around the Russian areas proper a zone in whose administration local differences were to be considered. Those areas might be looked upon as an experimental field for applying the ideals of the Age of Enlightenment. That zone was to include Finland.

When the Finnish deputation, led by Baron C. E. Mannerheim (who had been condemned to death for his participation in the Anjala League but later pardoned), arrived in St. Petersburg, it refused to act without the authority of the Diet. The Czar's benevolent response was that the Finnish Diet would shortly be convoked. Moreover, on the 1st of December, he decreed that matters pertaining to Finland were to be presented directly to him, bypassing the Russian ministers. This decree laid the basis for establishing Finland's special status; but it did not yet create a Finnish state, for that document alone did not provide the necessary substance of national autonomy.

The advocates of submission, like Tengström, attributed the favorable outcome to the magnanimity of the victor and the wise submissiveness of the vanquished. The change in the Czar's politics had taken place, however, precisely at the time when the Finnish forces were victoriously pushing forward; and, to a higher degree than people suspected at the time, current events on the world stage affected the fortunes of Finland. Yet, in the achievement of national autonomy, Col. Sprengtporten also played a part.

From Annexation to Autonomy

Those Finnish champions of national independence who had gone to Russia during the reign of Gustavus III did not remain inactive during the Finnish War. That incorrigible dreamer Jägerhorn imagined that the Czar would bestow on Finland not only autonomy but also a new form of government, which would closely follow the lines of the one in effect in Sweden-Finland during the Age of Freedom. After all, Russia had at that time endeavoured to maintain that system in Sweden which gave the Diet predominant control of affairs; and Jägerhorn and his small Finnish following did not seem to comprehend that a system favoured by one power in an opposing country would not be tolerated at home. Once again, Klick was more Russian than the Russians in demanding that

Finland be absorbed into the Czarist realm as a governmental district.

Sprengtporten, by contrast, combined realistic political thinking with a concern for the interests of Finland in his activities, and, thereby, the old man belatedly attained, in the last works of his life, the status of a true statesman. Before the outbreak of hostilities, he had experimentally broached the idea of setting up Finland as a separate state, to be ruled by some member of the Czarist family. To this proposal, the Czar would not agree, but the proclamation issued after the outbreak of war, with its promises to the Finnish people, bore the stamp of Sprengtporten. But his personal aversion to the constitutional laws passed by Gustavus III was so strong that he opposed their ratification. On the other hand, throughout the war, Sprengtporten had skillfully kept alive the idea of having the Diet convoked; and, in the beginning, he had had such a falling out with von Buxhoevden that he declined the offered post of Governor-General of Finland. When, however, his plan at last triumphed, he accepted the appointment and returned to his native land as her mightiest son. But, during his brief term in office, he was unable to close the gap between himself and his countrymen.

Upon the approach of a new Central European war, the Czar hastened to summon the Estates without waiting for the termination of hostilities with Sweden. The Diet met at the little episcopal town of Porvoo (Borgå) in March, 1809, and at that session Finland was established as an autonomous state. It would have been extremely difficult psychologically for the autocratic Czar to undertake the enactment of special constitutional laws for conquered lands. But, in pledging to respect the rights thitherto enjoyed by the inhabitants, he could also, without exciting amazement in Russia, ratify existing laws. The markedly monarchistic character of the constitutional laws in force in Finland—the Form of Government of 1772 and the Act of Union and Security that amended it in certain fundamental respects—made it easy in practice, too, for the Czar to observe them without needing to make much of a compromise with his absolute powers. Without Gustavus III's two *coups d'état,* the ratification of the constitutional laws inherited by Finland from Sweden would have demanded of the Czar a greater sacrifice than he would have been capable of, and the Finns would probably have been left without a constitution.

In the Diet the Finnish people pledged their fealty to the Russian Czar, who, in turn, ratified "the religion and fundamental Laws of the Land, as well as the privileges and rights which each estate in the said Grand Duchy, in particular, and all the inhabitants, in general, be their position high or low, have hitherto enjoyed." The moral inhibitions that perhaps troubled the members of the Diet, because they had to violate their oath of allegiance to the Swedish sovereign in order to swear one to the Czar, were removed a couple of weeks before the estates met at Porvoo by a *coup d'état* in Sweden. The ancient appellation of Grand Duchy that had been given Finland had now been endowed with real significance, and the Czar himself affirmed in his concluding speech that the Finns had been "elevated to membership in the family of nations." Any attempt to interpret the Czar's use of the word *nation* (in the French text) in merely the ethnic sense fails on both philological and textual grounds. Ethnically, the Finns had always been a nation, and no sovereign can create an ethnic nation by arbitrary decree. It has been demonstrated that in his correspondence in the French language, Alexander I used the word *nation* in the political sense. These words of the Czar were construed a few years later as the pillars of Finland's "political existence."

Thus the Finns made a contract with the Czar of Russia establishing their future status before the conclusion of peace. Finland never became a Russian province, as would have happened had the Diet been convened after the peace treaty had taken effect. In the Peace of Hamina, signed in September, Sweden ceded the eastern half of the kingdom to Russia. The boundary between the states was drawn to coincide with the Muonio and Tornio Rivers, or slightly farther west than the line between the administrative areas considered part of Finland and those designated as Swedish, but somewhat farther east than the limits of the territory inhabited by Finnish-speaking people. Sweden did her utmost to retain possession of the Aland Islands, even to the point of appealing to Napoleon. But it was all in vain. Since, at the express demand of the Russians, no clause was included in the treaty concerning the autonomy of the Finns, the status of Finland was not secured by an international agreement, such as that of another country conquered by the Russians—Poland—whose autonomy was guaranteed by the Congress of Vienna.

Finland had been part of the Swedish kingdom and her inhabitants had participated as subjects of the Swedish monarch in all administrative affairs. In their new position, the Finns had no share in political administration in Russia, of course, and the ruler of Finland was determined by the Russian order of succession. On the other hand, the Finns were able to exercise within the grand duchy all the authority not reserved for the Czar as grand duke. This authority did not amount to much, but the constitutional laws, which were reaffirmed by each Czar in turn, guaranteed a certain minimum extent of it. In Russian quarters, though, it was subsequently argued that what Alexander I had conferred on Finland came from his magnanimity and omnipotence and that his gift could be withdrawn at any time. The Finns responded (and their stand was supported by Western jurisprudence) that the matter was not one of a gift but of a contract binding on both parties; and they reminded the Russians that, in 1816, Alexander I extended the binding powers of the agreement to include his successors as well, upon his delivering a pledge to continue to uphold the fundamental laws of Finland "forevermore... under Our scepter and that of Our successors."

What, then, was the power of the grand duke according to the constitutional laws ratified by Alexander I? The Form of Government of 1772 and the Act of Union and Security had been drawn up by Gustavus III and approved by the Diet under his royal pressure. The power that belonged to the nation had been deliberately left vaguely defined in these documents. Not even all the indisputable clauses could be literally applied in autonomous Finland, moreover, since the laws had been drafted to serve an independent realm.

The executive power was totally vested in the sovereign. The Act of Union and Security catalogued a host of royal prerogatives, among them the right to "decide upon the offices of the realm." The Czar thus had a free hand to organize the administrative institutions of Finland. The authority of the sovereign to decide on public offices did not signify the right to dismiss officials without due legal examination and trial: on the contrary, the Act of Union and Security guaranteed irremovability to the majority of the officials.

Convocation of the Diet depended on the ruler, but without its consent he could not enact new laws or amend old ones, or require the payment of new taxes. Both of these fundamental rights of the Diet were, however, considerably restricted. The sovereign had the right to issue decrees in regard to all such matters as were not embodied in the laws enacted by the Diet. It was incontestable that the Czar was obliged to obtain the approval of the Estates in order to carry out any revisions of the law relating to the constitution, class privileges, general civil and criminal statutes, the foundations of the military establishment, the church system, and the state bank.

The Estates also possessed the right to determine the "weight and purity" of money, i.e., to enact the currency laws, and this provision eventually gave rise to many a theoretical controversy. The acceptability of paper, silver, or gold rubles as legal tender was one of the prime problems of monetary policy in Finland during the Russian régime; but the decisions did not concern the "weight and purity" of the ruble, which was something the Finnish Diet could have no authority to deal with. Finally, the Form of Government provided, in its vague way, that if "some new question of law should arise," the procedure should be the same as in enacting other laws. With a little good will, it was, of course, possible on the basis of this provision to add to the number of legislative fields that required the co-operation of the Diet. On the other hand, the sovereign was in position to decide important matters, too, by decree, provided that he avoided directly contradicting laws passed by the Diet.

The significance of the right to approve taxes was reduced by the fact that the state economy at the beginning of the nineteenth century was essentially based on the land rent, which the farmers had been forced to pay ever since medieval times and which they continued to pay year after year in unchanged amounts. In the kingdom of Sweden, it was also necessary to collect, in addition, special provisional taxes, which the Diet approved for a prescribed time. During the Russian régime, such taxes were required in Finland for only a short period, and the Diet could then be left unconvened for over half a century without violating its rights in the endorsement of taxes. The Diet had no say in levying customs duties, this being strictly the business of the Czar.

Evidence of Finland's attainment of the position of a state was the fact that—in addition to her own laws, her own Diet, her own administrative system, and her own agency for presenting matters to the attention of the Czar—Russian subjects enjoyed no civil rights in Finland and that she maintained a customs boundary against the rest of the empire.

In organizing the administration of autonomous Finland, the point of departure was furnished by the institutions of Sweden, which were altered to the extent necessitated by the personal absence of the sovereign. In 1809, a Government Council was established as the highest administrative organ of state. It was to be composed of Finnish citizens, and the Diet in session at Porvoo was requested to draw up a report concerning its regulations. In 1816, the Czar conferred upon this organ the name of *Senate*, in order to make plain the fact that it was not subordinate to the highest Russian administrative body of the same name but rather on the same plane with it.

The Senate was not intended to act as a Finnish regency and, in the beginning, it could not be compared to the ancient Swedish Council of the Realm. It was empowered to make decisions only in such matters of small moment as had been customarily decided by the collegia and did not come under the jurisdiction of "highest authority." In the course of time, the administrative sphere of the Senate was enlarged, and it developed more and more into a "home government." Whenever the Senate was not entitled, or did not dare, to make a decision itself, it drew up a report on the matter, and the Czar often took into account the views therein expressed.

The Committee for Finnish Affairs, established in St. Petersburg and composed of Finnish citizens—of whom later only its influential secretary, known as the Minister Secretary of State, was retained—, was, in a certain sense, the Senate's twin. Its function was to present the proposals of the Senate to the Czar, but it was entitled to advocate a different solution. Also, the governor-general of Finland, who, after Sprengtporten's term, was always a Russian (since he was appointed to represent the Czar), expressed his own views, which often radically deviated from the recommendations of the Senate. He had the right to act as chairman at meetings of the Senate, but, on account of their deficient command of the Swedish language, the governors-general usually did not attend. The power that the chairman's post or the single vote he was entitled to cast would have brought to the governor-general was trifling compared with the influence he could exert directly on the Czar. Moreover, he was in charge of maintaining public order throughout the country, and he was commander of the Russian military forces in Finland.

Thus, the sessions of the Senate were actually under the direction of its vice-chairman, who, in regard to his station and influence, might almost be compared to a prime minister. The Senate resembled a modern ministerial cabinet more than it did the old Swedish Council of the Realm: its members held office only for a set term and, naturally, the Czar re-appointed only those senators who managed to retain his confidence; and, like ministers, some of the senators served as heads of various departments of the administrative system. Other senators composed the supreme court of justice, which meant that the country's highest judges were not in a politically independent position.

The fate of the Finnish army was also dealt with at the Diet of Porvoo. Under the protection of the mighty Russian empire, Finland was free from attack— that was the claim of the assembled Estates. This claim was intended to conceal the fact that up to that time it was the Finnish border with Russia that had been the principal site of warfare involving the Finns. If war were to break out with Sweden, the Estates boldly pointed out, " the state of mind of the Finns would long remain such that they could not easily be prevailed upon to turn their weapons against their former brothers." In line with the wishes of the Diet, the Czar dismissed, for the time being, the Finnish troops maintained on farms throughout the land. Both the regular and non-commissioned officers, however, were granted the right to draw their former emoluments as long as they lived.

This display of magnanimity toward the defeated army had a potent effect on the sentiment that prevailed among the educated class, favorably disposed as it already had been toward the new régime.

Finns who had social standing regarded it as a further gain for themselves that high offices opened up to them in their own country, whereas corresponding posts had been difficult for Finns to obtain during the Swedish régime. "Now every honest Finn should endeavour with all imaginable means to do his part in promoting the Czar's noble intentions to bring good fortune to the land of our birth," wrote one army major. "As now, during peacetime, I enjoy all my former rights and personal security, I should, in my opinion, lack a human heart if I were to hope for war and the restoration of Finland's former status just to be allowed to bear the name of a Swede ruled by a French prince."

Far-sighted Finns, among them that old Gustavian, G. M. Armfelt, who had returned to his own country, perceived the unfavourable psychological effect on the people of the lack of a national army. Russia's involvement in a war with Napoleon provided a tactically appropriate opportunity to recommend, by making an appeal on the ground of Finnish solidarity with the Czarist realm, the establishment of a national Finnish army. Alexander I did not consent to the institution of general conscription in Finland, but he did permit the formation of small enlisted Finnish military units.

At the beginning of the year 1812, the territory called "Old Finland" (according to the Russian viewpoint) was joined to the Grand Duchy; it was the territory ceded by the kingdom of Sweden in the peace treaties of Uusikaupunki and Turku. It is extremely rare for a victor to return territory to a conquered land, even when it has been brought under the rule of the conqueror. The formal juridical condition for this measure may be found in the type of personal union that was created between the huge empire and the tiny country, and this act of statesmanship may be viewed as an instance of the Czar-Grand Duke's close concern for the welfare of his Grand Duchy. Alexander was personally convinced of how much better conditions were in "Swedish" or "New" Finland than in "Russian" or "Old" Finland, where an attempt had been made to force a Russian stem to grow out of the roots of the Swedish-Finnish social system. However, mere solicitude for the welfare of a couple of hundred thousand subjects, or fear that they might constitute a warning to the inhabitants of "New Finland" as to what the fate of the latter would be under Russian rule, could not have inspired the Czar to take such a surprising step. It required a combination of various factors and many advocates.

Napoleon was just then preparing to invade Russia, and this wholesale real estate dealer was once more offering Finland to Sweden, where the sentiment favoring a war of revenge was strong. It was, however, perfectly clear that, even under the worst of circumstances, Russia would not permit Sweden to expand all the way to the outskirts of St. Petersburg. If the Swedish hopes were fulfilled, newly re-unified Finland would become split up again; the Finns accordingly had a strong reason to oppose an attack by their former mother country. Doubtless, the Czar had the further motive of wishing to form nationally and religiously homogeneous administrative areas. And at least three, if not four, of his influential advisers advocated re-unification: Sprengtporten, whose Finnish state, mapped out on the eve of the Finnish War, also included the territories previously conquered by the Russians; Armfelt, who received the appointment to the chairmanship of the Committee for Finnish Affairs; Count D. Alopaeus, a native of "Old Finland," who had carved out a career for himself as a diplomat in the service of the Czar; and also, perhaps, the Czar's Polish favorite, Prince Czartoryski.

The transfer of territory from the imperial domain to the Grand Duchy provoked displeasure in certain Russian quarters, and on two later occasions the possibilities were considered of shifting the border once again to bring the communes situated closest to St. Petersburg, i.e., the western part of the Karelian Isthmus, back on the Russian side; but the plan led to no action.

After the fashion of the scattered realms of former times, "Old Finland," along with Estonia and Livonia, had had somewhat different social institutions from the Russian governmental districts of the Czarist domain; for instance, total serfdom had not been established there. Certain special rights had even been granted to the inhabitants of the western strip of territory ceded to Russia by the terms of the Peace of Turku, as provided for in the treaty. Nevertheless, the enforcement of Swedish laws wrought a great change in the conditions that prevailed in the territory long since separated politically from the Swedish-Finnish realm. The most difficult question of all concerned the fiefs bestowed on Russian aristocrats by the Czars, which contained a third of the farms of "Old Finland." The feudal system had been abolished in Sweden-Finland as far back as the close of the seventeenth century, and it was generally anticipated that, following reunification, the rights of the Russian landlords in regard to the peasants of "Old Finland" would be curtailed, or at least strictly regulated. The opposite happened; in 1826, the feudal estates were proclaimed to be the absolute property of the landlords.

In the same year that Viipuri province was restored to Finland, the Czar made another momentous decision: the capital of the autonomous grand duchy was established in the small fortified town of Helsinki, which was protected by the guns of Sveaborg and was situated farther from Sweden than the "frontier city" of Turku. It was resolved that the new capital had to be invested with the trappings becoming its dignity. The planning was facilitated by a conflagration in the center of town. In charge of the project was the ex-Gustavian J. A. Ehrenström, who later became a senator, and the public buildings were designed by the German architect C. L. Engel. However, the Czar himself inspected every detail. Truly, Helsinki was to become, as Ehrenström remarked, "one of the most illustrious memorials of his reign."

Only an imperial command makes comprehensible the creation — in a town of only four thousand people, excluding the military garrisons — of a building complex which was one of the most monumental in all Europe. The new central square was lined on three sides by edifices that represented the basic elements in the public life of Finland in the nineteenth century: the Government Palace, the Cathedral, and the University. After the catastrophic fire of Turku in 1827, the University was also transferred to Helsinki. Interestingly enough, when the central administrative offices had been transferred earlier, the official reason was that their proximity had a distracting effect on the work of scholars. Soon, however, the vigilant eye of the government just across the square was considered to be more salutary to the pursuit of higher learning than the freedom of a provincial city had been.

8

National Awakening in the Shelter of Autonomy

Finland's diet was not convened for over half a century after the Estates had met at Porvoo in 1809. Suppressing the representative assembly of the Finns had not been the original intention of Alexander I. Many new laws that were being drafted were of such a nature as to require the approval of the Diet for their enactment. And in 1818, by command of the Czar, a Finnish House of Nobles was founded, in the roster of which were registered all the noble families of the land, so that the highest Estate might be organized for representation in the Diet. The next year, the Czar toured Finland, captivating both high-born and low-born with his personal charm. The basic aim of the tour was probably to work up popular sentiment in favor of the government in case the Estates were shortly summoned to meet.

But the summons did not come. Possibly, the negative experience that the Czar had in dealing with the Polish *sejm* discouraged him from engaging in further experiments, or else the idea ceased to interest him after he had immersed himself in religious mysticism. There was a deeper reason, too: after the downfall of Napoleon and the stabilization of the system championed by the Holy Alliance, Alexander no longer felt prompted to pay special attention to Finnish affairs or show special benevolence toward the Finnish people.

Hailing from far-off France, the Swedish Crown Prince Charles John (Bernadotte) was able to pursue policies free of emotional factors and traditions: he pledged Finland to Russia in return for Russia's pledging Norway to Sweden; and in 1812, at Turku, he concluded a treaty of alliance with Alexander.

Public opinion in Sweden no longer aspired toward the reconquest of Finland after the loss in the east had been compensated for by the victory in the west: the acquisition of Norway through a personal union. Sweden's unexpected entry into an alliance with Russia bewildered the unflinching Finnish friends of their old mother country. The future of Finland was thus no longer a problem to Russia: the country was an inseparable part of the Czar's empire and was geographically situated within Russia's system of alliances.

In 1823, Finland received a governor-general, A. Zakrevsky, who, unlike his predecessors, cared little for her special status. The Committee for Finnish

Affairs was abolished and Zakrevsky obtained leave to submit matters concerning Finland personally to the Czar, even past the Secretary of State for Finland. He also played a prominent role in pushing through the surprise decision concerning the fiefs of "Old Finland." Immediately after the death of Alexander in 1825, Zakrevsky made the Finnish people take an oath of fealty that was drafted on the Russian pattern and referred to the Czar as absolute ruler. But he had bet on the wrong horse. To the Russian throne ascended, not Constantine, for whom the oath had been formulated, but his brother, Nicholas—and, in the middle of the mutiny raging in Russia, Secretary of State R. H. Rehbinder obtained from Nicholas a solemn affirmation that he would honor the special status of Finland. Thereafter, a new oath was taken in Finland that corresponded to the legal position of the country.

The July revolution of 1830 and the political ferment that followed it in many European countries also affected the situation in Finland. Poland, which from the Russian point of view might easily be placed in the same category with Finland, revolted, while the Finns made no hostile move. The system created by the Holy Alliance began to break up and liberal democratic ideals scored triumphs in western countries, including Sweden. Although Russia was still able to gain a renewed treaty of alliance with Prussia and Austria for the preservation of autocracy, the political constellation had changed, and Finland once more found herself in the front lines. Consequently, the defense of Finland had to be strengthened, for one thing, and, for another, attention had to be given to the sentiment that prevailed among her inhabitants. Finnish behavior during the restless year of 1830 indicated that, at least, for the time being, the Finns could be trusted. So they should be kept satisfied. One of the men closest to the Czar, Prince A. S. Menshikov, was appointed governor-general of Finland in 1831, and he avoided treading o the incontestable rights of the Finns.

Proceeding thus, the governor-general observed the Czar's principles. The personification of autocracy, Nicholas I ruled his vast empire as a general commands an army: he demanded blind obedience of his subjects and adhered to the principles of justice himself. But military severity also was regarded as natural in Finland, at least until the February revolution. Nor was Finland to Nicholas I "a frontier land inhabited by an alien people"—as it was to be to Nicholas II—but the homeland of one of the peoples Providence had entrusted to his paternal rule. Although Nicholas I did not once convene the Diet of the Grand Duchy, he did not violate Finnish rights by making laws that required the approval of the Estates. Only one definite exception can be cited, one going back to Zakrevsky's term as governor-general: the Czar decreed, contrary to the law, that Finnish citizens who belonged to the Eastern Orthodox Church also were entitled to hold government office in Finland. To the Czar, as head of the Orthodox Church, laws that prevented fellow believers from entering the government service of a country under his rule must have appeared quite insulting; and the Czar's decree included, as a sort of apology, the observation that "other administrative concerns and circumstances" had prevented the convocation of the Diet to amend the law. Nicholas I allowed an attempt to rewrite the laws of Finland according to the formula of the Russian code to lapse, although it had not been intended to change the content of the law.

It was autocratic rule that prevented the latent forces of nationalism from breaking loose in Russia and that shielded the foundations of Finland's political status at a time when counter-forces had not yet developed in Finland to combat Russification. Characteristic of the Czarist ideology was the fact that Zakrevsky acknowledged without argument the predominant position of the Swedish language in the Grand Duchy. "It is not necessary to speak Russian," he said, "to serve the sovereign loyally." The idea of systematically Russifying Finland did find expression toward the end of Nicholas I's reign. It was voiced by a man in as high an office as Interior Minister Perovsky, but it did not represent the Czar's thinking. Viewed from the lofty perspective of the imperial throne, all the nations resting at its foot, both large and small, appeared equally estimable; and this ideological basis provided a favourable point of departure during the autocratic period for the creation of close relations marked by mutual confidence between the Finns and Russians. Members of the Finnish educated class entered the service of Russia in a steady stream, seeking in the imperial realm opportunities to rise to the highest levels of society, where in their own small native land there was little room. An officer trained in Finland was eligible to join the Russian army, whereas a Russian could not enter the miniature Finnish army. Russian aristocrats gladly spent the summer in idyllic Helsinki, especially in times when the government, determined to protect its subjects from being infected by western liberalism, banned travel abroad. The Russian language was studied more eagerly in Finland in those days than later on, when it was made the main subject in the secondary schools. And one Russian Maecenas provided the money for the publication of a dictionary of the Finnish language. Some Finnish and Russian upper class families were united by the ties of marriage.

"If the public temper everywhere were as good as in Finland," Nicholas I once remarked to his wife upon leaving Helsinki, "one might calmly look forward to the future." A Finnish unit, the "Guards of Finland," took part in crushing the Polish rebellion, and the clergy readily set the Lutheran Church, which preached peace and order on earth, at odds with the Roman Catholic Church, which held sway in Poland and which excommunicated princes and overthrew sovereigns. The Czar conferred upon the Cathedral in Helsinki the name of St. Nicholas, after whom he himself had been named, and when in practice the "St." was omitted, the authorities did not object. The wars waged by Russia against the "heathen" Turks were regarded by the Finns as wars of their own. And when, during the Crimean War, the British bombed some Finnish harbours and seized Finnish merchant ships, the friendly feelings of the Finns toward Russia were intensified.

It is evident that the cult of the great power practiced by its small protégé took forms that—had they exclusively determined the trend of the times—would have paved the way to the eventual absorption of Finland by Russia. Simultaneously, however, patriotic sentiment grew stronger in Finland, and even far-reaching expressions of it were tolerated, thanks to the fact that loyalty to the throne was unwavering and was appreciated at its true value in St. Petersburg.

Only a few decades had elapsed after the war of 1808—09, in which the Finns and Russians had fought each other, when Johan Ludvig Runeberg, in his

"Tales of Ensign Stål," transformed this essentially Swedish—Russian power conflict into a kind of Finnish fight for national freedom. Runeberg's idealistic and yet realistic martial poetry was destined to inspire a patriotic spirit of sacrifice in the hearts of many generations of Finns. His work passed the strictly enforced censorship after the poet had changed or cut just a few words.

The Russians—or the Czar's appointed representatives of native birth — took a tolerant view of such general expressions of Finnish patriotism and even of the awakening Finnish nationalist movement, which aspired to promote the Finnish language and to create a Finnish-language culture. But this tolerance had its limits. If any measures taken by the government were criticized or if, through the ideological program, there shone a hint of contamination by the dreaded, democratic influence, then the censor struck.

In 1850, it was prohibited to publish in the Finnish language any literature whatsover except what "both in regard to the spirit in which it was written and in regard to its manner of presentation" was of a devotional character or gave economic guidance. Not only were contemporaries dumbfounded but also research scholars have puzzled over the problem of why the linguistic majority should have become the victims of such discrimination—for, in respect to literature in Swedish, the former strict but not stifling rules of censorship remained unchanged. That is why many an authoritative scholar had held the censorship decree to represent an attempt by the Swedish-language bureaucracy of Finland to nip the budding national Finnish movement.

That explanation is anachronistic, however, for the language strife was yet to come. Both the Finnish and the Russian administrative quarters viewed (apparently quite mistakenly) the Finnish-speaking part of the population as being more receptive to anti-monarchistic currents, which were sweeping from Paris across Europe as a result of the February Revolution. The aim of the authorities seems to have been to safeguard the ignorant common people from every western leaven. The censorship decree was pushed through by Menshikov, but the statements of local political spokesmen could not have failed to influence his decision. The decree ceased to be enforced in practice after only four years, while Nicholas I was still alive.

During the half century in which the Diet was not convened, a ruling bureaucracy arose whose chief political virtue was caution and who lacked the broader national outlook of the academic circles. This bureaucracy had still been refractory under coarse Zakrevsky, but while the gentlemanly Menshikov was in office there was little friction. Baron Lars Gabriel von Haartman, who was vice-chairman of the Senate for nearly two decades and at the same time served as the head of the Department of Finance—in modern parlance, prime minister and minister of finance rolled ito one—worked systematically to sever the old ties binding Finnish economic life to Sweden and to create new ties with Russia.

When von Haartman took office, more Swedish than Russian banknotes were still in daily circulation in Finland, although the Crown refused to accept them in payment of taxes. After Russia had shifted from a paper monetary standard to a silver standard, von Haartman let the Bank of Finland redeem all the Swedish currency in 1840; thereafter, this thitherto unimportant financial institution began to issue ruble notes on its own. Credit must be given to von Haartman for straightening out the confusion that had prevailed up to that time in the country's monetary system. Moreover, the first modest and perhaps unwitting step had been taken toward an independent currency. Haartman's masterwork was getting the Saimaa Canal dug and completed in 1856. It connected Finland's eastern and greatest chain of lakes with the Gulf of Finland and strengthened the commercial ties that had begun to form during preceding decades betweeen St. Petersburg and eastern Finland. But the canal also opened the gates to the world's markets for the timber resources of the Finnish interior and thereby promoted the sawmill industry, which exported its products westward. This trend did not please von Haartman.

When the question of building railroads came up in the 1850's, von Haartman opposed every line except a strategic one leading from St. Petersburg to the western coast of Finland. In this matter, the new Russian governor-general, Count Berg, took a more Finnish attitude than the Finnish prime minister.

The policy of von Haartman and his spiritual brethren is related to the program that at a later date became known as the "compliance line." Despite certain exaggerated aspects, it was probably the most expedient policy during the reign of Nicholas I. Simultaneously, Prof. J. J. Nordström, who held the chair of law at the University, impressed on the minds of future officeholders a vital realization of Finland's special status and the constitutional rights of Finnish citizens.

Under the conditions that prevailed during the period of autocracy, there was the danger that the Finnish Church would turn into an institution maintained to uphold mere superficial morality and mundane order, with the ecclesiastical offices being treated as administrative posts. The Word of God was preached in a spirit inherited from the Age of Enlightenment, which aspired to salvage those dogmas that reason saw fit to accept. The rank and file of the churchgoers could not be satisfied by this type of preaching, and their dammed-up religious needs led to the eruption of powerful revivalist movements. They were led by men of the people, of whom the most celebrated was a peasant from Savo named Paavo Ruotsalainen.

Both the ecclesiastical and lay authorities considered it undesirable that lay preachers deliver sermons and hold devotional meetings, and, consequently, they attempted to suppress any such movement. However, litigation against the pietists inspired sympathy for them also among the educated class, whose religious pursuits had been intensified by the romantic intellectual trend. Pietism emerged victorious. Gradually, more and more clergymen joined the pietist movement, which began to purge the church from within.

Finnish Nationalist Awakening

At the time Finland was separated from Sweden, the Finnish educated class spoke Swedish, and even during the early part of the period of national autonomy the son of every peasant, artisan, or haberdasher entering secondary school still adopted Swedish as his "mother tongue." Fearing the spread of the alien Russian language in Finland, the yeomen's Estate had requested, at the

Diet of Porvoo, that the language situation be left unchanged. This was granted: Russian was used only in the offices of the governor-general and secretary of state in St. Petersburg, and, in the latter, only in conjunction with Swedish. All the rest of the administrative and judicial affairs of the country were conducted in Swedish.

In spite of the prevalence of reading ability, the common people, except the Swedish-speaking inhabitants of a narrow strip of the coast, did not understand a word of the documents handed out to them in government offices; and the ability to write would not have been of much use to them, because official petitions and applications had to be written in Swedish and the minutes of the meetings of local selfgoverning agencies also had to be kept in Swedish. There was no guarantee even that officials—as, for instance, a judge interrogating a party or a witness in a dispute—would have understood spoken Finnish. All the schools were Swedish, except children's primary grades; and even though ministers preached their sermons in Finnish, their language was sometimes a gibberish that consisted half of words derived from Swedish. The difference in language also caused the social boundary betweeen the educated class and the rest of the population to be sharper than it otherwise would have been. Which social group an individual belonged to, the gentry or the common people, could not only be seen in the way he dressed and in other similar distinguishing marks but it could also be heard in the languages he spoke. One story has it that, as late as the end of the century, there was a shopkeeper who, in sheer astonishment, called to his wife in a back room: "Do come here, woman! Here's a customer wearing a bonnet, but even so speaks Finnish!"

It was among the educated class of that divided society that the romantic nationalism of the early nineteenth century spread. When the nations of Europe struggled free of the grip of Napoleon, they were inspired by the ideals of nationalism; and though the political system created by the Congress of Vienna was alien to this ideology and the government set-up of the Holy Alliance strove to squelch it, it fought to insure a future for itself. To the romanticists, a nation was not solely the sum of the individuals who composed it nor even purely the product of a historical evolution. A nation, they believed, possessed its own, inseparable character, based on its racial origin; and, above all, it possessed, as a unique treasure, its language, which in a mystical way interpreted its special traits. The national legacy was believed to live not through the medium of the native language but within the language itself.

Applied to Finland, the pattern of nationalistic romantic thought held that, although she was a newcomer in the family of nations, the country could acquire the attributes of a true nation only if the official language was Finnish. It also signified that creative cultural activity in the country was possible only in a Finnish linguistic environment. The educated class would therefore have to adopt the vernacular. No attention was paid at this stage to the small, Swedish-speaking rustic population.

The romantic ideology of nationalism came from Germany and Scandinavia in the second decade of the nineteenth century to the University of Turku, where it gained a hold on the minds of Porthan's pupils, or of their pupils. Under its influence, interest awakened in developing literary Finnish to satisfy other than religious needs, and toward this end, a Finnish grammar and the previously mentioned dictionary of the Finnish language were produced. Simultaneously, demands were raised for introducing Finnish as a language of instruction in the schools, and a practical result was the establishment of a teaching post in the Finnish language at the University.

What other Turku romanticists expressed in cool, matter-of-fact terms, Adolf Ivar Arwidsson proclaimed with prophetic vehemence: "Only a nation is an independent entity... It alone has a sovereign existence; the individual is ruled and guided by the totality and by his environment... A spirit hovers over it; everybody must act more or less in obedience to it, and all actions aimed against it amount to mutiny against divinity and nature."

Only so long as "our mother tongue" survives, Arwidsson declared, "can we feel ourselves to be a nation. When the language of its forefathers is lost, a nation, too, is lost and perishes. All speaking the same tongue naturally form an indivisible whole; they are bound together internally by ties of mind and soul, mightier and firmer than every external bond. For language forms the spiritual, and land the material, boundaries of mankind; but the former is the stronger, because the spirit means more than material."

On a more specific level, Arwidsson declared: "Since all the judicial documents are drawn up in the Swedish language, even a peasant able to write does not know what they contain; he is likely to carry Uria's letter in his pocket... Inasmuch as we are permitted to approach the Almighty with prayers and thanks offerings in our mother tongue, why then must His everlasting justice be obscured in the twilight of alien phraseology?"

Such outspoken criticism of the official system shocked the Finnish representatives in St. Petersburg. It was not fitting for voices to be raised in the Grand Duchy, not, at least, critical ones. Arwidsson's journal was suppressed and he was dismissed forever, in 1823, from his post at the University. After that he migrated in despair to Sweden.

From the beginnings of the romantic movement in Turku, the political history of Finland cannot be written without bringing in the history of the University—which soon was transferred to Helsinki. It was among the faculty and the students of this institution that the new ideas were born and matured: the expressions of academic opinion served as the barometer of enlightened public opinion, and the University initiated great nationalist undertakings. The first official institutions to adopt Finnish as the language in which to record the minutes of their meetings were a number of the student corporations. They were organized on a regional basis, and it was obligatory for each undergraduate to join one upon enrolling in the University.

Arwidsson's dismissal did not mean that the Russian authorities, who controlled the actions of the native officials, opposed the Finnish nationalist movement as such. Called "Fennomania" by contemporaries, it was seen, on the contrary, as a means of alienating Finland from Sweden. When, in 1831, the Finnish Literature Society was founded for the purpose of carrying on research in the field of national studies, ratification of its bylaws met with no difficulty; indeed, it was established at a favourable juncture, for, just at that time Russia was anxious, for reasons of international power politics, to keep the Finns contented.

When Nicholas I visited Finland a couple of years later, he was welcomed by the student leader Johan Wilhelm Snellman (1806—81), who was destined to become Finland's most famous statesman during the period of national autonomy. Snellman explained to the Czar that union with Sweden had been ruinous to Finnish nationalism, which could now be saved by the country's new political status and the sympathetic attitude of the sovereign. He petitioned him to allow Finnish to be introduced as a language of education and official communication for the benefit of "Your Imperial Majesty's Finnish subjects." Since the petition aimed at a radical change in prevailing conditions, the ruling bureaucracy did not give it favourable attention. Still, it is of historical interest because it shows that young Snellman's basic outlook on Finland's position and his program were the same as those of the senator of thirty years later who had experienced much adversity.

Snellman soon also found himself at odds with the authorities, for his intention had been to lecture on academic freedom, which brought him the threat of being banished to Siberia. He traveled to Germany, where he acquainted himself with the philosophy of Hegel, in line with whose school of thought he published such meritorious philosophical studies that on two occasions he was invited to accept a professorial chair in Sweden. However, Snellman considered it his moral obligation to remain in his native country and engage in an unrelenting struggle to gain for the Finnish language its rightful status.

The issue was national survival. "Whether the Russian or the Finnish language will win out," Snellman later remarked in a private conversation, "only God knows. I dare not hope for anything. But that the Swedish language will go down in defeat, I know for sure." In a letter to a friend, he wrote: "Now our good luck in misfortune lies in the fact that the national self-confidence of the Finnish people is being primarily weighed down by a different power (he meant the Swedish language) from that which is binding its political independence (Russia). If in their stead there was one, even then there would be no other choice but to lose or to win, i.e., to dare... Postpone things for the time being! Then the time will surely come when both powers will be one, when opposing the one will signify open mutiny against the other, too."

While the senators lived from day to day, Snellman looked to the future, to a time when Russification must inevitably start. Before that time, Finland must be Finnicized: "Swedes we are no longer, Russians we cannot become; we must be Finns."

The concluding part of Snellman's slogan (in history books erroneously attributed to Arwidsson) demanded that the educated Finns adopt Finnish as their mother tongue. "When the educated people of a country... speak one language and the rest of the nation, the masses, speak another, the language of the educated class has no power of survival. It may sound like obscure speech—to the uncomprehending—if we say: it is nowise supported by the national spirit. The matter becomes perhaps clearer if we say: to the common people it is quite the same whether this language be Swedish or Mesopotamian. When school is taught and law and justice are administered in a language the rank and file of the nation do not understand, the rank and file do not even notice when one language replaces another. ...The Swedish language as the language of education in Finland has been based on Swedish political hegemony. Now this basis has collapsed and the force of habit is too weak to protect that language from being bypassed... What is required is that the educated people of our country are truly capable of being what they ostensibly are, the educated class of the *Finnish* nation of Finland. The majority of this class is of original Finnish stock; it has at least been born and raised among a Finnish population. Relatively few are descended from Swedish stock or have learned to regard themselves as expressly belonging to the Swedish race. It is the language of this educated class that is being referred to here. The future language of the small Swedish population proper is a matter of relative inconsequence from this standpoint.''

Since the doors of the university remained closed to Snellman, he was forced to accept a post in the out-of-the-way town of Kuopio as principal of a secondary school. There he began, in 1844, to publish two newspapers, the Finnish-language *Maamiehen Ystävä* (The Farmer's Friend), for the ordinary country people, and the Swedish-language *Saima,* for the educated class. Snellman did not have a poet's pathos, but the keenness of his logic in argument proved effective, and his voice carried much farther than those of the Turku romanticists. The direct or indirect sphere of influence of the *Saima* included the entire educated class of Finland with the exception of the higher administrative quarters, which were hostile to Snellman. And, although the *Maamiehen Ystävä* did not directly advocate any linguistic policy, certain parishes would surely not have taken action without the stimulus of its teachings and sent the Senate a petition in which their inhabitants requested the right to receive documents from government offices in the Finnish language. The peasantry, incapable of grasping the philosophic connection between nationality and language, did comprehend the existence of a burning practical need.

The *Saima* was suppressed at the end of 1846. The reason was not, however, its language program, which the ruling circles regarded as the product of romantic daydreaming, but the propagation of "doctrines of reform with a pernicious effect on youthful minds." The steps leading to the suppression of the journal were taken in response to the criticism directed by the *Saima* at the miserable conditions that prevailed on the estates belonging to the Russian aristocracy in the former "Old Finland." Yet, the fact remains that the attitude of the high officials toward Fennomania was at best one of suspicion and contempt, rather than of sympathy. And the Finnish nationalist awakening was confronted by other obstacles as well. It was asked whether Finnish could serve as a language of culture and whether the Finnish people in general were capable of being cultured.

"Geese all speak the same tongue, it is true, but they do not form a nation, not even wild geese, which nevertheless are independent," a friend wrote to Snellman. "Without being a nation one cannot achieve, create, least of all petition, the bureaucrats to establish a national literature. Finnish, as a language of education and literature, cannot spawn anything but ABC-books." Nor was speedy action regarded as necessary to meet the danger of Russification that Snellman warned about in his private letters: "The Swedish language is a shell, needed to protect Finnish, the kernel, to which the present unfavourable conditions do not extend. The shell will rot, but the kernel will not spoil during the long winter, and it will germinate when its time comes." Weakening the position of the Swdish language, it was said, would only open the door to Russian.

The first answers to these questions and doubts had already been received before the appearance of the *Saima*. The physician Elias Lönnrot, while practicing medicine in the northwestern frontier region, had run across singers of folk *runos* among the Finnish rural population on both the Finnish and, especially, the Russian side of the border. From the lips of these backwoods people, he wrote down long passages of folk poetry. By combining them and filling in gaps, he created the heroic epos *Kalevala*— a short version in 1835 and the definitive version in 1849.

The *Kalevala* excited admiration all over Europe. Before the longer second edition had appeared, lectures on it were being delivered in Germany, and a French version was the sensation of literary circles in Paris; but most potent was the enthusiasm the work inspired in Finland. A people whose untutored folk had created an epic that was comparable to the masterpieces of world literature could not be incapable of assimilating culture; a people who had the memorable past that is described by the poems of the *Kalevala* could not be lacking a national history.

Researchers have subsequently demonstrated that the *Kalevala* is—to a higher degree than was realized at first—of Lönnrot's own authorship, and many students of folklore have disputed the historical actuality of its heroes; but no amount of controversy over such questions can deprive the songs out of which Lönnrot composed his epic of their poetic charm. Not long after the *Kalevala*'s publication, there emerged from the ranks of the common country folk a writer in the Finnish language who gave eloquent proof of the Finns' capacity for culture. That writer was Aleksis Kivi (1834—72), whose dramas gave birth to the Finnish-language theater.

The main practical problem arose from the inability of the members of the educated class themselves to use the language whose promotion provided the idealistic content of their lives. Snellman published all his own writings in Swedish; the records of the Finnish Literature Society were kept in Swedish. "Have the Irish Englishmen as their leaders?... The Finns themselves must provide the initiative and the inspiration to lead. If they do not lead," asserted the opposition, "the movement is premature."

Snellman's disciples, the Fennomen, produced the response with their deeds. In the 1840s, intellectuals began to found societies which bound members to use Finnish "at every opportunity"—those with a "knowledge of their mother tongue" immediately and the others as soon as they had learned enough. An unparalleled willingness to make sacrifices for the cause was demonstrated when whole families began to speak a different language from the one they had spoken since childhood. The study of Finnish often led members of the upper classes to seek the company of peasants, and such personal contacts across class lines helped to strengthen the democratic character of the Finnish nationalist movement. The process continued for a few decades, and the last stage, which

Snellman himself did not approve at all, was the changing of Swedish surnames into Finnish ones.

But as early as the 1860s, counterforces began to make themselves felt, eventually halting the process. As a result of the national ferment, the language boundary ceased to be a social boundary; but as the linguistic lines became congealed towards the close of the century, the proportion of intellectuals speaking Swedish was many times greater than that of common people speaking it. In numerous Finnish-speaking localities the upper classes clung to the Swedish language, so the only means of augmenting the ranks of the Finnish-speaking educated class was to increase social mobility in the lower strata of society. Hence, Finnish-language secondary schools were needed, and the first one was founded in 1858.

Swedish Nationalist Awakening

The outright opposition directed against the Fennomen before the 1860s, which attained its peak in the censorship act of 1850, did not come from the Swedish nationalist, or Svecomanian, movement, since such a movement had not yet arisen in Finland. The opposition came from the bureaucracy. The attitude of the high officials was partly due to a fear that every kind of activity and agitation for reform might provoke suspicion in St. Petersburg, and partly to the understandable tendency of politicians to condemn Fennomania as idealistic-daydreaming. Finally, a natural love of convenience was a further factor—since it would have required extra effort to learn Finnish, it was not granted the status of an official language. To the bureaucracy, the Swedish-speaking minority among the rank and file of the nation was as alien as the Finnish-speaking majority; and the nationalist Finnish movement, for its part, did not regard the question of the minority's status as a topical one, because in school and in public life that segment of the population had no linguistic difficulties.

Nevertheless, the existence of the question was a fact that could not be avoided. Around 1860, there developed, under the leadership of that student of Swedish A. O. Freudenthal, a movement among the academic youth whose aim was to make the Swedish-speaking common people conscious of their Swedish nationality and to inspire in them a love of their mother tongue. The older Fennomanian and the newer Svecomanian movements might have been able to get along side by side quite well, had their activities been solely directed toward enlightening the masses in the spirit of romantic nationalism. The difficulty was the position of the intellectuals. Rejecting the Fennomanian demand that the educated class adopt Finnish as their mother tongue, the Svecomanians emphasized that, speaking Swedish, the educated class formed, together with the Swedish-speaking common people, a Swedish "nationality," which must not be betrayed by forsaking the Swedish language.

Thus, there arose among the majority of the members of the educated class in Finland an unfriendly attitude toward the cause of the Finnish language. This attitude was nourished by the doctrine, which shortly before had been invented in France and rapidly propagated abroad, regarding the inequality of races. The

Aryans, it was stated, represented a master race with special creative gifts and a capacity for conquest and rule; other races were capable at most of assimilating culture and living as decent subjects but incapable of independently establishing states.

Certain Scandinavians, notably the Swedish journalist A. Sohlman, in his book *Det unga Finland* (1855), a new edition of which appeared in Finland in 1880, applied this theory to Finland. Had not the eminent Finnish philologist M. A. Castrén only shortly before—during his arduous travels in Siberia—discovered that the languages spoken by a number of tribes living in that region in an extremely primitive condition were dstantly related to Finnish? And had he not advanced the idea—later disproved—that the original home of the Finnish people had been in the Altain mountains of Asia? The Finns were, he had said, no solitary racial fragment but belonged to the widespread Turanian race. But now it was declared that this imagined kinship to these short-skulled and yellow-skinned people was no honour but something to be ashamed of. Without the benefit of Swedish culture, the Finns, asserted Sohlman, would be on the same level as their relatives in Siberia. "And if the foreign elements were removed and the Finnish nation started to build on its own foundation, and detached itself from contact with Swedish culture, it would cover the distance to barbarity and extinction in as many decades as it took centuries for the Swedish influence to uplift the Finns to civilization, self-esteem, and a life of law and social order."

Against this background, the more radical of the Svecomen viewed the increasingly fervent conflict between the Swedish and Finnish languages as a struggle between a superior and an inferior race. They cannot be blamed for the fact that the racial theory on which the argument was based has subsequently been proved fallacious. Furthermore, the argument overlooked the historical fact hat the division of the educated class in Finland into Finnish-speaking and Swedish-speaking factions was not determined by biological but by ideological factors. The members of the educated class were descended partly from the Finnish-speaking and partly from the Swedish-speaking native peasants, and partly from families that had migrated to Finland from Sweden and other foreign countries. The families of different origins had intermarried, and eventually some of the descendants—without inquiring in any way into their racial past—adopted Finnish as their mother tongue, while others clung fast to Swedish. But those who believed in racial inequality—including the unequal division of native gifts between the two linguistic groups—must have felt deep concern over the victorious advance of Finnish and the decline of Swedish, considered not only from the standpoint of language but also from that of the national culture. The Fennomen again took the talk about the racial superiority of the Swedes as an insult, and, accordingly, irreconcilable bitterness between the two language groups was generated.

Pan-Scandinavianism and Liberalism

The Swedish nationalist movement in Finland had received stimuli from Sweden, and, nourished by romantic nationalist ideas, a sense of blood kinship was aroused between the Swedes and the Swedish-speaking Finns. More substantial national ties had been the objective of an earlier movement, which, seen from the Finnish point of view, was primarily political in character: Pan-Scandinavianism, emphasizing the close affinity among the four countries of the north. Finland was brought into Scandinavianist schemes during the Crimean War (1853—56). Russia's defeat appeared certain, and the Czar's enemies, England, France, and Turkey, urged Swedento take advantage of the situation and reconquer Finland.

The idea of revenge was vigourously espoused in Sweden and had support even in the royal court. Especially fervent advocates of it were a group of emigrants from Finland. Men like the poet Emil von Qvanten would have liked to see Finland join the Swedish-Norwegian union as a third, Finnish-language member. Since the Norwegians would not have cared to give the proposed newcomer a status equal to their own, Finland would have become a part of Sweden, at best enjoying limited autonomy. Nor did the Pan-Scandinavianists of Sweden like the idea of a Finnish-speaking Finland as a member of the union. Peace was made without Sweden's having entered the fray, but political speculation continued.

The Pan-Scandinavianists thought that they were supported in Finland by a powerful, if concealed, public sentiment. Indeed, in the opinion of the philologist Freudenthal and the circle closest to him, the pledge given by Alexander I at the Porvoo Diet had contained the "most treacherous words" ever uttered to the Finnish people, because, he claimed, they had not been intended to be kept. However, Finnish citizens could appreciate the autonomy achieved by their country even during the period of autocratic bureaucracy, and Snellman employed the full power of his forensic talents against Pan-Scandinavianism. He declared that Sweden had ceded to Russia only a province, whereas now, by virtue of its new political connection, that province had become a state—one which, moreover, had expanded territorially beyond the area surrendered by Sweden. The events of 1808—09 had thus signified for Finland a decisive step forward. Besides, the Fennomen feared the suppression of the Finnish nationalist movement if their country were rejoined to Sweden.

Pan-Scandinavianism as a political force perished in 1864. In that year, Sweden-Norway refused to give the brotherly military aid that Denmark expected after being attacked by Prussia and Austria. Yet, in Finland, even after that, the furtive hope was sometimes whispered that she might one day find herself in the lap of the former mother country again.

In Sweden, the Form of Government of 1772 and the Act of Union and Security were not retained as constitutional laws. A new Swedish Form of Government was enacted in 1809 to create a balance between the powers of the monarch and the Diet, while in practice the position of the king steadily weakened and that of the Diet grew stronger. In Finland, the center of political gravity continued to rest on the throne. This was according to constitutional law, in addition to which the Czar's authority was bolstered by his exercising the full power of the Autocrat of All the Russias. Sweden enjoyed freedom of the press, while Finland was under strict censorship. Pan-Scandinavianism thus at first had closer ideological ties to liberalistic thought than to the awakening Swedish nationalistic movement.

The roots of liberalism in Finland can be traced back to the year 1848. Academic youth had at that time been won over by sympathy towards the February Revolution and the currents that followed in its wake, which aimed at breaking up the Holy Alliance and ending the oppression of subject nationalities. At the students' spring festival, F. Cygnaeus cast a spell over the crowd with his eloquence—tradition has endowed his speech with a most magical effect because the words have not been preserved—and the Finnish national anthem, set to a poem by Runeberg, was sung for the first time. A realistic political sense and the calmness native to the Finnish character prevented any unrest among the youthful element; and liberalism, which came to the fore later on, nourished mainly on influences from England, was cool and rationalistic.

To the liberals, language was not the mystic symbol it was to the romantic nationalists, but a practical instrument of culture and social activity. In their view, it was reasonable for the Finnish language to be granted more rights, but they believed that this would happen in time without any great fuss. The Swedish language, too, they thought, should be allowed the opportunities for development that it demanded in Finland. Whereas the Fennomen explained that in Finland there lived only one nation and that, therefore, only one language should be spoken there, and whereas the Svecomen argued that, since two languages were spoken there, it also meant that two nations lived in the country, the slogan of the liberals became: "One nation, two languages!" Declaring themselves to be members of a single nation proves that the liberals did not accept Sohlman's racial theory. A sympathetic attitude toward the Finns and the Finnish language separated the liberals of Finland from the Pan-Scandinavianists of Sweden, who wanted collaboration only with a Finland that preserved her Swedish heritage intact. One contemporary observer commented that Sohman had done an unwitting disservice to the Swedish cause in Finland.

It might be supposed that time was working in favour of the liberals, but such was not the case, for they were too much ahead of their time. The issue of language and nationality did not greatly concern the liberals. Their primary aim was to have the Diet made into an institution that convened regularly and acquired authority at the expense of the imperial throne. Their program included establishing freedom of the press, promoting local self-government, and liberating economic life from government controls. At times, the liberals interpreted Finnish autonomy in a recklessly loose way. For instance, the chief mouthpiece of the faction, the *Helsingfors Dagblad,* in 1863 discussed Finland's chance of declaring herself neutral in the event of the threatening outbreak of European hostilities, regardless of Russia's position. And a question that was insulting to Russia was raised in the House of Nobles: Did Finnish noblemen serving in Russian civil or military posts have the right to enter the Diet, because, according to the constitutional laws, participation was denied to those "in the service of foreign monarchs, masters, and states." The aspirations of the liberals in Finland were given particularly outspoken expression in the Swedish press.

Liberalism alienated the Finns from the Russians and loosened the bonds that had grown firm in previous decades. The liberals viewed with self-satisfied superciliousness the backward neighbouring realm, which was only then undertaking to free the serfs. To the liberals, in line with their basic outlook, the national antithesis between Finland and Russia was a secondary matter. What was decisive was the ideological and sociological difference between the two countries. Accordingly, they stressed, for the instruction of the Svecomen, that the culture of Finland was not menaced by the Finnish language but by Russian autocracy. But, in their progressive optimism, the liberals did not comprehend the boundless power given a state by faith in authority and blind obedience, and that is why they underestimated Russia. The popular idealistic writer Z. Topelius, who belonged to the liberal faction in the language conflict, declared in a private letter that the Finns had better await a day "when the Russian colossus would collapse from within." And yet, during the Crimean War, he had attracted attention and provoked annoyane as a journalist with his conspicuously pro-Russian writings.

Autonomy Gains Strength

The Russian colossus did not collapse, even though Czar Nicholas I died while the Crimean War was still raging. His son and heir, Alexander II (1855—81), had received a civilian education, unlike his father; and by nature, too, he was more gentle. The times were witnessing the culmination of European-wide liberalism, signifying that the intellectual basis on which the new grand duke was obliged to build up the Finnish system of government also had changed. Moreover, Russia was weak from the effects of defeat in the war. Wise statesmanship counseled treating the Finns benevolently—for had they not shown unswerving loyalty to their sovereign throughout the conflict? "My father relied on you," declared the new Czar, laconically. "All of you have fulfilled your duty."

The signs of the times were also marked by the Finns, and public sentiment was first given open expression from the lectern of the University Auditorium, underneath a portrait bust of Alexander I. In an address delivered on the occasion of the coronation of the new Czar, Professor (later Bishop) F. L. Schauman boldly emphasized the need to convene the Finnish Diet.

As governor-general of Finland, Alexander II appointed a Baltic German, Count F. W. Berg, an enterprising and progressive-minded, but imperious and quarrelsome character. He could not get along at all with old, conservative Baron von Haartman, who in 1858 had to step aside as vice-chairman. Haartman's resignation from the Senate made possible the initiation of economic reforms aimed at freedom of enterprise. Count Berg felt sympathetic toward the Fennomen and became friends with Snellman. Hitherto regarded as a dangerous agitator, Snellman was first named professor of philosophy at the University and in 1863 he was appointed minister of finance in the Senate. In 1858, Finnish was decreed the language of local self-government in those communes where it was spoken by the majority of the inhabitants. A couple of peasants' deputations ventured to request an audience with the Czar himself confidently to broach the matter of having Finnish adopted as the language of education and justice, and Snellman tried to influence the Czar along the same lines.

181

Visiting the Parola military encampment in 1863, His Imperial Majesty signed a language edict that signified the greatest victory the Fennomen could hope to achieve under the prevailing conditions. "It is and will continue to be a cornerstone of the future of the Finnish people," Snellman, who had attended the ceremony, declared later. "What the parties concerned have managed to eliminate will surely be restored, with interest." He was referring to the obstructive tactics used by the Senate and the lower government bureaus in applying the edict during the period of twenty years when it was to be gradually put into effect. The deficient knowledge of Finnish possessed by the public functionaries made it impossible to force its immediate adoption as a language of administration and justice. But the Senate was dilatory also about issuing orders concerning the linguistic qualifications of candidates for office to clear the way for the reform. Thus Snellman's language edict did not begin to make itself really felt until the termination of the period of grace. According to its provisions, Finnish was to have equal status with Swedish in bureaus and courts of justice when they had direct dealings with the public. The internal language of government bureaus remained Swedish.

Shortly after the Crimean War, Alexander II visited Helsinki and dictated into the records of the Senate a broad, if roughly drafted, program of reform, mainly along economic lines. When the details of this program and other deferred reforms were studied by the Senate, it continually encountered provisions of the law which would have to be amended to make the projected measures legal—and this required authorization from the Diet. The public impatiently awaited the summoning of the Diet, and even the governor-general advocated its convocation.

But when the Minister of Finance, Baron F. Langenskiöld, was afforded an opportunity to discuss the matter with Alexander, he received the impression that the Czar was disinclined to carry out the wishes of the Finnish people. The Czar's negative attitude was evidently due to the fact that his Polish and even Russian subjects were demanding the convocation of popular assemblies at the same time; a concession in one direction would have made it more difficult to maintain an uncompromising stand in another. Under the circumstances, in order to do something toward breaking up the jam in administrative affairs, Langenskiöld proposed to the Czar an unfortunate compromise. It was the so-called April Manifesto of 1861, which left Finland dismayed.

Not only did the Manifesto appear to postpone the convening of the Diet to a distant future but it also appeared to violate Finland's constitutional laws. It was tantamount to a *coup d'état*. It called for the formation of a 48-man committee to enact provisional laws for observance—since they were ratified by the Czar—"until circumstances permitted" the Diet to meet. Constitutional law was disregarded in providing for election to this body and for the procedures to be followed. When the Senate sent an address of thanks to the Czar in response to the notification, the minority of its members wanted to include a statement that the wording of the Manifesto left room for an "interpretation contrary to the Finnish constitution."

Politically vigilant groups of citizens drafted a popular petition of protest addressed to the Czar, and Helsinki witnessed the unusual spectacle of popular demonstrations (mainly to express sympathy for the senators voting in the minority). Motivated by good intentions, Baron Langenskiöld was dumbfounded by the fierce attacks against him; but he succeeded in quickly obtaining from the Czar an explanation regarding the purpose of the Manifesto—one that, in fact, amounted to a rectification—which removed the constitutional doubts: the resolutions of the committee could not be ratified into laws; it was authorized merely to make reports on proposed laws handed down by the Czar in order to facilitate the work of the future Diet.

Alexander II retreated without making the original phrasing of the Manifesto an issue of prestige, for, what with the concern displayed in the West over the stern policy pursued by Russia in Poland, he wanted to demonstrate that he could rule constitutionally over law-abiding subjects. The extremists among the liberals continued to sabotage the committee even after the rectification, but Snellman managed to win the public over to the committee's side by his determined stand in its favour. He himself described the press controversy provoked by the issue as the most violent he had ever experienced. For him, that was saying a great deal.

The history of this so-called January Committee is told here at such comparative length because it foreshadowed many of the subsequent constitutional conflicts; it taught the Finnish people the lesson that the preservation of autonomy meant scrupulous adherence to the letter of the law.

When the unrest in Poland broke out into a new open revolt and the Finns once more held their peace, the Czar issued a summons for the Finnish Diet to convene in Helsinki in September, 1863. The hiatus of more than half a century, which has exaggeratedly been called in Finnish history a "political night," was over. The sovereign himself was on hand to open the proceedings, and, in his ceremonial address from the throne, he underscored the principles of constitutional rule and promised to enlarge the rights of the Estates.

The Form of Government of 1772 and the Act of Union and Security contained only scanty and general stipulations regarding the work of the Diet or the election of its members, despised as it had been by Gustavus III; and, during the protracted hiatus, the tradition in Finland had also been broken. The enactment of a new law to regulate the functions of the Diet was accordingly called for, and the enlargement of the authority of the Estates that had been promised was thereby rendered less troublesome than if carried out by separate acts. Above all, there was reason to anticipate that such a Constitutional Law, specifically enacted for autonomous Finland and ratified by the Czar, would fortify the position of the grand duchy.

Other changes in the political system were discussed, notably in liberal quarters, including the transformation of the Senate into a parliamentary government. Even a new Form of Government was considered. Alexander I had not agreed to frame a new constitution for his new Finnish subjects but had preferred to keep the old one in effect. Now, however, the Pan-Scandinavian movement had made disagreeable to the Russians the idea that part of the realm was being governed according to Swedish constitutional laws. In the end, Alexander II did not want to give Finland a new Form of Government, either. The quip that the Finnish constitution was like a married man's illicit amorous affair proved to be true—everybody knew about it but nobody wanted to discuss it in public.

The Czar ratified the Diet Act in 1869, but it did not contain even those extensions of the prerogatives of the Estates that he had deigned to mention in his address opening the proceedings of the Diet. The Finns did gain a victory to the extent that they now had a constitutional law of their own, one in which the limits of the power of the sovereign and of the Diet were laid down more precisely than before—for example, the Czar was obliged to convene the Diet every five years. It soon became customary to summon it every third year. Later, the Czar granted the Diet a limited right to initiate legislation.

The question of extending the suffrage did not much interest the framers of the new constitution. It was feared that radical proposals might endanger the fulfillment of the reform. The structure of the Diet thus remained as before, unless one takes into account the abolition of the class division among the nobles and the extension to the teachers in the University and secondary schools of the right to elect representatives to the Estate of the clergy. A greater change took place in 1879, when the elections to one of the Estates, namely, that of the burghers, were arranged according to the general practice prevailing in the Europe of those times: the right to vote was no longer dependent in towns on pursuit of a "bourgeois" occupation but instead on exceeding a certain minimum income. The act was loosely drafted, however, and made it possible for each town to arrange its own electoral system.

Besides insuring the regular continuation of the work of the Diet, the chief objectives of the Liberals included freedom of the press. The first session of the Diet witnessed the enactment of a provisional press law to abolish censorship. But at the very next session, the Czar demanded the tightening of certain stipulations. The Liberals would not agree to this offer of compromise, with the result that no permanent press law whatsoever could be enacted and there was a reversion to varying administrative decrees and censorship of printed matter.

The vigorous legislative activity that began in the 1860s embraced the most varied spheres of social life, and it bore the stamp of liberalism. Trade, maritime commerce, and industry were liberated by degrees from government tutelage. At the same time, the government lowered the tariff; and, since Russian economic policy was likewise taking a cautious step toward free trade, there prevailed in commercial relations between Finland and Russia a higher degree of reciprocity than at any other time during the period of national autonomy. In the rural parts of the country, where local self-government had thitherto been confined to parish meetings headed by the ministers, a communal administrative organization was set up to handle lay affairs. The clergy had looked after the education of small children with praiseworthy zeal and made the Finns a literate nation; but the Church considered its educational objective to be achieved when the members of a parish had learned to read the Holy Bible and devotional literature, and could recite the main points of the Christian doctrine. Public opinion had begun to demand a more varied education for citizens, and the Rev. Uno Cygnaeus came out with a bold proposition: the schools should operate apart from the supervision of the Church, though on a Christian basis. In 1865, the municipalities and rural communes were granted the right to found State-subsidized elementary schools.

The Church Act passed in 1869, which had been drafted by Bishop Schauman, a Liberal, reduced the power of the State over the Church and let the laity participate in deciding ecclesiastical affairs in the Church's own representative institution, the Church Assembly. Since revivalist movements had purged the Lutheran Church of Finland, lay churchgoers had wrested a position for themselves in its leadership. The principle of freedom of worship was contained in the Church Act; but certain politically delicate questions relating to the members of the Eastern Orthodox Church caused the practical implementation of this reform to be postponed for a couple of decades. Not until 1889 did it become lawful to secede from the Lutheran State Church and found independent church congregations. But few exercised that privilege, for the effect of the collaboration between the Pietists and the clergy and of the new Church Act was to transform the State Church into a people's church.

One of the most noteworthy achievements during the reign of Alexander II was the gradual establishment of an independent Finnish monetary system. During the various stages of the process, Finnish statesmen displayed estimable diplomatic skill.

During the Crimean War, the Russian bank stopped redeeming banknotes with silver; and since the Bank of Finland had been issuing ruble banknotes, it had to follow suit. The inflation of banknotes in Finland did not cause more than about a twenty per cent rise in prices, at most, but even such a slight dislocation of the economy was frowned upon in the nineteenth century. The Bank of Finland would have been able to redeem its own banknotes if it had been released from the obligation of redeeming Russian ones, too. But Langenskiöld's plea to the Czar to let the grand duchy, regardless of the rest of the empire, go back to the silver standard was in vain. Instead, the Czar agreed to a measure which ostensibly, though not actually, gave Finland an independent monetary system: the Bank of Finland began to issue quarter-ruble notes called *markkas*.

In 1865, Snellman succeeded where his predecessor, Langenskiöld, had failed. The silver mark was designated as the monetary unit of Finland. The silver ruble continued to be legal tender in Finland, too; since Russia adhered to the paper standard, however, its silver rubles did not circulate but were buried at the bottom of household chests. Actually, if not yet formally, Finland now possessed an independent monetary system.

In the 1870s, the value of silver declined in relation to gold and numerous European states changed to a gold standard. In Finland, a corresponding change was deemed necessary because of the country's commercial relations with the West. Finance Minister C. H. Molander obtained the Czar's consent for the reform, even though the Russians suspected Finnish separatism in it. From the year 1878, the Finnish and Russian monetary system had nothing in common, since Finland was both formally and actually on the gold standard, while Russia was formally on the silver, but in reality on the paper standard. In its paired value the Finnish mark was no longer a fraction of the Russian ruble, either, but was valued on a par with the French franc. The first changes in the monetary system had been carried out without any supporting action by the

Diet; the last step was taken with the consent of the Diet. And thus the institution of an autonomous currency in Finland enjoyed the security that was granted by the law, which the Czar did not have the right to amend on his own initiative.

The Language Conflict

The three ideological trends that grew into national movements after the middle of the nineteenth century—Fennomania, Svecomania, and Liberalism—and produced separate organs of opinion of their own, collided with each other in the Diet also. No firm party organizations had been created yet, however. Some men gained recognition as party leaders, but they were unable to count their followers accurately, for many of the Diet members failed to identify themselves clearly with any faction.

In addition to the aging Snellman, the leaders of the Fennomen were G. Z. Forsman and Agathon Meurman. Eventually raised to the rank of nobility and dubbed Baron Yrjö-Koskinen, Professor Forsman was a historian with the first thorough history of Finland to his credit — a work imbued with the Finnish nationalist spirit. Meurman, the son of Arwidsson's sister, was a member of the landed gentry who exercised such an influence over the yeomanry that he could boast, only half in jest: "The yeoman's Estate, it is I."

As the most prominent figures among the Svecomen, there emerged C. G. Estlander, a professor of esthetics, Baron V. M. von Born, Baron R. A. Wrede, a professor of law, and A. Lille, a newspaper editor. Freudenthal was never elected to the Diet and he avoided other political activities as well. The party accordingly took on a more aristocratic color than the father of the Swedish nationalist movement had intended: keeping the Swedes in the majority among the educated class was regarded as more important than working for the benefit of the Swedish-speaking common people.

In 1880, the Liberals—under the leadership of Leo Mechelin, a professor of law—organized themselves more firmly than the other two factions and drew up a party program. Snellman, then in the last year of his life, responded to the publication of that program by pronouncing stern judgment on the party: "In our country, true liberalism is dedication to the task of liberating the majority from the tutelage and linguistic tyranny of the minority." In line with their basic outlook, the Liberals continued to be indifferent to the language question. But even though all the party leaders spoke Swedish, they considered it their duty—contrary to the Svecomen—to work in behalf of the Finnish-speaking inhabitants of the country also. "What would be the future of this nation," Mechelin asked rhetorically of Estlander, "if the rank and file of the great majority were denied an equal share in the benefits of Western, particularly Scandinavian, culture with the Swedish-language minority, who can and must, without giving up these benefits, work for the best welfare of the whole nation?"

The ferocity of the language conflict eventually crushed the Liberal party. Its program failed to attract popular support, and soon all that was left was a number of generals without an army. For lack of subscribers, the *Helsingfors Dagblad,* which had long been Finland's most prominent newspaper, ceased publication in 1889. Their mother tongue, together with bonds of family and friendship, drew the Liberal leaders into the ranks of the Svecomen. This shift signified the addition to the Swedish party of elements that held a more positive attitude toward the Finnish-speaking part of the population than Freudenthal's disciples. The Liberal heritage also partly accounts for the uncompromising constitutionalism that distinguished the Swedish party. The same year the *Helsingfors Dagblad* gave up the ghost, *Päivälehti*, a Liberal newspaper in the Finnish language began to appear. A little earlier, the Finnish party had become divided into "old" and "young" factions. The young faction represented cultural liberalism and was in close contact with the literary circles that belatedly, in the 1880s, had brought the naturalistic trend to Finland. Except for the early years of ferment in the movement, the "young" Finns maintained a more conciliatory stand in the language conflict than their rivals.

Snellman had been forced out of the Senate in 1868 after becoming involved in a quarrel with Governor-General N. Adlerberg. Thereafter, the Fennomen had no champion in the government, whose members, of course, remained aloof from the political parties and generally were reluctant to broaden the use of the Finnish language. This same trend was also supported by Adlerberg. On the other hand, the sympathy of his successor, F. L. Heiden (1881—97), was on the side of the Fennomen. During Heiden's term, the first modest symptoms of parliamentarism could be perceived when, in 1882, the Senate received three party leaders (Yrjö-Koskinen, Mechelin, and a fellow Liberal). That was an acknowledgment of their political standing.

The party division in the Diet became clearly defined at about the time the Liberal party faded out of existence, for, with few exceptions, the representatives of the different Estates joined either the Fennomen or the Svecomen. The Estates of the clergy and the yeomen were indisputably controlled by the former and the nobility by the latter. The Swedes held the majority in the ranks of the burghers as well, but it was only a slight majority. If the Finns could have gained the upper hand there, too, they could have dictated the decisions of the four-chamber Diet on the strength of three of the chambers. The more the electoral system was democratized in the towns, the slimmer became the chances of the narrow and mainly Svecomanian patriciate to pick the successful candidate or candidates in an election.

Every effort to amend the clause in the Diet Act that governed urban elections was condemned to defeat, for the Svecomen vigourously resisted all change liable to endanger their partisan interests. There remained, however, a possibility for the individual towns to draw up their own electoral system by virtue of the latitude allowed by the clause mentioned within the very loose framework of the law. Even this course was not easy to follow, for, in reaching decisions, urban dwellers had to vote according to the old electoral system. Still, at any rate, it was not impossible.

About 1880, a vehement struggle for the franchises that stemmed from the language strife began in nearly every town, and the adoption of new local electoral rules paved the way for Fennomanian victories. Finally, in the last two four-chamber Diets, the Fennomen commanded a majority in the burghers' Estate. But, under the political conditions of the period, this change in balance of power between the parties had no practical significance.

The full implementation of Snellman's Language Edict at the beginning of 1884 did not remove the causes of friction even from administration or justice. The extreme indignation of the Fennomen was excited when the attorney-general, supported by some Swedish newspapers, referred to the civil law inherited from the Swedish regime, according to which courts of justice must render judgment in the Swedish language. It was asked whether he wished to regard Finnish as a foreign tongue in Finland, and it was observed that in other respects as well, the laws dating back to Swedish times were to be read *mutatis mutandis*.

The Liberals and the Svecomen wanted the language question decided in the Diet by means of a law which would have safeguarded them from any surprise move by the Fennomen. Such a solution would have had the further advantage of legally preventing the Russian language from being established as the language of administration in Finland. Perhaps the Czar also had the latter point of view in mind when he opposed the enactment of the language law. The new language edict passed in 1886 supplemented Snellman's and signified a further step forward by the Finnish-speaking inhabitants. However, the length of the step depended in practice on each government office, which was entitled to decide for itself whether to use Finnish or Swedish as the internal language or in correspondence with other bureaus.

On the whole, Swedish was preferred by officials, for most of them had received their education in that language. Accordingly, a second front in the language war was established in the field of secondary school education. Snellman had wanted to have part of the curriculum of all schools that prepared pupils for matriculation taught in Finnish and part in Swedish. This would have obliged the educated class to learn both languages, thus keeping it intact as a group. While Snellman was still in the Senate, instruction in a number of schools actually had been arranged in this way; but when the majority of the educated people adopted the Swedish nationalistic point of view, the program could no longer be maintained. In 1869, the Fennomanian cause suffered another setback: up to that time, the secondary schools had been under the supervision of the ecclesiastical chapters, which favoured the Finnish nationalistic movement; but, as the school system became more secularized, the secondary schools were subordinated to a new agency, the national Board of Education.

To head the board, the Czar, in a surprise move, appointed Lieut.-General C. von Kothen, a bureaucrat from the era of Nicholas I, who in spirit belonged to bygone generations. As an anti-democrat, he advocated a total blockade of the channels of social flux whose opening the Fennomen deemed essential to the creation of a Finnish-speaking educated class. Like the other bureaucrats of his generation, he was no Svecoman. Nevertheless, in practice von Kothen's policy was directed against the pro-Finnish movement. But his excessive zeal in trying to make Russian the most important subject in secondary schools made him unpopular in other circles as well, and, after five years, he was forced to resign.

On von Kothen's orders, the only Finnish-language secondary school in Helsinki had been transferred to a provincial town; so, at heavy expense, the Finns founded a private Finnish-language lyceum in the capital. The same measure had to be taken in other communities, where the authorities had decreed Swedish to be the language of instruction in State schools. A change in educational policy did not take place until Yrjö-Koskinen took office as senator. By 1889, the enrollment in Finnish-language secondary schools was as large as in Swedish ones. The opposing sides had thus gained equal strength in the field of education, as well as in the Diet. The same situation existed in the student corps of the 1880's. The students commanded attention, not only because their position on the language question reflected that of the future body of civil servants, but also because of the prominent place occupied by the University in the public life of the nation. During the ensuing decade, the membership in the Senate also became just about evenly divided between Fennomen and Svecomen.

The even division of partisan strength heightened the pitch of the language struggle. A battle had to be fought for every inch of linguistic ground; the slightest shift of strength was liable to swing the balance to one side or the other. In many spheres, the Swedish language still held a position of absolute dominance. When, in 1894, Yrjö-Koskinen used Finnish to address the House of Nobles, one extremist among the Svecomen denounced it as an impertinence. And it was not until that same year that Finnish was spoken for the first time at a session of the consistory of the University—although many professors had long been lecturing in Finnish. But the fact that only one-seventh or one-eighth of the total population spoke Swedish spelled eventual defeat for the Svecomen, so many of them were pessimistic about the future.

While the Finnish people were wasting their strength on the language struggle that had begun during the sunny days of the 1860's, a small cloud arose, almost unnoticed, from beyond the Eastern horizon, growing steadily until, by the last decade of the century, it filled the whole sky with dark menace.

Finnish Autonomy Threatened

The two nationalist movements, reinforced by Liberalism, which held the autocracy of the East in contempt, made the gradual, uncoerced Russification of Finland impossible, even though it might have been conceivable during the period that immediately followed the year 1809. Despite the fact that Alexander II was sincerely honoured and even adored as a benefactor of the Finnish nation, a clear tendency to become alienated from Russia was felt even during his reign, while at the same time cultural and commercial relations with the West became more active and diversified than ever. The Russian nationalist movements—Slavophilism and Pan-Slavism—regarded the "decadent" West, to which Finland belonged spiritually, as inferior to the East. Despite their ardent nationalist ideology, these movements were nevertheless just part of a world-wide trend. Since Liberalism had reached its culmination during the third quarter of the nineteenth century, this trend led inexorably to the ascendancy of nationalism in intellectual life, to imperialism (notably competition in the acquisition of colonies) in politics, and to protectionism in economic affairs. Weak-willed Alexander II was swept along by the current, and at the end of the

1860's many of the Russian Liberal ministérs were forced to step aside to make room for nationalists. Russian Liberalism had viewed Finland as something of a Utopia, that might serve as an example to the rest of the Czarist realm, and this point of view had bolstered the special status of the grand duchy. The Slavophiles believed that Russification of the "frontier land" inhabited by an alien race would prove a blessing to the Finns themselves, who would thereby be saved from Western contamination.

Even during the hopeful decade of the 1860's, the Finns had received reminders of the limitations of their autonomy. Not all the reforms petitioned for had been gained, and at the close of the first Diet, the governor-general had complained that certain speeches had betrayed a lack of understanding of Finland's true position in the empire. However, at that time the Finns had been the active party and their constitutional rights had not been violated. A new phase was inaugurated when the Slavophilic press launched an offensive against the special privileges of "alien peoples," which represented an insult to the sacred autocracy, and demanded the consolidation of all the parts of the empire.

The Czar and his advisers, however, were not yet inclined to lend an ear to the chauvinists; and at the close of the 1870's, Finnish autonomy achieved two new victories: the afore-mentioned totally independent monetary system and, even more significant, a national army.

Responding to the call of the arms race and to the growing spirit of militarism, one European country after another adopted universal conscription. Russia followed suit in 1874. The grand duchy, the Finns realized, had two alternatives: either establishing an army of their own or submitting to the conscription of their men into the Russian military service. The idea of introducing conscription had been aired in some Finnish quarters long before preparatory measures in Russia had led to a solution. A committee, composed of members of the four Estates, drafted a proposal, and, although the Russian Minister of War criticized the separatism expressed in it, the Czar did not let the criticism affect the content of the law. In the Diet, The Fennomen and the Liberals supported the measure, albeit on quite different grounds. Snellman asserted that in Russian wars, the security of Finland was also indirectly at stake; so the Finns must expect to share in the sacrifice required. The Liberals thought—even if they did not say so—that the army would serve as an added pillar to support national autonomy.

The draft of the law was amended in the Diet to emphasize the autonomy of the country; for instance, the task of the army had been carefully defined in the bill as defending "the throne and the empire," but in the resolution of the Diet the word "empire" was changed to "fatherland." The final wording was designed to provide security against the use of the Finnish army beyond the national boundaries except in the extreme emergency of danger to the Czar's throne. The officer corps was to be composed of Finns. Some of the clauses of the act were proclaimed to be constitutional in nature, which meant that they could be amended only by the uniform consent of all four chambers of the Diet. According to the Russian custom, only part of the recruits were to be subject to compulsory military service, with the selection to be made by drawing lots; but the length of service was reduced in Finland to only half of that which prevailed in Russia, or three years. On the other hand, a short period of military training was also to be given to those Finnish youths who were exempted from the regular service. The Czar signed the Conscription Act in 1878, in the form amended by the Diet, and that success bolstered Finnish faith in the strength of their national autonomy.

Actually, Finland had only been enjoying a breathing spell, for Russian interests had been actively directed towards the Balkans. The traditional Czarist policy of expansion southwestward conformed to the Pan-Slavic ideology, since the Balkan countries were inhabited largely by Slavs of the Eastern Orthodox faith. The war of 1877—78 almost dealt Turkey a mortal blow, but the other European powers salvaged the wounded prey from the grip of Russia. The surprising termination of the victorious Balkan War was a humiliation hard for the Russian nationalists to swallow, and the defeatist mood simultaneously strengthened the anarchistic movement: within a short period, three attempts to assassinate the Czar were made.

In order to pacify the public, Alexander II hastily undertook to draft a constitution that provided for the establishment of a Russian representative assembly. He had already put his signature to it but it had not yet been promulgated when the fourth attempt on his life succeeded in March, 1881. According to the new constitution, Finland also was supposed to elect representatives to the imperial assembly, which thus would have enacted laws for the grand duchy as well. Although Alexander II doubtless had no desire to violate the rights of Finland, neither did he have sufficient power to protect them.

The Finns did not suspect how close the hangman's noose was hovering over their heads, and they did not become aware of it for decades. They retained an idealized image of Alexander II; even the passing of a popular national sovereign could scarcely have caused more sincere grief in Finland than the death of the Czar. The reign of Alexander II had been a time of progress in all areas in Finland, and nations always tend to personify the causes of good and bad times. The whole Finnish nation had reason to rejoice in the revival of constitutional life and in the gains made by the cause of national autonomy, and the Fennomen gratefully remembered the Language Edict and the fact that the Czar had wanted the opening ceremonies of the 1863 Diet also held in Finnish. A memorial statue to Alexander II was erected in the center of the monumental central square of Helsinki, before the entrance of the Government Palace.

The sincerity of Finnish grief was not diminished by the fact that it was mixed with a fear of the future. Old Snellman's comment contained a blunt complaint that Finland was powerless to hold the Russian anarchists in leash: "In a moment like the present, we are deeply depressed by the feeling that we belong to a small, weak, subject people. There is nothing we could have done to protect the life of our ruler, to protect ourselves. From the hands of a gang of bandits must we accept our destiny."

Finland actually did have to accept her destiny from the hands of the "gang of bandits" that had murdered the good Czar, though not in the shape of misfortune but a deferment of misfortune. The new, strong-willed Czar, Alexander III, was not so intimidated by public unrest as his father had been, and he put the proposed constitution *ad acta*. The sovereign was encouraged in this measure by his former tutor, the influential minister of education, Pobjedonostsev, for whom the destruction of Finland's special status was a positively religious duty. But in striving to save autocratic rule, which to him was the most precious thing on earth, he unwittingly saved Finland, too.

Czar Alexander III was personally attached to the grand duchy, in whose archipelago he used to cruise on his yacht during the summers, or he would stop at his fishing cottage, where he chopped the firewood himself, while Czarina Dagmar did the cooking. Dagmar was a Danish princess and in her Finland had an intercessor as near to the throne as it was possible to get. However, the Czar could not endlessly oppose the demands directed against Finland by the nationalists, especially when they were based on arguments citing the true interests of the empire.

After the Balkan War, the attention of the Pan-Slavists turned again to Finland. In his work "The Subjugation of Finland" (1889), K. Ordin, the Czar's major-domo, depicted Finland as a conquered Swedish province upon which Czar Alexander I, in his omnipotence, had bestowed certain rights; exercising that same omnipotence, any succeeding Czar might abolish those rights. Finnish scholars explained the invalidity of Ordin's thesis; it was criticized from the juridical standpoint by the Liberal Mechelin and from the historical standpoint by the Fennoman J. R. Danielson, whose work "Finland's Unification with the Russian Empire" was presented to the Czar himself through the mediation of the Danish royal house.

Ordin's influence could be clearly seen in the Russian members of the Russo-Finnish mixed committee charged with the task of drawing up a new Form of Government for Finland. It involved codifying all the laws and procedures based on established custom pertaining to the legal status of Finland. Governor-General Heiden leaned toward the Russian line and induced the Czar to appoint a new mixed committee to deliberate upon the question of the status of Finland. The report submitted by this so-called Bunge Committee recommended to the sovereign that in regard to those Finnish laws which concerned the interests of the empire as a whole, the Diet should be requested to give only its opinion; the Czar, in ratifying a law, thus would not be bound to the text of the law as approved in Finland. The best-informed circles in Finland feared a *coup d'état* as early as 1893, but Alexander III hesitated to sign the new code, and the next year, death freed him from the dilemma.

In certain lesser matters, on the other hand, Alexander III yielded. In connection with the reform of the Russian postal system, the Czar, in 1890— just after reading Ordin's book—ordered the abolition of the independent postal service of the grand duchy. The use of Finnish postage stamps was permitted for more than ten years thereafter; in other ways, too, the practical significance of the measure was slight. It has been conjectured that the Russian nationalists induced the Czar to take this step only in the hope that, having been slightly budged, the heavy rock of Finnish autonomy might later be rolled wholly out of place.

Actually, far more dangerous to Finland were the plans that were being considered to merge her tariff and monetary systems with the Russian ones. The tariff plan fell through, however, because Russian business quarters feared the competition from the more highly developed Finnish industry, while the monetary plan was demolished by the Czar's negative stand. Dismay was inspired in Finland by the Czar's retraction of his signature from Finland's new criminal code after Russian critics had assailed certain of its provisions. The action was a singular one with a constitutional political system, but it was not really a violation of Finnish autonomy.

There was an awareness in Finland that a chauvinistic outlook was gaining headway in ruling Russian quarters, although the Finns, perhaps, did not fully comprehend the deeper ideological bases of Slavophilism. At as early a time as the coronation of Alexander III, Meurman was shocked by the hostile attitude towards Finland that prevailed on that occasion, and he therefore exhorted the Fennomen and Svecomen to calm down in their attacks on each other; but this exhortation fell on deaf ears on both sides. Estlander spoke coarsely of the "higher" Swedish and "inferior" Finnish culture, while Yrjö-Koskinen proclaimed that in the struggle that was beginning in defence of national autonomy, the Fennomen alone represented the Finnish nation.

The more the Finnish and Russian nations drew apart, the more the Finns placed their hopes in the Czar, upon whom they continued to look as the national sovereign of their land. With a single exception, Alexander III had not destroyed the credulity of the Finns in his public decisions. Yet they did not know everything that took place within the walls of the imperial palace—for instance, they did not know that the Czar had completely accepted Minister of War Vannovski's plan to absorb the Finnish military units into the Russian army. Thus, the chairmen of the Finnish Estates aspired to gain a direct adience with the monarch in order to tell him about the concern of the Finnish people; the Czar's prestige allowed him to receive only the archbishop because, as head of the State Church, he was an appointee of the sovereign. And when, in 1894, Nicholas II ascended his father's throne and, after the custom of his predecessors, swore an oath to keep inviolate the constitutional laws of Finland, this oath was regarded as a guarantee that during the reign of the new and still unknown Czar the fundamental principles on which Finland's special status was based would continue to be honoured.

9

Autonomy Lost
and Independence Gained

The Coup d'État *of Nicholas II*

There is an often quoted saying of Snellman's: "If only, when critical times come, the Finnish people would be able to face their ordeal as a single-minded nation!" During the peiod of Russification that started at the turn of the century, this hope of national solidarity was not fulfilled. Yet, the Finland confronting the crisis was incomparably more resistant to alien pressure than she had been during the early part of the period of autonomy. Where before there had been a body of compliant public functionaries and slumbering masses of subjects, there was now a true nation, determined to defend its rights—a nation which Runebergian patriotism and the Finnish and Swedish nationalist movements had awakened to a consciousness of its separate identity, and Liberali m to a realization of its constitutional rights.

The significance of nationalist values was emphasized at the turn of the rentury by the neo-romantic current in the arts, characterized by a fervent interest in the *Kalevala*. The composer Jean Sibelius drew on the national epic for his tone poems, in whose monumental simplicity the influence of folk music can be traced. The close connection between political and cultural history is demonstrated by his world-famous "Finlandia," composed in 1899 as the finale to a series of historical tableaux staged at a patriotic festival. The artist Akseli Gallén-Kallela forsook naturalistic landscape and genre painting in favour of depicting episodes from the *Kalevala* in a synthetic manner. The poet Eino Leino wrote his most impressive verse on motifs borrowed from folklore and in the Kalevalian meter. The simultaneous appearance on the national scene of these and several other men of creative genius ushered in, at the turn of the century, a unique golden age of the Finnish spirit. The rank and file of the nation could not help being carried along by the rising tide of national self-esteem.

Thanks to the simultaneous play of numerous factors, the timber resources of the Finnish interior began to be drawn into the sphere of foreign trade around the 1870's, bolstering the economic foundations of both cultural and political life. The rural economy became commercialized and the hungry agrarian society slowly started to undergo industrialization. The export of forest products was directed towards the West. And when, around 1890, ice-breakers began to make it possible to keep a number of Finnish ports open right through the winter, Russia lost its dominant position in Finland's foreign trade. The rate of industrialization accelerated during the boom years at the very end of the century, and the humble cottagers of the Finnish countryside thronged into the towns and cities.

The basis for the labour movement was thus laid. The workers' organizations had been led by members of the educated class, who had been content to demand social reforms and voting rights for all but avoided the issue of opposition between labour and management. The organizations had not wanted the colour red on their banners because it was used abroad by "socialists and others." In 1899, organized Finnish labour broke loose from "bourgeois" tutelage and founded a separate political party under the leadership of Dr. N. R. af Ursin, who had been converted to the socialist creed. For a time, however, the party did not formulate its stand on Marxist theory. The working class movement opened the door to political life for the great masses of the people excluded from the Estates represented in the Diet and thus added depth to the front guarding the autonomous status of the country. On the other hand, there had opened up, in addition to the earlier chasm that separated the parties in the language strife, a new breach, which was no extension of the old one but was situated, in a sense, on a different level.

Such was the Finland of the period when the Russian nationalists started to decide *in toto* the Finnish policy of the empire. "We have not subjugated alien races in order to give them pleasure," declared one Russian minister somewhat later, "but because we need them." Evidently, Russia's realistic interest required re-organization measures in Finland. Thus, it seemed unreasonable that the military burden on the grand duchy should be proportionally lighter than that borne by the rest of the empire, or that Finns should enjoy greater rights in Russia than Russian subjects did in Finland. Conflicts on individual issues could have been settled, however, had not Russian nationalism—for ideological reasons—set as its goal the Russification of Finland. The Finns would not amicably submit but proceeded to resist, and the nation composed of the Czar's most loyal subjects for ninety years became hostile and unreliable. After matters had gone that far, Russia's practical interest began to require measures that earlier would have been downright harmful from the standpoint of the empire, such as the abolition of the Finnish army. Moreover, the very prestige of Russia as a great power made it necessary to force obedience on the small Finnish nation.

Russification of Finland for the sheer sake of Russification was what motivated the actions of Nicholas Bobrikov, who was appointed governor-general in 1898. He condemned the generally accepted "heresy" of the Finns, which held that the only bond between the empire and the grand duchy was a common sovereign. He had no patience with Finnish claims to constitutional government. "The dignity of Russia" required that Finland be attired in new garments in order to be recognized abroad as Russian. And, he declared, "the outbursts of evil and resistance bound to come during this work of reform must be quelled at all costs." Russians must be given the opportunity to serve in the public offices of the grand duchy, and Russian must be made the administrative language of Finland. Even in the girls' schools of Finland, Russian must be adopted as the principal subject in the curriculum, for only then would the language of the empire be sure to take root in Finnish soil—infiltrating "family life through the mediation of the women." Finland's national tariffs and monetary system must be abolished. The Finnish army must be merged into the Russian military establishment.

When Bobrikov took office as governor-general, the fate of the Finnish army was already hanging in the balance. The issue involved not only ideological but also concrete Russian interests.

A bill to revise the Finnish Conscription Act had been drawn up during the reign of Alexander III, at a time when the Czar had been negotiating with the French for a political agreement and his prospective ally had been pressing him to hasten measures designed to strengthen the Russian armed forces. The shelving of the bill for many years indicates that the question of the small Finnish military units was hardly a vital one to the empire. Governor-General Heiden, who as ex-chief of the imperial Russian staff was undoubtedly qualified to judge such matters, considered it futile to teach Finnish youth, which "was accustomed to eat salted herring, to eat buckwheat porridge"—that is, to force Finns to serve in the Russian army. Nevertheless, Nicholas II gave his approval to one of the merger plans, and a bill that called for the absorption of the Finnish army was presented to the Finnish Diet. As frightening as its provisions were, its formal aspects were even more shocking: the Diet was merely requested to render an opinion on it, and the apparent intent was to enforce the plan whether the Finnish Estates liked it or not. After recovering from the initial shock, the Estates decided to deal with the bill as if it had been submitted to them in strict accordance to the Diet Act. They agreed to a considerable increase of the national military burden and to the employment of Finnish troops in the "defense of the empire,"but they rejected the clauses that signified the abolition of the national army.

Before the Diet could work out the final form of the bill, which then gained its unanimous approval, the Czar carried out a *coup d'état*. The resistance of the Finns did not surprise the Russians; it was precisely for the purpose of overcoming the expected resistance that the Diet had been deprived of its power to amend the Conscription Act in advance. "The time has come to forget such antiquated laws as the Form of Government of 1772," the Czar wrote in his own hand on the discreetly drafted proposal vainly presented to him by the Finnish Senate as a new conscription law. Thus, the issue of the fate of the Finnish army forced into the open the question of Finnish national autonomy as a whole.

The report of the Bunge Committee had already created the concept of *imperial legislation*, i.e., legislation concerning the empire as a whole. Laws common to all the Russias—Finland included—as well as such laws in force in Finland alone which were of imperial concern were to be enacted by applying the principles of autocracy: after the Czar had received reports on a bill from the Finnish Diet, Senate, Minister Secretary of State, and Governor-General, as well as the Russian Imperial Council, he "enacted" the law quite regardless of the stand taken by any or all of those who had rendered opinions. This shortcut was to be used in reorganizing the Finnish military establishment, and when the Finns objected on the grounds that traffic along the route taken was illegal, the Russians proceeded to mark the new route on the official map.

By a manifesto issued on the 15th of February, 1899, the Czar confirmed the regulations for imperial legislation. Persuading Nicholas II to sign this unlawful document probably did not require nearly so great an effort from the high-placed Russian nationalists as was imagined in Finland. Monarchists at heart, the Finns were psychologically unprepared to believe that their sovereign had deliberately broken his pledge, given four years before, in which he had sworn to uphold the constitutional laws of the grand duchy. As the truth became known, however, His Imperial Majesty's attribute in Finnish parlance became "The Perjurer." Within a few weeks, three million of the Czar's most faithful subjects began to despise him.

During these weeks, the Finns suffered many a disappointment in trying to undo the damage. When the Manifesto was delivered to the Senate, a decision had to be made to publish it in the Statute Book of Finland; only from the moment of publication would it be in effect as law. Promulgation of every decree of the Czar's had till then been deemed an official duty that permitted no compromise. And such was the attitude of the Senate on this occasion, too, but a telegraphic message from St. Petersburg had aroused boundless indignation in Finland in advance, with the result that many of the senators began to nurse doubts. Other senators declared that the Senate, responsible as it was only to the Czar, had no business correcting him even when he was obviously guilty of lawlessness.

By a vote of ten to ten, the Senate decided to publish the Manifesto. The tie vote generally reflected the party lines without, for the time being, signifying any irreconcilable ideological split. The Senate also asked for an explanation from the Czar—as had been requested previously, and received, in the case of the April Manifesto—which would have made possible the augmentation of the Czar's authority, sought by the Russians, along legal lines, with the consent of the Finnish Diet. Representing the nation, the Diet was in a position to take a braver stand than the Senate, which was directly dependent on the Czar. The Estates declared the February Manifesto to be invalid in Finland.

Politically vigilant of old, the university students skied from farm to farm and from cottage to cottage across the far-flung, snowbound land and, in slightly more than a week, collected 523,000 signatures on a protest addressed to the Czar, petitioning him to bring the provisions of the Manifesto into harmony with the constitutional laws of Finland. This civic protest, in which nearly half the adult population took part, was an amazing demonstration of political alertness and unanimity. A slight breach was left in the popular front when the leaders of the underestimated labour movement were not invited to join the Protest Committee; but this breach was quickly repaired, and in the House of Nobles the Socialist leader Dr. Ursin called for active defence of Finland's "national existence." A deputation of five hundred men set forth to deliver the petition and the signatures, filling many volumes, to the Czar personally. Nicholas II, however, instructed the Minister Secretary of State to tell the deputation: "I shall not, of course, receive them, although I am not angry with them, either."

The name of Finland and an awareness of the peril threatening her political status spread—because of the Manifesto—throughout the civilized world. No less than 1,063 scientists, writers, and artists in different European countries drew up a petition addressed to the Czar, entitled "Pro Finlandia," which was entrusted to a deputation under the chairmanship of Senator Trarieux of France for delivery to Nicholas II.

"Scarcely a single famous name is missing from it," said the embarrassed minister of the court upon eyeing the petition. But after long deliberation the Czar nevertheless refused to receive the international deputation. On their way back home through Finland, the members of the deputation, who represented the intellectual élite of the world, were accorded an idolatrous reception, the like of which, in the words of one member, no Czar was likely to experience in that country for a long time.

It is not impossible that the international deputation slowed down the rate of Russification. At least, no attempt was made to enforce the Manifesto immediately. Still, the vacant post of Minister Secretary of State—that is, the official representative of Finland in St. Petersburg—was filled by a Russian, W. K. von Plehwe, who subsequently served at the same time as imperial minister of the interior.

Illegal Conscription Divides the Nation

In July, 1901, the Czar imposed on Finland, on the strength of the regulations for imperial legislation, a new conscription law. It was drafted wholly under the influence of Governor-General Bobrikov and Minister of War Kuropatkin. Not only the resolution of the Finnish Diet on the measure, and the opinions expressed at different stages for its passage by the Senate, but also the stand of the Imperial Russian Council towards it, were bypassed as too moderate. And, in the forms observed in handling the measure, even the stipulations of the February Manifesto were disregarded to accommodate the governor-general and the minister of war.

The existing Finnish army was dissolved. Finnish conscripts were to be situated "for the time being" in units recruited "for the most part" from Finland, but some of them could be ordered to report directly to Russian detachments stationed in Finland or in St. Petersburg as reinforcements. Moreover, Russian officers could be appointed to command detachments mainly composed of Finns, and a knowledge of the Russian language was required of their non-commissioned officers as well. As in the former Conscription Act of Finland, the task of the army was defined as the defense of "the throne and the fatherland," but this time fatherland meant, not the grand duchy, but the empire of Russia.

Right after the promulgation of the February Manifesto, a resistance organization was formed under the leadership of Mechelin. In response to the new conscription order, Mechelin drew up a protest, which once more was signed by about half a million citizens. When von Plehwe, the official representative of Finland, presented the document to the Czar, he drew attention to the fact that among the signatories were numerous civil servants. He concluded from this that, from the Russian point of view, the civil service corps in Finland was no longer trustworthy. Essential changes of personnel should therefore be made; at the worst, the corps should be Russified, though Russification was no end in itself to von Plehwe—as it was to Bobrikov—but only a means toward achieving other ends.

In Finland, it was perceived that objections were futile. The next thing a law-abiding citizen might resort to was refusing to obey illegal orders. Nobody should therefore report for military service, since the Conscription Act of 1878 was not adhered to. When the shift was thus made from open protests to disobedience, the leadership of the "passive resistance" movement was obliged to go underground, and for that purpose a secret society was founded, borrowing its name, *Kagal,* from the organization of the persecuted Jews of Russia. The Kagal exhorted the preachers not to announce military conscriptions from pulpits, the communes not to elect members to draft boards, physicians not to examine recruits and, above all, youths of conscription age not to report for service.

Only part of the populace accepted the instructions from the Kagal, and the opening of the disobedience campaign produced the most utterly irreconcilable party conflict thitherto seen in Finnish history: the division into Constitutionalists and "Compliants."

According to the constitutional point of view, the preservation of Finland's autonomy depended on the Finns themselves to maintain their rights uncompromisingly and to refuse to obey illegally imposed "laws" of the Czar or illegal decrees of the governor-general. Idealistically trusting in the triumph of justice, the unarmed nation must carry on the struggle with all the means available, without, however, resorting to violence. The Constitutionalists included nearly all the prominent judges and lawyers in the land.

The policy of compliance was pursued, on the other hand, by the majority of students of history and the members of this group did not believe in the triumph of justice. In advocating compliance, these men reasoned that considerations of prestige caused great powers to be unyielding. That is why they were prepared to yield up to a given point—how far, remained an open question, for the time being.

"In life there are many collisions of duty, but for us there can be only one course," declared V. M. von Born, one of the leaders of the Constitutionalists. "Read *Ensign Stål,* if you have forgotten your Bible, and the answer will be clear." It was essential to preserve the "bridge" by crossing which "the sovereign and the nation can once more find each other," wrote the history professor J. R. Danielson-Kalmari, a leader of the Compliants. "...A single stray step is liable to cause untold misfortune."

When Constitutionalists were ousted from official positions, Compliants stepped into the vacancies. Their excuse was that otherwise Russians would take over; as evident as the truth of this argument was, it did little to alleviate the bitterness of the expelled officials. The Constitutionalists sacrificed their jobs, their social position and their economic advantages for the good of their country. The Compliants also acted out of conviction, and their aim was also to serve the welfare of the fatherland, and it is only to their discredit that this conviction of theirs yielded them personal benefits. Among them should not be counted those who only advanced their own private interests with the aid of the foreign power; such characters did exist, and, later on, there were more of them.

Precisely because each party fought for the ideology it had adopted and not for the benefit of any special group, the chasm could not be bridged.

According to the "Citizen's Catechism" published by the Kagal, those who advocated compliance should be treated in daily life like carriers of the plague or violent criminals. Contacts between relatives and friends were broken off if they happened to take opposite sides in the conflict; they did their shopping in different stores and deposited their savings in different banks; and, in one town, a new secondary school was founded because families belonging to opposite political camps did not want their children to attend the same institution.

The course of history at first appeared to show that resistance, even at the risk of sacrificing momentary advantages, was not only morally a superior attitude to compliance but was effective as well, and therefore represented realistic politics. Consequently, the Constitutional outlook on the events of the Russification period dominated the Finnish interpretation of history with unchallenged authority between the two world wars, and all the presidents of the republic elected to office during that interval were former Constitutionalists, regardless of what party they had joined in the new political groupings. The first former member of the compliance faction to become president was J. K. Paasikivi.

When an outside threat confronts a country in which there are two fiercely opposed parties, like the Finland of the 1890's, the common peril is likely to have the fortunate effect of causing differences to be forgotten. But if disagreement arises concerning the manner of resisting the threat, as was the case in Finland after the turn of the century, the new front line is liable to be drawn close to the old one, and all the old rancour and bitterness are poured into the same cask along with new acids. The stands taken by the two language parties in the struggle to save the national autonomy were by no means the outcome of chance but the logical culmination of a long, ideological evolutionary process. The Svecomen had embraced the legacy of passionate devotion to constitutionalism left behind by the defunct Liberal party, whereas the great master of the Fennomen was Snellman, who had got close to the Czar and in his attitude toward foreign policy had represented what the Liberals viewed as a realism destitute of ideals.

Since the stronghold of the Fennomen in the Diet was the Estate of the clergy, the whole party had to some extent received a clerical colouring, and the Lutheran Church laid stress on unconditional dutifulness towards secular authority. Archbishop G. Johansson commanded the preachers to announce the illegal conscriptions in the churches: "The duty of a minister is to publicize the decrees issued by the government, and it is not his business to inquire into their legality." The majority of the ministers obeyed their superior, but the parishioners drowned out the voice from the pulpit by singing hymns.

The Svecomen suspected that the Fennomen were prepared to make concessions to the Russians just so long as the latter strengthened the status of the Finnish language. "You have presumably been told," Meurman, the

Fennoman leader, brusquely remarked to a group of foreign journalists during the Russification phase of Alexander III's reign, "that we are ready to sell our country's most cherished rights, provided the deed of sale is drawn up in Finnish." The charge was unjust, though not wholly unfounded. During Bobrikov's term as governor-general, the Compliants managed to have an edict passed that at last established Finnish in public affairs on a fully equal plane with Swedish. In any case, the language question was now of secondary importance to the Compliants, too: Fennoman Yrjö-Koskinen wanted to break off all relations with the Svecomen for the express reason that, by opposing the politics of compliance, they were, in his mind, a danger to the nation. Yet it must be noted that, ideologically, the line of compliance reverted to national romanticism: Finland's Western system of law and justice was not, according to its lights, as valuable a pillar of nationality as was the Finnish language. The national spirit expressed by the mother tongue was bound to survive, so the Compliants believed, through the trying times during which the constitutional laws were violated. Thus, the joy over the regulations passed in favour of the Finnish language was diminished among the Compliants also by the fact that previously it had been decreed that Russian should gradually be introduced into the higher administrative levels. Yrjö-Koskinen found consolation in the fact, however, that the civil servants continued to serve the public in the vernacular and that instruction was given in the schools "in the language of the land."

The old and the new battlelines lay a considerable distance apart, however. To be sure, the Svecomen, with very few exceptions, joined the Constitutionalist camp; but, of the Fennomen, the liberalistic Young Finns had been in opposition to the Senate already before the February manifesto because of its inclination towards compliance, and thereafter the party leadership failed to keep even the Old Finns in line. Some of them got together with the Young faction to found a pro-Finnish constitutional party, and aged Yrjö-Koskinen, who denounced the secessionists as the Svecomen's "Finnish-wagging tail," became the object, before his death in 1903, of abusive demonstrations. He was succeeded as party leader by the more moderate Danielson-Kalmari. The clash of opinion was, of course, by no means alleviated by the fact that the Constitutionalists one by one resigned or were removed from the Senate, which was finally left wholly in the hands of the Old Finns.

This gave Finland the equivalent of her first party Cabinet. The active policy of this government was directed towards clearly demarcating the regulations for imperial legislation by means of a law which the Finnish Diet would approve. This measure was supported by Russian moderates: influential Minister Secretary of State von Plehwe, whose nationalism did not seem to be very vehement, took an understanding attitude towards the aspirations of the Old Finns. But Governor-General Bobrikov strongly objected to the measure. He did not want to pay any price for the compliant policy of the Old Finns, and it would be unfair to imply that this party enjoyed the favour of the despot. After defeating their political opponents with the aid of the Russians, Bobrikov explained in his secret reports, the Old Finns would undertake to put up quite as tough a resistance as the Constitutionalists. The governor-general's evalution of the situation demonstrated that he understood conditions in the grand duchy even less than the Russian government did.

The Labour party was unable to elect delegates to the Diet, except in rare instances, but it had its own press and organization, and it supported the passive resistance of the Constitutionalists with the power of its masses of followers. The ideology of the international working class movement placed the party behind barricades erected against the Czar and those Finns whom it regarded as having submissively bowed down to autocracy. Although the majority of party leaders embraced the ideology of internationalism and belittled nationalist aspirations, the party nevertheless sided with the national front in the struggle against autocratic rule. In a country where the rightists systematically sabotage the decrees of the government, the leftists must be revolutionists; in a country where the ruler violates his oath and the authorities force citizens to obey illegal regulations, it is too much to expect the public to respect the law. It was the period of Russification that gave the Finnish labour movement its bold revolutionary outlook. It adopted the Marxist philosophy in 1903 and grimly took up the weapons of class strife. To the name of the party was added the description "Social Democratic," after the example of the corresponding political movements in Scandinavia and Germany, but the revisionism gaining ground in the ranks of labour in those countries remained, for the time being, more alien to the Finns.

From the standpoint of traditional parliamentary procedure, the arena that was chosen by the parties to test their strength for the first time was a strange one: the premises of draft boards during the illegal conscription of 1902. In order to ameliorate the common dread of Russian military service, the Czar decreed that in the initial conscription under the new regulations, only about one per cent of the recruits were to be taken into the army and were to be chosen by the drawing of lots. Nevertheless, three-fifths of the youths of conscription age—the proportion among the university students was as high as five-sixths—refused to report for the draft. Even moderate Old Finns were secretly gratified that participation was not total, although publicly they did exhort the youth to obey the sovereign. A heavy increase in the number of emigrants indicated that future recruits, too, sought to escape military service. The result was so embarrassing to Russia that Bobrikov's transfer to some other post appears to have been considered.

In the following two conscriptions, the resistance was less successful but still strong enough to cause the Russians to abandon their campaign in this field. The hope expressed by one member of the international deputation that the Russian bear would break its teeth on a Finnish rock was thus realized. The Finnish national army, of course, was not re-established; Russian doubts about its reliability were well founded after their five years of autocratic defiance of constitutional law. But the Finns were released from personal military service, and Finland was obliged to pay a small annual tax to the imperial treasury as compensation. The Constitutionalists had saved the young men of Finland from being sent to fight in the Russo-Japanese War.

The Dictator Is Assassinated

The failure of the conscriptions was aided by sabotage of public officials, the great majority of whom belonged to the Constitutionalist faction. Ever since the Swedish régime, government officeholders in Finland—with the exception of the governors and others who occupied so-called positions of trust—had been irremovable. The protection afforded by the law did not help much during the Russification period, however, for the Czar issued illegal decrees whereby he either assumed himself, or passed on to the governor-general, the power to dismiss civil servants. Among the civil servants removed from their posts was K. J. Ståhlberg, who was destined to become the first president of the Republic of Finland. The illegal conscription policy was the motive force that initiated the dismissals.

A peaceful demonstration, ostensibly directed against the Senate of Old Finns, was held in Helsinki. Cossacks on horseback dispersed the crowd with whips, which caused the Turku Court of Appeal to bring up an indictment against the Russian governor in Helsinki, who was chiefly responsible. The consequence of this action was that nearly the entire official staff of the court was changed —some members were discharged, some resigned. The chief justice, who followed the policy of compliance, became the target of abuse and insults from his own countrymen.

Censorship became more intolerable than ever, for the press constantly had to deal with questions about which the Russians were sensitive, and the governor-general, who had taken over the supervision of printed matter more and more, exercised his powers unscrupulously. When in October, 1903, according to the timetable previously drawn up, Russian became the language of plenary sessions of the Senate, Bobrikov was able to start acting as chairman and thus could directly influence the resolutions of the Finnish government. But even all this power was not sufficient to satisfy him.

The demonstrations that had taken place in connection with the removal of the members of the staff of the Turku Court of Appeal made the Czar more inclined to agree to demands put forward by Bobrikov which previously had been regarded even in Russia as risky: the granting of dictatorial powers. By a resolution passed in April, 1903, the Czar transferred that authority to him. The entire civil administration, including even the self-governing communes, was placed under the governor-general's authority. He was empowered to close down business establishments, suppress associations, and banish annoying individuals either to foreign countries or to other parts of the empire. The greatest bitterness was aroused by the power of banishment, which Bobrikov used to exile the Constitutionalist leaders. However, human values were still so highly regarded at the beginning of this century that even those exiles who were kept under surveillance in distant parts of the Russian empire were given tolerable treatment—as were those disobedient Finnish civil servants who, at a later stage, were shipped to prison in St. Petersburg. The exiles who were allowed a choice migrated to Sweden, whence they directed the activities of the Kagal in Finland, holding meetings secretly attended by participants from that country.

As the Russian yoke tightened, the passive resistance of the Finns began to seem ineffective and inadequate. The cosmopolitan writer Konni Zilliacus demanded that violence be met with violence, that passive resistance be abandoned for active resistance. At the "Diet of Stockholm", held in the autumn of 1903 under the chairmanship of Mechelin, Zilliacus was left in the minority; but after that he set off on his own course. With the aid of his wide circle of friends and acquaintances abroad, he maintained contact with the leaders of Russian national minorities and leftist parties, and during the Russo-Japanese War he performed valuable services for the Japanese. In Finland, kindred spirits of his occasionally exploded bombs without causing notable damage, and, at the end of 1904, Zilliacus organized an activist party to prepare for a rebellion. Before that, a young official named Eugen Schauman had rid Finland of the man who was regarded by the Constitutionalists as their chief enemy and who, in the opinion of the Old Finns, was the greatest obstacle to their policy of conciliation. That man was Bobrikov.

It was on the 16th of June, 1904, that Schauman, acting strictly on his own, without the support of any organization, shot the tyrant to death. He atoned for the murder by shooting himself immediately; but in the nationalistic view, the deed merited honour, and Schauman became a national hero. The Old Finns feared vindictive reprisals, but the vacant governor-general's post was filled by Prince Ivan Obolensky, who acted more moderately than Bobrikov, even though he obviously had the same ultimate goal. It was just around that time that the monarch abandoned his attempts to enforce his illegal conscription measures. When von Plehwe was also murdered, in Russia, a Finn of the Compliants' party was appointed Minister Secretary of State for Finland. Elections to the Diet were held at the same juncture, resulting in heavy defeat for the Old Finns, and exiles who were elected were permitted to return home and take their seats in the Diet. At the insistence of the Constitutionalists, the Estates refused to consider bills presented by the government until normal conditions were restored in the country; but the Czar announced his intention of adhering to the February Manifesto. When the external pressure was slightly relieved, the internal discord became extremely intensified. The attorney-general of Finland, E. Soisalon-Soininen, an Old Finn, was murdered. The assassin's defense lawyer was one of the jurists ousted from the Turku Court of Appeal, Pehr Evind Svinhufvud, who was to become one of the political leaders of the country.

The Czar Is Forced to Retreat

Russia was defeated in its war with Japan (1904—05). Its progress had been followed in Finland with the same enthusiasm as that of the Russo-Turkish wars during the preceding century—with the fundamental difference that, previously, Finnish sympathies had been for Russia and were now for her enemy. Neither did Russia's own persecuted opposition group grieve over the reverses on the field of battle sustained by the Czarist régime. And the peace treaty, involving acknowledgment of defeat, was such a blow to the prestige of the autocrat that the leftist political factions succeeded in calling a general strike in

October, 1905. Nicholas I was obliged to guarantee civil liberties for his subjects and to grant the authority to pass legislation to the advisory representative assembly that he had recently founded.

Just before the strike in Russia ended, it spread to Finland. The initiative was taken by organized labour, but the Finnish general strike was not aimed against management nor even against the bourgeois community, as is clearly shown by the fact that, on the whole, the employers, in order to demonstrate their solidarity, paid their employees wages for the period of the strike. The Constitutionalists also joined the strike, and the bureaus manned by Old Finns were compelled to shut their doors.

A high degree of unanimity prevailed in the negotiations between the Constitutionalists and the Socialists under the chairmanship of Svinhufvud. The February Manifesto and all the decrees and edicts issued on the strength of it would have to be abrogated, it was resolved, and both the Senate and the Minister Secretary of State would have to resign. Moreover, the Socialists firmly demanded a pledge for a thorough reform of the Diet, and the fundamentally conservative Constitutionalists acquiesced—although many of them without the slightest enthusiasm for it.

However, there was a boundary which the Constitutionalists refused to cross under any conditions because it would have signified the abandonment not only of party ideology but also of the sturdiest pillar of Finland's national autonomy: respect for constitutional law. The sole possibility of realizing the reform of the Diet along legal lines was, of course, to submit the measure to the four Estates for approval. Labour doubted that the Estates could bring themselves to introduce a wholly democratic parliamentary system, and past experience certainly justified such doubts. Moreover, national assemblies empowered to enact fundamental laws are part and parcel of the revolutionary tradition, and the Finnish Socialists, who, for lack of information, believed that the general strike in Russia was continuing, entertained the illusion that the hour of revolution was about to strike in Finland. Accordingly, they demanded in their so-called Red Declaration that the reform of the system of representation be left to a national assembly to be elected by universal suffrage. The understandable political inexperience of the working class was displayed by the election at a mass meeting, held in one of the squares of Helsinki, of a new Finnish government. Everybody present who appeared to be grown up was allowed to vote! Most of the members of this "government" did not personally take the election seriously, but the relations between the opposing sides grew critical, and both of them organized armed forces during the strike, the Constitutionalists a White Guard, and the Socialists a Red Guard.

After the despised Old Finns awakened to the realization that they had been thrust out of the stream of history, they decided to endorse the plan for a radical reform of the Diet; and, also, on the question of procedure, they approached the Socialists halfway. They thereby sought to calm the more radical elements, fearing that open revolutionary demands might cause the Russian army to take punitive action.

On November 4th, 1905, the Czar issued a proclamation that rescinded the decrees based on the February Manifesto (thus also cancelling the governor-general's dictatorial powers). The proclamation also declared the manifesto itself to be null and void "until the matters dealt with therein are arranged through legislative measures," and assigned to the Senate the task of drafting a law to democratize the structure of the Diet as well as laws to safeguard civil liberties. The Constitutionalists were satisfied and demanded an end to the general strike, but the most radical elements in the labour camp would not agree until after the White Guards had taken a hand in the matter.

Fratricidal strife was avoided by the margin of a hair's breadth. However, blood was shed the very next summer. The trouble started when the men of the Russian garrison in the island fortress of Sveaborg mutinied against their officers. Many members of the Red Guard in Helsinki joined the mutineers. The Red Guard commander, Captain John Kock, once more imagined that the revolution had dawned and called a general strike. This led to a small but ominous clash in the worker's section of town. Afterwards, the Senate disbanded the Red Guard, while the White Guard decided to disband of its own accord.

The consequence of the Great Strike was that the Senate composed of Old Finns resigned and was replaced by one composed of Constitutionalists. Mechelin took the chair. One of the senators was a Socialist, but the majority in his party considered it ill-becoming of a member to join a bourgeois government, and he was expelled from the party. For the first time, the Senate had resigned in a body and, for the first time, a homogeneous party government had been simultaneously appointed. The post of minister secretary of state was awarded to a personal friend of the Czar's, Major-General A. Langhoff, who later, under extremely difficult conditions, did his best for Finland. The post of governor-general was awarded to Privy Councillor N. Gerard, the first civilian to serve in this lofty capacity. The officials removed by Bobrikov returned to their former positions, and the Old Finns who had replaced them were forced to step aside. This was bound to open old wounds and stir up passions.

Since Finland's autonomy had been restored intact, the Constitutionalists condemned the course of action pursued by the Compliants as erroneous and took the credit for the victory. But the essential factor in its achievement had been the Russo-Japanese War and the revolutionary ferment in Russia. The political thinking of the masses of the people was profoundly influenced by the conclusion that violence was not only the surest means of defending their rights but also of bringing about the hoped-for reform of the system of representation.

Parliamentary Reform and the New Diet

The Czar's bill creating a unicameral Diet to be elected through universal and equal suffrage was presented in the spring of 1906. It was dealt with speedily and painlessly by the Estates, thus putting to shame the leftists who had doubted their ability to vote themselves out of existence. The bill was passed by the nobles by a big majority and by the other Estates unanimously; nor did any question stir up serious debate except whether the traditional system of election by the majority should be preserved or whether the proposed proportional system of elections should be adopted; the latter system was supported by all four Estates.

Thus, Europe's most radical parliamentary reform was carried out in a single sweep: the antiquated Diet of four Estates was replaced by a totally democratized system and the number of voters was multiplied tenfold (from 126,000 to 1,273,000). The increase was due not only to the fact that the unenfranchised classes gained voting rights, but also to the extension of suffrage to women.

The length of the step taken requires an explanation, especially considering that there still prevailed in Europe at that time a bicameral system of representation, in which only the lower chamber was elected by democratic elections. In Finland, plans had previously been laid to shift from the four-chamber system via the bicameral route to a single-chamber one, but, at first, internal disagreements and, later, Russification measures had forced a deferment even of minor changes. During the struggle for national rights, the sense of national solidarity had spread also to the unenfranchised elements of the population; it was desired to bring them into active participation in political affairs, "to call upon them for help in the fight". Consolation was sought in conservative quarters in the thought that, should the new parliament take on a radical hue, it would be counterbalanced by the Czar, without whom no legislative action could be completed. Even so, unanimity would doubtless have been hard to achieve had not the phrasing of the November Manifesto presupposed that suffrage would become universal and equal and the parliament one consisting of a single chamber. It was a choice of either adhering to the Czar's manifesto or leaving the Diet of four Estates as it was—and the second of the alternatives was no longer attractive to any quarter.

In the first elections under the new system, in 1907, the Constitutionalists suffered a crushing and, at least to them, wholly unexpected defeat, which proved that their ideology was incomparably more strongly represented in the privileged classes who were behind the old Diet of Estates than among the masses of the nation. The Young Finns won twenty-six of the 200 seats, and the Swedish People's party, supported by an overwhelming majority of the Swedish-speaking group, won twenty-four seats. Still more surprising—and positively stupefying to bourgeois circles—was the election success scored by the Socialists in a country where industrialization was only just beginning. The Social Democratic party captured eighty seats, and the cottagers and tenant farmers of rural areas obviously had voted heavily for labour. Also, the support of the Old Finns was stronger than might have been expected; they won fifty-nine seats. In addition, several small parties vied for votes. Among them, the Agrarian Union captured nine seats and the Christian Workers' party won two seats. The former lined up on important political decisions with the Constitutionalists and the latter with the Old Finns.

The tripartition of the new Parliament made the game of politics a complicated one, because the ground that separated the two main groups, the Constitutionalists and the Compliants, was altogether different from the ground that separated these two from the third, leftist group, the Socialists. The bourgeois parties included both conservative and radical elements, with the line of demarcation running inside the parties rather than between them, whereas the dividing factors consisted of policy in relations with Russia and, to a minor degree, the language question. On the whole, taking into account both the party programs and the positions taken in parliamentary debate, it may be said of the three old parties that the Swedish party stood farthest right, the Old Finns farthest left, and the Young Finns in between the two.

The free-for-all struggle fought by the three groups against each other is illustrated by a statement made in Parliament: "One day, Mr. Danielson-Kalmari (an Old Finn) thrusts his dagger into the heart of the Constitutionalist faction, while Mr. Sirola (a Social Democrat) rejoices that the wound is fatal. The next day, Mr. Jonas Castrén (a Constitutionalist) seizes his sledge hammer and, swinging it ferociously, shatters the Social Democratic party to smithereens. And on the third day, the Socialists and Constitutionalists join forces to kill the oft-slain Old Finns."

Collaboration was also made difficult by the uncompromising devotion of the leftists to the cause of class warfare. "We're never going to help any of you in any matter," asserted one Social Democrat to the rival bourgeois groups. Characteristic was the taking of sides in the vote on the first parliamentary interpellation in 1908: the Socialists voted no confidence and the Constitutionalists, of course, voted confidence in Mechelin's government, while the Old Finns refrained from voting. The outcome was a vote of censure, and the Mechelin Senate, honouring parliamentary principles, deemed it right to resign. In spite of Finnish wishes, the Czar had not agreed, in connection with the parliamentary reform, to making the government dependent on Parliament: but, since he himself was by no means statisfied with the Constitutionalist composition of the Senate, it was arranged for half of the senators to leave their posts, with the vacancies to be filled with Old Finns. Thus, the enemies found themselves sitting down around the same table.

Time after time, Parliament elected as speaker Constitutionalist Svinhufvud, whom the Social Democrats also supported, because they looked upon him as the most unyielding opponent of Czarism. Svinhufvud is a rare example of a man who never had to make compromises with his convictions, or even to practice diplomatic tact, and who nevertheless—even without wishing to—carved out for hiself a brilliant political career. A single anecdote suffices to depict this straightforward man's character. Every time he was elected speaker of Parliament, he used to pay a courtesy call on the governor-general. But when F. A. Seyn, a kindred spirit of Bobrikov's, took office, Svinhufvud began to neglect these calls. The governor-general dispatched an official to ask Svinhufvud whether the speaker's courtesy call was not in accordance with polite custom. "That's right," responded Svinhufvud, "but this time there will be no call." Once, the Czar dissolved Parliament right after the opening ceremonies because of the outspoken speech delivered by Svinhufvud. And when, after six years in the chair, he was obliged to hand the speaker's gavel to the Social Democrat Oskari Tokoi, the reason was his having served notice in advance that he would not hold his tongue in leash.

Svinhufvud was not alone to blame, however, for the fact that the work of Parliament was continually interrupted. There were various reasons why the Czar dissolved it four times within three years. Moreover, Nicholas II left unsigned numerous laws which Parliament had managed to enact in spite of the interruptions, and thus the work of political and social reform remained at a standstill. Accordingly, when Parliament passed a law to democratize the communal administrative system, which was controlled by a thin, privileged stratum of society, the Russian-born senators explained that unicameral legislative assemblies had not yielded positive results, for they had, it was asserted, become forums of "extreme radicalism, insufficient prudence and a deficient sense of responsibility"—and the law was not ratified. If the Socialists had branded the measures passed by the Diet of Estates as "class laws" as long as the workers were denied the vote, they now found the work of Parliament fruitless. It was bound to weaken the confidence of the working class in parliamentary procedures.

Finland Loses Her Autonomy

During the rejoicing after the victorious Great Strike, the Finns failed to perceive that upheavals boding no good for their country had occurred in Russia. Out of credulity and because they were blinded by hatred of Nicholas II for having violated his oath, the Finns even tended to interpret these upheavals as changes for the better as far as Finland was concerned. The Czar was no longer an autocrat, and his ministers and the two chambers of the imperial assembly (the Duma and the Imperial Council) became the strongholds of Russian nationalism. The opposition that had ostensibly prevailed thitherto only between the sovereign and his Finnish subjects had expanded to one between the Finns and the upper classes of Russia represented in the imperial assembly. Confronted by critical world opinion, the Czar could withdraw behind his nation's back.

Although, since the death of Alexander III, the Finns had been incapable of influencing the Czar's opinions, it was even more utterly hopeless to so much as try to make the Russian Council of Ministers or the assembly see the Finnish point of view. It did not take long for the Finns to grasp the fact that they had received merely a breathing spell and that they would be obliged to shift from the offensive—i.e., the endeavour to augment the power of their own Parliament—to defensive positions. The international situation had become more favourable for the empire, and the leftist movements on the home front had been suppressed. Russian ruling circles were annoyed over the fact that revolutionaries were finding asylum in freer Finland. It was in Finland that Lenin and Stalin, for instance, met each other for the first time.

In 1908, the Czar decreed that all matters relating to Finland were to be submitted to the Russian Ministerial Council for examination before being referred to him. This repealed the system of dealing with Finnish affairs established by Alexander I even before the Diet of Porvoo, a system that for a whole century seemed to show that between the Russian empire and the grand duchy of Finland there existed only a personal union. The next year, the Czar again issued a number of illegal decrees and edicts, one of which established Finland's participation in Russia's military expenditures on a permanent basis. The idea of drafting Finns into the imperial army had been abandoned once and for all, because the intensification of friction had made them untrustworthy in Russian eyes. At the same time, Finland's strategic importance to Russia grew, for, owing to the Swedish king's pro-German sympathies, it was believed that Sweden might join the Central Powers in the event of a major war.

The proclamation issued during the Great Strike had by no means solved the problem of establishing regulations for imperial legislation, as optimists had at first imagined, but had simply pointed the way to replacing the February Manifesto with a new instrument constructed according to legal formulae. But the demands of the Russians went even further than ten years before, and they knew full well that the Finnish Parliament would not voluntarily surrender its rights. Therefore, it was only asked to deliver a report on the new bill drafted in Russia. As one man, the otherwise dissension-torn Parliament refused to draw up a report on a matter in regard to which it had the right to enact a law or refrain from doing so. The Finns did not entertain the illusion, however, that they could prevent the Russian nationalists from carrying out their project. By a heavy majority, the bill was passed by both chambers of the Russian assembly, and the Czar signed it on June 30, 1910.

The act, providing regulations for imperial legislation, briefly signified that all the more important laws concerning Finland were thereafter to be enacted by the Duma of Russia, which at any time might arbitrarily add to the otherwise nearly endless catalogue of "matters of imperial concern." Like the other administrative districts of Russia, Finland was entitled to elect deputies to both chambers of the imperial assembly, but she never deigned to exercise this right. Finland's autonomy had been destroyed—or, more accurately, it had been reduced to the condition of a machine that is cut off from its source of power but is still running for a while on the momentum previously gathered. Finland no longer had her own legislation, but her old, independent laws remained in effect until the Russian assembly had time to enact new ones for the country.

Having gained this victory in principle, Russian nationalism did not immediately rush to carry out concrete measures. The first heavy blow was dealt Finland in 1912, when the so-called Parity Act, passed in the framework of the regulations on imperial legislation, awarded civil rights to Russians resident in the grand duchy. The reason for the enactment of this law could hardly have been the reluctance to apply for Finnish citizenship of some Russian haberdashers who had moved to Finland or their unwillingness to submit to minor restrictions imposed on the business activities of aliens. More important was the fact that the new law made it possible for Russians to man the Senate and key bureaus and to get at Finnish officials who refused to obey laws they considered illegal—which they did more on grounds of principle than for practical reasons. Numerous civil servants were ousted and sentenced to prison by Russian courts for violating the provisions of the Parity Act. Svinhufvud was banished to Siberia when he refused to recognize as his superior a Russian appointed to the lofty office of attorney-general. But this time no dictatorship was instituted, everything was arranged in accordance with the new "laws," and the press even enjoyed greater freedom than during the first period of Russification.

The post of governor-general was taken over in 1909 by the former chief of Bobrikov's bureau staff, F. A. Seyn, a man of the same general stamp as his late superior but more deceitful. The Constitutionalists resigned from the Senate in the spring of the same year, and the Old Finns remained only until autumn. On resigning, Senator Paasikivi remarked that this action ought to have proved to the Czar that all the Finns—and not only the minority consisting of Constitutionalists—opposed illegal rule. The parties that had fought each other tooth and nail during Bobrikov's time now approached each other, and the politics of compliance appeared to have ended in disaster, for the ruling Russian circles were totally lacking in desire for conciliation. The vacancies in the Senate were filled by personally ambitious climbers or Russians holding Finnish citizenship, who had the support of no political party, until the Parity Act opened the door to the Senate for Russian bureaucrats.

The Finns sought compensation for their political reverses in the non-political area of sports, and succeeded. At the Olympic Games held in Stockholm in 1912, Finland was dramatically projected on the map of the world by her runners and other athletes. Victories in sports were anything but insignificant in upholding national self-esteem during a period of political abasement.

Such was Finland when World War I (1914—18) brought on a commercial blockade, food rationing, and all the restrictions on civil liberties imposed during times of total war even in democratic countries, let alone the Czarist empire. Finland did not wage war, and, thanks to their previous passive resistance, the Finns once more escaped shedding their blood on the Russian front. Still, Finland was joined to a belligerent power.

Toward Independence

The program confirmed by the Czar for the total Russification of the grand duchy became public knowledge at the very start of the war. For a period of ninety years the Finns had been content with personal union with Russia, and—except for the quite limited circles favouring Pan-Scandinavianism during the years right after the Crimean War—they had never nursed separatist aspirations. Even the Constitutionalists had fought only for the preservation of Finland's national autonomy, without striving for more. But Arwidsson had already, in veiled language, sketched out political independence as the final goal of national development, and this dream had been plainly described during Bobrikov's time in speeches held behind closed doors. After the politics of compliance had gone bankrupt, the only alternative to national doom was complete secession from Russia. Everything had to be staked on one card: that card was Russia's defeat in the war, which would make armed rebellion possible.

It was characteristic of Finnish history that the initiative was once more taken by politically enlightened student circles. Immediately, in the autumn of 1914, student leaders fearlessly undertook negotiations both for foreign aid, without which no struggle for freedom was possible, and for the backing of the native political parties. Old party lines were shattered: in all the bourgeois groups, there were men of caution, who turned their backs on the students' appeal, but also men of courage, who, willing to risk both their personal freedom and the remaining shreds of national autonomy, were prepared to direct the new activist movement. Among those favourably inclined towards the undertaking was also the top leader of the Social Democrats, Oskari Tokoi, who, however, warned the students about elements in his party that were liable to turn a war of liberation into a civil war. Under the historian's magnifying glass, very few adventurers have been exposed among the *Jaegers;* the young men undertook their uncertain mission in the spirit of sacrifice for their native land.

Many activists would have preferred to establish their base of operations in neighbouring Sweden, but the Swedes held grimly fast to their neutrality. Thus the eyes of most activities became focused on Russia's chief enemy, Germany, which had won victories on the eastern front and in whose own interest it was to cut Finland off from the Czarist empire. Germany promised to give military training to Finnish volunteers, and men began to be enlisted systematically on all levels of society toward the creation of the core of an army of liberation for Finland. Many a recruiting agent and many a recruit was caught by Russian gendarmes, but a couple of thousand men managed to cross the border into Sweden and from there to make their way to Germany. There, the 27th Prussian Light Infantry Battalion, composed of these Finns, was given the promised training, but resentment was aroused when it was sent as a unit into open battle on the Baltic front.

The problem of arranging the status of the Finnish *Jaegers,* as the members of the battalion being trained by the Germans were called, and the question of Finland's political future compelled the activists to create a secret diplomatic apparatus. The people in charge of the Kaiser's foreign affairs were cautious and would not promise the Finns more than that Germany would try to secure international guarantees for Finland's autonomy at the peace conference. Toward the same end, certain private Finnish quarters turned to the American and British governments, but prevailing opinion considered it unrealistic to place any hopes in the Western Powers. If the latter were to win the war, their ally Russia would also be on the winning side and would refuse to make any concessions. This logical conclusion was not, however, destined to prove correct.

Decrepit Czarism was unable to endure the wear and tear of waging a major war that involved terrific casualties and territorial losses. The storm raised by the revolution of March, 1917, blew down the rotten tree. The provisional government set up to replace the Czar declared null and void all the illegal measures that had been directed against Finland and thereby restored the country to her constitutional, autonomous status. Finnish political prisoners in Russia were released and allowed to return home, and their persecutor, Governor-General Seyn, was arrested and sent to jail in St. Petersburg. Finland had won again; the objective of the passive resistance in defence of the country's rights had been gained once more. The happy twist of fate had the effect of bolstering again the idealism of the Finns and their faith in the triumph of justice in history.

In spite of her victory, Finland was teeming with questions. Since there had existed a personal union between Finland and Russia, as the Finns understood it, had the bonds been totally cut after the overthrow of the Czar? If the many-headed provisional Russian government was entitled to resume the full authority of the sovereign in Finland, did that mean that the same authority must automatically pass on to any organ whatsoever that exercised the ruling power in Russia? At any rate, should not a bigger share than before of the "supreme authority" be delegated to Finnish organs of government, and, if so, how much should go to the Parliament and how much to the Senate? Thus, the problem also took on an internal political aspect. And, since Finland now had attained the goal of her fight for justice, should not the activist movement cease?

The most influential political leader of revolutionary Russia, Kerenski, took a trip to Finland to exhort the Finns to be loyal, and the commander of the Russian Baltic Fleet engaged in negotiations with the Finnish student leaders. Neither succeeded: activism continued to live, and independence, which earlier had only been whispered about in trusted company, was discussed openly. To all the afore-mentioned questions, however, different answers were given, which eventually crystallized into political programs.

Finland gave *de facto* recognition to the provisional Russian government as the power that exercised "supreme authority" by carrying out its rulings. Thus, the provisional government appointed a new Senate for Finland. When the previous general elections had been held, the Czar had announced that the Parliament chosen would not be convened until the war was over; consequently, the turnout at the polls was extremely poor and the Socialists won an absolute majority— not of the votes, to be sure, but of the parliamentary seats (103 out of the 200). This exceptional distribution of power in home politics later had a fundamental effect on Finland's fortunes, owing to the disappointment felt by the leftists on losing their majority position at the following election. Until then, however, the parliamentary strength of the Socialists encouraged them to change their established tactics to the extent of agreeing to accept seats in the government of a capitalist country. All the political figures were represented in the new Senate. There were an equal number of Social Democrats and "bourgeoisie," but the president, Tokoi, belonged to the former.

The leftists' dominant position in Parliament tempted them to transfer to it as great a share of the Czar's authority as possible. Under the delusion of having obtained the consent of the Mensheviks, or Russian Social Democrats, the Finnish Social Democrats pushed through, in July, the so-called Power Act: Parliament declared itself to be vested with the "supreme authority" in Finland, leaving, however, foreign policy and military affairs in the hands of the Russian government. The act was criticized by bourgeois spokesmen on grounds of domestic politics: Under the circumstances that prevailed at the time, the measure threatened to lead to the dictatorship of a single party. Viewed from a longer perspective, it would have created a state in which the government would merely have amounted to a parliamentary committee. The bourgeois members of Parliament did not block the passage of the bill, however, even though they were in a position to do so,* because the alternative would have been to leave the "supreme authority" in the hands of the Russian government and because the law, in any case, took the country closer to its goal of national independence. Besides, the bourgeois deputies were subjected to extraparliamentary pressure

* According to the regulations that have been in force throughout the existence of the unicameral Parliament in Finland, any amendment of constitutional law requires a majority of two-thirds, or, if it is desired to amend a law without submitting it for reconsideration by the next Parliament, a majority of five-sixths.

from the extreme left. Violent strikes, mass demonstrations and harassment of the oligarchical municipal councils were part and parcel of the prevailing order.

The provisional government under Kerenski, in which the Mensheviks were participants, would not ratify the Power Act but ordered the dissolution of the Finnish Parliament. This decision had the effect of bringing the Finnish Socialists nearer to the Russian leftists who were outside the Kerenski government — the Bolsheviks. The attitude of the Finnish bourgeoisie stiffened. When the dissolution order reached the Senate, all the bourgeois senators voted in favour of its being carried out, and, contrary to custom, Governor-General Stakhovich cast a ballot, thereby breaking the tie vote. Accordingly, it was decided to obey the order. Parliament dissolved recalcitrantly, and the Social Democrats gradually resigned from the Senate.

The new elections dropped the leftists into the minority (92 seats). No political landslide had taken place, but the voting was heavy and the result thus reflected popular opinion better than the preceding general election had. Also the disproportion between the number of votes and that of seats among the parties was smaller. The Agrarian Union captured twenty-six seats and it thereby became a faction corresponding in size to the older bourgeois parties. The Socialists were surprised, disappointed, and bitter towards the bourgeoisie, who had co-operated with the Russian government in enforcing the dissolution order and even had openly rejoiced in it.

After labour had lost its majority position in Parliament, it became increasingly difficult for the parliamentary wing of the party to restrain the revolutionary wing. Paralysis of the import trade had brought the nation close to the brink of famine, and the paralysis of the export trade had caused heavy unemployment, which was no longer alleviated, as in earlier war years, by fortification works paid for by the Russian army. The act passed by the preceding Parliament to democratize communal administration had not till then been ratified by the "supreme authority." Social reform remained at a standstill, and many tenant farmers feared eviction after the temporary edicts that banned evictions lapsed. The formation of the political front was influenced by the fact that the bourgeois parties had drawn closer together throughout the second Russification period and by the fact that, after the Russian revolution, the issue dividing the Constitutionalists and the Compliants had completely lost its significance.

Two private armies were forming in the country, which now had no official military organization and whose police forces also were weak, because the Russian gendarmerie had been disbanded after the March revolution. The armies were the bourgeois Civil Guards, or White Guards, and the socialistic Red Guards. The activists had organized the Civil Guards to drive the Russian troops out of the country, only partly to advance any internal political interests. The parliamentary wing of the Socialists did not approve the formation of the Red Guards, but it was incapable of preventing their organization.

The revolutionary elements among the Finnish Socialists were strengthened by the radical trend of Russian sentiment; the influence spread either directly from St. Petersburg or through the agency of Russian troops stationed on Finnish soil. On the 7th of November, the Bolsheviks seized power in Russia, and, after this new revolution, events started to move in Finland in a mad rush.

The cautious bourgeois quarters that up to then had repudiated the activists' ideal of national independence were now ready to explain that Russia was in chaos and therefore the exercise of "supreme authority" there had ceased. The desire for independence of the revolutionary wing of the Finnish Socialists dwindled after the upheaval in Russia. The party as a whole wanted, at all events, to hold tight to the Power Act, if for no other reason than internal politics. It drew up a coarsely worded program that contained the Power Act and a collection of resolutions of principle in the sphere of social legislation, which by eliminating "futile formalities" were to be put into effect by the same rap of the gavel that decided the political status of Finland. To oppose this program in Parliament, a conservative plan was drawn up, entrusting the authority of the Czar to three regents; and this plan triumphed when the bourgeois deputies voted for it in a body. But the decision remained in force only for a week.

The labour union organization, which had fallen under the control of extremists, called a political general strike, and the weak police force was helpless to prevent violence. Some thirty peaceful citizens were murdered. Then, once again, the parliamentary elements among the Socialists gained the upper hand over the revolutionaries, and part of the bourgeois deputies submitted to a compromise solution: On November 15, Parliament resolved, by a considerable majority, to take over the "supreme authority... for the time being..., inasmuch as it has not yet been possible to elect the regents." No reservation was made on this occasion in respect to foreign policy and military affairs. *De facto,* Finland had declared herself independent. After Parliament, exercising the prerogatives of the Czar, had then ratified certain laws that had been championed by labour and passed during the summer, the strike was called off. A proclamation issued by the Central Revolutionary Council set up by the extremists on the left fairly bristled with threats, but the still weak counterforces who were determined to defend society gained time for organizing.

The bloodshed perpetrated by the strikers had destroyed the last possibilities of collaboration between the "Whites" and the "Reds." And the entire Social Democratic party had become compromised in the eyes of the bourgeoisie despite its great inner dissension. The new government consisted of bourgeois representatives alone, and the chair was taken by Svinhufvud, who had reaped fame by opposing Russification and who enjoyed a reputation of unyielding firmness. In practice, the powers assumed by Parliament were concentrated in the hands of the government, especially after the Senate on January 12, 1918, received broad authority from Parliament to create a firm system for maintaining law and order.

Because of the general strike, the resolution of November 15 did not receive wide recognition at home or abroad; moreover, it was not clearly formulated and was not a fitting declaration of independence. On December 4, while revolutionary Russian troops held a noisy meeting in front of the Senate building, Svinhufvud submitted to Parliament a proposal drafted by K. J. Ståhlberg for a Form of Government for an independent republic of Finland, and, on the same occasion, he delivered a brief, simple speech for Finnish independence. To this measure was added a still simpler public declaration by

Parliament, and its commemoration on December 6 is annually celebrated as Finland's Independence Day. So widely divergent were the paths already taken by the "Whites" and the "Reds" that, at that momentous turning point in the fortunes of the nation, it was not possible to arrive at a wording satisfactory to both camps. The leftists' proposal, which was rejected, stressed the necessity of reaching an agreement with the Bolshevik government on Finnish independence.

Independence could become a reality only after the foreign powers had granted recognition to it and the Russian troops had withdrawn from the country. The withdrawal depended on Russia alone, and in regard to foreign recognition, Russia also held the key position. But the Finnish Senate was at first unwilling to turn to the Soviet government, for it shared the view prevailing in Europe at the time that the Bolsheviks, who had suffered a defeat in the recently held elections of the national assembly, empowered to enact constitutional laws, would not remain in power long. It also feared that, by entering into relations with the Reds, it might prejudice the succeeding White government. The Germans were less biased, since they were then engaged in peace negotiations with the Soviet government; and Germany actually put pressure on Svinhufvud to ask Lenin to recognize Finnish independence. As has been pointed out, the Soviet government wanted to show the world that it alone possessed full power in Russia, and it had informed the Germans that it would respond favourably towards such a request, provided that the Finns initiated the negotiations. Recognition of Finnish independence was in line with the principle of national self-determinaton that was held by Lenin. As a recent study has brought to light, every nation had to be granted the right, according to the Bolshevik ideology, to secede from Russia in order to carry out its own revolution and finally return to the fold as a member of the federation of Soviet republics. In a speech made by Stalin at the time of the Red insurrection in Finland, he counted this country among the Soviet republics.

Svinhufvud traveled to St. Petersburg and, on New Year's Eve, the Council of People's Commissars reached a decision to recognize the sovereignty of Finland. Russian recognition was followed by most of the other countries; France, of the Entente powers, acted as quickly as her enemy, Germany, and neutral Sweden. And the Finnish Parliament announced that the newly established state would pursue a policy of neutrality in the world conflict, which was still raging. Only the American and British governments exercised caution and restraint in dealing with the question of recognizing Finland.

The War of Liberation that also Became a Civil War

Getting rid of the Russian troops stationed in Finland proved to be a more difficult task than gaining recognition abroad. The strength of the Russian land forces inside the Finnish boundaries was about 40,000 men, in addition to the Russian naval units anchored in Finnish harbours. The Soviet government wanted to keep some troops in Finland in order to prevent a military vacuum from forming along Russia's northwestern border and also, possibly, in order to be on hand to assist the Finnish revolutionaries. Viewed from the standpoint of Finland, the very existence of internal unrest made the presence of foreign troops dangerous — besides limiting, in principle, the sovereignty of the country.

The leaders of the activist movement deliberated slowly and squeamishly on security measures until there appeared among them a man who demanded a swift decision. This man was Lieutenant-General Gustaf Mannerheim, who had served in the Czarist forces and had returned to his native land after the revolution. At a meeting held in the middle of January, he declared: "If you gentlemen are able to travel north on tonight's train, you must start off immediately!"

Around the same time, Svinhufvud assigned Mannerheim the task of creating a military organization. And on the 27th of January, 1918, the Senate named him commander-in-chief. Simultaneously, it raised the Civil Guards to the status of the country's official armed forces. Now Finland no longer had two private armies, but troops under the authority of the lawful government facing illegal forces. No ministry of war was established; instead, the commander-in-chief decided all military questions.

The leadership of the young state had thus been placed in the hands of two strong men, Svinhufvud and Mannerheim. They differed greatly in personality, and the collaboration between them was not entirely without friction. One foreign diplomat has described the two tellingly: "On the one hand, rugged, angular, democratic Svinhufvud, who outwardly appears almost deliberately careless, but who, in his objectivity, straightforwardness, and clarity of judgment, rises above the whole of his surroundings and who is a passionate Russian-hater and unmistakably a Finn; on the other hand, the aristocratic, extremely elegant cavalry general, highly polished and suave, a favourite of the ladies, who feels sympathy for the Russians and the Swedes." With amazing skill, this general, who spoke Finnish poorly and who had become alienated from his native land during his long stay in Russia, gained the favour of the Ostroboth-nian peasantry and became the idolized national hero of the whole of White Finland.

Ostrobothnia, whence there were the best communications abroad, had been chosen as the main base of White operations in the War of Liberation. Considerable Russian forces were stationed there, but, on the other hand, there was only slight Red Guard activity. The taking of action was hastened by an order issued by the Soviet government's commissar of military affairs, Podvoi-ski, to the Russian forces stationed in Finland to disarm the Civil Guards. To be sure, the Finnish envoy to Petrograd persuaded Podvoiski to rescind his order; but Mannerheim was notified of the rescission too late to stay his hand. It was during the dark hours before the dawn of January 28, 1918, that Mannerheim started a systematic attack against the Russians in the southern part of the province. The undisciplined enemy troops were disarmed after slight skirmishes. Even before that, the insignificant Russian garrisons in northern and central Karelia had surrendered.

By an odd coincidence, the Reds started their insurrection in Helsinki on the very same night. At the Social Democratic party meeting that was held right after the general strike, where no less a personage than Josef Stalin had been a guest and had urged the Finnish workers to seize power, the advocates of democratic procedure had still managed to maintain the upper hand. The significance of the moderates' victory, however, had been diminished by the deliberate vagueness of the wording of the resolution that was passed at the meeting. But, in January, with the aid of the Red Guards, the extremist minority in the party executive usurped control at the suggestion of Trotsky, the Soviet Commissar for Foreign Affairs. Thereafter, the Social Democratic party resolved to seize the whole country. Thus was born a dictatorship of the minority of the minority.

To exercise ruling power, the Reds set up a People's Commission under the chairmanship of K. Manner. Among the other members, the best known today, by virtue of his later career, was O. V. Kuusinen. Out of feelings of solidarity with the working class, many a Socialist who possessed a fundamentally democratic outlook placed himself at the disposal of the People's Commission, even though his doubts were silenced by the rejoinder: "Now is not the time for questions but for obedience to orders!" Recently, it has been demonstrated by one research scholar that the administrative organization of the People's Commission had been borrowed, down to many of its details, from Russia. This provides additional evidence that the revolution did not grow spontaneously from within but was a foreign importation. It would have been surprising, as another scholar puts it, if in a country that had belonged to Russia during the Bolshevik revolution no attempt at staging a revolution had been made. Within a few days, the line of battle was established between the area under the control of the Reds and the area under Senate control (map 3).

This line was so situated that approximately half the population of Finland lived on the Red side and half on the White side. In the area ruled by the Reds, the national capital and the country's chief industrial centers were located, yet life went on more normally on the White Side. For twenty years, the Finnish nation had been fighting expressly for the cause of "legality" and against Russia. Therefore, no propaganda was needed to bring about a silent but all the more stubborn condemnation of the illegal government, which was backed, moreover, by Russia. The rather rare educated Social Democrats kept their hands clean of the insurrection, with a few exceptions, and now it was seen how difficult it was to govern without an educated class. Civil servants failed to report to their bureaus for work and teachers stayed away from school; the banks and most shops closed their doors, and the factories would have ceased production had not the People's Commission threatened to nationalize those that did not continue operations—under the presence of war activities, it had no time to carry out a general socialization of the country.

The Red government was helpless to cope with the passive resistance against it, and it was unable even to maintain discipline among its own followers. The People's Commission itself frowned on violence, but mass murders were instigated especially on a fairly high level by the Red Guard, and the investigations set into motion by the People's Commission were aborted by sabotage in the ranks of the Red Guard. The few White Guards taken prisoner by the Reds ran a high risk of execution. Some fifteen hundred persons were murdered. The lack of trained military personnel fundamentally handicapped operations of the Red troops, for they had scarcely any officers besides some Russians who had volunteered their services.

The White administrative apparatus was handicapped by the fact that most of the civil servants lived in Red Finland. The majority of the members of the Senate, among them, and at a late stage, even Svinhufvud, had succeeded in escaping to Ostrobothnia, while the rest went into hiding. The core of the White Army was composed of Civil Guard volunteers. The Ostrobothnians went to war singing hymns, as if on a holy crusade: but, as soon as their own province had been purged of Russians, they took the unmilitary liberty of making occasional trips to their homes. The manpower requirements for conquering Southern Finland could not be completely filled by calling for volunteers. Consequently, recruiting for compulsory military service was begun on the basis of the Conscription Act of 1878, which had been illegally repealed by Nicholas II. Fresh recruits were given hasty training and the *Jaegers* of the Finnish battalion, whom Germany permitted to return to Finland in February, received officers' commissions.

However, the front froze, bringing great distress to Red Finland. The problem of reinforcements came to the fore. Mannerheim had accepted the commission of commander-in-chief on the express condition that foreign troops would not be called upon to help. And the acting chairman of the Senate, Heikki Renvall, wrote to Edvard Hjelt, who was representing Finland in Berlin: "Foreign assistance would deprive our struggle for liberation of its nobility and cause the wild fire of class hatred to burn deep into the nation's soul, there to smoulder." Long before that Hjelt, on his own initiative, had requested that the German government send an expeditionary force to help the White army. When the Finnish government subsequently joined in the request, there ensued a dramatic episode, for Mannerheim announced that he would resign. The quest of a new commander-in-chief actually was instituted, but agreement was finally reached.

In Germany, the matter was complicated by the signing of the Peace Treaty of Brest-Litovsk on March 3, which led German foreign policy to closer relations with the Bolsheviks, whose opponents inside the Soviet Union were supported by the Western Allies. Germany was unwilling, therefore, to undertake any action liable to be construed as being directed against the Soviet government. On the other hand, according to the terms of the Treaty of Brest-Litovsk, the Russian troops were supposed to withdraw from Finland. The German military championed intervention, because "Finland is Germany's natural ally against Great Russia, not only with the final period of the war but also with the peace to follow in view," to quote Field Marshal von Hindenburg. But the German political leadership did not welcome the idea. Kaiser Wilhelm decided the question by siding with the military. The Germans even accepted certain terms laid down by the recipient of their assistance. First of all, the Germans announced that they were lending a hand not in order to "meddle in her domestic affairs but to help Finland in her fight against a foreign foe." Te German troops in Finland were to be subordinated to Mannerheim's orders— though they actually operated under the command of General von der Goltz, almost totally separated from the Finnish forces. Finland, for her part, submitted to a treaty that circumscribed its discretionary powers in foreign affairs by making concessions in Germany's favour and that gave Germany almost a monopolistic position in its foreign trade.

After the German promises had been received, Mannerheim actually pressed the Germans to hasten their aid, but he also accelerated the offensive operations of the White army in order to gain a decisive victory before the arrival of assistance from abroad. The stubbornly defended Red base of Tampere, an industrial city, was captured at the beginning of April, after a gory battle that lasted many days, and, at the same time, a strong Russian unit that had crossed the frontier was encircled and destroyed on the Karelian Isthmus.

On April 3, the Germans landed on the coast of the Gulf of Finland. In nine days, they advanced to Helsinki. Finnish Civil Guards came out of hiding to take part in capturing the city. With the Germans advancing from the south and the government troops from the north, the Reds were squeezed ever harder, and within a few weeks, in spite of their tough resistance, they were all forced to surrender. On May 16, which until World War II was celebrated in Finland as a kind of second Independence Day, Mannerheim, "a theatrical director by the Grace of God," rode at the head of his army into festive Helsinki. In arranging his victory parade, he evidently sought to turn the attention and overflowing admiration of the Whites of southern Finland away from the Germans to the exploits of their own army. At the end of the war, the country was free of uninvited foreign military forces, and this circumstance alone justifies use of the expression "War of Liberation."

The members of the People's Commission and the several other leaders managed to escape to Russia, but over 70,000 soldiers of the Red Guard had been taken captive by the Whites. The release of the prisoners after the end of hostilities was prevented, first, by fear of a new insurrection, which the Red fugitives threatened to foment, and, second, by a desire to separate the violent criminals who were guilty of plundering, arson, and murder from the group. Despite the special laws passed to speed up the machinery of justice, it was impossible to carry out the investigations overnight. Santeri Alkio, leader of the Agrarian Union, wrote during the war: "The Reds have started an insurrection to wipe out national independence just after its achievement." And the liberal poet Eino Leino noted that Lenin's idea of reunification had become realized on the part of Red Finland. Both statements by representatives of the political center reflect the prevailing sentiment in White Finland, and everybody on the defeated side was considered guilty of treason. Eight thousand Reds were shot—after more or less arbitrary courts-martial—at the end of the war. Of course, the victory of the People's Commission would surely have brought about Finland's absorption into the Soviet Union, but the Reds could scarcely have been aware of such a probability; they only aimed at a social revolution. Since even the free population was caught in an acute food shortage, the prisoners' rations were quite inadequate, and more than twelve thousand Reds perished in prison camps of hunger and disease. In later discussion relating to the war, excessive attention has been paid to the stand taken by the tenant farmers. The crofters remained fairly passive, however, and among the men killed in battle the percentage of crofters, fathers and sons, was about the same on both sides. The crofters did not compose the core of the Red forces, and they did not have any reason to join the Red ranks, either: Svinhufvud's government had submitted to Parliament a bill creating independent holdings of the tenant farms, whereas the People's Commission proclaimed their holders to be lessees of the State.

The conflict was over. But because it had been a war of liberation, a state of war continued to exist with the Soviet government, and because it had been a civil war, besides, it left wounds in the body and soul of the nation that were slow to heal.

10

Independent Finland

Internal and External Stabilization

Czar Nicholas II's treachery had reduced the traditional monarchistic sympathies of most Finns, and the draft of the Form of Government submitted by the Senate to the Diet in conjunction with the Declaration of Independence called for the establishment of a republic. But even in those days, there were monarchists, and the alternative solution championed by them was based on foreign policy. In requesting military aid from Germany, Hjelt, for instance, took the liberty of indicating that Finland, out of gratitude, would elect a German prince as king.

The Civil War had the effect of tremendously bolstering support for a monarchical system on the theory that so great an authority could be concentrated in the hands of the government that it would forestall any future attempt to stage a rebellion. In his speech on the occasion of the victory parade, Mannerheim, without making any direct reference to monarchy, gave expression to a growing sentiment: "The Army considers it its right to voice openly the hope that guarantees be given toward preventing a recurrence of such conditions by the creation of a social system and governmental authority which would forever safeguard us against a new régime of terror like the one our country has just been delivered from." And as witnesses he called upon those whom nobody dared gainsay: "The fallen demand that they will not have made their sacrifice in vain."

The army did not take a direct hand in politics, however, nor did it need to. Since nearly all the socialist M.P.'s were absent—having directly or indirectly participated in the rebellion—the monarchists controlled a majority in Parliament. The Civil War had broken out before the republican Form of Government could be dealt with; and since the view was that no revolution had taken place in Finland, it could be explained without resort to juridical sophistries that the fundamental laws that dated back to the reign of Gustavus III were still in force. The power that resided through these laws in the sovereign—at first the Swedish king and subsequently the Russian Czar—was now given to a native regent.

In May, 1918, Svinhufvud was elected regent. The new government appointed by him, with J. K. Paasikivi as Prime Minister, consisted wholly of monarchists. Neither of the monarchistic Forms of Government proposed by it could, however, muster the support of the required five-sixths' majority although in the latter, especially, the authority of the monarch had been considerably reduced from that enjoyed by the Czar. After suffering their second defeat, the monarchists made hasty preparations to elect a king on the basis of a certain clause in the Form of Government of 1772.

Since no Finn could even be considered as a candidate for the throne, the election also posed a problem of foreign politics. As soon as the Paasikivi government took office, Commander-in-chief Mannerheim surprised them by resigning. The reasons for the suddenly aggravated disagreement were pondered at the time and have been pondered since. Much attention has been given to the organization of the army. Svinhufvud and the government followed the program of the German military experts that had arrived in the country and sought to organize the Finnish army on the basis of preparedness for prompt action, and thus to be capable of supporting German policies during the raging world war, though at the risk of weakness in the future. Mannerheim worked with a long-range aim, it has been claimed, and, by proceeding slowly, sought to create a strong army. The fundamental reason for the conflict, however, was probably that Mannerheim, contrary to the Senate, did not believe in Germany's victory and wanted to avoid becoming compromised by holding a high post while the pro-German trend prevailed in Finland.

This trend caused the eyes of the king-seekers to focus on Germany, where princes had been an article of export in olden times. The Finnish monarchists were unwilling to settle for less than Wilhelm II's own son, Oscar, but the Germans were not attracted by the prospect of having Finland so firmly bound to their own destiny, for the preservation of the Finns' young independence looked pretty uncertain. The Finns were motivated by the same sense of uncertainty but drew the opposite conclusion: the Kaiser's son alone could give their country a guarantee of Germany's future military support against Russia. Regent Svinhufvud made a trip to Germany to exert personal pressure on Wilhelm II toward letting Oscar ascend the throne of Finland, but his efforts were to no avail. On the other hand, the political leadership of Germany expressed the hope that Finland would become a monarchy "in the interests of Finland and both parties." In October, 1918, Parliament decided to offer the Finnish crown to Friedrich Karl, Prince of Hessen.

When the monarchists, realizing that they were not supported by the majority of the nation, elected a king from a country on the verge of defeat in a major war, they demonstrated twofold political shortsightedness. Still, it should be borne in mind that the background of the monarchistic strivings was a yearning for security: in its perilous position, the nation reached out for support where it imagined it could be found. The same consideration of security also determined the policy in regard to East Karelia, the territory across the eastern frontier, although a further factor was the romantic nationalistic sentiment. Since Czarist Russia appeared to be splitting up into many segments and a British expeditionary force was advancing down from the Arctic coast into East Karelia, the sparse native population, closely related to the Finns, was caught up in a wave of separatism.

Map 4 A: The Finnish Winter War, 1939–40
       B: War with the U.S.S.R., 1941–42

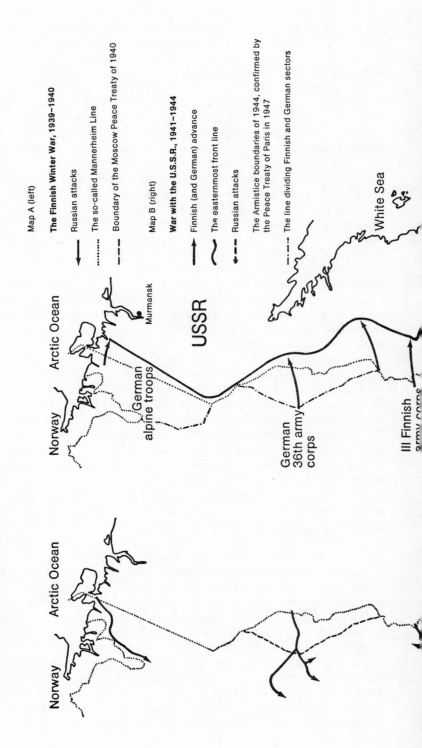

Map A (left)

The Finnish Winter War, 1939–1940

Russian attacks

The so-called Mannerheim Line

Boundary of the Moscow Peace Treaty of 1940

Map B (right)

War with the U.S.S.R., 1941–1944

Finnish (and German) advance

The easternmost front line

Russian attacks

The Armistice boundaries of 1944, confirmed by the Peace Treaty of Paris in 1947

The line dividing Finnish and German sectors

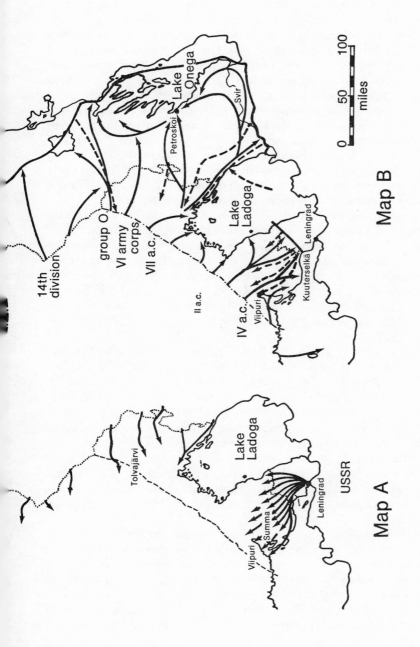

14th
division

group O

VI army
corps

VII a.c.

II a.c.

IV a.c.

Viipuri

Kuuterselkä

Leningrad

Lake
Ladoga

Petroskoi

Lake
Onega

Svir

Map B

0   50   100
miles

Tolvajärvi

Viipuri

Summa

Leningrad

Lake
Ladoga

USSR

Map A

In one pathetic order of the day that dated back to the War of Liberation, Mannerheim spoke of driving "Lenin's troops" out of "Viena Karelia" (northern East Karelia) too. All the bourgeois parties of Finland were interested in annexing the territory, because Finland thereby would secure a shorter and more easily defensible border in the east. The questions of forming a monarchy and conquering East Karelia were entwined in many ways. Without a monarchy, it would not be possible to obtain the support of Germany, observed Paasikivi, and, without the support of Germany it would not be possible to take possession of East Karelia. This line of argument, it was believed, would convert the Agrarian party from its republican to a monarchistic outlook. But the Germans double-crossed the credulous Finns. In August, Germany made an agreement with the Soviet government whereby the Germans and Finns would join forces to drive the British troops out of northwestern Russia, after which the army that was carrying out the operation would be withdrawn; no mention was made of compensation to Finland for participating.

Germany proved to be too near exhaustion, however, to undertake any hostilities in the far North. Every day brought it closer to collapse. When there could be no further doubt about the outcome of World War I, the Finnish government decided to enter into relations with the Western powers.

Svinhufvud swallowed his pride and summoned Mannerheim. The former commander-in-chief did likewise and responded. Conscious of his importance, the general said, "So now you want to play your trump card." Mannerheim traveled to England, where he was coolly received, and to France, where it was considered important to confine Bolshevism geographically through European collaboration and where Finland's fight for freedom had excited admiration. Mannerheim's courtly manners gained him personal esteem, and in spite of the fact that the White Russians were conspiring against Finland, his diplomatic skill bore fruit.

The opening of foreign relations called for changes in Finland. The German troops, which the Finns never considered to be an army of occupation, as they were branded by the Allies, left the country. Friedrich Karl, who had not yet accepted the Finnish Parliament's offer of the crown, now refused it. Svinhufvud resigned and Mannerheim was elected to take his place as regent. Parliament was dissolved in order to give the whole nation a chance to express its views on the planned constitution, and a new government took office. After the elections, Britain and the United States recognized Finnish independence. At first, they had laid down the condition that the Versailles Peace Conference decide the boundaries of Finland, but the Finnish government rejected this demand insofar as it concerned territory which, historically, had been part of the country.

The revision of Finnish foreign policy did not relieve the tension between Soviet Russia and Finland; on the contrary, it was the Entente powers that supported, albeit weakly, the counter-revolutionary armies pitted against the Red troops in Russia. During Mannerheim's tenure as regent, the question of intervention in Russia by the victorious Allies and, incidentally, by Finland, too, was constantly being aired as the military situation in that chaotic land continued to change from week to week. Mannerheim, however, found it impossible to reach an understanding with the ex-generals of the Czarist army, who even refused to acknowledge Finnish independence; but, regardless of them, Finnish forces kept a couple of East Karelian rural districts occupied and Finnish volunteers operated over an extensive area jointly with East Karelian "Whites" against the "Reds."

As early as the 1917 elections, the Old and Young Finns had merged for practical purposes; and, as the political picture changed, the supporters of these factions became realigned on new grounds. The issue of the new constitution at first formed the political watershed, but the realignment of parties remained even after this issue had been surmounted. The rightist party established in the autumn of 1918 selected a name that identified the merger, the National Coalition, and the centrist party founded around the same time adopted a name that stressed its program of reform, the National Progressive party.

The Finnish working class movement reorganized itself under the leadership of Väinö Tanner, who had been a member of Tokoi's government, as a revisionistic Social Democratic party on the Western model. By his strength of will and energy, Tanner managed to keep the working class in line even while the masses, instilled with the doctrine of class struggle, were still incapable of grasping his parliamentary point of view.

The parliamentary elections of March, 1919, relaxed internal tensions, and the Social Democratic party captured 80 of the 200 seats. Since the National Coalition won only 28 seats and the other monarchist party, the Swedish People's party, won 22, it was a foregone conclusion that Finland would become a republic. But even the Progressives and the Agrarians insisted on a strong executive, and at this stage the main controversy was between the bourgeois and the Social Democratic parties. In the case of the majority of the statutes, the point of view of the former won. Mannerheim reluctantly but loyally signed the new Form of Government on July 17, 1919.

Still in force, this constitution gives the Finnish head of State greater power than Western sovereigns enjoy, though less power than the president of the United States can exercise. The Finnish president is elected by delegates who represent the nation. The first president, however, was voted into office by Parliament. The Swedish People's party and the National Coalition cast their ballots for Mannerheim, while the Social Democrats, Agrarians, and Progressives joined forces to support the candidacy of K. J. Ståhlberg, a professor of law and a member of the Progressives, who deserves most of the credit for drawing up the new Form of Government. Performing the duties of president independently and above partisan disputes, Ståhlberg then laid a solid foundation for applying that constitutional law. Mannerheim was obliged to join that other leading figure of the War of Liberation, Svinhufvud, off the stage of public affairs, for he would not accept the post of commander-in-chief that was offered to him by Ståhlberg without certain political conditions. Mannerheim traveled to western Europe and from Paris sent Ståhlberg an open letter in which he urged Finland to join the offensive just then in progress under White Russian General Yudenich against Petrograd, whose "fate was in Finland's hands." Even Ståhlberg did not completely oppose joining the attack, but he demanded the support of the half-hearted Entente powers. The Red Army rallied to repulse

Yudenich. Lenin himself confirmed the general's view that had the Baltic states—including Finland—taken part in the operations, the Bolshevik regime might have collapsed.

The Finns did not show any interest in making peace with the Soviet government. When the negotiations finally did get under way at Tartu (Dorpat) in June 1920, their course was influenced by the fluctuations in the fortunes of war on the Russian—Polish front.

On October 14, 1920, the Finnish delegation, headed by Paasikivi, signed a peace treaty with Russia at Tartu. The Soviet Union reaffirmed its recognition of the independence of Finland, which, in addition to her historic boundaries, received a narrow corridor that leads to the Arctic coast, the territory of Petsamo. The Finns did not fully realize that the position of the Soviet government had become stabilized, and the Agrarian Union, in particular, had tenaciously kept alive hopes of annexation by Finland of the territory inhabited by "kinsmen" across the border. The extreme rightists spoke of a "shameful peace," but in Paasikivi's opinion the boundary was too advantageous to Finland to last. The Soviet government did promise, in a special declaration read on the occasion of the signing of the peace treaty, autonomy to the East Karelians. The Finnish interpretation of this declaration made Finland, in a way, party to a matter of internal Soviet policy. That act brought an added danger to Finnish—Soviet relations, already fraught with mutual suspicions.

In 1921, when the Soviet system began to be enforced in East Karelia, the local population revolted. Finland appealed to the League of Nations and supplied a refuge for the defeated East Karelians who fled across the border, but—in contrast to the policy of the regency of Mannerheim—the government looked with disfavour upon the Finnish volunteers who once more rushed to help their "brothers of the same race."

The young republic ran into difficulties in the field of foreign affairs in the opposite direction, too. In the autumn of 1917, the inhabitants of the Åland Islands, numbering some twenty thousand, had expressed their nearly unanimous desire to join Sweden. King Gustavus V, who had repeatedly been obliged to back down before the *Riksdag,* aspired to enhance his popularity through territorial expansion and he was supported by rightist quarters. During the Finnish civil strife, complicated situations developed in the Ålands, where Russian, Red Finnish, White Finnish, Swedish, and German troops operated on the small islands almost simultaneously. Sweden made stubborn efforts at the Versailles Peace Conference and in the League of Nations to gain possession of the group of islands, to no avail. To compensate the Swedes, Finland was instructed, in the Aland Pact of 1921, to give the inhabitants of the islands local autonomy and to keep the area demilitarized. So insignificant did the great powers hold the Soviet Union in those days that, in spite of its proximity, it was not admitted among the guarantors, which included, for instance, distant Italy.

11

Problems of Domestic Policy in the 'Twenties

Finnish domestic policy was rocked in the 1920s by the cross swell caused by a pair of currents generated by opposing forces. There was the language conflict inherited from the preceding century, and the relations between the "bourgeois" and socialist elements of the population had deteriorated on account of the civil war and its aftermath. At times, the antagonisms produced by the two currents mingled to some extent.

The language conflict gained renewed energy from the rise of nationalism in Europe to become the strongest ideological movement of the period between the two world wars. The point of departure of both the Finnish-speaking and the Swedish-speaking Finns was the national-romantic idea that nationality was based upon language—but the conclusions drawn were different on the two sides. At first, the Swedish side was on the offensive. If they had regarded themselves as simply a linguistic group, they should have been willing to settle for the parity expressly guaranteed by the constitution of the republic in proclaiming both Finnish and Swedish national languages; but insofar as the Swedish-speaking Finns were declared to represent a separate "nationality," it was logical to demand for this segment of the population an autonomous status. From the areas populated mainly by people who spoke Swedish would have to be formed districts with broad powers of self-government, districts under the common jurisdiction of a special Swedish executive and legislature. Separate army units would have to be formed with Swedish as the language in which commands were given. Of their far-reaching program, all the Swedes got were their own diocese and a department of their own in the national Board of Education. On the other hand, the pressure brought to bear by the Swedish-speaking segment of the population had the effect that when the first attempt was made to regulate the use of each of the official languages on the bureacratic level by legislative means, the initial law was quickly repealed and a new one, which was more to the Swedish taste, enacted. After that, however, the Swedes were obliged to shift from the offensive to the defensive; and they even regarded as a defeat the law governing the language of the University of Helsinki (1923), although it rested more on a practical than ideological basis.

This law laid down that instruction in all the faculties of the University had to be given in each language in the same proportion as there were students of each language group enrolled in them. As a result, many a professor whose mother tongue was Swedish was obliged to lecture in Finnish.

Efforts had been made by the Ambassador of Sweden in Helsinki as well as the Swedish universities and press to influence the content of the University Language Act, to no avail. The bid of the local Swedes for outside help in this matter, as in their strivings for autonomy, provoked the indignation of the Finnish-speaking public and was a contributing factor in the birth of the so-called True Finnish movement *(aitosuomalaisuusliike)*. Taking off from the national romantic idea that nationality—and therefore the State, too—was rooted in language as well as from the fact that only 11 % of the inhabitants of Finland spoke Swedish, the True Finns demanded the establishment of a monolingual Finland, where Swedish was entitled to recognition only as the local language in Swedish-speaking communities. The Agrarian Union incorporated True Finnish principles in its political program, but in practice it only "growled" but did not "bite." The conservatives of the National Coalition party and the liberals of the Progressive party, on the other hand, gave the movement only partial, reluctant support. The Social Democrats, for ideological reasons alone, regarded the language issue as a sixth-rate problem, besides which they had to consider the small Swedish-speaking segment of the party following.

The True Finnish cause received its most ardent backing from the Finnish-speaking students enrolled in the university. It was to be expected that the most dramatic scenes in the language struggle would be enacted at the University of Helsinki. And it was the antagonism between the two language factions that inspired philanthropists at least as much as interest in culture to make such sizable donations that two small private universities were founded in Turku; a Swedish one in 1918, and then, in 1922, a Finnish one.

Finnish students returning from East Karelia, where they had fought as volunteers against the Red Army side by side with the native East Karelians founded the Academic Karelia Society (AKS), whose primary purpose was the support of the nationalistic aspirations of kindred peoples. But when in time this activity became ever more fruitless and more dangerous from the standpoint of the country's position, the society began to concentrate with all its youthful zeal on the struggle to create a strong national state, and the idea of a national state included the idea of a single official language. The AKS, for practical purposes, dominated unchallenged the Finnish-speaking student world up to the collapse of the Lapua movement.

The labour movement split down the middle from the effects of the events of 1918. Its new, communist fork in Finland had two prongs, and at first it was both programmatically and organizationally but later only organizationally twofold. The Finnish Communist party (SKP) was founded by Red emigrés in Petrograd in the summer of 1918. When the Social Democrats, at their party rally in 1919, under the leadership of Väinö Tanner, embraced a parliamentary line that rejected violent action, the revolutionary minority received about one-third of the votes. The most fanatic opponents of the majority were expelled from the party; nevertheless, the opposition managed to gain control of quite a number of labour organizations, such as the women's and youth leagues. It failed in its attempts, however, to take over the party executive, and in 1920 a party to the left of the Social Democrats was formed under the leadership of Arvo Tuominen. This faction viewed as unrealistic the schemes of the Finnish Communist party based in Petrograd to smuggle arms into Finland for a new insurrection. Though its ultimate aim was also to establish a dictatorship of the proletariat, the Socialist Workers' party, as it was named, wanted to take part in parliamentary activity, too, and it was not prepared to take orders from a foreign country. It nonetheless found its way into Lenin's favour ahead of the emigrant Communists, whose political mill kept grinding thin air and whose ranks, moreover, had been thinned down in a gory fracas. O. V. Kuusinen spent a long time underground in Finland and skilfully led the new party into Moscow's lap. The dominant position in the party executive was held by members of the Finnish Communist party residing in this country, but these men were obliged to follow the orders of the Communist leadership based in Soviet territory.

In 1922, the Communists took part in the parliamentary elections, capturing 27 seats. But the following year, the Agrarian government headed by Kyösti Kallio indicted the whole Communist group in Parliament for treason and outlawed the party. The Communists thereafter took part in elections under the name of the "Socialist Workers' and Small Holders' Election Organization" and kept their illegal, underground operations separate from their public activities in order to secure for the latter the protection of the Finnish laws. The public generally identified the underground Communist party with the aboveboard election organization, and the latter was not looked upon as a legitimate member of the family of political parties. When President Relander noted in his diary during a government crisis that he had summoned all the party leaders for negotiations, he added, "not of course the Communists, whose leadership is stationed in Moscow"—and, in practice, President Ståhlberg had proceeded along the same lines.

In the trade union movement, where they were obliged to act jointly with the Social Democrats, the Communists for tactical reasons sometimes refused to obey commands issuing from party headquarters in Moscow. And the Trade Union Organization of Finland (*Suomen Ammattijärjestö*), although the majority of its membership lined up with the extreme left, did not join the Communist Profintern. To be sure, neither did the organization become a member of the Social Democratic Trade International based in Amsterdam. An aspiration to break loose from the guardianship of the SKP emerged also in the aboveboard party in Finland at the end of the decade. There is probably justification for speaking of a national Communists' group, which seems to have been on Tuominen's mind, too, when he was forming his party.

During the interwar period, it could not be said, as in the decades of the 1940s and 1950s, that the deepest breach between parties separated the Social Democrats from the Communists; but, starting in 1919, the labour movement was like a tree with two branches continuously growing in opposite directions. As in the other western revisionist labour parties, the socialization of the means of production became a theme that softened in the Finnish Social Democratic camp, too, to gentle background music, which had no direct connection with the political issues of the day. With respect to agrarian policy, the party began to lend support to the drive, powered especially by the Agrarian Union, to form independent small holdings. The guidelines accepted in 1926 set frth the taking of governmental responsibility, which till then had been rejected, as being quite as natural as in the case of the other parliamentary parties. On the other hand, the Communists, competing for votes with the Social Democrats, represented a challenge, which compelled the party from time to time to make certain radical gestures and in deciding certain issues on a personal level to take some steps leftward.

The first governments of the young republic were composed mostly of politicians from the parliamentary center—the Progressive party and the Agrarian Union; and they leaned for support now to the right—the National Coalition and the Swedish People's party—, now to the left—the Social Democratic party. These administrations continued to pursue the policy of pardoning civil war prisoners adopted by Svinhufvud and Mannerheim; and, as a result, Red Guards convicted of participating in the insurrection were released from prison one by one. A Military Service Act, which prescribed a term of service lasting between 12 and 18 months, was passed as the basis of the army. The Agrarian Union stressed the importance of the Civil Guards to national defense and, pointing to them, wanted at first, for reasons of economy, to reduce the term of service to nine months; and the Social Democrats, of course, who at this stage still took a sour view of the army, backed up the Agrarian proposal, aiming as it did at lightening the military burden as much as possible. The provisions of the law were probably affected by the threat of war experienced in the winter of 1922, while it was being debated. The work of social reform, which had been delayed by the struggle for legal rights, was given impetus. As early as 1918, the rump Parliament, with its rightist majority, had passed a law on the strength of which the tenant farmers could gradually gain ownership of their holdings, and the succeeding Parliament revised several of the clauses in the law in favour of the tenants. Compulsory education for children for a seven-year period was instituted, and freedom of worship was secured by law.

After the government in 1923 had imprisoned the representatives of the Socialist Workers' party, Parliament was again undersized, though not as much as following the Civil War. The Social Democrats demanded that the president dissolve Parliament, but the bourgeois parties were unanimously in favour of carrying on with the rump Parliament. President Ståhlberg dissolved it. In this way, he emphasized the ascendancy of the president in the Finnish Form of Government and laid a basis for future practice. He would have been re-elected president with near unanimity, but he was probably weary of the heavy task of governing. Feeling that he had already done his duty, he absolutely refused to run again for office. A combination of the Agrarian Union, the National Coalition and the Swedish People's party then voted into office for the 1925—1931 term a member of the Agrarian right wing, Governor Lauri Kristian Relander. The collaboration among the parties of the political center has been seen to have ended with this election. The Agrarian Union shifted perceptibly toward the right; but, to counterbalance this move, the Swedish People's party, which feared the True Finnish movement, began to collaborate on a tactical basis with the Social Democrats. For some years, the usual line-up in Parliament was the Finnish-speaking bourgeois groups, reinforced by a few Swedes, versus the leftists, reinforced by the majority of the Swedes. Only a few votes one way or the other decided issues. The Swedes gave votes of no confidence to bourgeois governments without, however, sharing in the responsibilities of rule with the Social Democrats. Under these circumstances, only minority governments of short duration emerged, giving parliamentarism a bad sound in extreme rightists' ears.

The most noteworthy of these governments was the one formed by the Social Democrats under Väinö Tanner in 1926. It provided evidence of the national integration achieved in the years following the Civil War, and the suspicions nursed particularly in rightist circles were proved unfounded: Tanner was even on hand in Helsinki's Senate Square to receive the customary annual parade held in commemoration of the end of the War of Liberation. With the backing of the Swedish People's party, Tanner pushed through a law restoring civil rights to those Red prisoners still deprived of them. But the bourgeois groups could not stomach the Tanner government's economic policy, and it fell as a result of disagreement over the tariffs on grain.

The Radical Rightist Movement and the Trend toward National Integration

In Finland's geopolitical situation, the activities of the Communists were felt to be a formidable threat to national independence. And with politically inspired strikes, they also disturbed domestic peace and public order. The long harbour strike damaged Finland's export trade in forest products at the precise juncture when the U.S.S.R. began to market timber abroad. On the other hand, the extraordinary legislative measures planned to combat communism violated civil liberties. Furthermore, the Social Democrats suspected that emergency laws might be aimed against them, too, before long; the conduct of the extreme rightists provided ample ground for such suspicions.

The question of special legislation to combat communism took on an urgent aspect in the autumn of 1929. "Does Parliament want to weaken further the country's position among nations, which running errands for a foreign power and acting for its benefit among our people signify?" asked ex-Prime Minister Vennola, a Progressive, when the bill facilitating the suppression of organizations guilty of any "punishable deed" was submitted to Parliament. Around the same time, when members of the Communist Youth League held a rally in the Ostrobothnian parish of Lapua wearing their red shirts, an incensed crowd tore these shirts into shreds and broke up the meeting. When the government, which was once more composed of Agrarians and headed by Kyösti Kallio, announced that it would not punish the perpetrators of the riot, it received a vote of confidence from all the M. P.'s except the Communists. An organization called *Suomen Lukko*—"the Lock of Finland"—was formed for the purpose of stamping out overt Communist activities by legal methods, and it received support from all the bourgeois parties. But it was superseded the following spring by the Lapua movement, which resorted to violent methods. Several dozen local Communist ringleaders were forced to step into a car, driven to the Soviet border in a backwoods area and there ordered to walk over to the other side. The rather limited circles that had never liked the democratic system of government took advantage of the confusion and engaged in acts of violence against certain influential politicians: the Social Democratic vice-speaker of Parliament, Väinö Hakkila, was subjected to rough handling and ex-President Ståhlberg, no less, was abducted and driven close to the Soviet border.

In the summer of 1930, President Relander submitted to Parliament, then under pressure from the Lapua movement, a set of bills aimed at preventing overt Communist activity. Some of the bills were passed, but the decision on the most important of them, which involved amending constitutional law and therefore required a five-sixths' majority, was postponed until the next parliamentary term. The president forthwith dissolved Parliament and called upon the nation to elect representatives ready to vote for the proposed constitutional amendments. The old breach opened up once more threateningly, for all the bourgeois parties declared themselves in favour of the anti-Communist laws, whereas the Social-Democrats opposed their passage. The parliamentary seats won in the elections by bourgeois candidates, (two-thirds of the total), sufficed to secure passage, in October 1930, of these laws, which were interpreted as democracy's weapons of self-defense.

Hardly had the laws been ratified when the presidential election was at hand. Ståhlberg agreed to become the Progressive party's candidate. The National Coalition turned to another elder statesman, Svinhufvud, whom Relander had named prime minister during the height of the excitement generated by the rightist radicals. Svinhufvud wavered, because he estimated Relander's chances of gaining the Agrarian vote and thereby defeating Ståhlberg to be better than his own. The Agrarian Union, however, would not accept Relander as its candidate, regarding him as not enough of a True Finn and too close to the Lapua movement. Nevertheless, the electoral bloc consisting of the conservative National Coalition, the Agrarian Union and the Swedish People's party hoped for by Svinhufvud became a reality and he himself was elected president for the 1931—1937 term by 151 votes as against 149 for Ståhlberg. As soon as he took his oath of office, he appointed Mannerheim chairman of the Defence Council. Thus did both heroes of the War of Liberation come back to public life from plaster portraits sitting on top of the nation's bookcases.

It was expected that the political crisis in the domestic sphere would blow over after the passage of the anti-Communist laws and the presidential election; but the Lapua movement did not fold up, although its original objective had been attained. It even began to demand that the Social Democratic party be also banned, and in February 1932 some 500 armed men rallied at Mäntsälä, not far from Helsinki, to dictate demands to the government. The situation was tense not so much because of fear that large masses of people might join the rebellion but because it was suspected that the Army and the Civil Guards would let even small forces carry on as they pleased. Using his authority and prestige, President Svinhufvud prevailed upon the rebels to disband without bloodshed. It was only then that the crisis blew over: the Lapua movement was suppressed on the strength of the emergency laws that it had been instrumental in getting passed itself. The rightist radicals founded a party of their own, the Patriotic People's Movement (*Isänmaallinen Kansanliike,* known as IKL, for short), and—unlike the original Lapua movement, which had sprung spontaneously out of the native soil—it drew inspiration from Nazism, just then rising to power in Germany. The parliamentary elections proved, however, that the IKL enjoyed only insignificant popular support.

Resenting the favourable stand taken by the AKS toward the abortive Mäntsälä mutiny, a number of its most prominent members quit the organization; the majority of them joined the Agrarian Union, fortifying the True Finnish spirit, which had already imbued the party.

The first government set up during Svinhufvud's term in office was composed of representatives of all the non-socialist parties. It broke up on account of disagreement inside its own ranks and at the same time with the president over measures to combat the great economic depression. It was succeeded by a government headed by Professor T. M. Kivimäki, a member of the Progressive party, that, in spite of the weakness of its parliamentary base, held on for nearly four years (1932—36), or longer than any other government in the annals of the Republic. It stayed but partly because it could depend on the president's support and partly because nobody knew how to replace it. It kept the rightist radicals under leash but also attempted to tighten the anti-Communist legislation further. The Social Democrats, which scored gains in two successive parliamentary elections and saw their political brethren take over the reins of government in the other Nordic countries, started to reach for power in Finland, too. In the fall of 1936, the Kivimäki government received a parliamentary vote of censure by a majority of one. But the uncompromising president refused to entrust the Social Democrats with any ministerial portfolios. In response, they determined to prevent Svinhufvud's re-election by every means in their power. In the approaching election, the Progressive party nominated once more as its candidate ex-President Ståhlberg, who it was supposed could also count on the support of the Social Democrats. Owing to Svinhufvud's popularity, his list won so many votes across party lines in the elections to the electoral college that the Social Democrats became uncertain whether Ståhlberg could defeat him; so they swung their support to the Agrarian candidate, Kyösti Kallio, a prosperous farmer from northern Ostrobothnia, who went on to win the presidential election. In the sphere of foreign affairs, which was soon destined to become the President of the Republic's central arena of activity, all three rivals for the office of chief executive were rather inexperienced. There was, however, a notable difference between Ståhlberg and Kallio in that collaboration between the former and Mannerheim, who was destined to gain increasing authority in the administration of the country's foreign affairs, was impossible to imagine, whereas the general got along splendidly with Kallio.

After this, both of the major parties, the Social Democrats and the Agrarians, agreed upon sharing governmental responsibility and decided to offer the post of prime minister to an outside referee, Professor A. K. Cajander, who belonged to the Progressive party. The post of foreign minister went to Rudolf Holsti, who had made a name for himself in the early years of the republic. The "red earth government," as the coalition was popularly called, had stronger parliamentary backing than a single one of its predecessors; and, during a period marked by the threat of war, it came to symbolize national solidarity. Paradoxically enough, the Lapua movement had hastened the process of the Social Democrats' becoming rooted in the democratic Finnish society, which it had defended by making common cause with the democratic forces in the bourgeois camp—and if there still remained loose ends, they were certainly tied during the period the Cajander government sat in office.

Mannerheim had had to cope with formidable obstacles to obtain appropriations for the building up of the national defenses, which had been neglected during the preceding decade. The needs of the military establishment had to be weighed against other needs, however, for Finland was still predominantly an agrarian and, as such, poor country. President Svinhufvud's program—"First, the borders must be secured; after that, we can cut thicker slices of bread"—evoked no sympathetic response from the political left, until administrative responsibility had shifted their way—and not much from the center, either. In 1938, Parliament approved—by practically a unanimous vote—a military procurement program that involved the expenditure of about three thousand million *markkas,* a remarkable appropriation in any Finnish budget. But the decision was made too late, for only a small part of the arms could be purchased before World War II broke out. The next summer, the nation demonstrated its defensive will in a unique way: thousands of men from all classes of society spent their summer vacation participating, without pay, in fortifying the Karelian Isthmus. Both the approval of the basic procurement program and the speeches made by leading Social Democrats proved that, as regards the will to defend the country, there no longer existed any essential difference between the bourgeoisie and the working class. The latter were evidently influenced by the example of Sweden, which had taken energetic measures under the direction of Social Democratic politicians to strengthen the nation's defenses.

The opposition between labour and the non-socialist segments of Finnish society received its stubbornest and most concrete expression in the attitude toward the Civil Guard organization. The Civil Guard units, which had formed the nucleus of the White Army in the War of Liberation, were retained as auxiliary troops to bolster the regular army—which meant that they enjoyed a legally recognized status in the republic. Theirs was an unmilitarily democratic system of self-rule, and their commander-in-chief was the president of the republic. Their function was not only to defend the country but also, especially, to safeguard the prevailing social order; they therefore sought to keep out of their ranks men who were felt to be politically unreliable, and the Social Democrats steered clear of them on account of both the manner of their original establishment and the character of their membership.

After Mannerheim, on the occasion of the May Parade in 1933, spoke his historical words, "We need no longer ask where the other fellow was fifteen years ago," the rift in the work of national defense began to close. During World

War II, the Civil Guards were integrated into the regular army; and mutual hard feelings were rooted out by an agreement concluded between the Social Democratic party and the Civil Guards. Together with the corresponding women's auxiliary organization, *Lotta Svärd*, the voluntary militia was perceived to be a cheap and at the same time most effective means of reinforcing the armed forces of a small nation.

The language dispute of the University of Helsinki was also settled, and the settlement proved lasting. The Swedish People's party had no part in the Cajander government. And the Social Democratic view that language legislation was a sixth-class question could also be interpreted to mean that for the sake of harmonious collaboration in administrative matters they were ready to go a long way to meet the Agrarians. In 1937, Parliament enacted a law that established Finnish as the language of the University of Helsinki, except that in the most important subjects parallel instruction also had to be given in Swedish. Dissatisfaction was felt in both extreme camps. But there can be no doubt that this solution — by removing a grievance generally felt in Finnish-speaking circles — hastened the end of the language conflict, which was inflicting one defeat after another on the Swedes.

Isolation in Foreign Relations

Even before the Peace of Tartu (Dorpat), Finland sought to establish collaboration with the so-called border states that had emerged along the western frontiers of Russia. In 1921, at a time when the East Karelians were in revolt against the communist system imposed upon them, Poland, Latvia, Estonia and Finland delivered notes to the Soviet government protesting its failure to abide by peace terms. The Finnish government specifically accused the Russians of violating the autonomy of East Karelia. This complaint Finland also brought to the attention of the League of Nations, which in Soviet eyes was nothing better than a family union of victorious capitalistic powers. Frightened by notes issued by the Soviet government and the movements of certain Red Army units, Finland then closed its frontier to prevent volunteers from crossing over into East Karelia. The consequences of the crisis appeared in many ways. Disappointed that open conflict had not broken out between the Soviet Union and Finland, the Finnish Communist party engineered what became known as the "pork mutiny" in the logging areas of Lapland, an aborted surprising that took on the aspect of a farce. A rightist fanatic assassinated Interior Minister H. Ritavuori, whose responsibility it was to keep the eastern border sealed off. The most notable consequence was the opening of negotiations, which interested the Progressives and Agrarians in particular, with the border states with a view to military collaboration. Foreign minister R. Holsti signed a political pact with Warsaw, but the combined right and left gave him a vote of no confidence, with the result that the pact was never ratified. The negative stand of the National Coalition was probably influenced by the caution maintained by Paasikivi and the former Old Finnish group in their Russian policy. Later on, the western powers, too, warned Finland against any alliance with the Baltic countries, whose position externally was regarded as weak. And Poland's evident aspirations to achieve hegemony, again, did not please the Finns. Although one of President Relander's pet ideas was an alliance among the Scandinavian and Baltic countries, the border-state policy gradually withered away and was forgotten.

After this, external affairs stirred the interest of Finnish politicians very little and no disagreements worth mentioning cropped up between the parties in this sector. Finland became a member of the League of Nations in 1920 and from 1927 to 1930 was represented on the council of the League. The Finns were among the most ardent supporters of the world organization. After the border-state policy was wrecked and British interest in the Baltic sphere waned, Finland fell back on the pious hope that the League of Nations would secure the country against the threat from the East. The League and the Soviet Union were set up as actual alternatives when, in 1926, Moscow offered non-aggression pacts to neighbouring states. "It's better to take guarantees from fifty-five states than from one country," Holsti declared unrealistically. Disagreement concerned not only the aspect of the problem involving principle but also concrete details of the proposed treaty. Finland let the discussions break off, and when Moscow took the matter up again after the Social Democrats formed their government (p. 00), it turned out that the faith of the foreign minister in the League of Nations was even firmer than that of his bourgeois predecessor. The Soviet move was repulsed once more.

That domestic politics were not essentially bound up with foreign policy is shown by the fact that a non-agression treaty with the U.S.S.R. was eventually concluded during Svinhufvud's presidential term, in 1932, when the rightist factions were waxing strongest. At points disputed during the preceding rounds of negotiations, both sides retreated, the Finns more than the Russians. The reason for the Finnish government's conciliatory attitude was the strengthening of the international position of the U.S.S.R. Nor did the Soviet government try to mix Finland's domestic politics with its foreign policy: its reactions to the Lapua movement and the resulting outlawry of communist activity were mild. Moscow did not, in fact, begin to pay attention to Finnish "fascism" until after Hitler's rise to power, when the unrest in Finland had passed its culminating point but the situation in European foreign politics in general had begun to come to a head. This chronology lends support to the unadulterated Paasikivian concept that the prime considerations in Moscow's Finnish policy were the Soviet interests in the military arena and the sphere of foreign affairs.

During the period between the two world wars, the U.S.S.R. was shunned throughout non-communist Europe, and in Finland anti-Russian sentiment was intensified by the memory of the many wars of the past and the last Czar's short-sighted politics. More intensely than ever before, the Finns felt that they were holding an outpost of the West against the East. The Finnish attitude of the 1920s and 1930s was reflected in the opening lines of a frequently quoted poem by Uuno Kailas:

> Sinister lies the borderland —
> Before me, Asia, the East.
> Like a sentry, on guard I stand —
> Behind me, Europe, the West.

The anxiety of the Finns was certainly not ameliorated by the many airfields and the branch lines of the Murmansk railroad reaching out toward Finnish territory that the Russians had built in the wilds of East Karelia.

The national leaders saw the weaknesses in the defenses and therefore sought foreign support. Where it could be found, after the hopes naïvely placed in the League of Nations had collapsed in the mid-'thirties, was a puzzle. Britain was militarily weak and its interest in the Baltic region has always been slight. Thus those people considered themselves smart that, pointing to the days of World War I, could argue: the expansion of Russian power in the northwest could not be in accord with the interests of Germany. Svinhufvud counted on help from Germany in case of a Soviet attack, but even he did not want any political agreement with the Germans. Orientation toward Germany did not—except in the case of the small IKL faction—signify approval of Nazism, and it did not determine the country's foreign policy. Out of caution, Finland would not even accept the non-agression treaty offered by Germany; and it was during the presidency of the pro-German Svinhufvud that Finland solemnly declared its intention of following the Scandinavian line in its foreign policy.

The Nordic states never got around, however, to agreeing on military collaboration. It has been said that Denmark feared Germany, Finland feared Russia, Norway feared nobody and Sweden was never able to decide whom to fear most (*Jakobson*). Since, however, the appearance of any major power in the demilitarized Åland Islands would have been a danger to Sweden, too, the Swedes and Finns jointly undertook in 1938 to nullify the Åland Pact and build fortifications at that crossing of sea lanes. The parties to the agreement, including Germany, acceded to the request made by Finland and Sweden, but the League of Nations avoided a clear decision because the U.S.S.R. opposed the measures planned. Under these circumstances, Sweden did not dare to undertake the fortification of the Aland Islands, and Finland was also obliged to give up the project. This was not only a local strategic setback for Finland, but the issue had more far-reaching consequences: Finland had become entirely isolated in its foreign policy; and this, perhaps, had been considered by the Soviet government to be a more important objective than the fate of the islands as such.

Even though they had miscarried, however, the discussions that had taken place called the attention of the Swedes to Finland's problems and increased their willingness to help in case of need. And since the same type of artillery and the same caliber of guns were taken into use in Finland as in Sweden, the Finns were able, when the war clouds darkened in the autumn of 1939, to obtain guns quickly and without time-consuming negotiations from their next-door neighbours to the West.

After Hitler's rise to power, there appeared many signs of growing suspicion and mistrust between Finland and its giant eastern neighbour. The head of the Soviet mission in Helsinki spelled it out to the foreign minister in the Kivimäki government that in the event of armed conflict in central Europe, the Soviet Union would feel compelled to occupy part of Finland. The party secretary of the Leningrad district, A. Zhdanov warned in one speech—at least, according to the version published in Finland—that the Red Army might take steps to investigate what was going on in the little countries bordering on the U.S.S.R. Suspicions were increased, on the one hand, by aggressive pronouncements published by representatives of the AKS and the IKL and, on the other, the instigations of the Finnish communist emigrés in the Soviet Union. Holsti made a visit to Moscow as foreign minister without achieving anything to write home about; at bottom, in fact, it was more important to him to follow the lead of France and England in opposing Germany than to court the favour of Moscow.

In August 1938, a secretary of the Soviet legation in Helsinki named Yartsev, who despite his modest position had received his assignment from Stalin himself, took up with the political leaders of Finland the question of a possible German attack on the Soviet Union through Finnish territory. If German troops were allowed to land in Finland unopposed, he warned, the Red Army would "not wait at the river" marking the boundary between the two countries. Yartsev did not utter threats alone; he also offered Finland military assistance because the Russians doubted, besides Finland's willingness, its ability, too, to repel a landing on its coast by military forces of a major power. The Finns responded to Yartsev's proposals with a restraint approaching indifference. His lowly status on the diplomatic ranking list was confounding, and the Finns failed or refused to grasp the scope of the discussions; but, above all, the Finns were dismayed by the very thought of Soviet troops marching into the country, where, once in, the Finns felt, they would stay. All the Finns were prepared to do was merely to state that Finland would allow no foreign power to gain a foothold on Finnish soil. The talks led nowhere. And after the Soviet Union was left on the sidelines in the settlement of the Czechoslovakian crisis in September 1938, the Finnish stand grew still stiffer. Late the following winter, the treaty of assistance offered by Yartsev was changed to a proposal of territorial readjustments, but also the requested cession of small islands in the Gulf of Finland to the U.S.S.R. met with unqualified opposition.

In the spring of 1939, the well-known negotiations began in Moscow between the British and French governments and the U.S.S.R. Against the danger of a German attack, a treaty on aid to the countries—among them Finland—situated between Germany and the Soviet border was supposed to be drafted. Stalin wanted military assistance to be forced on the little border states, even against their will, if necessary, and even in the event of an "indirect attack," by which was meant, for example, a specially friendly attitude taken by some small nation towards Germany. The border states rigidly opposed the unsolicited "guarantees," which would have violated their independence. Great Britain, in particular, made an effort to uphold the sovereign rights of the small powers, but the negotiations broke up. The reason for the failure to reach an understanding was that Germany offered Stalin more than the others. The division of eastern Europe was made in a secret pact signed on August 23, and in it Finland was placed in the Soviet sphere of interest. The pact was followed by Hitler's invasion of Poland.

The Winter War

At the beginning of October 1939, the Soviet government wanted to take up for discussion with the Finns certain "concrete political questions." The chief demands made by Stalin to the negotiators appointed by the Finnish government, J. K. Paasikivi and Väinö Tanner, were the cession of a small area on the Karelian Isthmus to the U.S.S.R. and the leasing of the Hanko peninsula at the mouth of the Gulf of Finland, or at least the outlying islands, as a military base; in return, Finland was to be given a slice of territory in East Karelia. They refused to accept at face value the concern expressed by the Russians that some foreign power might attack Russia across Finland and that therefore the territories demanded were of military importance. The Finns were sincerely anxious to stay neutral, and their military experts asserted that Finland would be able to defend itself against any potential foe that might attempt to land on the Finnish coast. Stalin considered the Finnish armed forces too weak to defend the country. "This is where a big power would make a landing," he said, placing his hand on a map of Finland over the Hanko area, "and from this point it would continue to advance regardless of your resistance."

The stand of the Finnish government, on which Paasikivi and Tanner were dependent, was influenced by a suspicion that Moscow's ultimate objective was the conquest of all Finland. The territorial cessions demanded would have fatefully weakened the Finnish defenses; and if the Soviet government were to make new demands after the proposed border revisions, Finland would be even less capable of resistance than before. Paradoxically enough, the uncompromising policy of the Finnish government was bolstered by quite the opposite line of thought: the Finns did not believe the Red Army would move into action.

An invisible background factor that influenced the decision of the Finns to stand fast was the traditional constitutional ideology according to which the country's rights—including the right to keep its territory inviolable—must be adamantly upheld. In his youth, President Kallio had attended a meeting held in Sweden by the Finnish Constitutionalists who had been exiled by Governor-General Bobrikov, and Foreign Minister Eljas Erkko's father had been one of the exiles. The significance of the position taken by the political leaders in their dilemma should not, however, be exaggerated, for the entire nation stood behind the government with a unanimity that is unparalleled in Finnish history. No party advocating compliance appeared on the scene. There cannot be the slightest doubt that the rightist parties, which were not represented in the government, would have pursued the same line of policy. And the conduct of the labour organizations appeared to prove that the wounds inflicted by the Civil War had healed so completely that not even a scar was visible. "Only a few weeks before, I would still have qualified use of the word fatherland by putting it within quotation marks, but not any more," wrote one young working-class novelist. The most enduring significance of the autumn and winter of 1939—1940 in Finnish history lies in the fact that the young republic achieved the national solidarity that is matter-of-course among old and politically mature nations in making vital decisions.

The meeting of Scandinavian heads of state held during the negotiations in

Moscow made it only too apparent that Finland had no hope of getting help from the neighbouring countries in the West. And Foreign Commissar Molotov made public the demands of his government, after which there was reason to fear that, with its prestige as a major power at stake, the Soviet Union would be unwilling to make any compromises. Even so, the Finnish government let the negotiations break off. Since history cannot be re-enacted, like an unsuccessful scene played before a movie camera, it is impossible to tell what actually would have happened if Finland had yielded to Soviet pressure—at best, there are only the probabilities suggested by later events.

During the negotiations in Moscow, Finland had had time to mobilize its defence forces, escaping the dangers of a surprise attack. On the other hand, the Finnish position was even more perilous than had been taken into account in the defence plans, for Finland was forced to grapple, all alone, with a major power that had avoided involvement in the general European war.

When the Red Army on November 30 crossed the eastern frontier in every sector, the odds pitted against Finland were so overwhelming that observers abroad expected the Finnish resistance to collapse in a short time. It is possible that the national solidarity so unshakingly demonstrated by the Finns during the negotiations in Moscow might have begun to crack and their morale to weaken under the burden of privations and sufferings of war; people might have begun to ask whether it was worth the sacrifice of blood, sweat and tears to keep even important pieces of territory. But nobody had a chance to ask such questions before the Soviet government took a step that aroused the Finns to superhuman efforts. Stalin set up a puppet Finnish government at the very outset of the war. When the Finnish Communist leader Arvo Tuominen, who had fled to Russia during the heyday of the Lapua movement and was in Stockholm at this juncture as a Comintern agent, declined the dubious honour, the post of prime minister was handed over to O. V. Kuusinen, who at the time the Peace of Tartu was made had dismissed the independent Republic of Finland as an "extremely transitory phenomenon." Now, every Finn knew that not merely some pieces of strategic territory were at stake, but national independence and everything the Finnish people "held dear and sacred," as Mannerheim later put it in a famous order-of-the-day. The war was waged with religious fervor, which has been depicted most pithily by Yrjö Jylhä in his poem *The Weary Soldiers*. When the exhausted Finnish fighters plead to be admitted into the ranks of Heaven's army, God responds:

'Tis on earth my cohorts contend.
Whosoever layeth down his arms
Him shall I disown.

The Finnish government that had sat in office during the Moscow negotiations resigned as soon as the war broke out, and the president replaced it with a new government, composed of all the parties except the IKL. Risto Ryti was appointed to the post of prime minister, Tanner took over the foreign office and Paasikivi was named minister without portfolio. The new government appealed to the League of Nations, and that helpless organization responded by showing its last sign of life: it declared that the Soviet Union had placed itself outside the pale of the League by its unprovoked aggression against Finland. Russia's expulsion from the dying organization had no more effect on the course of the war than did the printer's ink expended by the world press to glorify Finnish exploits in battle, the praises of Finland sung by statesmen like Churchill, or the humanitarian aid and the token forces of volunteers from abroad. The world had taken the position of a spectator in a theatrical arena, first to weep over the tragedy of the hapless Finns and later to applaud their fighting spirit. Platonic sympathy could bring no realistic help to Finland's military or political position, but the psychological effect momentarily bolstered Finnish resolve. Of greater value were the shipments of arms that arrived in substantial quantities, especially from Sweden.

Finnish leaders worked energetically to persuade Sweden to enter the war. Their argument was that, if the Soviet border were shifted over to the Tornio river, Sweden would become the next-door neighbour of the great Eastern power. A veritable mass movement to help Finland was stirred up in Sweden, and two reinforced Swedish volunteer battalions managed to reach the fighting front before the hostilities ended; but responsible Swedish politicians considered joining the war a hazardous adventure.

For the first two months of the war, the poorly armed Finnish forces held their main defensive positions on the Karelian Isthmus, the humble scattered row of pillboxes that became famous as the "Mannerheim Line." North of Lake Ladoga, the Finns scored their first victory with a direct attack across the frozen Tolvajärvi. After that, the Finnish troops, which were accustomed to forest terrain, kept smashing the invading divisions in the vast wilds along the eastern frontier into small fragments. The rings of encirclement became popularly known as *mottis,* after the Finnish term for a cord of firewood. One by one, these encircled enemy forces were wiped out.

The Finns' meager resources of manpower and matériel, together with the invaders' extraordinarily stubborn defence inside the *mottis,* slowed down the completion of the mopping up operations. But, at Suomussalmi, in a single sector, the main part of two Red divisions was annihilated by *motti* tactics. One of the most amazing chapters in world military history had been written, and the Finns' defensive triumph was not left without political consequences. Contrary to its attitude at the beginning of December, Moscow was now willing to discuss peace with the legal government of Finland. The independence of the nation had been saved, but now that Sweden no longer faced its recent peril, Finland lost the last shred of hope of receiving military aid from its closest Western neighbour.

The Winter War had not, however, yet ended. The U.S.S.R. now demanded much more territory than it had in the fall; and, to press its demands, it launched an offensive on the Karelian Isthmus at the beginning of February with a heavier concentration of forces than ever. After two weeks of heavy fighting, the Mannerheim Line cracked at Summa, and the Finns had to retreat to the vicinity of Viipuri. Exceptionally cold weather froze Viipuri Bay to such a depth that the enemy was able to attack over the ice and threaten the weak right flank of the Finnish forces.

Public opinion in Great Britain and, especially, France clamored ever more loudly for aid to be sent to Finland. The route any expeditionary army would have had to take ran through Norway and Sweden—and the plan was to have part of the force remain in Swedish territory to block the shipment of iron ore to Germany. Thus the issue of dispatching an expeditionary force was bound up in the toils of the greater war, and the Swedish government was compelled at this juncture really to take into account Germany, the attitude of which the Swedes had previously used as a pretext for their refusal to provide Finland with effective aid. Germany was liable to consider Western military operations in Scandinavia as grounds for attacking Sweden. The offer of assistance to Finland given by the big Allied European powers did not remain a meaningless gesture, however, for the consequences of its acceptance were most likely taken under advisement by the Soviet government at the time the decision to make peace was reached. Since the help promised to Finland was slight and its arrival would have taken a long time, the Finns felt there was no realistic alternative to accepting the peace terms laid down by Moscow. In the Finnish government, Ryti, Tanner and Paasikivi worked hard, sometimes even on their own individual responsibility, to achieve peace. They thus formed a kind of "compliance" group, which was supported by the man who knew best the limited lasting power of the Finnish defences, Mannerheim. In favour of continued resistance, in both the government and Parliament, was one faction of the Agrarian Union.

The peace treaty signed in Moscow on March 13, 1940, forced Finland to cede to Russia the part of southeastern Finland that extends approximately to the border drawn in the centuries-old Peace of Uusikaupunki (Map 4), plus a slice of territory along the northeastern frontier. In addition, the Finns had to lease to the Russians as a military base the peninsula of Hanko. The inhabitants of those areas, who numbered 11 % of the total Finnish population, moved over to the Finnish side of the new boundary. Their resettlement—mainly as farmers on newly created holdings—proved to be a colossal task, which the nation proceeded to carry out in the shadow of the great war and under persistent political harassment from the Soviet Union. The people of Finland, who had taken a confident attitude toward the war, received the tidings of peace by hanging out flags of mourning. And Foreign Minister Tanner deemed it necessary in his radio speech to defend the peace policy pursued by the government; on the other hand, there was not a hint in his words to the effect that the nation might have responded critically to the inflexibility of the Finnish leaders in the autumn negotiations.

In the Shadow of a New War Threat

Appointed to the post of envoy to Moscow, Minister Paasikivi applied all his diplomatic skill to resist new Russian demands, while trying to persuade his government to yield to such demands as he felt to be inescapable. Accordingly, Finland had to grant the U.S.S.R. military transit rights by rail to the Hanko base. The greatest concern was aroused in Finland by the Soviet government's meddling in domestic Finnish affairs. When the Communists attempted to emerge from underground into the open again, taking advantage of the depressed public spirits in the wake of defeat, and demonstrators shouted cheers for a speedy revolution, Foreign Commissar Molotov made a speech in which he took them under his protective wing. It was not until December, when the pressure had eased up a bit, that the Finnish authorities dared to enforce the law to deal with camouflaged Communist organizations. After Molotov had asserted in a private conversation that the relations between Finland and the U.S.S.R. would remain bad as long as Tanner held a minister's portfolio, the Social Democratic leader quit the cabinet. When President Kallio's paralytic stroke necessitated holding an emergency election to choose a new president to finish his term, Molotov announced the names of four national Finnish leaders as being *personae non gratae:* Tanner, Mannerheim, Svinhufvud, and Kivimäki, recently appointed envoy to Berlin. In practice, Molotov's warning had no effect, however, because it was a foregone conclusion that Kallio's successor would be Risto Ryti, who had earned general respect by his vigorous and at the same time skilful management of political affairs as prime minister. The vote was practically unanimous in Ryti's favour. Ryti took personal charge of foreign policy, especially while his first cabinet, headed by J. W. Rangell, sat in office. His second prime minister, Edwin Linkomies, a strong-willed man, also took a share of the responsibility for foreign policy.

After the Peace of Moscow, the question of close collaboration between Finland and Sweden was revived in both countries, and the Finns' feeling of insecurity kept interest in the matter continuously alive. Even prior to the signing of the Peace of Moscow, Sweden and Norway had held out hopes of a defensive alliance with Finland, but discussion was nipped in the bud by Molotov's announcement of his stiff opposition to the idea. When Finland made inquiries about potential Swedish military assistance, not even the amount given during the Winter War could be promised. A slightly more favourable stand was taken by the Swedes later on toward the idea of a political federation, for, as the stronger partner, Sweden would have had the decisive say in foreign policy. But the plan had to be abandoned on account of the opposition of both Moscow and Berlin. When Molotov called on Hitler in Berlin in November and was asked how he might solve the Finnish problem, he responded that he intended to settle the score with Finland in the same way as he had done with the Baltic countries.

The political isolation of Finland had become nearly total after the German occupation of Denmark and Norway in April. The maintenance even of economic ties with the West was difficult. The annexation in the summer of the Baltic countries by the Soviet Union did not worsen the strategic position of Finland, but it came to the Finns as a political shock, as it is movingly described by Paasikivi in his diaries. In desperation, Finland strove to build up strength to the utmost of its slim resources: the period of military service was extended from one to two years, in addition to which the Civil Guards were formally integrated into the army; the new border was fortified and weapons were procured to the extent that the defence forces were far better equipped than they had been during the Winter War. It was realized, however, that Finland could never be strong enough to stand alone and that the only foreign power in a position to help the Finns in a pinch was Germany—if so willing.

It was not known in Finland then that as early as July, 1940, Hitler had decided to make war on the Russians the next year; but the Finns felt immensely relieved when, in August, Germany requested military transit rights through Finnish territory to Norway. Though sensitive about its neutrality, Sweden had nevertheless already granted the Germans similar rights — and incomparably many more troops were transported over Swedish than Finnish territory. It is also noteworthy that the Soviet Union had acquired similar transit rights across southern Finland to the Red base at Hanko. Finland could not be accused, therefore, of having abandoned its policy of neutrality in making the same sort of concession to the Germans. The internal democratic system prevailing in Finland was never—either before or during theig joint action against the common enemy—violated by the Germans. One Finnish Anglophile, who, under a pseudonym, published in Sweden a pamphlet dealing with the political position of Finland and criticizing the Finnish government, tellingly described the state of mind of his fellow countrymen: "To let the Russians into the country would be the same to the Finn as letting a fire break loose; to open the door for the Germans has so far been the same to him as calling in the fire brigade."

In ringing a fire alarm, it is not the practice to prepare elaborate documents, and the German-Finnish military transit agreement was only loosely constructed. When the transit traffic began, all that existed was a technical agreement signed by the Finnish General Staff and the German Air Force. The agreement on the governmental level was concluded later. Moscow lodged no protest, although Molotov did make an attempt, on his afore-mentioned visit to Berlin, to call a halt to the German transport operations. Following this visit, the German authorities let the Finns understand that Germany was prepared to support them, and they were urged to stand fast in the face of any Soviet demands.

During the winter, the idea took hold among the Finnish political leaders, headed by Ryti and Mannerheim, that collaboration with Germany was inevitable. Starting in the month of December, unofficial negotiations took place between officers representing the two nations, and the Finns requested reinforcements for the defence of, in especial, northern Finland. The first political contact was made as late as the end of May, when Minister Schnurre brought to Helsinki the initial German offer of military assistance. It was a matter that called for closer military negotiations, which were speedily arranged both in Helsinki and in Germany. As regards the decision made, the joint memorandum drawn up by the Finnish military leaders and government was deliberately vague: "Provided the political aspect of the question is clarified...., the proposed measures may be taken." That "political aspect" was not clarified definitely and publicly until the Finnish Parliament on June 25 issued its declaration that a state of war existed between Finland and the U.S.S.R. Insofar as the secretive political leadership calculated on the Soviet Union's giving grounds in one way or another for affirming the existence of a state tf war, it calculated correctly.

In the meantime, those buttons were pushed that set the machinery of war into motion. German troops poured into Finnish Lapland via the ports along the coast of Finland and overland across the border from Norway. Mannerheim ordered the Oulu river to be the boundary dividing the areas of German and Finnish operations.

In Finland, a general mobilization was carried out that was one of the most drastic known to history, for no less than one-sixth of the entire population—counting the women and children, too—was called to colors. But the Finnish forces were lined up strictly for defence.

In his famous proclamation of June 22, 1941, Hitler declared that German troops stood on the Arctic coast side by side with their Finnish comrades to defend the territory of Finland in joint action with the Finnish "heroes of liberty." The Finnish Ministry of Foreign Affairs notified all its envoys that the nation intended to remain neutral. When, however, German aircraft taking off from bases in Germany bombed Leningrad by curving over Finnish territory, the Soviet air force dropped bombs on a number of towns in southern Finland. The Finns had not drifted into war as the unwitting victim of two major powers in conflict; they had purposefully chosen war but for reasons of both internal and external policy waited for the enemy to strike first. The alternative, however, would have been to submit passively to the reduction of their country to a battleground overrun by German and Soviet armies. What the Finnish government and Parliament had to take into account further was the mood of the nation, which hoped fervently for the recovery of the Finnish territory lost through the Peace of Moscow.

The Continuation War

The new war has been called the "Continuation War" in Finnish history because the Winter War is regarded as having set into motion the sequence of events leading to its outbreak. It has also been called the War of Retribution. There was unanimous agreement among the Finnish people that, what with the nation's having been drawn into hostilities again, every effort should be made to recapture what had been lost. The whole nation had become overtaken by the spirit of resistance, now active instead of merely passive, as during the Czarist regime. Just as, during the period of national autonomy, the Finns had twice pressured Russia to restore to their grand duchy the legal status wrested from it, they now grimly insisted on reclaiming the territorial rights that had so recently been theirs. This frame of mind was given classical expression in an exclamation by a character in Väinö Linna's novel *The Unknown Soldier*. When the advancing Finnish forces crossed the boundary drawn by the Peace of Moscow, Second Sergeant Hietanen snapped: "Of all the damned posts they've set up all over the woods! I don't like it."*

The Finns knew that they had the sympathy of the entire non-Communist world. And when Karelia was recaptured at the end of August after hard fighting, United States Secretary of State Cordell Hull actually congratulated Finland on its military success. Parliament proclaimed the territory ceded to the U.S.S.R. in the Peace of Moscow rejoined to the rest of Finland. The displaced population returned to its native province and began the work of reconstruction amid the ruins of two wars.

---

* This utterance is missing from the freely rendered English version of the novel.

The Finnish forces advanced also into East Karelia in the autumn in order to shorten the front and to gain strategically better defense positions for the protection of the home front against air raids, which could be launched from many bases just across the border (see Map 4). Certain expressions of opinion, like, above all, an order-of-the-day issued by Mannerheim, which caused a great public stir, revived old dreams, cherished a quarter of a century before, of the annexation of East Karelia by Finland. But, since these dreams were regarded as unrealistic, the East Karelian question was wrapped up in an official blanket of silence; and the government never considered the occupied territory to be anything more than a pawn likely to prove of value at future peace negotiations.

Finland never budged from its uncompromising position that the Finnish war was a defensive struggle separate from the war of the great powers, and the Finnish government strove to act at all times on the basis of this policy. Neither the military nor the political leadership would yield to German demandsthat Finnish forces take part in operations against Leningrad and, later, the Murmansk line.

The Finnish offensive was called to a halt at the beginning of December, 1941, just one day before the British government, under Stalin's pressure, declared war on Finland—a war that never resulted in the shedding of blood. Up to June, 1944, the Soviet-Finnish front was quiet, except for a few local attacks made by Red troops. In the meantime, Finland put out peace feelers several times—even at the risk of affronting Germany, which penalized every such move by reducing or even completely blocking shipments of goods vitally necessary to Finland. A speech delivered by Stalin in November, 1943, made it plain to the stunned Finns that the Soviet government held fast to the boundary drawn by the Peace of Moscow. And when, the following spring, he at last laid before the Finnish government his armistic terms in detail, new demands had been added: Finland would have to give up the Petsamo corridor to the Arctic coast, reduce its army to peacetime strength, pay war reparations amounting to $600 million and drive the Germans out of Finnish territory within a month. Fulfilling the two last-mentioned conditions did not appear to be possible no matter from what angle they were regarded. Disarmed, Finland could have been immediately occupied by German troops; and then, as these would have gradually retreated to Norway, Russian troops would have followed in pursuit as a new army of occupation. Parliament rejected the armistice terms offered by Stalin by a unanimous vote.

At the very same time as the Western allies landed in Normandy, the Russians launched a major offensive on the Karelian Isthmus. The artillery concentration was one of the heaviest in world military annals: in some places, there were as many as 400 pieces of artillery firing away along a stretch of only slightly over half a mile. The Finnish front line was smashed immediately. And there was not enough time after that to concentrate adequate strength on the still unfinished main defence line, which also broke at Kuuterselkä. The front had to be pulled back speedily behind the city of Viipuri. Halting the enemy attack appeared to be a more overwhelming task than during the fighting over the same terrain in the final days of Winter War. In order to reinforce the critical Viipuri sector, the Finns withdrew from East Karelia, where they were forced to repulse heavy assaults on their right flank.

When Finland sued for peace, Stalin demanded unconditional surrender. On the very same day that Stalin's demand was received, Foreign Minister von Ribbentrop arrived in Helsinki to pressure the Finns into accepting an agreement not to make peace without Germany's consent. Mannerheim regarded such acceptance as vital to continued resistance at the front because agreement also called for armed assistance from the Germans. Since, however, passage of the agreement through Parliament was uncertain, Ribbentrop was persuaded to accept instead a personal letter from President Ryti to Hitler. Even this measure caused the United States to break off diplomatic relations with Finland. And the Social Democratic ministers threatened to resign from the cabinet. The prompt assistance received from Germany was by no means unimportant: the Red offensive was stopped by dint of utmost exertions. The achievement of this last defensive victory demonstrated, in any event, that the Finns had not become demoralized in spite of the protracted stagnant trench warfare and the relentless American and British radio propaganda campaign, which had tried to drum into the heads of the Finns that they were not, after all. fighting for but against democracy.

Just as soon as the Finnish front had become stabilized, Ryti handed in his resignation as president. Elected by emergency arrangements as his successor, Mannerheim announced that he was not bound by Ryti's personal pledge to Germany. New peace feelers were put out, and Stalin proposed conditions that were harsh but not, like those of the preceding spring, impossible to fulfill. Germany had weakened during the summer to such an extent, moreover, that driving out the German troops operating in northern Finland no longer appeared overwhelming. Besides, no deadline was now set for the completion of this task. If the Germans had been given sufficient time to transport their equipment and stores with them, they would evidently have withdrawn without a fight. But Molotov pressed the Finns to speed up operations. Owing to the Germans' fierce resistance and scorched-earth tactics in retreating, it took the outnumbered Finns several months to drive them back over the northwestern boundary of Finnish Lapland. So fearsome was the prospect of setting forth on a new and unknown course that the decision to break off relations with Germany could not be made unanimously by Parliament, as most of the major decisions of the war years had been, but by a vote of 108 to 45. The armistice terms did not involve negotiations, even to the extent of four years before, but were dictated; and on September 19, 1944, Finland signed the new treaty in Moscow.

12

Postwar Chronicle

The national boundary laid down by the Peace of Moscow after the Winter War in the southeast was not altered, and the Karelians who had moved back into the reconquered territory during the hostilities took to the road once more as refugees, with their loads of salvaged possessions. Petsamo had to be ceded to the U.S.S.R. and the peninsula of Porkkala, a short distance west of Helsinki, had to be handed over to the Russians as a naval base on a 50-year lease. Finland's anti-Communist laws had to be repealed, and the Finnish Communist party now emerged for the first time as a legal organization, duly registered in Finland. Nevertheless, it saw fit, with an eye to elections, to form a front organization under the name of the People's Democratic Union, in which the Communists would be the controlling force. The Finnish army was to be reduced to peacetime strength within two and a half months. The Civil Guards, which had become organic parts of the Defence Establishment, were required to be abolished, together with the *Lotta Svärd* women's auxiliaries, on the ground of a clause in the Armistice Treaty banning "Fascist" organizations. The Peace Treaty signed in Paris in 1947 specified the maximum size of the various branches of the Finnish defence forces, and it also included other stipulations that imposed permanent restrictions on Finnish independence.

War reparations set at $300 million had to be paid within six years. Moscow later agreed to extend the period to eight years and to reduce the total sum by $73.5 million. If the value of the reparations deliveries had been estimated according to the prices prevailing at the time, Finland actually paid the equivalent of $570,000,000. The discrepancy is due to the pricing basis that was applied. During the first reparations year, this uncompensated export exceeded Finland's commercial exports. But, by accepting a lowered standard of living, the Finns managed to fulfill this obligation. Its fulfillment was taken by the Finns from the very outset as a point of honour. At the same time as the Finns were forced to create a considerable metal industry in order to satisfy Soviet demands for reparations in kind, instead of in money, they were also faced with the necessity of dealing with an acute supply shortage, resettling the uprooted Karelian population, and rebuilding devastated Lapland and cities damaged by bombs.

Great internal difficulties were caused, on the other hand, by the clause in the Armistic Treaty that, based on decisions reached jointly by the U.S.S.R. and the Western powers, obligated Finland "to collaborate with the Allied powers in the apprehension of persons accused of war crimes" and in their trial. It turned out that not only the issue of "war crimes" was involved but also the issue of political responsibility for the war. The criminalization of Finland's wartime policy, which in the beginning had been unanimously supported by Parliament and later on by a large majority of the M.P.'s, required the establishment of an emergency tribunal as well as the enactment of a special retroactive law that violated the nation's traditional system of justice. There was no alternative. An emergency tribunal had to be set up and the retroactive unconstitutional law passed. And thus were President Ryti, wartime Prime Ministers J. W. Rangell and Edwin Linkomies, Foreign Minister Henrik Ramsay, Ministers Väinö Tanner, Antti Kukkonen and Tyko Reinikka, as well as Minister T. M. Kivimäki, the wartime envoy to Berlin, sentenced to prison.

After serving their sentences, during which Ryti's health broke down, most of these men were once more invited to accept high positions of public trust. After the "War Guilt" trial, Mannerheim, who felt a bond of solidarity with the accused, resigned as president. Elected to succeed the aged Marshal of Finland was another elder statesman, who had kept out of politics since the outbreak of the Continuation War, J. K. Paasikivi. His aim—the so-called Paasikivi Line— was to cling uncompromisingly fast to national independence, yet to handle foreign relations in such a way as to avoid the slightest conflict with Soviet interests and to inspire the Soviet rulers with confidence in the sincerity of this realistic Finnish policy. The Paasikivi Line came clearly into sight in a practical application for the first time in 1947, when Finland turned down the U.S. offer of Marshall aid.

The next year, Finland concluded a Treaty of Friendship, Cooperation and Mutual Assistance with the U.S.S.R. It was Stalin who took the initiative, but Paasikivi and the Finnish Parliament succeeded in making such revisions in the text as to result in a treaty fundamentally different from the documents it was patterned after—the treaties Moscow had signed with Hungary and Romania. The clause calling for mutual assistance takes effect only if Germany, or some state allied with Germany, attempts to attack the Soviet Union across Finnish territory; and, in the event of such an attack, Soviet military assistance to Finland cannot be given automatically, but only after negotiations on the matter. Although Finland's desire to steer clear of the conflicts of interest between the major powers is mentioned in the introductory section of the treaty, the country could not maintain its neutrality, even in the loosest sense of the word, as long as the Russians kept the military base of Porkkala, which was an enclave inside the territorial bounds of Finland. However, Finnish adherence to the Paasikivi Line was crowned with success: in January of 1956, just before the end of Paasikivi's second presidential term, Moscow handed the leased area back to Finland. At about the same time, the Finns' freedom of action in the field of foreign policy broadened with their admission to membership in the United Nations (1955).

In the first three cabinets after the war, People's Democrats held portfolios, once even the post of prime minister. The 1948 elections, however, saw their parliamentary representation cut down by a quarter (from 49 to 38). The Treaty of Peace had been ratified and the Treaty of Friendship with the Russians had stabilized the line of foreign policy. Mr. K. A. Fagerholm formed a one-party Social Democratic government, which threw the Communists out of the key posts they had succeeded in capturing. The Fagerholm administration restored the security of the citizenry under the law, which had been abused, notably through arbitrary arrests by the Communist-controlled state police. The Communists strove to overthrow the government by calling wildcat strikes on a large scale; but law and order were maintained with a firm hand.

During this period, collaboration began between the Social Democrats and the small bourgeois parties to the right of the Agrarian Union, and it was this coalition that re-elected Paasikivi president in 1950 for his second six-year term. Characteristic of these years were cabinets jointly controlled by the Agrarians and the Social Democrats, usually with Dr. U. K. Kekkonen serving as prime minister. Yet, despite collaboration on the administrative level, relations between the two ruling parties remained cool; and, in the 1956 presidential election, the Agrarian candidate, Kekkonen, was pitted against the Social Democratic candidate, Fagerholm. With minor exceptions, the electors representing the small bourgeois parties cast their ballots for Fagerholm; but, in addition to the backing of his own party, Kekkonen received all the electoral votes of the People's Democrats. Kekkonen therefore emerged victorious in the electoral college by 151 votes to 149. His first term of office started with the outbreak of a general strike, which for three weeks paralyzed the nation's economy. The strike brought to a dramatic end the period of postwar unrest in the labour market. The trade-union movement had finally come into its own in Finland as a social and political force to be reckoned with, and the Social Democrats were obliged to engage in a hard struggle to keep under leash the new masses of workers that had joined the unions. Under these circumstances, the party was obliged to make far-reaching demands.

President Kekkonen adhered to the line of foreign policy laid down by Paasikivi, which as a result now began to be referred to as the "Paasikivi-Kekkonen Line." In 1956, Finland became a member of the Nordic Council and, in 1961, an associate member of the European Free Trade Association (EFTA). In 1973, Finland concluded the same kind of free trade agreement as Sweden and Norway with the European Economic Community (EEC), or Common Market. Two years later, Finland had the honour of hosting the Congress for Security and Cooperation in Europe, which brought together under the same roof, in Helsinki, a larger number of national leaders than any previous international conference in history.

Relations between Finland and the U.S.S.R., however, were even marked in the beginning by serious crises. At the end of 1958, Fagerholm's second government — a coalition of all the parties except the People's Democrats (and a splinter faction of left-wing socialists that had broken with the parent Social Democratic party) — was forced to quit when Moscow plainly showed a lack of confidence in its intentions. Then, in the autumn of 1961, the Soviet government, pointing to the Berlin crisis, called for negotiations towards implementing the military provisions of the Treaty of Friendship, Cooperation, and Mutual

Assistance. The Russians later withdrew their demand at Kekkonen's request; but, at the height of the crisis, the so-called Honka coalition, which the Social Democrats and certain bourgeois groups had formed to prevent Kekkonen's re-election, was dissolved. Kekkonen was then re-elected for a second six-year term by a large majority of the electors.

During the early years of this term, the cabinet portfolios were divided up mainly among non-socialists, but the year 1966 formed a watershed in domestic politics. The parties of the left won a majority in Parliament (103 of the 200 seats). This division of strength did not last, however, for in the three following elections the leftists slipped back into the minority. A more lasting political change than the temporary leftist triumph in 1966 was wrought by the long stride leftward taken by the Social Democrats: they showed a greater willingness to work hand in hand with the Communists than at any other time since the latter became organized as a separate party. The result was a so-called popular-front government, which consisted at first of the Social Democrats, the Centre party (formerly the Agrarian Union), and the People's Democrats. Much the same coalition lined up for the 1968 election to keep President Kekkonen in office. After this third presidential term was extended an extra four years by special legislative action, Kekkonen was re-elected in 1978 for a fourth term as President of the Republic and this time also won the support of the conservative National Coalition party.

Index